WORKSHOPS IN COMPUTING
Series edited by C. J. van Rijsbergen

Also in this series

Graham Birtwistle (Ed.)

IV Higher Order Workshop, Banff 1990

Proceedings of the IV Higher Order
Workshop, Banff, Alberta, Canada
10–14 September 1990

Published in collaboration with the
British Computer Society

Springer-Verlag
London Berlin Heidelberg New York
Paris Tokyo Hong Kong
Barcelona Budapest

Graham Birtwistle, BSc, PhD, DSc
Department of Computer Science
University of Calgary
2500 University Drive
Calgary, Alberta T2N 1N4
Canada

ISBN-13:978-3-540-19660-0   e-ISBN-13:978-1-4471-3182-3
DOI: 10.1007/978-1-4471-3182-3

British Library Cataloguing in Publication Data,
Higher Order Workshop (4th: 1990: Banff, Canada)
Proceedings of the IV Higher Order Workshop, – (Workshops in
computing)
I. Title   II. Birtwistle, Graham M. (Graham Mark), *1939–*   III. Series
005.1
ISBN-13:978-3-540-19660-0

Library of Congress Cataloging-in-Publication Data
Higher Order Workshop (4th: 1990: Banff, Alberta,)
IV Higher Order Workshop, 10-14 September 1990. Banff, Canada /
Graham Birtwistle (ed.)
p. cm. – (Workshops in computing)
"Published in collaboration with the British Computer Society."
Includes index.
ISBN-13:978-3-540-19660-0 (alk. paper)
1. Parallel processing (Electronic computers) –Congresses   2.
Programming languages (Electronic computers)–Congresses.   3.
Automatic theorem proving–Congresses.   I. Birtwistle, G.M. (Graham
M.)   II. Title.   III. Title: Fourth Higher Order Workshop, Banff 1990.   IV.
Title: 4th Higher Order Workshop, Banff 1990   V. Series.
QA76.58.H54 1990   91-15861
004.'.35–dc20   CIP

34/3830-543210   Printed on acid-free paper

Preface

It is many years since Landin, Burge and others showed us how to apply higher order techniques and thus laid some foundations for modern functional programming. The advantage of higher order descriptions – that they can be very succinct and clear – has been percolating through ever since. Current research topics range from the design, implementation and use of higher order proof assistants and theorem provers, through program specification and verification, and programming language design, to its applications in hardware description and verification.

The papers in this book represent the presentations made at a workshop held at Banff, Canada, September 10–14 1990 and organised by the Computer Science Department of the University of Calgary. The workshop gathered together researchers interested in applying higher order techniques to a range of problems. The workshop format had a few (but fairly long) presentations per day. This left ample time for healthy discussion and argument, many of which continued on into the small hours.

With so much to choose from, the program had to be selective. This year's workshop was divided into five parts:

1. Expressing and reasoning about concurrency: Warren Burton and Ken Jackson, John Hughes, and Faron Moller.
2. Reasoning about synchronous circuits: Geraint Jones and Mary Sheeran (with a bonus on the fast Fourier transform from Geraint).
3. Reasoning about asynchronous circuits: Albert Camilleri, Jo Ebergen, and Martin Rem.
4. Categorical concepts for programming languages: Robin Cockett, Barry Jay, and Andy Pitts.
5. Automated reasoning: Dan Craigen and Mark Saaltink, Mike Fourman and Roberto Hexsel, and Lars Rossen.

Acknowledgements. The workshop was made possible through an operating grant from the Natural Sciences and Engineering

Research Council of Canada. The workshop was held at the Banff Centre, whose ever obliging staff made sure that everything ran smoothly and to plan. Brian Wyvill gave a memorable talk on some spectacular climbing on Patagonia's Cerro Torre on the final evening to bring the event to a close. Banff National Park supplied the bear.

Graham Birtwistle
University of Calgary

March 1991

Contents

List of Authors

F. Warren Burton
School of Computer Science, Simon Fraser University, Burnaby,
British Columbia V5A 1S6, Canada

Albert J. Camilleri
Hewlett-Packard Laboratories, Filton Road, Stoke Gifford,
Bristol BS12 6QZ, UK

J. Robin B. Cockett
School of Mathematics and Computing, Macquarie University,
New South Wales 2109, Australia

Dan Craigen
Odyssey Research Associates, 265 Carling Avenue, Suite 506,
Ottawa, Ontario K1S 2E1, Canada

Jo C. Ebergen
Computer Science Department, University of Waterloo, Waterloo,
Ontario N2L 3G1, Canada

Michael P. Fourman
Laboratory for the Foundations of Computer Science, University of
Edinburgh, Edinburgh EH9 3JZ, UK

Roberto A. Hexsel
Laboratory for the Foundations of Computer Science, University of
Edinburgh, Edinburgh, EH9 3JZ, UK

John Hughes
Computing Science Department, University of Glasgow,
Glasgow G12 8QQ, UK

W. Ken Jackson
School of Computer Science, Simon Fraser University, Burnaby,
British Columbia V5A 1S6, Canada

C. Barry Jay
Department of Computer Science, University of Edinburgh,
Edinburgh EH9 3JZ, UK

Geraint Jones
Programming Research Group, Oxford University Computing
Laboratory, 11 Keble Road, Oxford OX1 3QD, UK

Faron Moller
Department of Computer Science, University of Edinburgh,
Edinburgh EH9 3JZ, UK

John O'Donnell
Computing Science Department, University of Glasgow,
Glasgow G12 8QQ, UK

Andrew M. Pitts
University of Cambridge Computer Laboratory,
New Museums Site, Pembroke Street, Cambridge CB2 3QG, UK

Martin Rem
Department of Mathematics and Computer Science,
Eindhoven University of Technology, PO Box 513,
5600 MB Eindhoven, The Netherlands

Lars Rossen
Department of Computer Science, Building 344,
Technical University of Denmark, DK-2800 Lyngby, Denmark

Mark Saaltink
Odyssey Research Associates, 265 Carling Avenue, Suite 506,
Ottawa, Ontario K1S 2E1, Canada

Mary Sheeran
Computing Science Department, University of Glasgow,
Glasgow G12 8QQ, UK

Partially Deterministic Functions

F. Warren Burton* and W. Ken Jackson

School of Computing Science
Simon Fraser University
Burnaby, British Columbia
Canada V5A 1S6
burton@cs.sfu.ca

Abstract

A partially deterministic function is a function that is deterministic except that it may be more or less well defined. That is, if a partially deterministic function returns a complete result, that result is unique. If it returns a partial result, or no result at all, then at least what is returned is consistent with the unique complete result. This is analogous to the partial correctness of a program.

If f is a (deterministic) function and g is a partially deterministic function such that for any use of g, $f \sqsubseteq g$, then f may be used to reason about a lower bound for possible results that can be returned by a program.

We will illustrate the use of partially deterministic functions in the context of parallel combinatorial search algorithms.

---

*This work was supported by the Natural Sciences and Engineering Research Council of Canada.

1   Introduction

A nondeterministic expression is an expression that may evaluate to any of several values. For example, McCarthy [7] has proposed a nondeterministic function *amb* defined so that the value of *amb a b* may be either *a* or *b* subject to the restriction that *amb a b* is not ⊥ unless both *a* and *b* are ⊥.

Nondeterminism is useful in a number of ways: a nondeterministic program may omit the exact details of execution and thus be written at a higher level; or an application may require nondeterminism to handle events that cannot be predicted by the program, such as when a sensor fires in a real-time system. Our interest is in nondeterministic programs that adapt their behavior based on factors not determined by the program. In particular, a parallel algorithm should adapt its behavior to the number of processors available. If this adaptation is transparent to the program then the behavior of the program is nondeterministic.

There are two problems with nondeterminism in computer programs. First, it is hard to reason about nondeterministic programs. (For example, [6] contains an explanation for why equational reasoning breaks down.) Second, it is difficult to experimentally debug nondeterministic programs because different results may be produced on different runs. This makes it rather difficult to confirm that a nondeterministic program is correct.

We solve both these problems by restricting our attention to a limited class of nondeterministic expressions. A *partially* deterministic expression may evaluate to any of several values but all of these values are bounded by an upper and a lower bound. That is, for any partially deterministic function g there are deterministic functions f and h such that $f \sqsubseteq g \sqsubseteq h$. Often the lower bound can be used to demonstrate the correctness of an algorithm: If we substitute f for g throughout a program we can reason about or debug the resulting deterministic program. The result returned by the deterministic program using f will be a lower bound for any possible result that may be returned by the nondeterministic program using g. The upper bound guarantees that the set of possible results is consistent.

Section 2 presents a more thorough description of partially deterministic functions. We then illustrate the use of partially deterministic functions in the context of parallel combinatorial search algorithms: for decision problems in section 3 and for optimization problems in section 4.

2   Partially Deterministic Functions

A nondeterministic expression denotes a set of possible results. Formally, these sets are elements in a powerdomain. We are interested in *erratic* non-determinism (nothing is done to prevent non-termination) so for our purposes the Plotkin powerdomain [1, 8] (also called the Egli-Milner powerdomain) is appropriate. The Plotkin powerdomain, $\mathcal{P}(D)$, on a domain D ordered by $\sqsubseteq$, uses the ordering, $\sqsubseteq_S$, where for all $A \in \mathcal{P}(D)$ and $B \in \mathcal{P}(D)$,

$$A \sqsubseteq_S B \text{ iff } (\forall a \in A . \exists b \in B . a \sqsubseteq b) \wedge (\forall b \in B . \exists a \in A . a \sqsubseteq b).$$

If D is a flat domain then the elements of $\mathcal{P}(D)$ are the non-empty subsets of D that are either finite or contain ⊥. If D is a non-flat domain then it is possible that two distinct subsets of D are computationally equivalent and should be considered equal. In this case, the usual trick is to consider equivalence classes of subsets of D (see [8] for the details).

A nondeterministic expression can denote any set but the set denoted by a partially deterministic expression must have an upper bound.

Definition: A function g is *partially deterministic* if there exists a deterministic function h such that $g \sqsubseteq_S \{h\}$.

A partially deterministic function cannot return inconsistent results. The only form of nondeterminism is the extent to which a result is produced. This is analogous to partial correctness of a program.

The function *amb* is not partially deterministic since it has no upper bound. The simplest partially deterministic function is perhaps the partially deterministic *or* function. There are several standard variants of the *or* function. The function *strict_or* is strict in both arguments and is defined by the axioms

$$strict\_or \ True \ True = True$$
$$strict\_or \ True \ False = True$$
$$strict\_or \ False \ True = True$$
$$strict\_or \ False \ False = False$$
$$strict\_or \ \bot \ y = \bot$$
$$strict\_or \ x \ \bot = \bot$$

The conditional *or*, strict only in its first argument, is defined by

$$cond\_or \ True \ y = True$$
$$cond\_or \ False \ y = y$$
$$cond\_or \ \bot \ y = \bot$$

Finally, parallel *or* is not strict in either argument. It is defined by

$$para\_or \ True \ y = True$$
$$para\_or \ x \ True = True$$
$$para\_or \ False \ y = y$$
$$para\_or \ x \ False = x$$
$$para\_or \ \bot \ \bot = \bot$$

Parallel *or* is said to be nonsequential since there is no sequential strategy for evaluating its arguments; the arguments must be evaluated in parallel. In theory this is a very nice function. In practise, *para_or* must evaluate its arguments in parallel and fairly. This leads to substantial time and space overheads.

A partially deterministic *or* function might choose to behave like *cond_or* or choose to behave like *para_or*. By defining

$$pd\_or \ x \ y = \{ cond\_or \ x \ y, para\_or \ x \ y \},$$

pd_or $\bot$ *True* returns *True* if it behaves like *para_or* or it returns $\bot$ if it behaves like *cond_or*.

Rather than provide a programming language with some type of nondeterministic choice construct, we use the functional language Miranda[1] [9, 10] and assume

---

[1]Miranda is a trademark of Research Software Ltd.

that some identifiers, such as pd_or[2], denote partially deterministic functions. Let the semantic function S map expressions plus environments to their denotations so that $S[\![\text{pd\_or x y}]\!]\rho = \{cond\_or\ x\ y, para\_or\ x\ y\}$. Note that S maps deterministic expressions to singleton sets. When f and g denote deterministic functions, we will abuse the notation somewhat and write

$$\text{f} \sqsubseteq_S \text{g} \sqsubseteq_S \text{h} \quad \text{to mean} \quad S[\![\text{f}]\!]\rho \sqsubseteq_S S[\![\text{g}]\!]\rho \sqsubseteq_S S[\![\text{h}]\!]\rho$$

A language is partially deterministic if the nondeterministic constructs in the language are all partially deterministic functions. We will limit our attention to partially deterministic languages for the remainder of this paper.

Reasoning with nondeterministic functions is more difficult because equational reasoning breaks down or extra machinery is needed to maintain equational reasoning (for more details see [6]). We attempt to avoid these difficulties by reasoning with deterministic lower bounds. After all, laziness is a tradition in the functional programming community. Thus we are interested in partially deterministic functions that have nontrivial lower bounds. Suppose we have a partially deterministic function g such that

$$\text{f} \sqsubseteq_S \text{g} \sqsubseteq_S \text{h},$$

where f and h denote deterministic functions and g is used in a program P. We can reason about the program P[f/g] with the knowledge that P[f/g] $\sqsubseteq_S$ P. Since it is usually necessary that a program meet its specification, but permitted for a program to exceed its specification (i.e. *specification* $\sqsubseteq_S$ *program*), this is usually sufficient. This approach will be illustrated in the next sections.

3 Decision Problems

Often combinatorial decision problems are solved by searching a solution space structured as a tree. For simplicity of presentation, we assume that the search tree is finite, binary, and only leaf nodes are potential solutions (a common tree organization for the decision 0/1 Knapsack problem has these properties).

With these assumptions, it is easy to specify how to search such a decision tree. The function dsearch below is such a specification.

```
dsearch root
    = is_solution root, if is_leaf root
    = subtree_search,    otherwise
      where
      subtree_search = strict_or (dsearch (lchild root))
                                 (dsearch (rchild root))
```

For any node, node, is_leaf node is true if node is a leaf node and is false otherwise. For any leaf node, node, is_solution node is true if node is a solution and is false otherwise. For any non-leaf node, node, lchild node and rchild node are the left and right children of node. It is natural to use strict_or in a specification because of its symmetry. Using strict_or also gives an implementation maximal freedom in that it does not require that any potential solution be avoided.

---

[2]Miranda expressions are written in a typewriter font.

When `dsearch` is viewed as an algorithm, every node in the search tree must be visited because `strict_or` is strict in both arguments. The algorithm is highly parallel because each subtree can be explored in parallel but the exhaustive search may more than offset the advantage of parallelism.

We can transform this exhaustive search algorithm into a backtracking algorithm by substituting `cond_or` for `strict_or`. Of course the two algorithms are not strictly equivalent. For example, if the left subtree contains a solution and the right subtree contains an infinite path (contrary to our original assumption), then the backtracking algorithm will return `True`, but the exhaustive search will fail to terminate. It is usually considered safe to go from the exhaustive search to the backtracking algorithm, since we loose nothing. That is, our backtracking algorithm meets (and exceeds) its specification, since `strict_or` $\sqsubseteq$ `cond_or` forces `dsearch` $\sqsubseteq$ `dsearch[cond_or/strict_or]`. It is not usually considered safe to go the other way unless we are certain that nontermination is not a problem. The backtracking algorithm has little potential for parallelism.

Using `para_or`, the subtrees can be searched in parallel. When a solution is found in either subtree the result is `True` and the processes searching the other subtrees can be terminated. However, the time and space overheads involved in fairly evaluating the subtrees may offset the advantages of parallelism. The `para_or` can behave nondeterministically: on a subsequent run a solution in a different subtree might be found. The semantics are deterministic since the overall result is `True` if any solution is found regardless of where the solution is found.

Speculative evaluation [2, 3] offers an interesting alternative. Semantically, `spec_or` is equivalent to `cond_or`. With `spec_or`, the first argument must be evaluated. The second argument may be evaluated in parallel, but if the first argument evaluates to `True` then the evaluation of the second argument may be terminated. On a single processor, `spec_or` behaves like `cond_or`. On a large number of processors, `spec_or` behaves like `para_or` except the leftmost solution must be found. Thus `spec_or` may behave nondeterministically, but has deterministic semantics. The time and space overheads associated with speculative evaluation will likely be significant but not as severe as with nonsequential functions. The problem with using `spec_or` is that even if a solution is very quickly found in the right subtree by the speculative computation, the search of the left subtree must be completed.

What we would really like is the best of both worlds. We would like to be able to evaluate a right subtree if there are plenty of processors available and to terminate the search of the left subtree if a solution is found in the right subtree. At the same time, we do not want to be required to evaluate the right subtree. To solve this problem, we use the partially deterministic function `pd_or`. For example, the value of (`pd_or` $\perp$ `True`) may be either `True` or $\perp$. If only a single processor is available then `pd_or` behaves like `cond_or` resulting in backtracking behavior. If more than one processor is available then `pd_or` may behave more like `para_or` and the subtrees may be searched in parallel. In order to reason about a program, we require that `strict_or` $\sqsubseteq_S$ `pd_or` and this is satified with

$$\mathcal{S}[\![\text{pd\_or x y}]\!]\rho = \{cond\_or\ x\ y, para\_or\ x\ y\}.$$

For example, `strict_or` $\sqsubseteq_S$ `pd_or` forces

$$\text{dsearch} \sqsubseteq_S \text{dsearch[pd\_or/strict\_or]},$$

so partially deterministic search meets and may exceed the specification `dsearch`.

4 Optimization Problems

In many combinatorial problems it is necessary to search a solution space for the best solution to the problem. In this section, we consider minimization problems where "best" means smallest and we call the measure of a solution the *cost* of the solution. As with decision problems, it is easy to specify an exhaustive search using strict functions, however a more efficient algorithm would use a lazy maximum and a lazy minimum. We discuss two possible implementations of the lazy maximum and lazy minimum: one implementation uses speculative evaluation and the other uses partially deterministic functions.

Again, for simplicity assume that the solution space is organized as a binary tree with solutions at the leaves. The function osearch, defined below, specifies a simple exhaustive search algorithm for an optimization problem represented by such a tree.

```
osearch root
    = (cost root, root),  if is_leaf root
    = osubtree_search,      otherwise
      where
      osubtree_search = osearch (lchild root) min
                        osearch (rchild root)
```

The function, osearch, returns an ordered pair, consisting of the cost of the best solution together with that solution. For any node, node, is_leaf node is a bool indicating whether or not the node is a leaf. For any leaf node, cost node is the cost of the solution. If the node is not a leaf, then (lchild node) and (rchild node) are the left child and right child of node. The functions max and min are binary infix versions of the maximum and minimum functions. Both max and min fully evaluate both arguments.

Suppose there is a function lower_bound such that lower_bound node is a lower bound on the least cost solution to be found in the subtree rooted at node. Also nil_node is a special node such that nil_node < node for any node, node, that may be encountered during a search. Then for any root of a subtree, root, replacing subtree_search with

$$\text{(lower\_bound root, nil\_node)} \; \underline{\text{max}} \; \text{subtree\_search}$$

has no effect on the outcome of the search, even when the bound is tight, since

$$\text{(lower\_bound root, nil\_node)} < \text{subtree\_search.}$$

The exhaustive algorithm can be improved by using the lower bound to decide when a minimal solution cannot exist in a subtree and to prune the subtree when this is the case (the essential idea behind branch-and-bound). We would like to use lazier versions of min and max to do this pruning. For example, suppose a left child, s, is a leaf with cost 3 and the right child has a lower bound of 5, then we would like

$$\text{lazy\_min (3,s) (lazy\_max (5,nil\_node) } \bot)$$

to evaluate to (3,s). Of course, ⊥ may be replaced by any expression and the result still holds. We may read an expression like `lazy_max 5 ⊥` as "at least 5". To maintain correctness, we require that $\underline{\text{max}} \sqsubseteq_S$ `lazy_max` and $\underline{\text{min}} \sqsubseteq_S$ `lazy_min`.

However, things are not quite this simple. We need a richer value space in order to be able to represent values such as "at least 5". We adapt the "improving value" abstract data type described in [4, 5]. The type signature for improving values is as follows:

```
abstype improving *
with make :: * — > improving *
     break ::  improving * — > *
     lazy_max ::  improving * — > improving * — > improving *
     lazy_min ::  improving * — > improving * — > improving *
```

The `make` function converts a value into an improving value while `break` converts an improving value into a value. A simple lazy search algorithm, using improving values, is given by the function `losearch` (lazy optimization search) defined below.

```
losearch = break.losearch'

losearch' root
   = make (cost root, root),            if is_leaf root
   = lazy_max bound losubtree_search', otherwise
     where
     bound = (make (lower_bound root, nil_node))
     losubtree_search' = lazy_min (losearch' (lchild root))
                                  (losearch' (rchild root))
```

In practice, priorities should be associated with the expansion of subtrees, so available computing power can be put to best use. This is discussed in [3] and will not be considered further here.

Rather than give axioms for `make`, `break`, `lazy_max`, and `lazy_min`, we will simply require that any implementation satisfy the following properties:

$$\text{make (a } \underline{\text{min}} \text{ b)} \sqsubseteq_S \text{ lazy\_min (make a) (make b)} \qquad (1)$$
$$\text{make (a } \underline{\text{max}} \text{ b)} \sqsubseteq_S \text{ lazy\_max (make a) (make b)} \qquad (2)$$
$$\text{break.make} = \text{id} \qquad (3)$$
$$\text{make.break} \sqsubseteq_S \text{id} \qquad (4)$$

where "." is the infix composition operator in Miranda. These properties are sufficient to prove that `losearch` exceeds the specification `osearch`. The proof is a straightforward induction on the tree. All we need now is an implementation that satisfies the above properties. We discuss two: the first, based on [4, 5], uses speculative evaluation and the second uses partially deterministic functions.

Improving values may be represented by a list of strictly increasing values. If the list is finite, the final element of the list will be the exact value that the previous elements bound. For example, the list [5, 7, 10], represents the value 10, while the partial list, 5:⊥, represents a value that is at least 5. The following code implements `make` and `break`.

```
improving * == [*]
```

```
make a = [a]
break x = last x
```

To differentiate them from the partially deterministic functions defined later, lazy_max is called spec_max and lazy_min is called minimum. The function spec_max evaluates its first argument to give lower bounds on the result then appends any bounds from its second argument that are better. Its definition is

```
spec_max xs ys = spec (monotonic_append xs) ys
```

```
monotonic_append xs ys = xs ++ dropwhile (≤ last xs) ys
```

Note that the evaluation of the second argument is started as a speculative computation. On the other hand, minimum merges two lists, removing duplicates to maintain monotonicity. In addition, the merge ends as soon as either list ends (which occurs when one of its arguments produces an exact value and the other argument produces a lower bound that exceeds the exact value).

```
minimum xs ys = short_merge xs ys
```

```
short_merge [ ] [ ] = [ ]
short_merge (x:xs) [ ] = [ ]
short_merge [ ] (y:y) = [ ]
short_merge (x:xs) (y:ys)
   = x:short_merge xs ys,      if x = y
   = x:short_merge xs (y:ys), if x < y
   = y:short_merge (x:xs) ys, if x > y
```

It is straightforward to show that this implementation satisfies properties (1)-(4) and thus,

$$osearch \sqsubseteq_S losearch[spec\_max/lazy\_max, minimum/lazy\_min].$$

In [4] a different approach is taken. A lengthy set of axioms is given for improving values. The above implementation is shown to satisfy these axioms and properties (1)-(4) can be deduced from the axioms.

A problem with improving values is that sometimes the result is not as strong as it could be. For example, spec_max is not commutative when viewed as a binary operation:

$$break (minimum (make\ 5) (spec\_max \perp (make\ 7))) = \perp$$

but

$$break (minimum (make\ 5) (spec\_max (make\ 7) \perp)) = 5.$$

The make 7 is sufficient information for this expression to evaluate to 5. However, making spec_max commutative would require a nonsequential para_max function (analogous to para_or) because the $\perp$ has to be avoided without examining it. We would like to avoid the overheads associated with nonsequential functions and so we turn to a partially deterministic maximum function.

Consider the partially deterministic function, pd_max defined by

$$\mathcal{S}[\![\texttt{pd\_max x y}]\!]\rho = \{spec\_max\ x\ y, spec\_max\ y\ x\}.$$

Now,

```
break (minimum (make 5) ( pd_max ⊥ (make 7)))
```

may be either $\perp$ or 5. This means that an implementation is free to return 5 once it it has sufficient information, but is not required to gather this information fairly (within a finite amount of time). Operationally, if only a single processor is available then pd_max can behave like spec_max and evaluate the left argument before looking at the right argument. If more than one processor is available then pd_max can evaluate both arguments in parallel until either one produces sufficient information to prune the other.

Notice that since max is commutative,

```
make (a max b)  ⊑  spec_max (make a) (make b)
make (a max b)  ⊑  spec_max (make b) (make a)
```

so that make (a max b) $\sqsubseteq_s$ pd_max a b. More generally, properties (1)-(4) are satisfied with pd_max/lazy_max and minimum/lazy_min. Therefore a partially deterministic search, using pd_max, meets the specification, osearch. That is,

```
osearch ⊑_s losearch[pd_max/lazy_max, minimum/lazy_min].
```

No matter which possible result is returned by the partially deterministic search, that result always exceeds the specification.

5   Conclusion

A partially deterministic function is a function that is nondeterministic only to the extent that the result returned may be more or less well defined, within known bounds. We have seen that partially deterministic functions permit an adaptive parallel implementation where the result returned may depend on the number of processors available and perhaps other information known only at runtime. At the same time, it is easy to reason about the partially deterministic functions since one can reason about the lower bound, which is a simple deterministic function.

References

[1] Manfred Broy. A theory for nondeterminism, parallelism, communication, and concurrency. *Theoretical Computer Science*, 45(1):1–61, 1986.

[2] F. Warren Burton. Controlling speculative computation in a parallel functional programming language. In *Proceedings of The Fifth International Conference on Distributed Computing Systems*, pages 453–458, Denver, Colorado, May 1985.

[3] F. Warren Burton. Speculative computation, parallelism, and functional programming. *IEEE Trans. Comput.*, C-34(12):1190–1193, Dec. 1985.

[4] F. Warren Burton. Indeterminate behavior with determinate semantics in parallel programs. In *Functional Programming Languages and Computer Architecture*, pages 340–346, 1989.

[5] F. Warren Burton. Encapsulating nondeterminacy in an abstract data type with determinant semantics. *Journal of Functional Programming*, to appear about January, 1991.

[6] John Hughes and John O'Donnell. Expressing and reasoning about nondeterministic functional programs. In *IV Higher Order Workshop*, Banff, 1990. Springer-Verlag.

[7] John McCarthy. A basic mathematical theory of computation. In P. Braffort and D. Hirschberg, editors, *Computer Programming and Formal Systems*, pages 33–70. North Holland, Amsterdam, 1963.

[8] David A. Schmidt. *Denotational Semantics: a Methodology for Language Development*. Allyn and Bacon, Inc., Boston, 1986.

[9] David A. Turner. Functional programs as executable specifications. In C. A. R. Hoare J. Shepherdson, editor, *Mathematical logic and programming languages*, pages 29–54. Prentice-Hall, 1985.

[10] David A. Turner. An overview of Miranda. *SIGPLAN Notices*, 21(12):158–166, Dec. 1986.

Nondeterministic Functional Programming with Sets

John Hughes and John O'Donnell
Computing Science Department
Glasgow University
Glasgow G12 8QQ, Scotland

Abstract. Nondeterminism can be introduced into a functional language, along with a set of laws for reasoning about the behaviour of programs, without disturbing referential transparency. We show how to do this by adding a new type constructor for sets and a carefully selected family of operations on sets. Instead of specifying a nondeterministic choice explicitly with choose or amb, a programmer specifies the set of values which the program might compute. Operations on sets are restricted in order to maintain laws for reasoning about programs; in particular, no function can choose an element from a set. The implementation is specified via rewrite rules that transform a program in the nondeterministic language into an ordinary functional program augmented with amb (which is not directly accessible to the programmer). The denotational semantics for this language is based on the Hoare powerdomain, so it includes bottom as a possible result even when the implementation will definitely not produce bottom. Since the denotational semantics fails to capture all the properties of the implementation, we present an additional method for reasoning about the productivity of a program. Productivity can be used to place additional constraints on the implementation which are not expressible in the powerdomain semantics. All of these techniques are illustrated by defining a "processor farm" program and proving several of its properties.

1. Introduction

The need for nondeterminism in programming arises from several distinct sources. Some problems are inherently nondeterministic, others can be solved more efficiently or elegantly with nondeterminism, and parallel algorithms sometimes require nondeterminism in order to schedule machine resources.

Inherently nondeterministic problems have nondeterministic specifications, so their implementations must also be nondeterministic. Most of the classic operating system problems, such as the dining philosophers problem, are inherently nondeterministic.

Nondeterminism aids elegance and efficiency in some programs that could, in principle, be written deterministically. For example, consider an interactive programming environment. Usually the system simply computes and prints responses to the user's inputs. However, it must always be able to interrupt its output when the user types a control-C. This can be implemented efficiently by having the system choose nondeterministically whether the next output character should come from the running program or a new prompt (in case the user typed control-C). A deterministic polling solution is possible, but unfortunately it requires some support from the input device, and it also requires the programming environment to simulate an abstract machine interpreting the current expression. This approach is ugly and inefficient; nondeterminism gives a superior solution.

Exploiting parallelism in a deterministic algorithm sometimes requires choices in the computation to depend on execution times. Since execution time is invisible to the functional programmer, such choices appear to be nondeterministic. A typical example is the processor farm, presented later in this paper.

Many nondeterministic constructs have been proposed for functional languages; some of them are briefly described in [1]. An important example is McCarthy's amb, which satisfies

$$\text{amb } x \perp = x$$
$$\text{amb } \perp y = y$$
$$\text{amb } x \, y = \text{either } x \text{ or } y$$

These equations say informally that amb makes an arbitrary choice between its arguments x and y, except that it avoids choosing bottom if possible. In addition, it should satisfy an operational property: if neither x nor y is bottom, but their evaluation times are sufficiently different, then ambxy should return the one whose evaluation takes less time. This property is usually stated informally, because we do not want to formalise the notion of "sufficiently different." The intended implementation of amb $x \, y$ is to evaluate x and y concurrently, through either timeslicing or parallelism. Whichever value reaches head normal form first is returned.

It is easy to write nondeterministic programs with amb. Unfortunately, adding amb to a functional language violates referential transparency. For example, amb $1 \, 2 = $ amb $1 \, 2$ can be reduced to $1 = 2$, which is false. So we cannot use amb in an unrestricted way without losing equational reasoning, which is one of the primary reasons for using a functional language in the first place.

We present an alternative nondeterministic language construct based on sets. Nondeterministic sets are rich enough to express a wide range of useful algorithms, but they are weak enough to maintain referential transparency. In particular, it is impossible to define amb using nondeterministic sets.

A denotational semantics for the nondeterministic set language can be defined using powerdomains. Unfortunately, the denotational semantics serves only to define which values could be produced by a program, but is not useful for reasoning about termination. In order to support reasoning about total correctness, we give an inference system useful for reasoning about the output produced by some nondeterministic programs.

We could specify the implementation of nondeterministic sets by describing the necessary modifications to a graph reducer. That approach would push the specification of the implementation to an unnecessarily low level, and would constrain the implementation too much. For example, we don't want to specify whether the implementation must use timeslicing or parallelism. Instead, we specify the implementation more abstractly by showing how a program using non-deterministic sets can be transformed into an equivalent program with no non-deterministic sets — but which uses amb. Many ways to implement amb are already known, and amb can simply be added to an existing functional language as a new primitive, without changing the compiler.

The rest of this paper is organised as follows. Section 2 introduces the language of nondeterministic sets and gives a few simple examples. Section 3 outlines a denotational semantics based on the Hoare powerdomain and discusses the limitations of this semantics. Section 4 specifies the implementation and shows how to implement nondeterministic sets by program transformations. Section 5 uses the notion of productivity to develop a method for reasoning about termination and deadlock avoidance in the presence of infinite lists. Section 6 illustrates non-deterministic sets through a nondeterministic solution to a significant problem in functional operating systems, the processor farm. Section 7 summarizes the results and presents our conclusions.

2. The nondeterministic set language

The central idea is to separate the language which the programmer reasons about from the language of operations that are actually executed:

- The programmer uses the *set language* to specify and reason about the set of possible values which the program could compute. This is an ordinary functional language augmented with a new type $\{\alpha\}$ for each existing type α, along with several new operators on set types. The set language is referentially transparent, and ordinary functional and mathematical reasoning are valid.

- The *target language* is the base functional language augmented with amb. The implementation transforms programs written in the set language into equivalent programs in the base language. The set $A :: \{\alpha\}$ in the set language becomes a representative element $a :: \alpha \in A$ in the base language. In order to pick a representative, the implementation sometimes uses amb to make a nondeterministic choice.

Some of the standard mathematical set operators don't make sense for non-deterministic sets, and must be excluded from the language. Some operators would violate referential transparency, while others would not work with the intended implementation. Every nondeterministic set operator must satisfy the following properties:

(1) A set operator must map sets to sets. Once nondeterminism is introduced, it cannot be removed. This property is needed both to keep referential transparency and to allow the implementation to represent a set by one of its elements. It prohibits the definition of choose:

$$\text{choose} :: \{\alpha\} \rightarrow \alpha$$
$$\text{choose } X = \text{arbitrary element chosen from } X$$

A consequence is that amb cannot be defined using nondeterministic sets:

$$\text{amb } x\, y \;=\; \text{choose} \left(\{x\} \cup \{y\}\right)$$

This limits the expressiveness of the language, which is a good thing: we want to limit the language enough to keep referential transparency. This restriction also prevents a function from folding the elements of a set into a single value, disallowing functions like max, min and sum over sets. If we allowed folding a set, then the implementation would need to remember all the elements of the set, and the efficient implementation we intend would not work.

(2) Choices are irrevocable. Thus for any operator $op :: \{\alpha\} \rightarrow \{\beta\} \rightarrow \{\gamma\}$, there must exist an operator op' such that

$$\text{choose}\,(X\ op\ Y) = (\text{choose}\,X)\ op'\ (\text{choose}\,Y)$$

where $X :: \{\alpha\}$, $Y :: \{\beta\}$ and $X\ op\ Y :: \{\gamma\}$. (We can use *choose* to reason about programs, even though it cannot be defined in the language.) This property allows the implementation to represent a set X by an element x, without ever having to backtrack and pick a different representative. The implementation actually applies op' to the representatives, instead of applying op to the sets. This restriction disallows set intersection because there is no operator op' that satisfies

$$\text{choose}\,(X \cap Y) = (\text{choose}\,X)\ op'\ (\text{choose}\,Y)$$

for arbitrary sets X and Y. In a similar way, the restriction prohibits us from filtering a set.

(3) A set operator op *must distribute over union, so* $op\,S \cup op\,T = op\,(S \cup T)$. This constraint allows the implementation to make nondeterministic choices early, which is essential for efficiency.

Given these constraints, we can introduce the set operations that will be included in the language. Section 3 gives their denotational semantics, and Section 4 describes their implementation.

Given a value $x :: \alpha$, we can construct the singleton set

$$\{x\} :: \{\alpha\} \qquad\qquad (singleton)$$

Given two sets, $X :: \{\alpha\}$ and $Y :: \{\beta\}$, the cross product can be defined:

$$X \times Y :: \{(\alpha, \beta)\} \qquad\qquad (product)$$

A function $f :: \alpha \rightarrow \beta$ can be mapped over a set $X :: \{\alpha\}$:

$$f * X :: \{\beta\} \qquad\qquad (map)$$

We can generalize this to functions that take n arguments by defining a comprehension. Let $f :: \alpha_1 \rightarrow \ldots \rightarrow \alpha_n \rightarrow \beta$. Then a comprehension can map f over sets with types α_1 to α_n, producing a set of values of type β:

$$\{f\ x_1 \ldots x_n \mid x_1 \in X_1, \ldots x_n \in X_n\} :: \{\beta\} \qquad\qquad (comprehension)$$

Only the union operators introduce nondeterminism. We can take the union of two sets $X :: \{\alpha\}$ and $Y :: \{\alpha\}$

$$X \cup Y :: \{\alpha\} \qquad\qquad (union)$$

and we can take the "big union" of a set of sets $Xs :: \{\{\alpha\}\}$

$$\bigcup Xs :: \{\alpha\}$$ *(big union)*

Finally, it is sometimes necessary to require an expressions e_2 to be $\bot$ if e_1 is $\bot$. This allows us to avoid choosing e_2, even when e_2 is not $\bot$. The expression

$$e_1 \gg e_2$$ *($\gg$)*

is defined to be $\bot$ if e_1 is $\bot$, and otherwise e_2.

3. Semantics of nondeterministic sets

Let D be the value domain for the base language. Since each type α in the base language induces a new type $\{\alpha\}$ in the set language, we need a new domain D' which includes subsets of D as elements. Therefore we need a powerdomain semantics.

There are three standard powerdomains, and the choice of powerdomain will affect what the semantics can say about the language. The union operator should be bottom-avoiding, and this constrains the choice of powerdomain. Bottom avoidance requires that

$$S \cup \bot = \bot \cup S = S$$

for any set S. In particular,

$$\{1\} \cup \{\bot\} = \{1\}$$
$$\{1\} \cup \{2\} = \{1, 2\}$$

Since $1 \sqsubseteq 1$ and $\bot \sqsubseteq 2$, monotonicity of $\cup$ and $\{\cdot\}$ require $\{1\} \sqsubseteq \{1, 2\}$ to be true in the powerdomain. This is true in the Hoare powerdomain, but not in the Egli-Milner nor the Smythe powerdomains. So the elements of D' will be the non-empty Scott-closed subsets of D ordered by subset. (The Scott-closed subsets of D are the downward-closed subsets of D augmented with the limit of any chain whose elements lie in D.) We will frequently need to build an element of D' from a subset of D, so we define an operator for this purpose: X^* is defined to be the Scott closure of X.

We can define the semantics of the nondeterministic set operators by specifying the set S of values which we intend the implementation to compute (which will not in general be an element of the powerdomain D') and then taking the *-closure:

$$\mathcal{E}[\![\{x\}]\!]\rho = \{\mathcal{E}[\![x]\!]\rho\}^*$$ *(singleton)*

$$\mathcal{E}[\![X \times Y]\!]\rho = \{(x, y) \mid x \in \mathcal{E}[\![x]\!]\rho, y \in \mathcal{E}[\![Y]\!]\rho\}$$ *(product)*

$$\mathcal{E}[\![f * X]\!]\rho = \{\mathcal{E}[\![f]\!]\rho x \mid x \in \mathcal{E}[\![X]\!]\rho\}^*$$ *(map)*

$$\mathcal{E}[\![\{f\ x_1 \ \ldots \ x_n \mid x_1 \in X_1 \ \ldots \ x_n \in X_n\}$$
$$= \{\mathcal{E}[\![f]\!]\ \rho\ v_1 \ \ldots \ v_n \mid v_i \in \mathcal{E}[\![X_i]\!]\rho\}^* \quad (comprehension)$$

$$\mathcal{E}[\![X \cup Y]\!]\rho \ = \ \mathcal{E}[\![X]\!]\rho \cup \mathcal{E}[\![Y]\!]\rho \qquad\qquad (union)$$

$$\mathcal{E}[\![\textstyle\bigcup Xs]\!] \ = \ \{x \mid X \in \mathcal{E}[\![Xs]\!]\rho,\ x \in X\} \qquad (big\ union)$$

The semantics of the rest of the language is entirely unaffected by the presence of nondeterminism; for example

$$\mathcal{E}[\![I]\!]\rho \ = \ \rho I$$
$$\mathcal{E}[\![\lambda I.E]\!]\rho \ = \ \lambda x.\mathcal{E}[\![E]\!]([x/I]\rho)$$
$$\mathcal{E}[\![E_1\ E_2]\!]\rho \ = \ (\mathcal{E}[\![E_1]\!]\rho)\,(\mathcal{E}[\![E_2]\!]\rho)$$

The denotational semantics given above is too weak to capture all the properties of the implementation. For example, we know that the implementation will represent the singleton set $\{1\}$ by the representative 1, but the Scott closure forces us to use $\{\bot, 1\}$. So the denotational semantics cannot be used to prove that the program $\{1\}$ will produce any output at all! The denotational semantics is useful for proving partial correctness of programs, but we need a separate method for proving total correctness. Section 5 addresses that problem.

4. The implementation

The implementation of the nondeterministic set language can be specified in terms of any implementation of the base language by showing how to transform a program in the set language into the amb language. This section gives a set of rewrite rules that define such a transformation. First we specify a number of constraints which the implementation must satisfy (4.1), and then we give the rewrite rules (4.2).

4.1 Abstract specification of the implementation

The implementation of nondeterministic set functions should be specified precisely enough to justify a set of laws adequate for reasoning about nondeterministic programs. But the specification should also be abstract enough to avoid irrelevant details. For example, it should not require the compiler to use a G Machine or Tim abstract machine. In particular, the implementation must not constrain the evaluation strategy; it should allow both timeslicing and parallelism.

We specify the implementation by giving an inference rule for each operator op on sets, relating op to another operator op' which the implementation applies to the set representative. The general form of an inference rule says: given an element x of set X (above the line), the implementation can apply op' to x in order to compute a representative of $op\ X$ (below the line):

$$\frac{x \in X}{op'\ x \ \in \ op\ X}$$

A singleton set is represented by its element:

$$\frac{}{x \in \{x\}} \qquad\qquad (singleton)$$

The cross product of two sets is represented by the pair of representatives from the sets.

$$\frac{x \in X \quad y \in Y}{(x,y) \in X \times Y} \qquad (product)$$

The implementation maps a function f over a set X by simply applying f to the set representative x.

$$\frac{x \in X}{f\,x \in f * X} \qquad (map)$$

More generally, we can map a function that takes n arguments over n sets with a set comprehension of the form

$$\{f\,x_1 \ldots x_n \mid x_1 \in X_1, \ldots, x_n \in X_n\}.$$

The implementation applies f to the representatives:

$$\frac{y_1 \in X_1 \quad \ldots \quad y_n \in X_n}{f\,y_1 \ldots y_n \in \{f\,x_1 \ldots x_n \mid x_1 \in X_1, \ldots, x_n \in X_n\}} \qquad (comprehension)$$

The crucial set operation is bottom-avoiding union, which plays the same role as bottom-avoiding choice or amb in other nondeterministic systems. The advantage of bottom-avoiding union is its referential transparency. As a result, its specification allows a richer set of laws for reasoning about programs than choice or amb. There are two inference rules:

$$\frac{x \in X}{x \in X \cup Y} \qquad \frac{y \in Y}{y \in X \cup Y} \qquad (union)$$

The implementation must nondeterministically choose which rule to use; the following section shows how it does so.

While union allows us to pick an element from one of two sets, "big union" allows us to pick an element from any of a set of sets:

$$\frac{x \in X \in Xs}{x \in \bigcup Xs} \qquad (big\ union)$$

4.2 The implementation: from sets to amb

We could implement nondeterministic sets with a three-phase compiler. The first phase typechecks the original program, which may contain set types. The second phase transforms the program, removing all the sets and set operations and (possibly) introducing applications of amb. The third phase compiles the transformed program, using ordinary compilation techniques.

Typechecking ensures that the set operations are used in a valid manner. No additional typechecking machinery is needed: set types can be treated as a built in algebraic type, just like lists and tuples.

After typechecking, the compiler transforms a nondeterministic program containing set expressions into an equivalent one in the base language. The only remaining vestige of nondeterminism is the presence of amb in the transformed program. Ordinary deterministic programs are unaffected by this transformation.

We can define the transformation by a set of rewrite rules from terms in the set language into terms in the base language. These rules are closely related to the specification rules in the previous section. The difference is that the specification rules state properties of semantic values, while the rewrite rules transform expressions into expressions.

The transformed program represents a set by an element, so the compiler transforms $\{e\}$ into the value in that set. Since e (a term in the set language) may itself contain set expressions, the rewrite rules must be applied recursively to transform it into e' (a term in the base language).

$$\frac{e \Rightarrow e'}{\{e\} \Rightarrow e'} \qquad\qquad (singleton)$$

Cartesian products are similar: the implementation makes a pair of the representatives it is given.

$$\frac{e_1 \Rightarrow e_1' \quad e_2 \Rightarrow e_2'}{e_1 \times e_2 \Rightarrow (e_1', e_2')} \qquad\qquad (product)$$

Set mappings become ordinary function applications:

$$\frac{f \Rightarrow f' \quad e \Rightarrow e'}{f * e \Rightarrow f' \, e'} \qquad\qquad (map)$$

The term $E(x_1, \ldots, x_n)$ denotes an expression E with free variables $x_1, \ldots, x_n$. A nondeterministic set comprehension consists of such an expression, along with definitions of the free variables. The compiler recursively transforms $E(x_1, \ldots, x_n)$ into $E'(x_1, \ldots, x_n)$ and replaces the sets with their representatives:

$$\frac{e_i \Rightarrow e_i' \quad E(x_1, \ldots, x_n) \Rightarrow E'(x_1, \ldots, x_n)}{\{E(x_1, \ldots, x_n) \mid x_i \in e_i\} \Rightarrow \atop \text{let } x_1 = e_1' \text{ in } \ldots \text{ in let } x_n = e_n' \text{ in } E'(x_1, \ldots, x_n)} \qquad (comprehension)$$

The rule provides sharing by binding the expressions e_i to variables x_i. For example,

$$\{x + x \mid x \in \{1\} \cup \{2\}\}$$
$$\Rightarrow \quad \text{let } x = \text{amb } 1 \, 2 \text{ in } x + x$$

which is quite different than amb $1\,2$ + amb $1\,2$. The transformed expression can evaluate to 2 or 4, but not to 3. Sharing improves efficiency by avoiding duplicated computation. It is also needed for referential transparency:

$$\{x = x \mid x \in \{1\} \cup \{2\}\}$$

evaluates to $1 = 1$ or $2 = 2$, but it cannot evaluate to $1 = 2$.

The specification of bottom-avoiding union consists of two rules. The transformed program uses amb to decide nondeterministically which of these rules to apply:

$$\frac{e_1 \Rightarrow e_1' \quad e_2 \Rightarrow e_2'}{e_1 \cup e_2 \Rightarrow \text{amb } e_1' \, e_2'} \qquad\qquad (union)$$

Even though union is "safer" than choice, we use choice to implement it!

Big union is implemented the same way as singleton; it differs only in the types.

$$\frac{e \Rightarrow e'}{\bigcup e \Rightarrow e'} \qquad\qquad (big\ union)$$

The rewrite rules leave all the base language constructs unchanged:

$$\overline{x \Rightarrow x}$$

$$\frac{e_1 \Rightarrow e_1' \quad e_2 \Rightarrow e_2'}{e_1\ e_2 \Rightarrow e_1'\ e_2'}$$

$$\frac{e \Rightarrow e'}{\lambda x.e \Rightarrow \lambda x.e'}$$

5. Reasoning About Infinite Lists

In this section we digress a little to discuss termination proofs for programs operating on infinite lists. Infinite lists arise naturally when, for example, processes are modelled as functions from input channels to output channels [2]. When there is a cycle of communications then the lists representing the channels are even recursively defined. Thus in areas like functional operating systems we must expect to need to reason about nondeterministic recursively defined lists.

Unfortunately such programs can be awkward to reason about. Consider the recursive definition

$$nats = 0 : map\,(+1)\,nats.$$

Clearly the infinite list of naturals is a solution of this equation. But it is also a solution of

$$nats = map\,(-1)\,(tl\,nats).$$

Taken as a definition, the latter equation produces nothing (its value is $\bot$), while the former produces the entire infinite list of naturals.

How can we tell which recursive equations produce defined results? One approach is to reason independently about the *values* satisfying the equations, and the *definedness* of the least solution. This idea motivated Sijtsma to study a calculus for proving the *productivity* of recursive definitions [4]. Such an approach is attractive to us, because our present denotational semantics permits us *only* to reason about the possible values of an expression. We cannot prove the definedness of nondeterministic programs at the same time as we prove their partial correctness. A calculus of productivity may enable us to give separate proofs of termination.

The first subsection sketches a deterministic calculus of productivity for the λ-calculus with lists and **case** expressions. This calculus is inspired by Sijtsma's work, although it is presented very differently, and indeed differs also in substance. It can be used to prove the productivity of the *nats* definition above. The following subsection extends the calculus to cover sets and the operations on them introduced above.

An important difference between Sijtsma's calculus (or the deterministic calculus presented here) and the nondeterministic one is that the former can be justified from a denotational semantics, while the latter cannot. Because the set language's semantics does not capture termination, a calculus of termination cannot be justified with respect to it. Instead, the productivity calculus must be regarded as an independent part of the language specification.

5.1 Productivities

We want to reason about degrees of definedness: let us therefore define formally what we mean by such a thing.

Definition. A *productivity* π for a type σ is a limit-closed subset of the domain of values of type σ. (That is, if there is a chain $\{x_i\}$ whose elements all belong to π, then $\sqcup_i x_i$ must also belong to π)*. We say an expression e is π-productive, denoted $e \rightsquigarrow \pi$, if e evaluates to an element of π.

Four useful productivities for a type σ are

$$\perp_\sigma = \{\perp\}$$
$$\Delta_\sigma = \{x | x : \sigma\} - \{\perp\}$$
$$T_\sigma = \{x | x : \sigma; x \text{ total}\}$$
$$\text{Any}_\sigma = \{x \mid x : \sigma\}$$

(The type-subscript will usually be omitted on such productivities).

Given an indexed family of productivities $\{\pi_k\}$, we define

$$(\forall k.\pi_k) = \bigcap_k \pi_k.$$

Clearly

$$e \rightsquigarrow \forall k.\ \pi_k \iff \forall k.e \rightsquigarrow \pi_k.$$

It's useful to define ways of forming productivities for compound types from productivities for simpler ones. Clearly the cartesian product $\pi_1 \times \pi_2$ is a productivity for pair types:

$$(e_1, e_2) \rightsquigarrow \pi_1 \times \pi_2 \iff e_1 \rightsquigarrow \pi_1 \wedge e_2 \rightsquigarrow \pi_2$$

For function types we'll define

$$\pi_1 \Rightarrow \pi_2 = \{f \mid \forall x \in \pi_1.\ f\ x \in \pi_2\}$$

so, for example, the fact that $(+)$ maps total arguments to total results can be expressed as

$$(+) \rightsquigarrow T \times T \Rightarrow T.$$

For lists, π^0 is defined to be lists all of whose elements are π-productive, and π^k to be lists which, in addition, have k or more elements:

$$\pi^0 = \{\perp, []\} \cup \{x : xs \mid x \in \pi,\ xs \in \pi^0\}$$
$$\pi^{k+1} = \{x : xs \mid x \in \pi,\ xs \in \pi^k\}$$

---

* The properties Sijtsma defines correspond to *upwards-closed* productivities. The non-monotonicity of nondeterministic choice forces us to relax this seemingly natural condition.

In addition,
$$\pi^\omega = \forall k.\pi^k$$

A π^ω-productive list has infinitely many π-productive elements, so to show that *nats* defined above really does evaluate to the infinite list of naturals, it has to be shown to be T^ω-productive. The next subsection introduces a calculus that enables us to do so.

5.2 A Calculus for Productivity

We define a calculus for proving judgements of the form $e \rightsquigarrow \pi$ as a collection of axioms and inference rules. The axioms give the productivities of constants: for example

$$(+) \rightsquigarrow T \times T \Rightarrow T$$
$$[\,] \rightsquigarrow \pi^0$$
$$(:) \rightsquigarrow \forall k.\pi \times \pi^k \Rightarrow \pi^{k+1}$$
$$hd \rightsquigarrow \pi^0 \Rightarrow \pi \cup \bot$$
$$hd \rightsquigarrow \pi^{k+1} \Rightarrow \pi$$
$$tl \rightsquigarrow \pi^0 \Rightarrow \pi^0$$
$$tl \rightsquigarrow \pi^{k+1} \Rightarrow \pi^k$$

Axioms must be given for each primitive in the language.

The inference rules prescribe how productivities of compound expressions can be inferred from the productivities of their subterms. The rules for lambda-expressions, applications, fixpoints, and case expressions are

$$\frac{e \rightsquigarrow \pi \qquad \pi \subseteq \pi'}{e \rightsquigarrow \pi'} \qquad \text{(Weakening)}$$

$$\frac{f \rightsquigarrow \pi_1 \Rightarrow \pi_2 \qquad e \rightsquigarrow \pi_1}{fe \rightsquigarrow \pi_2} \qquad \text{(Application)}$$

$$\begin{array}{c} [x \rightsquigarrow \pi_1] \\ \vdots \\ \dfrac{e \rightsquigarrow \pi_2}{\lambda x.e \rightsquigarrow \pi_1 \Rightarrow \pi_2} \end{array} \qquad \text{(Abstraction)}$$

$$\frac{\bot \rightsquigarrow \pi \qquad f \rightsquigarrow \pi \Rightarrow \pi}{\text{fix} f \rightsquigarrow \pi} \qquad \text{(Recursion)}$$

$$\begin{array}{c} [x \rightsquigarrow \pi] \\ [xs \rightsquigarrow \pi^0] \\ \vdots \\ \dfrac{e_0 \rightsquigarrow \pi^0 \qquad e_1 \rightsquigarrow \pi' \qquad e_2 \rightsquigarrow \pi'}{\textbf{case } e_0 \textbf{ of } [\,] \rightarrow e_1; \; (x : xs) \rightarrow e_2 \textbf{ end } \rightsquigarrow \pi' \cup \bot} \end{array} \qquad \text{(Case)}$$

$$[x \leadsto \pi]$$
$$[xs \leadsto \pi^k]$$
$$\vdots$$

$$\frac{e_0 \leadsto \pi^{k+1} \qquad e_2 \leadsto \pi'}{\textbf{case } e_0 \textbf{ of } [\,] \to e_1; \ (x:xs) \to e_2 \textbf{ end } \leadsto \pi'} \qquad \text{(Case nonempty)}$$

In the following the calculus is applied to programs in a richer language with, for examle, recursive definitions. Such constructs are regarded as syntactic sugar for the λ-calculus in the standard way. We also assume that unfolding definitions preserves productivity. Using these rules it can be shown, for example, that if $f \leadsto \pi_1 \Rightarrow \pi_2$ then $map\ f \leadsto \forall k.\pi_1^k \Rightarrow \pi_2^k$.

Returning to the nats example,

$$nats = 0 : map\ (+1)\ nats.$$

We start with a simple lemma: from

$$1 \leadsto T$$
$$(+) \leadsto T \times T \Rightarrow T$$

we conclude

$$(+1) \leadsto T \Rightarrow T$$

and hence

$$map\ (+1) \leadsto \forall k.T^k \Rightarrow T^k$$

The goal is to prove $nats \leadsto T^\omega$ — that is, $nats$ is really an infinite list. The proof is by induction, showing $nats \leadsto T^k$ for all k.

The base case is $nats \leadsto T^0$; that is, all the elements of nats are total (but we say nothing about how many are produced). Since the definition of nats is a sugared use of fix, the recursion rule is applicable if we can prove

$$\bot \leadsto T^0$$
$$nats \leadsto T^0 \Rightarrow 0 : map\ (+1)\ nats \leadsto T^0$$

The first of these is true trivially, and the second holds because if $nats \leadsto T^0$, then

$$map\ (+1)\ nats \leadsto T^0$$

by the lemma above, and since

$$0 \leadsto T$$
$$(:) \leadsto \forall k.\pi \times \pi^k \Rightarrow \pi^{k+1}$$

we have

$$0 : map\ (+1)\ nats \leadsto T^1 \subseteq T^0$$

as required.

For the step case of the induction, suppose that $nats \leadsto T^k$ for a particular k. Then, by the map theorem

$$map\,(+1)\, nats \leadsto T^k$$

and so

$$0\,:\,map\,(+1)\, nats \leadsto T^{k+1}.$$

So by unfolding its definition,

$$nats \leadsto T^{k+1}$$

It follows by induction that

$$nats \leadsto \forall k.T^k = T^{\omega}$$

which is what we wanted to prove*.

As a more complex example, consider the following well-known definition of the list of Hamming numbers (that is, numbers whose only prime factors are 2, 3 and 5).

$$ham = 1\,:\,combine\,(map\,(2*)\,ham)\,\big(combine\,(map\,(3*)\,ham)\,(map\,(5*)\,ham)\big)$$

where $combine$ takes two sorted lists and merges them into another sorted list. Sijtsma proves that the straightforward definition of combine has the property

$$combine \leadsto \forall j,k.\pi^j \Rightarrow \pi^k \Rightarrow \pi^{\min(j,k)}$$

This fact also holds in the system presented here. Now ham can be shown to be productive by the same kind of reasoning used above. First use the recursion rule to show that $ham \leadsto T^0$ and then use induction to show that $ham \leadsto \forall k.T^k = T^{\omega}$.

5.3 The Productivity of Sets

The first step in defining a similar calculus for nondeterministic programs is to define the notion of productivity for a set type. We do not take it to be a set of sets: instead a productivity for a set type $\{\sigma\}$ will be a productivity for σ. The interpretation is that the element chosen from the set by the implementation will have the given productivity.

The new inference rules are:

$$\frac{e \leadsto \pi}{\{e\} \leadsto \pi}$$

$$\frac{e \leadsto \pi}{\bigcup e \leadsto \pi}$$

---

* If we followed the spirit of Sijtsma's work more closely, we would define π^0 to be the set of all lists, and the base case of this induction would then become trivial. While this would be advantageous for deterministic programs, it would render untrue some of the theorems we wish to prove about nondeterministic ones.

$$\frac{e_1 \rightsquigarrow \pi_1 \quad e_2 \rightsquigarrow \pi_2}{e_1 \times e_2 \rightsquigarrow \pi_1 \times \pi_2}$$

$$\frac{f \rightsquigarrow \pi_1 \Rightarrow \pi_2 \quad e \rightsquigarrow \pi_1}{f * e \rightsquigarrow \pi_2}$$

$$\frac{e_1 \rightsquigarrow \pi_1 \quad \cdots \quad e_n \rightsquigarrow \pi_n \quad \begin{array}{c}[x_1 \rightsquigarrow \pi_1 \ldots x_n \rightsquigarrow \pi_n] \\ \vdots \\ e \rightsquigarrow \pi\end{array}}{\{e \mid x_1 \in e_1 \ldots x_n \in e_n\} \rightsquigarrow \pi}$$

$$\frac{e_1 \rightsquigarrow \pi_1 \quad e_2 \rightsquigarrow \pi_2}{e_1 \cup e_2 \rightsquigarrow \pi_1 \cup (\pi_2 - \bot)}$$

$$\frac{e_1 \rightsquigarrow \pi_1 \quad e_2 \rightsquigarrow \pi_2}{e_1 \cup e_2 \rightsquigarrow (\pi_1 - \bot) \cup \pi_2}$$

$$\frac{e_1 \rightsquigarrow \bot}{e_1 \gg e_2 \rightsquigarrow \bot}$$

$$\frac{e_1 \rightsquigarrow \Delta \quad e_2 \rightsquigarrow \pi}{e_1 \gg e_2 \rightsquigarrow \pi}$$

The two rules for $\cup$ capture its bottom-avoiding nature: it's possible to avoid a bottom in either operand, but not both. We can increase our confidence in these rules by noting that each operation has the same productivity as its base language translation. The translation of $\cup$, of course, involves amb, for which no productivity has so far been defined.

As an example of applying these rules, we'll show that nondeterministic merge satisfies

$$merge \rightsquigarrow \forall j, k.\pi^j \Rightarrow \pi^k \Rightarrow \pi^{j+k}.$$

The proof is fairly long, but simple in principle. The starting point is the following definition of merge:

$$
\begin{aligned}
merge\ xs\ ys\ &=\ bias\ xs\ ys\ \cup\ bias\ ys\ xs \\
bias\ xs\ ys\ &=\ \textbf{case}\ xs\ \textbf{of} \\
&\quad [\,]\ \rightarrow \{ys\} \\
&\quad (x : xs') \rightarrow \{x : zs \mid zs \in merge\ xs'\ ys\}
\end{aligned}
$$

The proof is by a very similar induction to those above, but this time the induction is on $j + k$. Once again, the base case depends on the recursion rule.

To show

$$merge \leadsto \pi^0 \Rightarrow \pi^0 \Rightarrow \pi^0$$

first note that

$$\perp \leadsto \pi^0 \Rightarrow \pi^0 \Rightarrow \pi^0$$

(since $\perp \leadsto \pi^0$). Now suppose that the i'th approximation to merge ($merge_i$) has this property. Then the $i+1$'th approximation to $bias$ has the property

$$bias_{i+1} \leadsto \pi^0 \Rightarrow \pi^0 \Rightarrow \pi^0.$$

To see this, assume that $xs \leadsto \pi^0$ and $ys \leadsto \pi^0$ in the body of bias. Then by the singleton rule, $\{ys\} \leadsto \pi^0$ and, under the assumptions $x \leadsto \pi$ and $xs' \leadsto \pi^0$,

$$merge_i \ xs' \ ys \leadsto \pi^0$$

$$\{x : zs \mid zs \in merge_i \ xs' \ ys\} \leadsto \pi^1 \subseteq \pi^0$$

and so applying the case rule to the body of $bias$,

$$bias_{i+1} \ xs \ ys \leadsto \pi^0 \cup \perp = \pi^0.$$

It now follows easily that

$$merge_{i+1} \leadsto \pi^0 \Rightarrow \pi^0 \Rightarrow \pi^0$$

and so, by the recursion rule,

$$merge \leadsto \pi^0 \Rightarrow \pi^0 \Rightarrow \pi^0.$$

For the step case, assume that

$$merge \leadsto \pi^j \Rightarrow \pi^k \Rightarrow \pi^{j+k}$$

for all $j + k \leq n$. First observe that if this property holds for a particular j and k then

$$bias \leadsto \pi^{j+1} \Rightarrow \pi^k \Rightarrow \pi^{j+k+1}.$$

This can be shown by applying the case-non-empty rule to the body of $bias$ and using the induction hypothesis. Suppose now that $j + k = n + 1$. If neither j nor k is zero, then in the body of $merge$ we can assume $xs \leadsto \pi^{(j-1)+1}$ and $ys \leadsto \pi^{(k-1)+1}$, and so by the observation above

$$bias \ xs \ ys \leadsto \pi^{j+k}$$
$$bias \ ys \ xs \leadsto \pi^{j+k}$$

Applying the union-rule, we have

$$merge \ xs \ ys \leadsto \pi^{j+k}.$$

However, one of j or k might be zero. Assume without loss of generality that $j = 0$, and so $k = n + 1$. Applying the case rule to the body of *bias* and using the induction hypothesis, we find

$$bias \rightsquigarrow \pi^0 \Rightarrow \pi^{n+1} \Rightarrow \pi^{n+1} \cup \bot.$$

So if $xs \rightsquigarrow \pi^0$ and $ys \rightsquigarrow \pi^{n+1}$ then

$$bias\ xs\ ys \rightsquigarrow \pi^{n+1} \cup \bot$$

$$bias\ ys\ xs \rightsquigarrow \pi^{n+1}$$

and so, by the union rule avoiding $\bot$ in the left operand,

$$merge\ xs\ ys \rightsquigarrow \pi^{n+1}$$

so

$$merge \rightsquigarrow \pi^j \Rightarrow \pi^k \Rightarrow \pi^{j+k}$$

in this case too. Now by induction

$$merge \rightsquigarrow \forall j, k . \pi^j \Rightarrow \pi^k \Rightarrow \pi^{j+k}$$

as required*.

Using this result we can prove a nondeterministic Hamming program to be productive: if

$$H = \bigcup\bigcup\Big\{\{\{1 : xs \mid xs \in merge\,(map\,(2*)\,h)\,ys\}$$
$$\mid ys \in merge\,(map\,(3*)\,h)\,(map\,(5*)\,h)\}$$
$$\mid h \in H\Big\}$$

then we can show

$$H \rightsquigarrow T^\omega$$

by a very similar argument to that used for *ham*.

6. Example: the processor farm

This section offers a slightly larger non-deterministic program: a *processor farm*. Consider the problem of computing

$$map\ f\ xs$$

---

* Note that this result would not hold if we had chosen to restrict productivities to be upwards-closed, and therefore defined π^0 to be the set of all lists. While the element chosen from $merge \bot [1,2,3]$ is certain to be $(1 : 2 : 3 : \bot)$, which is indeed T^3-productive, the element chosen from $merge[\bot][1,2,3]$ could be $(\bot : 1 : 2 : 3 : \bot)$, which is not. Thus if we include $[\bot]$ in the set of T^0-productive lists, we cannot hope to prove the result just shown.

in parallel, where xs is a long list. We could evaluate all the applications of f in parallel, but this would create a very large number of parallel processes which, on some architectures, could fill up the store and prevent the machine from working efficiently. Therefore we might prefer to use a limited amount of parallelism, perhaps corresponding to the number of processors available. We will create a fixed collection of processes, each of which applies f to all the inputs it is supplied with, and divide up the computation of $map\ f\ xs$ between them. Non-determinism will arise because we shall assign each computation of f to the next free worker. Thus the division of labour will depend on the execution times of the calls of f.

For simplicity, consider a farm with just two 'worker' processes — a processor small-holding. Assume also that the list xs of inputs to be processed is infinite; that is, Any^ω-productive.

Dividing up the Work

We begin by defining a *schedule* along with some useful operations. A schedule specifies which of the two workers should process each element of the input. It is represented by a list of values of type *tag*, defined as follows:

$$data\ tag\ ::=\ L\ |\ R$$

Given a schedule and a list of inputs, we can filter out those inputs destined for the left worker, or those destined for the right, with the functions

$$
\begin{aligned}
left\ (L{:}s)\ (x{:}xs) &= x : left\ s\ xs \\
left\ (R{:}s)\ (x{:}xs) &= left\ s\ xs \\
right\ (L{:}s)\ (x{:}xs) &= right\ s\ xs \\
right\ (R{:}s)\ (x{:}xs) &= x : right\ s\ xs
\end{aligned}
$$

Moreover, given a schedule and two lists xs and ys, the lists can be merged according to the schedule by the function

$$
\begin{aligned}
mux\ (L{:}s)\ (x{:}xs)\ ys &= x : mux\ s\ xs\ ys \\
mux\ (R{:}s)\ xs\ (y{:}ys) &= y : mux\ s\ xs\ ys
\end{aligned}
$$

It's straightforward to prove that if xs is infinite then

$$mux\ s\ (left\ s\ xs)\ (right\ s\ xs) \sqsubseteq xs$$

Similarly an easy induction * shows that

$$map\ f\ (mux\ s\ xs\ ys) = mux\ s\ (map\ f\ xs)\ (map\ f\ ys)$$

Now for any s,

$$
\begin{aligned}
&map\ f\ xs \\
&\quad \sqsupseteq map\ f\ (mux\ s\ (left\ s\ xs)\ (right\ s\ xs)) \\
&\quad = mux\ s\ (map\ f\ (left\ s\ xs))\ (map\ f\ (right\ s\ xs))
\end{aligned}
$$

---

* This is in fact one of the "free theorems" [5] that holds for all functions with mux's type. A proof is therefore unnecessary.

So given any schedule we can compute an approximation to *map f xs* by dividing up the inputs, processing them in two potentially parallel *maps*, and multiplexing the results together again. If the schedule *s* is infinite, then we can also prove these two terms equal.

Scheduling the Tasks

The result above holds for any schedule at all — so we could simply define one by, for example,

$$s = L : R : s$$

Such a schedule would send jobs to the first worker and the second worker alternately. But this would not necessarily lead to an average parallelism of two, because if one job took a particularly long time, the other worker would be held up waiting after processing one more element. A better strategy is to assign jobs to the next free worker. This requires non-determinism.

Let us therefore define a non-deterministic function *schedule* which takes two lists and returns a schedule specifying the order in which the elements of the lists become available. Its type is

$$schedule :: [*] \rightarrow [*] \rightarrow \{[tag]\}$$

and it can be defined by

$$schedule \; xs \; ys = \left(hd \; xs \gg \{L{:}s \mid s \leftarrow schedule \; (tl \; xs) \; ys\} \right)$$
$$\cup \left(hd \; ys \gg \{R{:}s \mid s \leftarrow schedule \; xs \; (tl \; ys)\} \right)$$

Note that it is the union operation in *schedule* that causes *xs* and *ys* to be evaluated in parallel. This is the only source of parallelism in the processor farm. Note also that we force the *heads* of *xs* and *ys* before choosing between them: this ensures that the schedule constructed reflects the order in which the list elements become available, not the list spines. The function *schedule* is generally useful: for example, a version of non-deterministic *merge* could be defined as follows:

$$merge \; xs \; ys = \{mux \; s \; xs \; ys \mid s \leftarrow schedule \; xs \; ys\}$$

An important lemma about *schedule*'s productivity is

$$schedule \rightsquigarrow \forall j, k. \; \Delta^j \Rightarrow \Delta^k \Rightarrow T^{j+k}$$

The proof is similar to the proof about *merge* above.

A schedule for the processor farm can be constructed from the function *schedule* as follows: the first job is always sent to the left worker and the second job to the right one, and thereafter jobs are allocated to the first available worker.

$$farm \; f \; xs = \{ans \mid (ans,s) \leftarrow X\}$$
$$\textbf{where } X = \bigcup \{ \; \textbf{let } l = map \; f \; (left \; s \; xs)$$
$$\textbf{and } r = map \; f \; (right \; s \; xs)$$
$$\textbf{in } \{(mux \; s \; l \; r, \; L : R : s') \mid s' \leftarrow schedule \; l \; r\}$$
$$\mid (ans,s) \leftarrow X\}$$

To prove partial correctness, note that

$$\{(mux\ s\ l\ r,\ L{:}R{:}\ s') \mid s' \leftarrow schedule\ l\ r\} \quad \sqsubseteq \quad \{(map\ f\ xs,\ \ldots) \mid \ldots\}$$

by the result above, and so

$$X \sqsubseteq \bigcup \{\textbf{let } \ldots \textbf{ in } \{(map\ f\ xs,\ \ldots) \mid \ldots\} \mid \ldots\}$$
$$= \{(map\ f\ xs,\ \ldots) \mid \ldots\}$$

Therefore

$$farm\ f\ xs \sqsubseteq \{map\ f\ xs\}$$

as desired. To complete the proof of correctness of the processor farm we need only show that the result is indeed infinite.

Suppose therefore that xs is α^ω-productive, $f \rightsquigarrow \alpha \Rightarrow \beta$, and $\beta \subseteq \Delta$. We must show $farm\ f\ xs \rightsquigarrow \beta^\omega$. This will follow from proving $X \rightsquigarrow \beta^\omega \times T^\omega$. Let F therefore be the function whose fixpoint X is

$$
\begin{aligned}
F\ X = \bigcup \{\ &\textbf{let } l = map\ f\ (left\ s\ xs) \\
&\textbf{and } r = map\ f\ (right\ s\ xs) \\
&\textbf{in } \{(mux\ s\ l\ r,\ L{:}R{:}\ s') \mid s' \in schedule\ l\ r\} \\
&\mid (ans,s) \in X\}
\end{aligned}
$$

Lemma. $F \rightsquigarrow \forall k.\ Any \times T^k \Rightarrow \beta^k \times T^{k+2}$

Proof. We have to show, from the assumption $s \rightsquigarrow T^k$, that

$$\textbf{let } l = \ldots \textbf{ in } \ldots \rightsquigarrow \beta^k \times T^{k+2}.$$

But for any $s \rightsquigarrow T^k$, there exists $0 \le i \le k$ such that

$$left\ s \ \rightsquigarrow \pi^\omega \Rightarrow \pi^i$$
$$right\ s \ \rightsquigarrow \pi^\omega \Rightarrow \pi^{k-i}$$
$$mux\ s \ \rightsquigarrow \pi^i \Rightarrow \pi^{k-i} \Rightarrow \pi^k$$

In fact i is the number of Ls in the first k elements of s, and these three facts follow by easy inductions. Now since $xs \rightsquigarrow \alpha^\omega$, we have

$$l \rightsquigarrow \beta^i$$
$$r \rightsquigarrow \beta^{k-i}$$
$$mux\ s\ l\ r \rightsquigarrow \beta^k$$

and, by the schedule lemma and $\beta \subseteq \Delta$,

$$schedule\ l\ r \ \rightsquigarrow T^k$$

It follows that

$$\textbf{let } l\ =\ \ldots \textbf{ in } \ldots \ \rightsquigarrow \beta^k \times T^{k+2}$$

End of proof.

Now, since $\perp \rightsquigarrow Any \times T^0$ and $\beta^k \times T^{k+2} \subseteq Any \times T^0$, we have by the fix rule that

$$X = \text{fix } F \rightsquigarrow Any \times T^0$$

By induction, and another use of the lemma, we have

$$X = \text{fix } F \rightsquigarrow Any \times T^\omega$$

and so, by a final use of the lemma,

$$X \rightsquigarrow \beta^\omega \times T^\omega.$$

It follows that

$$farm\ f\ xs \rightsquigarrow \beta^\omega$$

as desired.

7. Conclusion

We have shown how to obtain nondeterminism by adding sets of values to an ordinary functional language. A set contains all the values which might be output by the program, but the implementation will output just one representative from the set.

It isn't possible to introduce all the operators of set theory into the language without destroying referential transparency. The first major result of the paper is that a restricted class of set operators is sufficient for solving interesting nondeterministic problems, while remaining weak enough to retain referential transparency.

We have given a denotational semantics for the language based on the Hoare powerdomain. This semantics is useful for reasoning about what the program produces. For example, it can be used to show that certain race conditions do not cause outputs to appear out of order. However, the semantics is not able to capture all the properties of the intended implementation. In particular, it cannot be used to prove that programs terminate.

One way around the termination problem would be to resort to an operational semantics. We chose instead to stick with the denotational semantics, and to introduce an external method for reasoning about the productivities of programs. This is the second main result of the paper. The semantics is not sufficient to prove that the productivity laws are true. We view the productivity laws as additional constraints that must be satisfied by any valid implementation.

We have illustrated the expressiveness of these techniques by presenting a solution to the processor farm problem, along with a proof of its productivity. This example (both the program and the theorems we were able to prove about it) provides a concrete way to compare the effectiveness of nondeterministic sets with alternative approaches to nondeterminism. For example, the processor farm example falls outside the class of algorithms that can be expressed with Burton's 'improving values.' Further case studies of this kind will help to clarify the tradeoffs among the competing methods for nondeterministic programming.

References

1. John Hughes and John O'Donnell, "Expressing and reasoning about non-deterministic functional programs," *Functional Programming, Glasgow 1989*, Springer-Verlag (1990) 308–328.

2. G. Kahn and D. McQueen, "Coroutines and networks of parallel processes," *Information Processing 77*, North-Holland, Amsterdam (1977).

3. John McCarthy, "A basis for a mathematical theory of computation," *Computer Programming and Formal Systems*, North-Holland (1963) 33–70.

4. B. A. Sijtsma, *Verification and Derivation of Infinite-List Programs*, PhD Thesis, University of Groningen (1988).

5. Philip L. Wadler, "Theorems for free!," *4'th International Conference on Functional Programming Languages and Computer Architecture*, ACM (1989).

Process Algebra as a Tool for Real Time Analysis

Faron Moller[*]

Department of Computer Science
University of Edinburgh
Edinburgh EH9 3JZ Scotland

fm@uk.ac.ed.lfcs

Abstract

In this paper, we investigate the use of Process Algebra for reasoning about real time behaviours. We do this by describing a process algebra model based on Milner's *Calculus of Communicating Systems* (CCS), in which timing constraints are introduced as another level of observable behaviour beyond the usual observation of a system's functional (atomic action) behaviour. Though the language is simple, we demonstrate how to define several important derived operators.

We present a structured operational semantics for our language in the form of a transition system defined over syntactic terms, and define two bisimulation-based relations with respect to this semantics. The first is an equivalence giving a natural definition for when two terms should be equated, while the second is a preorder giving an equally natural definition for when two terms should be deemed equivalent except for the fact that the first may be faster than the second. We then present equational theories for these two relations.

---
[*]Research supported by ESPRIT BRA No 3006 — CONCUR

1 Introduction

The study of process algebra as the foundation of the semantics of concurrent computation has been a fruitful endeavour, giving a decade of almost continuous discoveries on the mathematical nature and practical development of concurrent processes, be they mechanical or otherwise. One of the original process algebra approaches studied as a mathematical model of concurrency was Milner's *Calculus of Communicating Systems* (CCS) of [10] and more recently [12], and this algebra continues to be studied and extended in many directions. Other important approaches to process algebra include Hoare's *Communicating Sequential Processes* (CSP) of [9] and [4], Bergstra and Klop's *Algebra of Communicating Processes* (ACP) of [2], Boudol's *Meije* calculus of [3], and Hennessy's process language of [7].

Each of the above approaches allows an elegant presentation of the causal and concurrent natures of processes, and each has been studied and exploited for this reason. Thus we are standing at a point in time now where a great deal of understanding has been developed of concurrent processes from different viewpoints, and we are now discovering the relative merits of the approaches and forming an idea as to the real issues which need to be captured by this aspect of the theory of concurrency.

There is (at least) one common deficiency in each of the above approaches to concurrency theory. This deficiency is that there is no concept of *time* embodied in any of the algebras. Though each of the languages allows the analysis of the temporal ordering of events, there is no way of specifying the relative speeds of the events. The closest approximation to such a desirable element of the theory until recently has been the approach taken in [11] of timestepping events synchronously in a modified version of CCS (*Synchronous* CCS, or SCCS). Such an approach mimics the global clock notion of synchronous computation, but is quite restrictive as a foundation to the theory of the temporal properties of concurrent systems.

Recently however, there has been a spate of developments aimed at eliminating this deficiency within process theory. As a sample of these developments we cite [12, 5, 8, 14, 13, 17, 19]. Each of these introduces some notion of timing into an existing approach to process theory, but in often distinctly diverse fashions. We see synchrony sometimes being enforced again, and also the methods often admit only discrete timestepping rather than a more general continuum of time passing. Thus we are again at a point of being unsure as to the correct direction to proceed in this aspect of concurrency theory, and debate is open as to the relative merits of the above (and other) approaches to the problem of describing the temporal properties of processes.

In this paper, we introduce the language TCCS, the *Temporal Calculus of Communicating Systems* of [13]. This language is founded on Milner's CCS, as well as the work of [18], and is in the consideration of the author a viable approach to timing in process algebra which avoids flaws such as those listed above which exist in other approaches. Some of the advantages of the approach are listed as follows: the framework is simple yet powerful in its expressive ability; it is based on well-founded existing technology; it is algebraic, or modular; it allows for modelling within a dense time domain (though the framework equally allows for modelling within a discrete time domain as well); it allows for the definition of natural equivalences and pre-orders; it admits of a logic for specification; and it can conceivably be automated within existing tools, namely the *Edinburgh Concurrency Workbench*.

2 The Language TCCS

Our language TCCS is a timed extension of CCS, Milner's *Calculus of Communicating Systems* of [10] and [12]. To define the language, we first presuppose a set Λ of *atomic action symbols* not containing τ or ε, and we define Act $= \Lambda \cup \{\tau\}$. We assume that Λ can be partitioned into two equinumerous sets with a *complementation* bijection $\bar{\ }$ defined between them extended by $\bar{\bar{a}} = a$. These complementary actions form the basis of the handshake communication method in our calculus, analogous to that of CCS. We also presuppose some set Var of *process variables*, and take T to represent some time domain (that is, a linearly ordered, lower-bounded set), be it for instance the discrete domain of positive integers, or the dense domain of positive rationals, or the continuous domain of positive reals. We shall for the most part not put any restriction on the time domain, but we will present some results which hold only over a discrete time domain such as the integers.

The collection of TCCS expressions, ranged over by P, is then defined by the BNF expression given in Figure 1, where we take $a \in$ Act, $X \in$ Var, $t \in T$, and S ranging over *relabelling functions*, those $S :$ Act $\rightarrow$ Act such that $\overline{S(a)} = S(\bar{a})$ for $a \neq \tau$ and $S(\tau) = \tau$. The intuitive interpretation of these terms can be given as

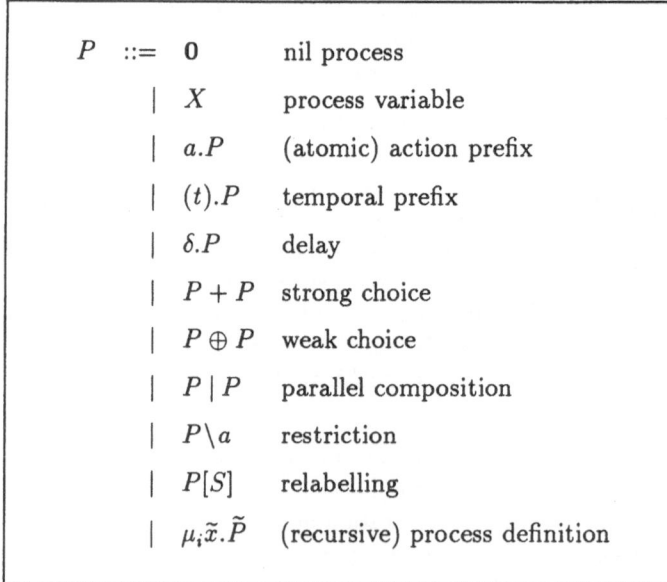

$$
\begin{array}{lll}
P & ::= & \mathbf{0} & \text{nil process} \\
& \mid & X & \text{process variable} \\
& \mid & a.P & \text{(atomic) action prefix} \\
& \mid & (t).P & \text{temporal prefix} \\
& \mid & \delta.P & \text{delay} \\
& \mid & P + P & \text{strong choice} \\
& \mid & P \oplus P & \text{weak choice} \\
& \mid & P \mid P & \text{parallel composition} \\
& \mid & P \backslash a & \text{restriction} \\
& \mid & P[S] & \text{relabelling} \\
& \mid & \mu_i \tilde{x}.\tilde{P} & \text{(recursive) process definition}
\end{array}
$$

Figure 1: Syntax of TCCS

follows.

- **0** represents the completely dead process. It can neither perform any computation, nor can it witness the passage of any time. In terms of a concrete machine, it may be thought of as one which is shut down or with its "plug pulled". One of the consequences is that whenever **0** is a component of a machine, then the whole machine will be temporally dead; the local temporal deadlock gives rise to a global temporal deadlock.

- X represents the process bound to the variable X in some assumed environment.

- $a.P$ represents the process which can perform the (atomic) action a and evolve into the process P upon so doing. The process cannot progress through time before performing the action a, and the action is assumed to occur instantaneously in time. If we wish to model a system where actions have some amount of duration (for instance, if we wish to talk of the computation of some hardware component with a certain known propagation delay), then we can naturally treat the action as a composite action consisting of the two atomic actions or events a_s (start action a) and a_f (finish action a), with the two actions separated in time by the appropriate duration t_a. Thus this composite action would be written as $a_s.(t_a).a_e$. Also note that atomic actions can be *causally* related without one being *temporally* dependent on the other. For instance, if we consider the process $a.b.P$, the action b is causally dependent on the action a in that it cannot have occurred *unless* (notice that we do not say *until*) the action a has occurred; however, the two actions are considered to happen simultaneously in time.

- $(t).P$ represents the process which will do no computation for an amount t of time, but at that point in time will commence behaving as the process P.

- $\delta.P$ represents the process which behaves as the process P, but is willing to wait some amount of time before actually proceeding. Here the understanding is that P has the capability to communicate with its environment, but the environment may at the present moment not allow the communication to occur; $\delta.P$ allows for the process P to delay its communication until such time as the communication can occur. Note that though the process $\delta.P$ may proceed with an action once the environment permits it, that action might not occur immediately. Such would be the approach of *maximal progress* as propounded for example by [19]. We choose to avoid maximal progress in our approach for two reasons. Firstly, we will have other approaches for analysing how soon an action can occur, so we can within our framework decide the (maximum) speed of the process assuming that maximal progress held. Secondly, we want to permit the possibility of modelling unexpected events. For example, in modelling a chemical plant, we may wish on top of the normal modelling of the system to model a disasterous scenario, called say *act-of-God*, which would be accomplished simply by the inclusion of the component process $\delta.act\text{-}of\text{-}God.P$, where P behaves as a disasterous event, a sort of "spanner thrown into the works". This process is ready to perform the "*act-of-God*", and this action can occur at any time, but it is not forced to occur by any maximal progress requirement imposed on the modelling framework.

- $P + Q$ represents a choice between the two processes P and Q. The process behaves as the process P or the process Q, with the choice being made at the time of the first action. Thus for instance any initial passage of time must be allowed by both P and Q. This operator is referred to as *strong* choice.

- $P \oplus Q$ represents a slightly different choice between the two processes P and Q. The process behaves as the process P or the process Q, with the choice being made at the time of the first action, or else at the occurrence of a passage of time when only one of the operands may allow the time passage to occur. In this case, the second *"stopped"* process is dropped from the computation. This operator is referred to as *weak* choice.

- $P \mid Q$ represents the parallel composition of the two processes P and Q. Each of the processes may do any actions independently, or they may synchronise on complementary actions, resulting in a τ action. Any passage of time must be allowed and recorded by each of P and Q.

- $P \backslash a$ represents the process P with the action $a \in \Lambda$ (as well as its complement action $\overline{a}$) restricted away, that is, not allowed to occur.

- $P[S]$ represents the process P with its actions renamed by the relabelling function S.

- $\mu_i \widetilde{x}.\widetilde{P}$ represents the solution x_i taken from the solutions to the mutually recursive definitions of the processes $\widetilde{x} = \{x_1, x_2, \ldots, x_n\}$ defined as particular (least fixed point) solutions to the equations $\widetilde{x} = \widetilde{P}$.

Some points worth noting which arise from the above informal description are as follows.

- As was described above, the process **0** acts as a deadlock process in that it cannot perform any actions, nor witness any passage of time. Hence, by the definitions of the strong and weak choice operators + and $\oplus$, and the parallel composition operator $\mid$, the constant **0** acts as an annihilator with respect to strongly adding to or composing with time-guarded processes, and as a unit with respect to the weak choice operator $\oplus$. Thus again in particular, local temporal deadlock will imply global deadlock — if only time derivations are possible from each component of a parallel composition involving **0**, then the whole composite process is deadlocked. Hence, of interest is the derived *nontemporal deadlock* process $\delta.\mathbf{0}$, which will allow any time to pass, but can never perform any actions. This process thus stands as a unit with respect to the strong choice operator + and the parallel composition operator $\mid$. We shall emphasize the importance of this derived concept by abbreviating it to $\underline{\mathbf{0}}$.

- The description given above of the delay prefix δ is such that it is only meaningful to follow it with action terms. $\delta.P$ represents a process which is delaying the *actions* of P until the environment in which the process is executing will allow the actions to proceed. Thus for instance, the process $\delta.(1).a.\mathbf{0}$ can never perform its action a, as it can never get past the delaying δ. Hence, this process will be identified with $\underline{\mathbf{0}}$ the nontemporal deadlock. Of importance then is the delayed action prefix $\delta.a.P$, and we emphasize its importance by abbreviating it to $\underline{a}.P$.

- The subcalculus given by replacing $\mathbf{0}$ and $a.P$ by $\underline{\mathbf{0}}$ and $\underline{a}.P$ respectively defines only processes which can never deadlock temporally; every process term must allow time to pass. This proves to be a useful subcalculus, both practically and theoretically. Practically, we can imagine its utility for example in modelling hardware components which are connected in a pipelined fashion in which the components have different propagation delays. One component will be ready to communicate its data to the next component, but this component will not be prepared to receive the data. In this case, the data signal will remain at the output port of the first component until such time as the receiving component is prepared to accept it. Theoretically, this subcalculus will be important when we consider comparing the relative speeds of behaviourally functionally equivalent processes. Furthermore, this subcalculus is seen to be simpler by noting that in the absence of temporal deadlock, the two choice operators collapse into the same operation, and there is no longer any need for the general delay operator δ. We shall henceforth emphasis the importance of this subcalculus by referring to it by ℓTCCS, or *loose* TCCS.

As a point of notation, we shall occasionally omit the dot when applying the prefix operators, and also drop trailing $\mathbf{0}$'s, thus for instance rendering $\delta.a.\mathbf{0} + (t).b.\mathbf{0}$ as $\underline{a} + (t)b$. Also, we shall allow the prefix operators to take equal precedence over the concurrency operator, which will take precedence over the recursion operator, which finally in turn will take precedence over the choice operators; outside of this, the binary operators will be left associative, and we shall freely use parentheses to override the precedence rules. Finally, we shall allow ourselves to specify processes definitionally, by providing recursive definitions of processes. For example, we shall write $A \stackrel{\text{def}}{=} a.A$ rather than $A \stackrel{\text{def}}{=} \mu x.a.x$.

2.1   Useful Derived Concepts

Besides the two important derived operators nontemporal deadlock and delayed action prefix, we can define other useful derived operators. We list only a few of the possibilities here. Firstly, we can define a *loose time prefix* as follows.

$$[t].P \stackrel{\text{def}}{=} (t).\delta.P$$

This allows a process to wait for a certain fixed time to pass before being willing to participate in a communication, and then to await any length of time afterwards for another process in the environment to participate in the communication.

Next we can define a *process prefix* operator as follows.

$$\text{INIT}_t(P) \stackrel{\text{def}}{=} P \mid (t).\mathbf{0}$$

This allows a process to execute normally for a certain fixed time t, and then die when it cannot perform any actions without possibly first allowing some further amount of time to pass.

Finally we can define a *timeout* operator as follows.

$$\text{TIMEOUT}_t(P, Q) \stackrel{\text{def}}{=} \delta.P + (t).Q$$

This allows a process P to commence execution through a communication with the environment at any instant over a certain fixed time, but then allows another process Q to execute after that time, thus preempting the first possibility. This operator is especially useful for modelling timeouts in fault-tolerant systems such as protocols, or as a method of forcing a computation to commence at some time within the next t units of time, by instantiating the process Q to **0**.

2.2   Some Simple Examples

For the remainder of this section we shall present several examples which will demonstrate the utility of the calculus.

Example 2.1 Suppose we have some collection of (distinct) times $t_i \in \mathcal{T}$ $(1 \leq i \leq n)$, and we define the simple processes H_i by

$$H_i \stackrel{\text{def}}{=} (t_i).finish_i.\mathbf{0}.$$

These processes can be viewed as horses competing in a race; the time which horse i takes to cross the finish line is given by t_i.

Following this interpretation, if we denote then a race to be the parallel composition of the horse processes, that is,

$$Race \stackrel{\text{def}}{=} \prod_{1 \leq i \leq n} H_i = H_1 \mid H_2 \mid \cdots \mid H_n,$$

then we discover that

$$Race = (t_m).finish_m.\mathbf{0},$$

where we interpret equality in a sense (to be made more precise later) as "having the same behaviour", and where m is such that $t_m < t_i$ for each $i \neq m$. Hence the effect of a *race* is to report the winning horse.

If we now denote another process $Race'$ by

$$Race' \stackrel{\text{def}}{=} \sum_{1 \leq i \leq n} H_i = H_1 + H_2 + \cdots + H_n,$$

then we can discover in fact that

$$Race = Race'.$$

This is a natural consequence of the fact that elements of a choice pass time together until the choice is actually made. This anomoly, where parallel computation is confused with nondeterministic choice, has an analogy in computation theory, where the process *Race* is viewed as the Turing Machine concept of nondeterministic acceptance — try each path in parallel, and accept if one of the paths succeeds.

Note that if we alter the definition of our horses slightly by defining the processes as

$$\widetilde{H_i} \stackrel{\text{def}}{=} (t_i).finish_i.\mathbf{0},$$

then this analogy breaks down. The corresponding race processes $\widetilde{Race}$ and $\widetilde{Race}'$ no longer have the same behaviour, as $\widetilde{Race}'$ still only reports the winning horse, whereas $\widetilde{Race}$ reports the times of all subsequent horses. That is, $Race'$ sorts the values t_i into ascending order.

Example 2.2 Here we present an example which is best suited to a discrete time model, but which works equally well in a more generous time model under the proviso that the components in the system may delay their communication capabilities. Consider the following two recursively-defined processes.

$$A \stackrel{\text{def}}{=} a.A' \oplus (1).B$$
$$B \stackrel{\text{def}}{=} b.B' \oplus (1).A$$

Here we are representing a system which is allowing one of two possible computation paths to be followed, and furthermore allowing the choice to be determined by time, in that the first path can be followed only at even time units, whilst the second path can be followed only at odd time units. This system can be considered for example as the description of a multiplexing system based on polling or sampling, or as the basis of a mutual exclusion algorithm for two independent processes sharing a common critical section. We can see this by interpreting the actions a and b as the first and second processes entering the critical section, respectively. Then the processes A' and B' can be reasonably defined by $A' \stackrel{\text{def}}{=} c.B$ and $B' \stackrel{\text{def}}{=} d.A$, where the actions c and d represent the first and second processes exiting the critical section, respectively. This system may be imagined as looking like the following picture.

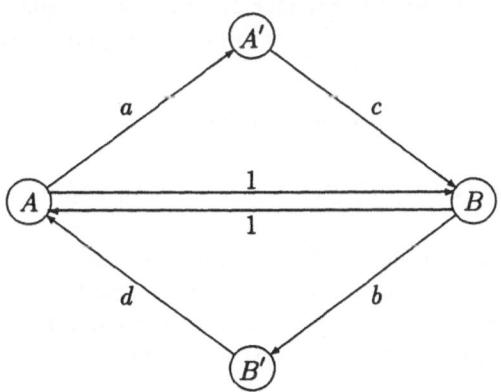

We can trivially generalise this system to give a simple mutual exclusion algorithm for any number of processes sharing a common resource.

Example 2.3 In this example, we describe a possible timed implementation of the Alternating Bit Protocol.

There are three components to our protocol: the sender, the receiver, and the medium. These three components are described as follows. First the sender S has the following definition.

$$S \stackrel{\text{def}}{=} S_0 \qquad \qquad S_b \stackrel{\text{def}}{=} send.S_b'$$
$$S_b' \stackrel{\text{def}}{=} \overline{s_b}.\text{TIMEOUT}_{t_r}(rack_b.S_{1-b} + rack_{1-b}.S_b', S_b')$$

Here, t_r is the amount of time which the sender will wait after sending a message before assuming the message has been lost and retransmitting the message. So the sender receives a request to send a message (the "*send*" action), immediately sends the message to the medium tagged with an appropriate binary digit (the "$\overline{s_b}$" action), and then waits for the appropriate acknowledgement to arrive from the medium (the "$rack_b$" action). If it receives the wrong acknowledgement, or is left waiting for the full duration of the retry time t_r, then it shall retransmit the message.

Next the receiver R has the following definition.

$$R \stackrel{\text{def}}{=} r_0.R_0 \qquad \qquad R_b \stackrel{\text{def}}{=} receive.R_b'$$
$$R_b' \stackrel{\text{def}}{=} \overline{sack_b}.\text{TIMEOUT}_{t_r}(r_{1-b}.R_{1-b} + r_b.R_b', R_b')$$

This definition is completely symmetric to the definition of the sender, with the exception that it starts in a state where it is awaiting the first message to appear from the medium (the "r_0" action).

Finally, the medium has the following definition.

$$M \stackrel{\text{def}}{=} s_0.(t_t).\overline{r_0}.M + s_1.(t_t).\overline{r_1}.M + sack_0.(t_t).\overline{rack_0}.M + sack_1.(t_t).\overline{rack_1}.M$$

Here, t_t represents the transmission time. Hence the medium at some point in time receives either a message from the sender or an acknowledgement from the receiver, suitably tagged, and passes the message or acknowledgement straight through after a delay of t_t, the transmission time.

We can then define our protocol as follows.

$$\text{ABP} \stackrel{\text{def}}{=} (S \mid M \mid R) \backslash \{s_0, s_1, r_0, r_1, sack_0, sack_1, rack_0, rack_1\}$$

With these definitions, under the assumption that $t_r > 2t_t$ (that is, that the sender and receiver will wait at least twice the transmission time, the amount of time required for a message to get across the medium and have an acknowledgement return, before timing out and retransmitting its message or acknowledgement), we can show that

$$\frac{}{(t).P \uparrow s}(s \le t) \qquad \frac{P \uparrow t,\ Q \uparrow t}{P + Q \uparrow t} \qquad \frac{P \uparrow t,\ Q \uparrow t}{P \mid Q \uparrow t}$$

$$\frac{P \uparrow t_0}{(t).P \uparrow s}(s \le t_0 + t) \qquad \frac{P \uparrow t}{P \oplus Q \uparrow t} \qquad \frac{P \uparrow t}{P \backslash a \uparrow t}$$

$$\frac{}{\delta.P \uparrow t} \qquad\qquad \frac{Q \uparrow t}{P \oplus Q \uparrow t} \qquad \frac{P \uparrow t}{P[S] \uparrow t} \qquad \frac{P_i\left\{\mu\tilde{x}.\tilde{P}\big/\tilde{x}\right\} \uparrow t}{\mu_i\tilde{x}.\tilde{P} \uparrow t}$$

Figure 2: Delay capabilities of TCCS terms

$$\text{ABP} = \text{SPEC},$$

where

$$\text{SPEC} \stackrel{\text{def}}{=} send.(t_t).receive.(t_t).\text{SPEC}.$$

and equality again is interpreted as "having the same behaviour", but now modulo the occurrence of some number of τ transitions.

3 The Semantics of TCCS

Up until now, we have only described informally what it means for two process terms to be deemed "the same". In this section, we define this notion in a rigorous fashion, by providing a mathematical semantic definition of the language.

The semantics of TCCS is *transition based*, structurally presented in the style of [16], outlining what actions and time delays a process can witness. In order to define our semantics however, we must first define a syntactic predicate which will allow us to describe when a process may idle for a particular amount of time. This function is defined as follows.

Definition 3.1 *The relation* $\uparrow \subseteq \text{TCCS} \times \mathcal{T}$ *(written* $P \uparrow t$ *for* $(P,t) \in \uparrow$*) is defined to be the least relation satisfying the natural deduction style inference rules laid out in Figure 2. These rules are to be read as follows: if the relation(s) above the inference line can be inferred, then we can infer the relation below the line.*

Informally, $P \uparrow t$ means that the process term P may idle for time t without performing any computation.

In Figure 3, we present the operational rules for our language. Again they are presented in an identical natural deduction style. Our transitional semantics over TCCS then is given by the least relations $\longrightarrow \subseteq \text{TCCS} \times \text{Act} \times \text{TCCS}$

$$\frac{}{a.P \xrightarrow{a} P} \qquad \frac{P \xrightarrow{a} P'}{P \oplus Q \xrightarrow{a} P'} \qquad \frac{P \xrightarrow{a} P', \ Q \xrightarrow{\bar{a}} Q'}{P \mid Q \xrightarrow{\tau} P' \mid Q'}$$

$$\frac{P \xrightarrow{a} P'}{\delta.P \xrightarrow{a} P'} \qquad \frac{Q \xrightarrow{a} Q'}{P \oplus Q \xrightarrow{a} Q'} \qquad \frac{P \xrightarrow{a} P'}{P \backslash b \xrightarrow{a} P' \backslash b}(a \neq b, \bar{b})$$

$$\frac{P \xrightarrow{a} P'}{P + Q \xrightarrow{a} P'} \qquad \frac{P \xrightarrow{a} P'}{P \mid Q \xrightarrow{a} P' \mid Q} \qquad \frac{P \xrightarrow{a} P'}{P[S] \xrightarrow{S(a)} P'[S]}$$

$$\frac{Q \xrightarrow{a} Q'}{P + Q \xrightarrow{a} Q'} \qquad \frac{Q \xrightarrow{a} Q'}{P \mid Q \xrightarrow{a} P \mid Q'} \qquad \frac{P_i\left\{\mu\tilde{x}.\tilde{P}\big/_{\tilde{x}}\right\} \xrightarrow{a} P'}{\mu_i\tilde{x}.\tilde{P} \xrightarrow{a} P'}$$

$$\frac{}{\delta.P \overset{t}{\leadsto} \delta.P} \qquad \frac{P \overset{t}{\leadsto} P', \ Q \overset{t}{\leadsto} Q'}{P + Q \overset{t}{\leadsto} P' + Q'} \qquad \frac{P \overset{t}{\leadsto} P', \ Q \overset{t}{\leadsto} Q'}{P \mid Q \overset{t}{\leadsto} P' \mid Q'}$$

$$\frac{}{(s + t).P \overset{s}{\leadsto} (t).P} \qquad \frac{P \overset{t}{\leadsto} P', \ Q \not\overset{t}{\leadsto}}{P \oplus Q \overset{t}{\leadsto} P'} \qquad \frac{P \overset{t}{\leadsto} P'}{P \backslash a \overset{t}{\leadsto} P' \backslash a}$$

$$\frac{}{(t).P \overset{t}{\leadsto} P} \qquad \frac{Q \overset{t}{\leadsto} Q', \ P \not\overset{t}{\leadsto}}{P \oplus Q \overset{t}{\leadsto} Q'} \qquad \frac{P \overset{t}{\leadsto} P'}{P[S] \overset{t}{\leadsto} P'[S]}$$

$$\frac{P \overset{s}{\leadsto} P'}{(t).P \overset{s+t}{\leadsto} P'} \qquad \frac{P \overset{t}{\leadsto} P', \ Q \overset{t}{\leadsto} Q'}{P \oplus Q \overset{t}{\leadsto} P' \oplus Q'} \qquad \frac{P_i\left\{\mu\tilde{x}.\tilde{P}\big/_{\tilde{x}}\right\} \overset{t}{\leadsto} P'}{\mu_i\tilde{x}.\tilde{P} \overset{t}{\leadsto} P'}$$

Figure 3: Operational Rules for TCCS

and $\leadsto \subseteq \text{TCCS} \times \mathcal{T} \times \text{TCCS}$ (written $P \xrightarrow{a} Q$ and $P \overset{t}{\leadsto} Q$ for $(P, a, Q) \in \longrightarrow$ and $(P, t, Q) \in \leadsto$ respectively) satisfying the rules laid out in Figure 3. Notice that these rules respect the informal description of the constructs given in the previous section.

We can also give operational rules directly for our two derived operators, non-temporal deadlock $\underline{0}$ and delayed action prefix $\underline{a}.P$. These are presented in Figure 4. These rules are redundant along with those of Figure 3; however, they will be needed for the subcalculus which we consider later.

3.1 A Semantic Equivalence

We can now define an equivalence relation $\sim$ on closed terms of TCCS based on Park's notion of a *bisimulation* ([15]) as follows.

$$\overline{0 \overset{t}{\leadsto} 0} \qquad\qquad \overline{\underline{a}.P \overset{a}{\longrightarrow} P} \qquad\qquad \overline{\underline{a}.P \overset{t}{\leadsto} \underline{a}.P}$$

Figure 4: Operational Rules For Derived Operators

Definition 3.2 *A binary relation* $\mathcal{R}$ *over terms in* TCCS *is a* $\mathcal{T}$*-bisimulation if and only if for all* $(P, Q) \in \mathcal{R}$ *and for all* $a \in$ Act *and for all* $t \in \mathcal{T}$,

> *(i) if* $P \overset{a}{\longrightarrow} P'$ *then* $Q \overset{a}{\longrightarrow} Q'$ *for some* Q' *with* $(P', Q') \in \mathcal{R}$;
> *(ii) if* $Q \overset{a}{\longrightarrow} Q'$ *then* $P \overset{a}{\longrightarrow} P'$ *for some* P' *with* $(P', Q') \in \mathcal{R}$;
> *(iii) if* $P \overset{t}{\leadsto} P'$ *then* $Q \overset{t}{\leadsto} Q'$ *for some* Q' *with* $(P', Q') \in \mathcal{R}$;
> *(iv) if* $Q \overset{t}{\leadsto} Q'$ *then* $P \overset{t}{\leadsto} P'$ *for some* P' *with* $(P', Q') \in \mathcal{R}$.

$\sim \overset{\text{def}}{=} \bigcup \{\mathcal{R} : \mathcal{R}$ *is a* $\mathcal{T}$*-bisimulation*$\}$ *is then the largest* $\mathcal{T}$*-bisimulation.*

In [13], it is shown that this relation defines a congruence over TCCS terms. This congruence satisfies the laws given in Figure 5, and these laws are conjectured to be complete with respect to reasoning about finite sequential TCCS terms, those terms in the subcalculus not involving the parallel composition or recursive process definition. These laws are complete for reasoning over this subcalculus in the discrete time domain of positive integers when we include the further axiom

$$(\oplus_{10}) \qquad \delta a x = a x \oplus (1)\delta a x$$

which can replace the two laws $(\oplus_8)$ and $(\oplus_9)$ in this case.

When we add concurrent composition to this subcalculus, we get a conjectured complete axiomatization by adding the laws of Figure 6. Again, this axiomatization is complete for the discrete time domain when we include the axiom the axiom

$$(E_7) \quad \delta X \mid (Y \oplus (1)y) = \bigoplus_{1 \le i \le m} a_i(x_i \mid (Y \oplus (1)y)) \oplus \bigoplus_{1 \le j \le n} b_j(\delta X \mid y_j)$$

$$\oplus \bigoplus_{a_i = \bar{b}_j} \tau(x_i \mid y_j) \oplus (1)(\delta X \mid y)$$

which can replace the law (E_5) in this case.

3.2 Relating Processes With Respect To Speed

In this section, we wish to consider a preorder which relates the relative speeds of functionally behaviourally equivalent processes.

In the previous section, we defined and analysed an equivalence in which two processes were identified roughly when they were identical in both their functional

(P_1) $\quad (s)(t)x = (s+t)x$ $\qquad$ (P_2) $\quad \delta\delta x = \delta x$

(P_3) $\quad \delta(t)x = \delta\mathbf{0}$

$(\oplus_1)$ $\quad (x \oplus y) \oplus z = x \oplus (y \oplus z)$ $\qquad$ $(\oplus_2)$ $\quad x \oplus y = y \oplus x$

$(\oplus_3)$ $\quad x \oplus x = x$ $\qquad$ $(\oplus_4)$ $\quad x \oplus \mathbf{0} = x$

$(\oplus_5)$ $\quad \delta x \oplus \delta y = \delta(x \oplus y)$ $\qquad$ $(\oplus_6)$ $\quad (t)x \oplus (t)y = (t)(x \oplus y)$

$(\oplus_7)$ $\quad (t)\underline{\mathbf{0}} = \underline{\mathbf{0}}$ $\qquad$ $(\oplus_8)$ $\quad \underline{a}x = ax \oplus \underline{a}x$

$(\oplus_9)$ $\quad \underline{a}x = \underline{a}x \oplus (t)\underline{a}x$

$(+_1)$ $\quad (x+y)+z = x+(y+z)$ $\qquad$ $(+_2)$ $\quad x+y = y+x$

$(+_3)$ $\quad x+x = x$ $\qquad$ $(+_4)$ $\quad x+\underline{\mathbf{0}} = x$

$(+_5)$ $\quad \mathbf{0}+(t)x = \mathbf{0}$ $\qquad$ $(+_6)$ $\quad \mathbf{0}+ax = ax$

$(+_7)$ $\quad \mathbf{0}+\delta x = \mathbf{0}+x$ $\qquad$ $(+_8)$ $\quad ax+(t)y = ax$

$(+_9)$ $\quad ax+\delta y = ax+y$ $\qquad$ $(+_{10})$ $\quad \delta x+\delta y = \delta(x+y)$

$(+_{11})$ $\quad (t)x+(t)y = (t)(x+y)$ $\qquad$ $(+_{12})$ $\quad \delta x+(t)\delta x = \delta x$

(D) $\quad x+(y \oplus z) = (x+y) \oplus (x+z)$ $\qquad$ (C) $\quad ax+by = ax \oplus by$

(A_1) $\quad \mathbf{0}\backslash a = \mathbf{0}$ $\qquad$ (R_1) $\quad \mathbf{0}[S] = \mathbf{0}$

(A_2) $\quad (b.P)\backslash a = \begin{cases} \mathbf{0}, & \text{if } a=b,\bar{b} \\ b.(P\backslash a), & \text{o/w} \end{cases}$ $\qquad$ (R_2) $\quad (b.P)[S] = b.(P[S])$

(A_3) $\quad ((t).P)\backslash a = (t).(P\backslash a)$ $\qquad$ (R_3) $\quad ((t).P)[S] = (t).(P[S])$

(A_4) $\quad (\delta.P)\backslash a = \delta.(P\backslash a)$ $\qquad$ (R_4) $\quad (\delta.P)[S] = \delta.(P[S])$

(A_5) $\quad (P+Q)\backslash a = P\backslash a + Q\backslash a$ $\qquad$ (R_5) $\quad (P+Q)[S] = P[S]+Q[S]$

(A_6) $\quad (P \oplus Q)\backslash a = P\backslash a \oplus Q\backslash a$ $\qquad$ (R_6) $\quad (P \oplus Q)[S] = P[S] \oplus Q[S]$

Figure 5: Equational Theory for Sequential TCCS Terms

$$(|_1) \quad (x\,|\,y)\,|\,z \;=\; x\,|\,(y\,|\,z) \qquad\qquad (|_2) \quad x\,|\,y \;=\; y\,|\,x$$

Let $X = \displaystyle\bigoplus_{1\le i\le m} a_i x_i$ and $Y = \displaystyle\bigoplus_{1\le j\le n} b_j y_j$

$$(E_1) \quad X\,|\,Y \;=\; \bigoplus_{1\le i\le m} a_i(x_i\,|\,Y) \;\oplus\; \bigoplus_{1\le j\le n} b_j(X\,|\,y_j) \;\oplus\; \bigoplus_{a_i=\bar b_j} \tau(x_i\,|\,y_j)$$

$$(E_2) \quad X\,|\,(Y\oplus(t)y) \;=\; \bigoplus_{1\le i\le m} a_i(x_i\,|\,(Y\oplus(t)y)) \;\oplus\; \bigoplus_{1\le j\le n} b_j(X\,|\,y_j)$$
$$\oplus\; \bigoplus_{a_i=\bar b_j} \tau(x_i\,|\,y_j)$$

$$(E_3) \quad (X\oplus(t)x)\,|\,(Y\oplus(t)y) \;=\; \bigoplus_{1\le i\le m} a_i(x_i\,|\,(Y\oplus(t)y))$$
$$\oplus\; \bigoplus_{1\le j\le n} b_j((X\oplus(t)x)\,|\,y_j))$$
$$\oplus\; \bigoplus_{a_i=\bar b_j} \tau(x_i\,|\,y_j) \;\oplus\; (t)(x\,|\,y)$$

$$(E_4) \quad \delta X\,|\,Y \;=\; \bigoplus_{1\le i\le m} a_i(x_i\,|\,Y) \;\oplus\; \bigoplus_{1\le j\le n} b_j(\delta X\,|\,y_j) \;\oplus\; \bigoplus_{a_i=\bar b_j} \tau(x_i\,|\,y_j)$$

$$(E_5) \quad \delta X\,|\,(Y\oplus(s+t)y) \;=\; \bigoplus_{1\le i\le m} a_i(x_i\,|\,(Y\oplus(s+t)y)) \;\oplus\; \bigoplus_{1\le j\le n} b_j(\delta X\,|\,y_j)$$
$$\oplus\; \bigoplus_{a_i=\bar b_j} \tau(x_i\,|\,y_j) \;\oplus\; (t)(\delta X\,|\,(s)y)$$
$$\oplus\; \delta X\,|\,(Y\oplus(s+t)y)$$

$$(E_6) \quad \delta X\,|\,\delta Y \;=\; \delta\!\left(\bigoplus_{1\le i\le m} a_i(x_i\,|\,\delta Y) \;\oplus\; \bigoplus_{1\le j\le n} b_j(\delta X\,|\,y_j) \;\oplus\; \bigoplus_{a_i=\bar b_j} \tau(x_i\,|\,y_j) \right)$$

Figure 6: Equational Theory for Parallel Terms

and their temporal behaviour, as viewed by an external observer. Now we wish to define a *"faster than"* precongruence which will hold between two process terms if they are functionally behaviourally equivalent, but where the first term can execute its function faster (*ie*, sooner) than the second term.

There is an immediate problem which arises in defining such a notion in TCCS. Within the language of TCCS, we saw that we can describe *timeout* contexts which will allow a certain computation to take place within a given amount of time, but will preempt the computation and proceed with an alternate computation if that amount of time is allowed to pass without the desired computation being performed. For example, the derived TCCS term $\text{TIMEOUT}_2(P, b.\mathbf{0})$ will allow the process P to proceed within 2 units of time, but will subsequently perform the action b and evolve into a deadlocked nil process if the process P does not proceed within the required time. Hence the behaviour of this timeout process will depend greatly on the *speed* of the context in which it is placed.

A slightly simpler version of this timeout context is $P + (2).b.0$. If we were to replace P in this expression with each of the terms $(1).a.0$ and $(3).a.0$ which represent the processes which will perform an a action after 1 and 3 units of time respectively, then in the first case, we would result in the process (behaviour) $(1).a.0$, whereas in the second case we would result in $(2).b.0$ due to the different timeout scenarios. Clearly we would want to consider the process term $(1).a.0$ to be *faster than* the process term $(3).a.0$. However, if we further desired that our *faster than* preorder be a precongruence (that is, that it be substitutive), then we would be led to deduce that the process term $(1).a.0$ is *faster than* the process term $(2).b.0$. This is undesirable though, as these two terms are not even functionally behaviourally equivalent.

The problem arises due to the preemptive nature of passing time in the semantics of the operators — it is possible to lose the capability of following a particular computation path through idling. To solve this dilemma, we work within the subcalculus ℓTCCS defined earlier, where such preemptive behaviour is eliminated, as *all* processes may idle indefinitely. In this calculus, though we can have timeout events made available in the environment after some amount of time, we can never lose the ability to do some other event due to the passing of time. This is not an unreasonable restriction, particularly in the design of hardware circuits, as this is precisely how an implementation behaves — if a port is prepared to communicate, then it is a reasonable assumption to make that this communication capability can only be removed through an actual change in state, and not through idling.

Using the transitional semantics defined here, we can define our *faster than* preorder $\lesssim$ using the following bisimulation-like definition. In this definition, and throughout the sequel, we shall allow ourselves to write the term $(0).P$, and to allow the transition $P \overset{0}{\leadsto} P$; for $(0)P$ we shall read P, and for $P \overset{0}{\leadsto} Q$ we shall read "Q is *syntactically identical to P*".

Definition 3.3 *A binary relation $\mathcal{R}$ over terms of ℓTCCS is a $\lesssim$-bisimulation if and only if for all $(P, Q) \in \mathcal{R}$ and for all $a \in \mathrm{Act}$ and for all $t \in \mathcal{T}$,*

> (i) *if $P \overset{a}{\longrightarrow} P'$ then $Q \overset{s}{\leadsto} Q' \overset{a}{\longrightarrow} Q''$ and $P' \overset{s}{\leadsto} P''$ for some s, Q', Q'', P'' with $\left(P'', Q''\right) \in \mathcal{R}$;*
>
> (ii) *if $Q \overset{a}{\longrightarrow} Q'$ then $P \overset{a}{\longrightarrow} P'$ for some P' with $(P', Q') \in \mathcal{R}$;*
>
> (iii) *if $P \overset{t}{\leadsto} P'$ then $Q \overset{t}{\leadsto} Q'$ for some Q' with $(P', Q') \in \mathcal{R}$;*
>
> (iv) *if $Q \overset{t}{\leadsto} Q'$ then $P \overset{t}{\leadsto} P'$ for some P' with $(P', Q') \in \mathcal{R}$.*

$\lesssim \overset{\text{def}}{=} \bigcup\{\mathcal{R} : \mathcal{R} \text{ is a } \lesssim\text{-bisimulation}\}$ *is then the largest $\lesssim$-bisimulation.*

Thus the only difference between this definition and the definition of the equivalence given above appears in the first clause: if the first (*faster*) process term can perform a particular action, then the second (*slower*) process term can either perform that action right away and evolve into a new process state which is *slower than* that into which the first process evolved, or else it can idle for some amount of time t and reach a state in which it can perform the action and thus evolve into a state which, while not necessarily itself *slower than* that into which the first process evolved, but *slower than* that state once the idling time is accounted for. As an example, we would want that

$$\underline{a} \mid (1)\underline{b} \lesssim (1)\underline{a} \mid (1)\underline{b}.$$

Now in the *faster* term, the action transition

$$\underline{a} \mid (1)\underline{b} \xrightarrow{a} \underline{0} \mid (1)\underline{b}$$

is matched in the *slower* term by the sequence of transitions

$$(1)\underline{a} \mid (1)\underline{b} \xrightarrow{1} \underline{a} \mid \underline{b} \xrightarrow{a} \underline{0} \mid \underline{b}$$

and while we have that $\underline{0} \mid (1)\underline{b} \not\lesssim \underline{0} \mid \underline{b}$, by the definition of $\lesssim$, we only require that $\underline{0} \mid \underline{b} \lesssim \underline{0} \mid \underline{b}$, as $\underline{0} \mid (1)\underline{b} \xrightarrow{1} \underline{0} \mid \underline{b}$.

The relation $\lesssim$ is a preorder: it is reflexive, as clearly

$$Id \stackrel{\text{def}}{=} \left\{ (P,P) : P \in \ell\text{TCCS} \right\}$$

is a $\lesssim$-bisimulation, and it is transitive, as given $\lesssim$-bisimulations $\mathcal{R}_1$ and $\mathcal{R}_2$ we can show that $\mathcal{R}_3 \stackrel{\text{def}}{=} \mathcal{R}_1 \mathcal{R}_2$ is a $\lesssim$-bisimulation. We can furthermore show that this relation is a precongruence over the finite operators of ℓTCCS.

It is clear from the similarities in the definitions of $\sim$ and $\lesssim$ that for P and Q being two terms of ℓTCCS, if $P \sim Q$ then $P \lesssim Q$ (and symmetrically, $Q \lesssim P$). However, the reverse implication does not hold; that is, $P \lesssim Q$ and $Q \lesssim P$ does not necessarily imply $P \sim Q$. A suitable counter-example is provided by the following two process terms which demonstrate a convex-closedness property of our relation:

$$A \stackrel{\text{def}}{=} \underline{ab} + \underline{a}(1)\underline{b} + \underline{a}(2)\underline{b} \qquad\qquad B \stackrel{\text{def}}{=} \underline{ab} + \underline{a}(2)\underline{b}$$

These two processes are equally fast by the above definition, yet are not equivalent, as $A \xrightarrow{a} (1)\underline{b}$, but for no $B' \sim (1)\underline{b}$ does $B \xrightarrow{a} B'$. Hence another equivalence of interest is $\lesssim \cap \gtrsim$, which we represent by $\cong$.

We have another general anomaly with this (or indeed any) *faster than* preorder for nondeterministic processes: we cannot guarantee that if $P \lesssim Q$, then P will *necessarily* execute faster than Q, but only that it has the capability of so doing. We would for example insist by reflexivity that for the above process A, $A \lesssim A$; but in executing the two instances of A, the first (supposedly *faster*) version may start with an a transition to the state $(2)\underline{b}$, whereas the second version may start with an a transition to the state $\underline{b}$. However, this problem only arises in the presence of nondeterminism, and also vanishes if we assume some form of built-in priority allowing faster computation paths to be followed whenever possible.

(L_0) $x \leq (t)x$

(L_1) $(x + y) + z = x + (y + z)$ (L_2) $x + y = y + x$

(L_3) $x + x = x$ (L_4) $x + \underline{0} = x$

(L_5) $(s)(t)x = (s + t)x$ (L_6) $(t)x + (t)y = (t)(x + y)$

(L_7) $x + (t)x = x$ (L_8) $(t)\underline{0} = \underline{0}$

(L_9) $\mathbf{0} \backslash a = \mathbf{0}$ (L_{10}) $\mathbf{0}[S] = \mathbf{0}$

(L_{11}) $\big(b.P\big) \backslash a = \begin{cases} \mathbf{0}, \text{ if } a = b, \overline{b} \\ b.\big(P \backslash a\big), \text{ o/w} \end{cases}$ (L_{12}) $\big(b.P\big)[S] = b.\big(P[S]\big)$

(L_{13}) $\big((t).P\big) \backslash a = (t).\big(P \backslash a\big)$ (L_{14}) $\big((t).P\big)[S] = (t).\big(P[S]\big)$

(L_{15}) $\big(P + Q\big) \backslash a = P \backslash a + Q \backslash a$ (L_{16}) $\big(P + Q\big)[S] = P[S] + Q[S]$

Figure 7: Inequational Theory for Sequential ℓTCCS Terms

A complete axiomatization for the finite sequential subcalculus is presented in Figure 7. Note that the completeness result here holds for any time domain.

Unfortunately, we have no analog in ℓTCCS to the Expansion Theorem. For example, the term $\underline{a} \mid (1)\underline{b}$ has no equivalent sequential form. We would want to be able to express this term by its expansion, namely as $\underline{a}(1)\underline{b} + (1)(\underline{a} \mid \underline{b})$ (where we can then recursively expand the subterm $\underline{a} \mid \underline{b}$ to $\underline{ab} + \underline{ba}$). However this term is clearly not equivalent to the original, as the expanded term can idle one unit of time, then perform an a action and evolve into a state where it must idle for one more unit of time before being capable of performing the b action, whereas the parallel term after idling one unit of time and then performing the a action, will always be capable of immediately performing the b action.

Though this common expansion of a parallel term is not necessarily equivalent to the term itself, we do have the result that it is related in one direction to the parallel term in the *faster than* relation; the parallel term is guaranteed to be *faster than* the sequentialised expanded term. These expansion principles are presented in Figure 8.

Hence, we thus cannot use the usual technique in comparing two terms of expressing the terms as equivalent sequential terms and then comparing these sequential terms using our complete set of laws for such terms. However, the expansion of a (parallel) term is so very close to being equivalent to the term itself, that we conjecture that it is not possible to find a sequential term which falls in the *faster than* relation strictly between a term and its expanded version.

$$(|_1) \quad (x \,|\, y) \,|\, z \;=\; x \,|\, (y \,|\, z) \qquad\qquad (|_2) \quad x \,|\, y \;=\; y \,|\, x$$

Let $X = \sum_{1 \le i \le m} \underline{a}_i x_i$ and $Y = \sum_{1 \le j \le n} \underline{b}_j y_j$

$(E_1) \quad X \,|\, Y \;=\; \sum_{1 \le i \le m} \underline{a}_i(x_i \,|\, Y) + \sum_{1 \le j \le n} \underline{b}_j(X \,|\, y_j) + \sum_{a_i = \bar{b}_j} \underline{\tau}(x_i \,|\, y_j)$

$(E_2) \quad X \,|\, (Y + (t)y) \;\le\; \sum_{1 \le i \le m} \underline{a}_i(x_i \,|\, (Y + (t)y)) + \sum_{1 \le j \le n} \underline{b}_j(X \,|\, y_j)$
$$+ \sum_{a_i = \bar{b}_j} \underline{\tau}(x_i \,|\, y_j) + (t)(X \,|\, (Y + y))$$

$(E_3) \quad (X + (t)x) \,|\, (Y + (t)y) \;\le\; \sum_{1 \le i \le m} \underline{a}_i(x_i \,|\, (Y + (t)y))$
$$+ \sum_{1 \le j \le n} \underline{b}_j((X + (t)x) \,|\, y_j)$$
$$+ \sum_{a_i = \bar{b}_j} \underline{\tau}(x_i \,|\, y_j) + (t)((X + x) \,|\, (Y + y))$$

Figure 8: Expansion Laws for ℓTCCS

4 Future Development

The work reported in this paper is part of an ongoing study into the temporal properties of concurrent processes, and represents only the start of this research programme. Some open problems were described in the main text, but there are several directions to pursue the study in the future. Here we briefly describe but three of the more important notions currently under consideration.

4.1 Treating Dense Times

The calculus TCCS admitted of an arbitrary time domain $\mathcal{T}$, so that we could for instance define and reason about process terms with temporal properties defined over the real numbers. However, in working within a dense time domain, we failed to prove any completeness results for our axiomatisation. The reason for this is that the expressive power of our sequential subcalculus is insufficient for expressing all parallel behaviour. If we consider ourselves working over a discrete time domain, then we can express every finite process term as an equivalent sequential process term, and thus we only need to concern ourselves with reasoning in this sequential subcalculus. For instance, over the discrete (integral) time domain, we can make the following identification:

$$\underline{a} \,|\, (1)b \;=\; a(1)b \oplus (1)(ab \oplus ba)$$

However, this identification is incorrect over any dense time domain (such as the rationals or the reals), and in this case it is in fact impossible to identify the concurrent process term on the left hand side of the equality with *any* sequential process term in TCCS.

To remedy this situation, both to facilitate completeness proofs and to simplify the theory (in the sense that parallel composition should be a nonprimitive construct in this interleaving semantic model), we need to introduce a more powerful construction into the language. The promising candidate is some form of *"integral"* operation such as that used in [1].

If we consider the above example in the dense time domain of the positive reals, we realise that we actually want the expression to read as

$$\underline{a} \,|\, (1)b \;=\; \bigoplus_{0 \leq t \leq 1} (t)a(1-t)b \;\oplus\; (1)ba.$$

That is, we want to express the term $\underline{a} \,|\, (1)b$ as an infinite continuous sum. For this reason, we use the notation given by the integral sign

$$\underline{a} \,|\, (1)b \;=\; \oint_{t=0}^{1} (t)a(1-t)b \;\oplus\; (1)ba.$$

This arises from the general description of the delayed time prefix as

$$\underline{a} \;\stackrel{\text{def}}{=}\; \oint_{t=0}^{\infty} (t)a.$$

To carry out this effort, we would need to introduce time variables into the language TCCS, and to define the transitional semantics of this new operator. We would need to be especially careful with the situation of introducing a negative time prefix into the language, for then we would either have to find an explanation for what such a concept was modelling (perhaps moving backwards in time in some fanciful quantum mechanical reasoning fashion) or else we would need to somehow syntactically restrict this possibility from arising.

4.2   A Logic for Specification

In the usual case of CCS with bisimulation semantics, we have a powerful logic for specification in the form of *Hennessy-Milner Logic (HML)* as described in [6]. It would be an ideal situation if the logic would extend itself to the calculus TCCS in some analogous fashion.

The logic in question would consist of the following formulae, which we refer to as *timed HML* formulae.

$$\phi \;::=\; true \;|\; \neg\phi \;|\; \phi_0 \wedge \phi_1 \;|\; \langle a \rangle \phi \;|\; \langle t \rangle \phi$$

We can define the rest of the typical formulae as derived notions in the expected fashion:

$$false \stackrel{\text{def}}{=} \neg true \qquad\qquad [a]\phi \stackrel{\text{def}}{=} \neg\langle a\rangle\neg\phi$$

$$\phi_0 \vee \phi_1 \stackrel{\text{def}}{=} \neg(\neg\phi_0 \wedge \neg\phi_1) \qquad\qquad [a]\phi \stackrel{\text{def}}{=} \neg\langle a\rangle\neg\phi$$

Terms in TCCS (or in ℓTCCS) would then satisfy such formulae according to the following rules.

$$
\begin{aligned}
&P \models true && \text{for all } P \\
&P \models \neg\phi && \text{iff } \ P \not\models \phi \\
&P \models \phi_0 \wedge \phi_1 && \text{iff } \ P \models \phi_0 \text{ and } P \models \phi_1 \\
&P \models \langle a\rangle\phi && \text{iff } \ P \stackrel{a}{\longrightarrow} P' \text{ for some } P' \text{ such that } P' \models \phi \\
&P \models \langle t\rangle\phi && \text{iff } \ P \stackrel{t}{\rightsquigarrow} P' \text{ for some } P' \text{ such that } P' \models \phi
\end{aligned}
$$

We can then define an equivalence $\simeq$ between terms according to the timed HML formulae which the terms respectively satisfy. That is, we could allow $P \simeq Q$ if and only if

$$\text{for all timed HML formulae } \phi, \qquad P \models \phi \ \textit{iff} \ Q \models \phi.$$

The question then would be, what is the connection between this equivalence and the equivalences which have been described in the main body of this paper? The expectation would be that this equivalence coincides with $\mathcal{T}$-bisimulation. We would also be interested in finding an asymetric relation based on this (or some similar) logic which would coincide with $\lesssim$-bisimulation. To do so, we could imagine having to define a faster-than relation over timed HML formulae to capture the asymmetry in the definition of $\lesssim$-bisimulation. Furthermore, we would have to capture the *"borrowing-of-time"* notion from the first clause of the definition of $\lesssim$-bisimulation.

4.3   Abstracting Away Silent τ's

In the theory of CCS, we have the notion of a *weak* bisimulation, where two process terms are identified roughly if they behave the same modulo the performance of the special τ action which results from an internal communication and therefore is considered to be unobservable to the external environment. Hence for instance we make the identification $a.\tau.P = a.P$, taking note that the occurrence of the τ action performed by the first process term is invisible to the observer of the system.

To define weak bisimulation in CCS, we first need to define the composite action derivation for $a \in$ Act,

$$\stackrel{a}{\Longrightarrow} \stackrel{\text{def}}{=} \stackrel{\tau}{\longrightarrow}^* \stackrel{a}{\longrightarrow} \stackrel{\tau}{\longrightarrow}^*;$$

that is, $\stackrel{a}{\Longrightarrow}$ represents an a-transition preceded and followed by some arbitrary number of τ-transitions. We can then equally define this relation over arbitrary sequences of actions, rather than single actions, allowing arbitrary sequences of τ-transitions between the actions. For TCCS, we would further need to define the composite temporal derivation

52

$$\stackrel{t}{\Rightarrow} \stackrel{\text{def}}{=} \stackrel{\tau}{\longrightarrow}{}^* \stackrel{t_1}{\leadsto} \stackrel{\tau}{\longrightarrow}{}^* \stackrel{t_2}{\leadsto} \ldots \stackrel{t_n}{\leadsto} \stackrel{\tau}{\longrightarrow}{}^*$$

(where $t = t_1 + t_2 + \cdots + t_n$), meaning and arbitrary number of τ-transitions evolving over time t. Our equivalence would then be given as follows.

Definition 4.1 *A binary relation $\mathcal{R}$ over terms in TCCS is a weak $\mathcal{T}$-bisimulation if and only if for all $(P,Q) \in \mathcal{R}$ and for all $s \in \Lambda^*$ and for all $t \in \mathcal{T}$,*

(i) if $P \stackrel{s}{\Longrightarrow} P'$ then $Q \stackrel{s}{\Longrightarrow} Q'$ for some Q' with $(P',Q') \in \mathcal{R}$;

(ii) if $Q \stackrel{s}{\Longrightarrow} Q'$ then $P \stackrel{s}{\Longrightarrow} P'$ for some P' with $(P',Q') \in \mathcal{R}$;

(iii) if $P \stackrel{t}{\Rightarrow} P'$ then $Q \stackrel{t}{\Rightarrow} Q'$ for some Q' with $(P',Q') \in \mathcal{R}$;

(iv) if $Q \stackrel{t}{\Rightarrow} Q'$ then $P \stackrel{t}{\Rightarrow} P'$ for some P' with $(P',Q') \in \mathcal{R}$.

$\approx \stackrel{\text{def}}{=} \bigcup \{\mathcal{R} : \mathcal{R}$ *is a weak $\mathcal{T}$-bisimulation*$\}$ *is then the largest weak $\mathcal{T}$-bisimulation.*

As for the subcalculus of CCS, this equivalence is not a congruence, since for example $a \approx \tau a$, but $a + b \not\approx \tau a + b$. Hence we take interest in the largest congruence $\approx^c$ contained in $\approx$.

This congruence is clearly a more interesting and useful definition of process equality, and so we would like to develop this theory more fully. There are no immediate complications appearing in this endeavour, but there is much to be accomplished before full understanding of this observational congruence is acquired.

Acknowledgements

The work presented in this paper has been developed in the most part with Chris Tofts at the University of Edinburgh and the University of Bath.

Bibliography

[1] Baeten, J.C.M. and J.A. Bergstra, *Real Time Process Algebra*, Preliminary Draft, 10/20/89, 1989.

[2] Bergstra, J.A. and J.W. Klop, *Algebra for Communicating Processes with Abstraction*, Journal of Theoretical Computer Science, Vol 37, 1985.

[3] Boudol, G., *Notes on Algebraic Calculi of Processes*, Logics and Models of Concurrent Systems, NATO ASI Series f13 (K. Apt, ed), 1985.

[4] Brookes, S.D., C.A.R. Hoare and A.W. Roscoe, *A Theory of Communicating Sequential Processes*, Journal of ACM, Vol 31, 1984.

[5] Groote, J.F., *Specification and Verification of Real Time Systems in ACP*, Research Report No CS-R9015, Centre for Mathematics and Computer Science, Amsterdam, 1990.

[6] Hennessy, M.C. and R. Milner, *Algebraic Laws for Nondeterminism and Concurrency*, Journal of the ACM, Vol 32, No 1, 1985.

[7] Hennessy, M.C., **Algebraic Theory of Processes**, MIT Press, 1988.

[8] Hennessy, M. and T. Regan, *A Temporal Process Algebra* Technical Report No. 2/90, University of Sussex Computer Science Department, April, 1990.

[9] Hoare, C.A.R., *Communicating Sequential Processes*, Communications of ACM, Vol 21, 1978.

[10] Milner, R., **A Calculus of Communicating Systems**, Lecture Notes in Computer Science 92, Springer-Verlag, 1980.

[11] Milner, R., *Calculi for Synchrony and Asynchrony*, Theoretical Computer Science, Vol 25, 1983.

[12] Milner, R., **Communication and Concurrency**, Prentice–Hall International, 1989.

[13] Moller, F. and C. Tofts, *A Temporal Calculus of Communicating Systems*, Proceedings of CONCUR'90 (Theories of Concurrency: Unification and Extension), Amsterdam, August 1990.

[14] Nicollin, X., J.L. Richier, J. Sifakis and J.Voiron, *ATP: An Algebra for Timed Processes*, Proceedings of IFIP Working Conference on Programming Concepts and Methods, North Holland, 1990.

[15] Park, D.M.R., *Concurrency and Automata on Infinite Sequences*, Lecture Notes in Computer Science 104, Springer–Verlag, 1981.

[16] Plotkin, G.D., **A Structural Approach to Operational Semantics**, Report DAIMI FN-19, Computer Science Department, Århus University, Denmark, 1981.

[17] Reed, G.M. and A. Roscoe, *A Timed Model for Communicating Sequentail Processes*, Proceedings of ICALP'86, Lecture Notes in Computer Science No 226, Springer Verlag, 1986.

[18] Tofts, C., *Proof Systems and Pragmatics for Parallel Programming*, PhD Thesis, University of Edinburgh, 1990.

[19] Wang Yi, *Real-time Behaviour of Asynchronous Agents*, Proceedings of CONCUR'90 (Theories of Concurrency: Unification and Extension), Amsterdam, August 1990.

The study of butterflies

Geraint Jones
Programming Research Group
Oxford University Computing Laboratory
11 Keble Road
Oxford OX1 3QD
England

Geraint.Jones@comlab.oxford.ac.uk

Mary Sheeran
Department of Computing Science
University of Glasgow
Glasgow G12 8QQ
Scotland

ms@dcs.glasgow.ac.uk

Abstract

Butterfly networks arise in many signal processing circuits and in parallel algorithms for many sorts of message-passing computers. This paper attempts to explain why this should be, and what butterfly networks are, using a new and elegant formulation based on a language of relations.

Most of the material covered by this paper has appeared in a less tractable form in earlier papers [6, 7]. The novelty here is in the simplicity and elegance of the presentation, which derives from an appropriate choice of high-level structures. These structures are represented by functions which are used to compose circuits from components, and are chosen to have simple mathematical properties.

This presentation makes it easier to explain how the design comes about, showing that butterflies are natural implementations of divide-and-conquer algorithms. We are then able to go on to explain many of the properties of butterfly networks, and of their implementations.

1 A language of relations

The important things in Ruby [5] are the structuring functions, and the interesting things to know are encapsulated by the mathematical properties of those functions. Nevertheless we will need to have some idea of what the component parts being composed are. These are the things that model the components of a circuit, or the nodes of a network of computers. You can think of these components as being relations: that is the simplest interpretation of what is happening. You should however keep in mind that this is just one interpretation, and that the important things to watch are the functions that put them together and the algebra of those functions.

The principal way of putting components together is (sequential) composition, which we write $R;S$. If you are thinking of relations, composition of relations means

$$x\,(R\,;S)\,z \;\equiv\; \exists y.\ x\,R\,y \;\&\; y\,S\,z$$

but the thing to keep at the front of your mind is that it is an associative way of putting circuits together, $(R\,;S)\,;T = R\,;(S\,;T)$.

In particular that means that it will make sense to talk about 'reducing' composition over a finite ordered set of indices, and we write

$$\overset{n}{\underset{i=1}{\overset{\bullet}{,}}}\, R_i \;=\; R_1\,;R_2\,;\ldots;R_n$$

at least in the case that $n > 0$, and we write R^n for $\overset{\bullet n}{,}_{i=1}\, R$.

The other extreme way of putting components together leaves them entirely unconnected. The parallel composition $[R, S]$ is defined by

$$\langle p,q\rangle\,[R,S]\,\langle t,u\rangle \;\equiv\; p\,R\,t \;\&\; q\,S\,u$$

and the thing to keep in mind is that sequential and parallel composition have the property $[P,Q]\,;[R,S] = [(P\,;R),(Q\,;S)]$ which Richard Bird [1] calls the *abides* property: that sequential composition abides with parallel composition.

The *inverse* (some people say more properly the 'converse') of a relation, R^{-1}, is defined by

$$x\,R^{-1}\,y \;\equiv\; y\,R\,x$$

and we will write R^{-n} for $(R^{-1})^n$ and so on. Beware of doing arithmetic in the exponent! A relation and its inverse cannot necessarily be cancelled, so $R^p\,;R^{-q}$ need not necessarily be the same as R^{p-q}.

Converse distributes over parallel composition, $[R,S]^{-1} = [R^{-1}, S^{-1}]$, and in a modified sense over sequential composition, for $(R\,;S)^{-1} = S^{-1}\,;R^{-1}$.

Because we will want to be using relations and their converses to translate data from one representation to another, we will find useful the abbreviation $R \setminus S = S^{-1}\,;R\,;S$, read 'the *conjugate* of R by S'.

The *sum* of two relations R and S (their relational sum, or their union) is a relation $R + S$ for which

$$x\,(R + S)\,y \;\equiv\; x\,R\,y \;\vee\; x\,S\,y$$

Most of the operations introduced so far distribute over sum, so that for example $(R + S)\,;T = (R\,;T) + (S\,;T)$. The exceptions are the operations like repeated composition that are not linear: because

$$
\begin{aligned}
(R + S)^2 &= (R + S)\,;(R + S) \\
&= (R\,;R) + (R\,;S) + (S\,;R) + (S\,;S)
\end{aligned}
$$

it is not generally the same as $R^2 + S^2$. Similarly the conjugation $R \setminus S$ is not linear in S, although $(P + Q) \setminus S = (P \setminus S) + (Q \setminus S)$.

We write $R : A \to B$ to mean that R relates things of type A to things of type B, and by this we mean that $R = A\,;R\,;B$. A type is just an equivalence relation, which is to say that it is a relation A for which $A = A^2 = A^{-1}$ and so $A = A^n$ for all positive and negative n. When we speak of a circuit R, we will have in mind particular domain and range types $R^{\dashv}$ and $R^{\vdash}$, for which $R : R^{\dashv} \to R^{\vdash}$, although we may not make them explicit. Do not think of $R^{\dashv}$ as being some function of R, it is just one element of a triple $\langle R^{\dashv}, R, R^{\vdash} \rangle$ which we misleadingly identify with R, on the grounds that it is usually obvious which $R^{\dashv}$ and $R^{\vdash}$ is meant. When $R^{\dashv} = R^{\vdash}$ we will write this as R^0, which is suggestive of $R^0\,;R^n\,;R^0 = R^{0+n+0} = R^n$. Such an R we will call *homogeneous*.

On the whole we will only need to talk about the types of lists of a given length: we write n for the type of lists of length n, meaning that $x\,n\,y$ if and only if $x = y$ and has n components. There is a notational trap lurking here, for we will write 2^n for the type of lists of length two-to-the-n: it should not be read as the n-times repeated sequential composition of 2. Since 2 is a type, the latter is just 2 and we will never need to write it.

A sum $R + S$ is *disjoint* if $R^{\dashv}\,;S^{\dashv} = \emptyset = R^{\vdash}\,;S^{\vdash}$ where $\emptyset$ is the unit of relational sum. In that case both $R^{\dashv} + S^{\dashv}$ and $R^{\vdash} + S^{\vdash}$ are types as you can check by calculation. (The sum of two types is not in general a type.) Moreover, since $R + S : R^{\dashv} + S^{\dashv} \to R^{\vdash} + S^{\vdash}$, repeated composition distributes over disjoint sum.

Sum is associative, commutative and idempotent, so we can write $\sum_i$ for the continued sum over any set of indices.

2 Transposing and shuffling

Most of this paper turns out to be about certain sorts of permutations: those that can be understood in terms of transposition operators. The transposition relation *trn* relates two 'rectangular' lists of lists, in such a way that

$$
x\;trn\;y \;\equiv\; x_{i,j} = y_{j,i}
$$

You can think of it as taking a row-of-columns enumeration of a two-dimensional array and turning it into a column-of-rows enumeration.

The easiest way of describing the relation *halve* is to say that its inverse $halve^{-1}$ relates a pair of equal-length lists to the even-length list obtained by concatenating them

$$
\langle x_0, x_1, \ldots x_{2n-1} \rangle \; halve \; \langle \langle x_0, x_1, \ldots x_{n-1} \rangle, \langle x_n, x_{n+1}, \ldots x_{2n-1} \rangle \rangle
$$

and similarly the relation *pair* is the converse of $pair^{-1}$ which relates a list of pairs to the even-length list obtained by concatenating the pairs

$$
\langle x_0, x_1, \ldots x_{2n-1} \rangle \; pair \; \langle \langle x_0, x_1 \rangle, \langle x_2, x_3 \rangle, \ldots \langle x_{2n-2}, x_{2n-1} \rangle \rangle
$$

Figure 1: layouts for $12\,;halve$, $12\,;pair$, and $12\,;riffle = (12\,;halve)\,;trn\,;(12\,;pair)^{-1}$

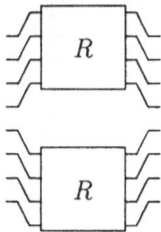

Figure 2: an interpretation of **two** R as a circuit arrangement

The reason we need *halve* and *pair* is to define

$$riffle \;\equiv\; halve \,;\, trn \,;\, pair^{-1}$$

which is a permutation of even-length lists. Think of the professional card-player's shuffling of a pack: the pack is divided in two, *halve*; the corners of the two half-packs are flicked together to interleave them, *trn*; and then the pack is straightened up to give the same status to cards from either half-pack, $pair^{-1}$. This 'riffling' operation is sometimes called a 'perfect shuffle'. It is harder to give a convincing account of how to unriffle a deck of cards, as described by $riffle^{-1}$!

Sometimes we will need to know how wide a list is being permuted, particularly because n successive rifflings of a list of length 2^n will restore it to its original order, which is to say that

$$2^n \,;\, riffle^n \;=\; 2^n$$

so that

$$2^n \,;\, riffle^{n-i} \;=\; 2^n \,;\, riffle^{-i}$$

Note that this is not directly related to an almost useless fact which any card-sharp will know, that $52 \,;\, riffle^8 = 52$.

3 A language of homogeneous relations

Suppose R is a length-homogeneous circuit, that is one which relates lists of signals only when they have the same length, so that $n\,;R = R\,;n$. One way of making

58

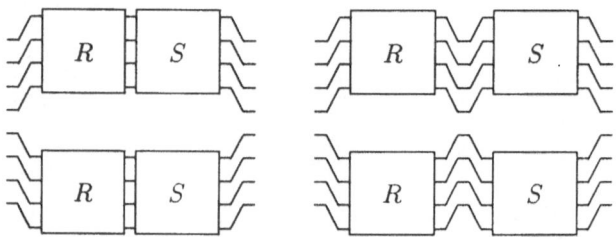

Figure 3: two circuit forms suggesting $\mathsf{two}(R\,;\,S) = \mathsf{two}\,R\,;\,\mathsf{two}\,S$

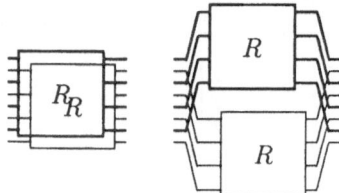

Figure 4: two different interpretations of $\mathsf{ilv}\,R = \mathsf{two}\,R \setminus \textit{riffle}$

a bigger length-homogeneous circuit is to take two copies of R, and to divide the inputs and outputs of the new circuit equally between the two copies.

$$\mathsf{two}\,R \;=\; [R, R] \setminus \textit{halve}^{-1}$$

So long as we confine ourselves to length-homogeneous relations, two distributes over composition, meaning that

$$\mathsf{two}(R\,;\,S) \;=\; \mathsf{two}\,R\,;\,\mathsf{two}\,S$$

and so $\mathsf{two}\,R^n = (\mathsf{two}\,R)^n$.

The restriction to length-homogeneous circuits is necessary. Consider the relation R which relates $\langle * \rangle$ to both $\langle * \rangle$ and $\langle *, * \rangle$, and the relation S which relates $\langle * \rangle$ to $\langle a \rangle$ and $\langle *, * \rangle$ to $\langle b \rangle$. Then $R\,;\,S$ relates $\langle * \rangle$ to both $\langle a \rangle$ and $\langle b \rangle$, so $\mathsf{two}(R\,;\,S)$ relates $\langle *, * \rangle$ to all four of $\langle a, a \rangle$, $\langle b, a \rangle$, $\langle a, b \rangle$ and $\langle b, b \rangle$. However $\mathsf{two}\,R$ relates $\langle *, * \rangle$ only to $\langle *, * \rangle$ and $\langle *, *, *, * \rangle$, and $\mathsf{two}\,S$ relates each of these to $\langle a, a \rangle$ and $\langle b, b \rangle$, so $\mathsf{two}\,R\,;\,\mathsf{two}\,S$ is a strictly smaller relation than $\mathsf{two}(R\,;\,S)$.

A different way of making a length-homogeneous circuit from two components of half its size is suggested by figure 4. The *interleaving* of two components is defined by

$$\mathsf{ilv}\,R \;=\; (\mathsf{two}\,R) \setminus \textit{riffle}$$

and – following from the distribution result for two – if R and S are both length-homogeneous then

$$\mathsf{ilv}(R\,;\,S) \;=\; \mathsf{ilv}\,R\,;\,\mathsf{ilv}\,S$$

What may be more surprising is that applications of two and ilv commute, for

$$\mathsf{two}\,\mathsf{ilv}\,R \;=\; \mathsf{ilv}\,\mathsf{two}\,R$$

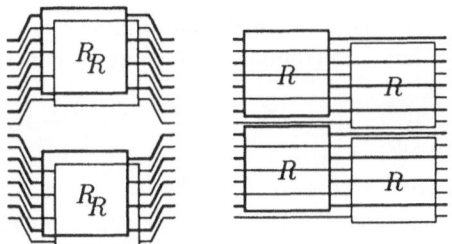

Figure 5: two views of two ilv R = ilv two R

This means, by an induction on the number of constructors, that any term consisting of applications of **two** and **ilv** to a relation is determined solely by the number of applications of **two** and the number of applications of **ilv**, and that the order in which they are applied is immaterial.

The meaning of the equality is suggested by figure 5, and the proof goes something like this

$$halve \; ; [riffle^{-1} \; ; halve, riffle^{-1} \; ; halve]$$
$$= \quad halve \; ; [pair \; ; trn, pair \; ; trn]$$
$$= \quad pair \; ; halve \; ; [trn, trn]$$
$$= \quad pair \; ; trn \; ; [halve, halve] \; ; trn$$
$$= \quad riffle^{-1} \; ; halve \; ; [halve, halve] \; ; trn$$

so

$$\text{\textbf{two} ilv } R \quad = \{ \text{definitions of \textbf{two} and ilv and collecting terms} \}$$
$$[[R, R], [R, R]] \setminus ([halve^{-1} \; ; riffle, halve^{-1} \; ; riffle] \; ; halve^{-1})$$
$$= \{ \text{calculation above, taking inverses on both sides} \}$$
$$([[R, R], [R, R]] \setminus trn) \setminus ([halve^{-1}, halve^{-1}] \; ; halve^{-1} \; ; riffle)$$
$$= \{ [[A, B], [C, D]] \setminus trn = [[A, C], [B, D]] \}$$
$$[[R, R], [R, R]] \setminus ([halve^{-1}, halve^{-1}] \; ; halve^{-1} \; ; riffle)$$
$$= \{ \text{collecting terms and replacing definitions} \}$$
$$\text{ilv \textbf{two} } R$$

The details are tedious, but we need never see them again: just remember that two ilv R = ilv two R.

4   Divide and conquer algorithms

Suppose you want to solve some problem by a binary divide and conquer strategy: that is, you know how to solve (conquer) some problems by an algorithm C, and you have a technique D for dividing up any problem that is too big to be dealt with by C. A problem divided has then become two smaller problems that can be tackled in the same way. The algorithm is a solution Φ to

$$\Phi \; = \; C + (D \; ; \text{two} \, \Phi)$$

You can read this as an equation in which the unknown is a relation, and in which the $+$ sign means relational sum (union). The solution can be found by unwinding the recursion:

$$
\begin{aligned}
\Phi &= C + D \,;\, \text{two}\,\Phi \\
&= C + D \,;\, \text{two}\, C + D \,;\, \text{two}\, D \,;\, \text{two}^2\,\Phi \\
&= C + D \,;\, \text{two}\, C + D \,;\, \text{two}\, D \,;\, \text{two}^2\, C + D \,;\, \text{two}\, D \,;\, \text{two}^2\, D \,;\, \text{two}^3\,\Phi \\
&= \sum_{i=0}^{n}\Big(\mathop{;}_{j=0}^{i-1} \text{two}^j\, D\Big) \,;\, \text{two}^i\, C + \Big(\mathop{;}_{j=0}^{n} \text{two}^j\, D\Big) \,;\, \text{two}^{n+1}\,\Phi
\end{aligned}
$$

and because (at least if there are no empty lists in the range of Φ) the range of $\text{two}^i\,\Phi$ contains only lists of length at least 2^i long, this unfolding eventually defines Φ, by

$$
\Phi = \sum_{i=0}^{\infty}\Big(\mathop{;}_{j=0}^{i-1} \text{two}^j\, D\Big) \,;\, \text{two}^i\, C
$$

We will suppose that C and D are length-homogeneous, and that $C : k \rightarrow k$ for some small number k. There is no harm in supposing that we can only conquer small problems: that is of the essence of how divide-and-conquer works. Of course there remains the problem of how to divide very large problems.

Suppose that D can itself be implemented by divide-and-conquer, and that $D = R + S \,;\, \text{two}\, D$. If we are to make progress S had better be simple: we could assume that S was the identity relation. In that case $D = \sum_i \text{two}^i\, R$ and if $R : k \rightarrow k$ as well as C, it follows that $\Phi = \sum_i (\text{two}^i\, R)^i \,;\, \text{two}^i\, C = \sum_i \text{two}^i(R^i \,;\, C)$. This is not very interesting, because it says that Φ can be applied to a list of a give size just by allocating each k-wide piece to a calculation independent of all the others.

Butterflies arise in the case where large division problems can be tackled by *interleaving* smaller division algorithms, for suppose that $D = R + \text{ilv}\, D$, then under the same assumptions

$$
\Phi = \sum_{i=0}^{\infty}\Big(\mathop{;}_{j=0}^{i-1} \text{two}^j\, \text{ilv}^{i-j}\, R\Big) \,;\, \text{two}^i\, C
$$

and if $R = C$

$$
\Phi = \sum_{i=0}^{\infty}\bowtie_i R
$$

$$
\text{where } \bowtie_i R = \mathop{;}_{j=0}^{i} \text{two}^j\, \text{ilv}^{i-j}\, R
$$

The right-hand side of this definition suggests a way of laying out the circuit which is illustrated in figure 8 for the case of $\bowtie_3 R$ where $R : 2 \rightarrow 2$. We define the butterfly of R by the sum

$$
\bowtie R = \sum_{i=0}^{\infty}\bowtie_i R
$$

The sum is disjoint, at least if $R^0 = k$ for some fixed number k, an assumption which we make in what follows.

(If you are comparing this paper with the discussion of butterflies in reference [6], notice that in that paper the definition is slightly different, being $\bowtie R = 1 + \sum_{i=0}^{\infty} \bowtie_i R$. The difference is unimportant, and only slightly alters the discussion in the following section.)

5   Recursive decomposition of butterflies

Because we arrived at the butterfly by solving a recursion equation, it comes as no surprise that it has a recursive decomposition. There are however a great number of other decompositions. Suppose p and q are at least zero, then

$$
\begin{aligned}
\bowtie_{p+q+1} R &= \overset{p+q+1}{\underset{i=0}{\text{\Large;}}}\; \text{two}^i\,\text{ilv}^{(p+q+1)-i}\,R \\
&= \overset{p}{\underset{i=0}{\text{\Large;}}}\; \text{two}^i\,\text{ilv}^{p-i}\,\text{ilv}^{q+1}\,R \;;\; \overset{q}{\underset{i=0}{\text{\Large;}}}\; \text{two}^{p+1}\,\text{two}^i\,\text{ilv}^{q-i}\,R \\
&= \overset{p}{\underset{i=0}{\text{\Large;}}}\; \text{two}^i\,\text{ilv}^{p-i}(\text{ilv}^{q+1}\,R) \;;\; \overset{q}{\underset{i=0}{\text{\Large;}}}\; \text{two}^i\,\text{ilv}^{q-i}(\text{two}^{p+1}\,R) \\
&= \bowtie_p\,\text{ilv}^{q+1}\,R \;;\; \bowtie_q\,\text{two}^{p+1}\,R \qquad\qquad (1)
\end{aligned}
$$

and

$$
\bowtie_{p+q+1} R = \text{ilv}^{q+1}\,\bowtie_p R \;;\; \text{two}^{p+1}\,\bowtie_q R \qquad\qquad (2)
$$

In particular, by taking one or other of p and q to be zero in each of equations 1 and 2, it follows that

$$
\begin{aligned}
\bowtie_{n+1} R &= \text{ilv}^{n+1}\,R \;;\; \bowtie_n\,\text{two}\,R &(3)\\
&= \text{ilv}^{n+1}\,R \;;\; \text{two}\,\bowtie_n R &(4)\\
&= \bowtie_n\,\text{ilv}\,R \;;\; \text{two}^{n+1}\,R &(5)\\
&= \text{ilv}\,\bowtie_n R \;;\; \text{two}^{n+1}\,R &(6)
\end{aligned}
$$

each of which suggests a layout for the implementation. The four decompositions of $\bowtie_3 R$, for a component $R : 2 \to 2$ that takes pairs to pairs, are illustrated in figures 6 to 9.

Results about the general $\bowtie$ follow from taking sums on both sides of each of these equations, for example from equation 3

$$
\begin{aligned}
\bowtie R &= \bowtie_0 R + \sum_{i=1}^{\infty} \bowtie_i R \\
&= R + \sum_{i=0}^{\infty}(\text{ilv}^{i+1}\,R \;;\; \bowtie_i\,\text{two}\,R) \\
&= \text{ilv}^0\,R \;;\; R^0 + (\sum_{i=0}^{\infty}\text{ilv}^{i+1}\,R) \;;\; (\sum_{i=0}^{\infty}\bowtie_i\,\text{two}\,R) \\
&= \text{ilv}^0\,R \;;\; R^0 + (\sum_{i=1}^{\infty}\text{ilv}^i\,R) \;;\; \bowtie\,\text{two}\,R \\
&= (\sum_{i=0}^{\infty}\text{ilv}^i\,R) \;;\; (R^0 + \bowtie\,\text{two}\,R)
\end{aligned}
$$

62

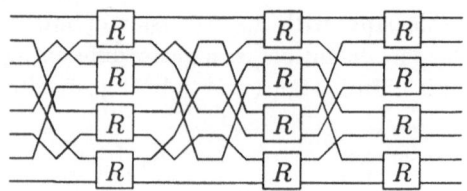

Figure 6: $\bowtie_2 R = \mathsf{ilv}^2 R$; $\bowtie_1 \mathsf{two}\, R = \mathsf{ilv}^2 R$; $\mathsf{ilv}\,\mathsf{two}\, R$; $\bowtie_0 \mathsf{two}^2 R$

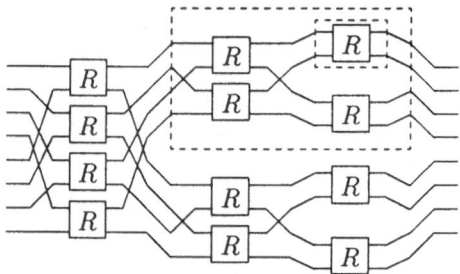

Figure 7: $\bowtie_2 R = \mathsf{ilv}^2 R$; $\mathsf{two}\bowtie_1 R = \mathsf{ilv}^2 R$; $\mathsf{two}(\mathsf{ilv}^1 R$; $\mathsf{two}\bowtie_0 R)$

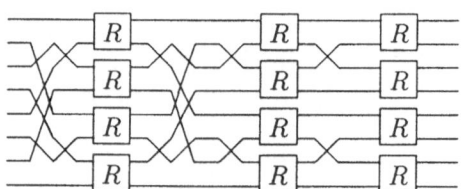

Figure 8: $\bowtie_2 R = \bowtie_1 \mathsf{ilv}\, R$; $\mathsf{two}^2 R = \bowtie_0 \mathsf{ilv}^2 R$; $\mathsf{two}\,\mathsf{ilv}\, R$; $\mathsf{two}^2 R$

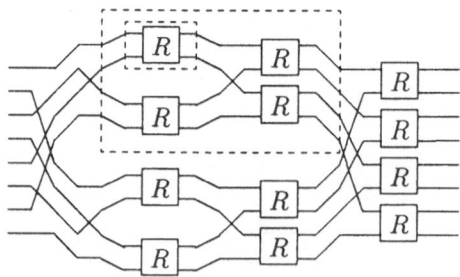

Figure 9: $\bowtie_2 R = \mathsf{ilv}\bowtie_1 R$; $\mathsf{two}^2 R = \mathsf{ilv}(\mathsf{ilv}\bowtie_0 R$; $\mathsf{two}\, R)$; $\mathsf{two}^2 R$

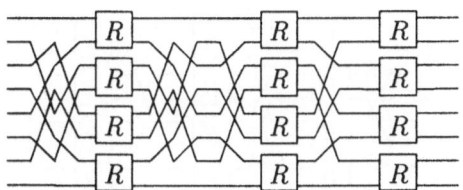

Figure 10: $\bowtie_2 R = \overset{2}{\underset{i=0}{\text{\large ;}}} \text{two}^2 R \setminus \text{riffle}^{2-i}$

because the various cross-terms are empty and so disappear from the sums. In the same way it can be shown that

$$\bowtie R = (R^0 + \bowtie \text{ilv } R) \; ; \; \sum_{i=0}^{\infty} \text{two}^i R$$

an so on.

6 Shuffle networks

Although the recursive decompositions of butterflies are elegant and easy to reason about, when it comes to laying out circuits they have the disadvantage of having differently shaped wiring in different places. Even if the R components can be replicated and laid out in a regular way, each column of wiring is different and there is an amount of work about 16^n involved in laying out the differently shaped parts of it.

Recall that because $\text{two ilv } R = \text{ilv two } R$, the only thing that matters in a term like $\text{two}^p \text{ ilv}^q R$, or the equivalent $\text{ilv}^q \text{ two}^p R$, is the number of applications of ilv and two. This is encapsulated in the equality

$$\text{two}^p \text{ ilv}^q R = (\text{two}^{p+q} R) \setminus \text{riffle}^q$$

which can be proved by an induction on q. The case of $q = 0$ is easy, and

$$
\begin{aligned}
\text{two}^p \text{ ilv}^{q+1} R &= \{\text{ commuting terms }\} \\
&\quad \text{ilv two}^p \text{ ilv}^q R \\
&= \{\text{ definition of ilv }\} \\
&\quad (\text{two two}^p \text{ ilv}^q R) \setminus \textit{riffle} \\
&= \{\text{ commuting terms }\} \\
&\quad (\text{two}^p \text{ ilv}^q \text{ two } R) \setminus \textit{riffle} \\
&= \{\text{ inductive hypothesis }\} \\
&\quad (\text{two}^{p+q} \text{ two } R) \setminus (\textit{riffle}^q \; ; \; \textit{riffle}) \\
&= \text{two}^{p+q+1} R \setminus \textit{riffle}^{q+1}
\end{aligned}
$$

This now suggests that the composition of terms that make up a butterfly has an expression in terms of $\textit{riffle}$ and $\text{two}^n R$.

$$\bowtie_n R = \overset{n}{\underset{i=0}{\text{\large ;}}} \text{two}^i \text{ ilv}^{n-i} R$$

64

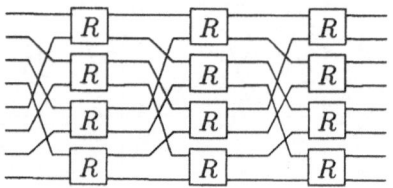

Figure 11: $riffle^3 ; \bowtie_2 R = (riffle ; \mathsf{two}^2 R)^3$

$$= \overset{n}{\underset{i=0}{;}} (\mathsf{two}^n R \setminus riffle^{n-i})$$

$$= \overset{n}{\underset{i=0}{;}} (riffle^{-(n-i)} ; \mathsf{two}^n R ; riffle^{n-i})$$

in which the columns of Rs are all the same, but the wiring between them, as illustrated in figure 10, is different for each column and unnecessarily complex.

By the associativity of sequential composition one of the three parts of each column can be carried forward to the next, and

$$
\begin{aligned}
riffle^{(n+1)} ; \bowtie_n R &= riffle^{(n+1)} ; \overset{n}{\underset{i=0}{;}} (riffle^{-(n-i)} ; \mathsf{two}^n R ; riffle^{n-i}) \\
&= \overset{n}{\underset{i=0}{;}} (riffle^{n+1-i} ; riffle^{-(n-i)} ; \mathsf{two}^n R) ; riffle^0 \\
&= \overset{n}{\underset{i=0}{;}} (riffle ; \mathsf{two}^n R) \\
&= (riffle ; \mathsf{two}^n R)^{n+1}
\end{aligned}
$$

in which each column is the same, and each is wired in the same way to its neighbours, as illustrated in figure 11. This arrangement of components is commonly known as a 'shuffle network'.

Since if $R : k \to k$, any term like $\mathsf{two}^i \, \mathsf{ilv}^j R$ has width $2^{i+j}k$, and in case $k = 2$, it is immediate from its definition that $\bowtie_n R : 2^{n+1} \to 2^{n+1}$, and the $riffle^{n+1}$ on the left-hand side can be cancelled yielding

$$\bowtie_n R = (riffle ; \mathsf{two}^n R)^{n+1}$$

Although there is still a great number of wire crossings in the resulting circuit – about 4^n in each of the $n+1$ columns – it has the advantage that each column is the same as all of the others, so only one column's worth of the circuit need be laid out and replicated.

By a symmetrical argument, it is also true that

$$\bowtie_n R = (\mathsf{ilv}^n R ; riffle)^{n+1}$$

Acknowledgments The presentation of divide and conquer algorithms owes much to several attempts to explain it to colleagues, and in particular to Richard Bird.

References

[1] R. S. Bird, *Lectures on constructive functional programming*, in [2]. (Programming Research Group technical monograph PRG–69)

[2] M. Broy (ed.), *Constructive methods in computing science*, NATO advanced study institutes, Series F: Computer and systems sciences, Springer-Verlag, 1989.

[3] G. David, R. T. Boute and B. D. Shriver (eds.), *Declarative systems*, North-Holland, 1990.

[4] K. Davis and J. Hughes (eds.), *Functional programming, Glasgow 1989*, Springer Workshops in Computing, 1990.

[5] G. Jones and M. Sheeran, *Circuit design in Ruby*, in [8].

[6] M. Sheeran, *Describing hardware algorithms in Ruby*, in [3]. (Revised form appears as [7])

[7] M. Sheeran, *Describing butterfly networks in Ruby*, in [4].

[8] Jørgen Staunstrup (ed.), *Formal methods for VLSI design*, North-Holland, 1990.

It may be said, therefore, that on these expanded membranes Nature writes, as on a tablet, the story of the modifications of species, so truly do all changes of the organisation register themselves thereon. Moreover the same colour patterns of the wings generally show, with great regularity, the degrees of blood-relationship of the species. As the laws of nature must be the same for all beings, the conclusions furnished by this group of insects must be applicable to the whole organic world; therefore, . . . the study of butterflies – creatures selected as the types of airiness and frivolity – instead of being despised, will some day be valued a one of the most important branches of Biological science.

W. H. Bates (1864) *The Naturalist on the River Amazons*

Sorts of butterflies

Mary Sheeran
Department of Computing Science
University of Glasgow
Glasgow G12 8QQ
Scotland

ms@dcs.glasgow.ac.uk

Abstract

This paper shows how Ruby is used to describe and analyse permutation
and comparator networks. It describes two merging networks, the bitonic
merger and the balanced merger, and shows how they are related. Both of
these networks can be used to build recursive sorters. The balanced merger
is also the building block of a periodic sorting network that is suitable for
implementation on silicon. The correctness of this sorter is demonstrated. As
always the key to success in understanding a circuit or algorithm is in finding
suitable structuring functions and studying their mathematical properties.
This paper uses the notation and to a large extent the structuring functions
introduced in reference [4] (in this volume) and that paper should be read
first.

1 Permutation networks

As well as the wiring permutation *riffle*, we will need some other permutations. The basic building blocks are $[id, id]$ and *swp* where $\langle a, b \rangle$ *swp* $\langle b, a \rangle$. The permutation $\mathbf{two}^n$ *swp* swaps adjacent pairs in a list of length 2^{n+1}. For example, $\langle 0, 1, 2, 3, 4, 5, 6, 7 \rangle$ is related by $\mathbf{two}^2$ *swp* to $\langle 1, 0, 3, 2, 5, 4, 7, 6 \rangle$. The permutation ilv^n *swp* switches the two halves of a list so that

$$\mathsf{ilv}^n \; swp \;\; = \;\; 2^{n+1} \; ; \; halve \; ; \; swp \; ; \; halve^{-1} \tag{1}$$

For example, $\langle 0, 1, 2, 3, 4, 5, 6, 7 \rangle$ is related by ilv^2 *swp* to $\langle 4, 5, 6, 7, 0, 1, 2, 3 \rangle$. The relation ilv^n *swp* commutes with $\mathbf{two}\, R$ for any homogeneous R.

$$
\begin{aligned}
\mathsf{ilv}^n \; swp \; ; \, \mathbf{two}\, R \;\; &= \{\, \text{equation 1 and definition } \mathbf{two} \,\} \\
& \quad 2^{n+1} \; ; \; halve \; ; \; swp \; ; \; halve^{-1} \; ; \; halve \; ; \; [R, R] \; ; \; halve^{-1} \\
&= \{\, halve \; ; \; swp \; ; \; halve^{-1} \; ; \; halve = halve \; ; \; swp \,\} \\
& \quad 2^{n+1} \; ; \; halve \; ; \; swp \; ; \; [R, R] \; ; \; halve^{-1} \\
&= \{\, swp \; ; \; [R, R] = [R, R] \; ; \; swp^{-1} \text{ and } R \text{ homogeneous} \,\} \\
& \quad halve \; ; \; [R, R] \; ; \; swp^{-1} \; ; \; halve^{-1} \; ; \; 2^{n+1} \\
&= \{\, \text{reversing the above calculation} \,\} \\
& \quad (\mathsf{ilv}^n \; swp \; ; \, \mathbf{two}\, R^{-1})^{-1} \\
&= \{\, \text{taking inverses, } swp^{-1} = swp \,\} \\
& \quad \mathbf{two}\, R \; ; \, \mathsf{ilv}^n \; swp \tag{2}
\end{aligned}
$$

For any $R : 2 \to 2$, the relations $\mathbf{two}^n R$ and $\mathsf{ilv}^n R$ are related by

$$\mathbf{two}^n R \;\; = \;\; (\mathsf{ilv}^n R) \setminus riffle$$

since $2^{n+1} \; ; \; riffle^n = 2^{n+1} \; ; \; riffle^{-1}$. So we can take the *riffle* conjugate of each side of equation 2 to get

$$\mathbf{two}^n \; swp \; ; \, \mathsf{ilv}\, R \;\; = \;\; \mathsf{ilv}\, R \; ; \, \mathbf{two}^n \; swp$$

The relation *prm*, for 'permute', defined by

$$prm = [id, id] + swp$$

relates a 2-list to each of its two permutations (and vice versa). Since $prm = prm^{-1} = prm^2$, it is the type of unordered 2-lists.

Switching networks can be built from *prm*. For example, $\mathbf{two}\, prm$ relates a list of length four to each of the four permutations that are obtained by choosing whether or not to swap adjacent pairs. These four possibilities are shown in figure 1. Similarly, $\mathbf{two}^n \, prm$ relates a list of length 2^{n+1} to each of 2^{2^n} permutations since each *prm* can be either $[id, id]$ or *swp*. Note that while $\mathbf{two}^n[id, id]$ and $\mathbf{two}^n \, swp$ both commute with $\mathsf{ilv}\, R$ for homogeneous R, $\mathbf{two}^n \, prm$ does not.

The network $\bowtie_n prm$ is an interesting one that has been much studied. For example, it is presented and analysed in reference [2] where it is called the *omega network*. It has $(n+1)2^n$ *prm* elements each of which has two possible settings.

2 Comparator networks

A two-input comparator is a permuting element whose range is constrained to be sorted. Let inc_i be the identity on sorted lists of length 2^i and $up = inc_1$ be the identity on sorted two-lists. Then $inc = \sum_{i=0}^{\infty} inc_i$ is the identity on sorted lists. Define

$$cmp = prm \mathbin{;} up$$

Then because prm and up are both types,

$$prm \mathbin{;} cmp = cmp = cmp \mathbin{;} up$$

so the type of cmp is $prm \to up$ which says that it relates an unordered 2-list to an ordered one. Because up is strictly smaller than the identity, $cmp < prm$.

The number of pairs in a sequence that are in order ($x_i \leq x_j$ for $i < j$) is a measure of the sortedness of the sequence. The relation $\mathbf{two}^n cmp$ increases the sortedness of a sequence by swapping the value at index $2i$ with the value at index $2i + 1$ if necessary. For example, the sequence $\langle 7, 6, 5, 4, 3, 2, 1, 0 \rangle$ is related by $\mathbf{two}^2 cmp$ to $\langle 6, 7, 4, 5, 2, 3, 0, 1 \rangle$. If the sequence in the domain of $\mathbf{two}^n cmp$ consists of two interleaved sorted sequences, then the related sequence in the range also consists of two interleaved sorted sequences. We write this as

$$\mathsf{ilv}\ inc \mathbin{;} \mathbf{two}^n cmp \;=\; \mathsf{ilv}\ inc \mathbin{;} \mathbf{two}^n cmp \mathbin{;} \mathsf{ilv}\ inc \qquad (3)$$

The relation $\mathsf{ilv}\ inc$ is the identity on sequences whose even-numbered elements and odd-numbered elements both form sorted sequences. Here we are using restricted identities as predicates. We will say that a sequence *satisfies* an identity if it is in the domain of the identity. The equation $Pre \mathbin{;} R = Pre \mathbin{;} R \mathbin{;} Post$ says that if an element in the domain of R satisfies Pre then the related element in the range of R satisfies $Post$.

It can be proved that if $k \leq n$

$$\mathsf{ilv}^{k+1}\ inc \mathbin{;} \mathbf{two}^{n+1} cmp \;=\; \mathsf{ilv}^{k+1}\ inc \mathbin{;} \mathbf{two}^{n+1} cmp \mathbin{;} \mathsf{ilv}^{k+1}\ inc \qquad (4)$$

from equation 3 and the properties of permutations.

3 Batcher's bitonic merger

Perhaps the best known comparator network of all is Batcher's bitonic merger. It is a butterfly of comparators and it sorts some but not all sequences. In particular, Batcher notes that $\mathcal{B}_n = \bowtie_n cmp$ sorts any sequence (of length 2^{n+1}) whose two halves are sorted into opposite orders (see references [1, 6]). It sorts many other

Figure 1: The four permutations realised by $\mathbf{two}\ prm$

sequences, but that does not matter. Knowing that it sorts sequences of that particular form gives us the classic recursive bitonic sorter.

The interesting properties of the bitonic merger derive from the fact that it is a butterfly. For example,

$$\begin{aligned} \mathcal{B}_0 &= cmp \\ \mathcal{B}_{n+1} &= \mathsf{ilv}^{n+1} \mathcal{B}_0 \, ; \mathsf{two}\, \mathcal{B}_n \\ &= \mathsf{ilv}\, \mathcal{B}_n \, ; \mathsf{two}^{n+1} \mathcal{B}_0 \end{aligned}$$

These are the two standard recursive decompositions often presented in the literature. The properties of $\bowtie$ give us many more, including

$$\mathcal{B}_{p+q+1} = \mathsf{ilv}^{q+1} \mathcal{B}_p \, ; \mathsf{two}^{p+1} \mathcal{B}_q$$

This is the equation that underlies the K-way bitonic sort which is presented in [5]. It is not really a new algorithm, but another way of decomposing an old one.

We can build networks with the same behaviour as $\mathcal{B}_n$ but with a different connection pattern by putting the wiring relation swp in front of selected comparators. This transformation preserves behaviour since $swp \, ; cmp = cmp$. Replacing every cmp by $swp \, ; cmp$ turns out to be uninteresting but we can replace the $\mathsf{two}^n \, cmp$ in the rightmost column by $\mathsf{two}^{n-1} \mathsf{one}\, swp \, ; \mathsf{two}^n \, cmp$ since

$$\begin{aligned} \mathsf{two}^{n-1} \mathsf{one}\, swp \, ; \mathsf{two}^n \, cmp &= \mathsf{two}^{n-1}(\mathsf{one}\, swp \, ; \mathsf{two}\, cmp) \\ &= \mathsf{two}^{n-1} \mathsf{two}\, cmp \\ &= \mathsf{two}^n \, cmp \end{aligned}$$

Abbreviate $\mathsf{two}^{n-1} \mathsf{one}\, swp$ to alt_n and let $alt = \sum_{i=1}^{\infty} alt_i$. For $n > 0$

$$\mathcal{B}_n = \mathsf{ilv}\, \mathcal{B}_{n-1} \, ; alt_n \, ; \mathsf{two}^n \, cmp$$

We want to move the alt leftwards so that it appears as a wiring relation on the domain. Define a new structuring function vee by

$$\mathsf{vee}\, R = (\mathsf{ilv}\, R) \setminus alt$$

We can compose alt on the left of both sides of this equation to give $alt \, ; \mathsf{vee}\, R = \mathsf{ilv}\, R \, ; alt$. Now

$$\mathcal{B}_n = alt_n \, ; \mathsf{vee}\, \mathcal{B}_{n-1} \, ; \mathsf{two}^n \, cmp$$

and by induction (using properties of vee that are discussed in the next section)

$$\mathcal{B}_n = (\overset{n-1}{\underset{i=0}{\overset{\bullet}{,}}} \mathsf{vee}^i \, alt_{n-i}) \, ; \overset{n}{\underset{i=0}{\overset{\bullet}{,}}} \mathsf{vee}^{n-i} \, \mathsf{two}^i \, cmp$$

We have shown that the bitonic merger can be rewritten as the composition of a wiring permutation $\overset{n-1}{\underset{i=0}{\overset{\bullet}{,}}} \mathsf{vee}^i \, alt_{n-i}$ with something that looks very like a butterfly except that it is made with vee instead of with ilv. The butterfly-like thing is the balanced merger proposed in reference [3] as the building block of a periodic sorter.

4   Networks built using vee

The next step is to study the properties of **vee**. Assume that R and S are length-homogeneous. Because ilv distributes over composition, so does **vee** (see figure 2).

$$\mathsf{vee}(R\,;S) = \mathsf{vee}\,R\,;\mathsf{vee}\,S$$

Because $alt_{n+1} = \mathsf{two}\,alt_n$ and ilv commutes with **two**

$$\mathsf{two\,vee}\,R = \mathsf{vee\,two}\,R$$

It is altogether more surprising to find that (for $R : 2^n \to 2^n$)

$$\mathsf{vee\,ilv}\,R = \mathsf{ilv\,ilv}\,R$$

Instances of these two equalities are shown in figures 3 and 4, for $R : 2 \to 2$.

If a sequence in the domain of $\mathsf{two}^{n+1}\,cmp$ satisfies $\mathsf{vee}\,inc$ then the related sequence in the range satisfies $\mathsf{ilv}\,inc$ since

$$
\begin{aligned}
\mathsf{vee}\,inc\,;\mathsf{two}^{n+1}\,cmp\ &=\ \{\text{ definition } \mathsf{vee}\ \}\\
&\quad alt^{-1}\,;\mathsf{ilv}\,inc\,;alt\,;\mathsf{two}^{n+1}\,cmp\\
&=\ \{\ alt\,;\mathsf{two}^{n+1}\,cmp = \mathsf{two}^{n+1}\,cmp\ \}\\
&\quad alt^{-1}\,;\mathsf{ilv}\,inc\,;\mathsf{two}^{n+1}\,cmp\\
&=\ \{\text{ equation 3 }\}\\
&\quad alt^{-1}\,;\mathsf{ilv}\,inc\,;\mathsf{two}^{n+1}\,cmp\,;\mathsf{ilv}\,inc\\
&=\ \{\text{ reversing the steps in the above calculation }\}\\
&\quad \mathsf{vee}\,inc\,;\mathsf{two}^{n+1}\,cmp\,;\mathsf{ilv}\,inc
\end{aligned}
\tag{5}
$$

Each comparator 'operates' on one value from each of the sorted sequences in the domain. An example of a sequence that satisfies $\mathsf{vee}\,inc$ (but not $\mathsf{ilv}\,inc$) is $\langle 0,4,5,1,2,6,7,3\rangle$; one that satisfies $\mathsf{ilv}\,inc$ (but not $\mathsf{vee}\,inc$) is $\langle 0,4,1,5,2,6,3,7\rangle$. These two sequences are related by $\mathsf{two}^2\,cmp$.

We have now proved

$$\mathsf{vee\,ilv}^k\,inc\,;\mathsf{two}^{n+1}\,cmp\ =\ \mathsf{vee\,ilv}^k\,inc\,;\mathsf{two}^{n+1}\,cmp\,;\mathsf{ilv}^{k+1}\,inc \tag{6}$$

because if $k = 0$ it reduces to equation 5, and if $k > 0$, since $\mathsf{vee\,ilv}\,R = \mathsf{ilv\,ilv}\,R$, it reduces to equation 4.

Let rev be the relation between each sequence and the corresponding sequence with the same elements in the reverse order. The relation $\mathsf{vee}^n\,swp$ reverses a sequence of length 2^{n+1}

$$\mathsf{vee}^n\,swp = 2^{n+1}\,;rev$$

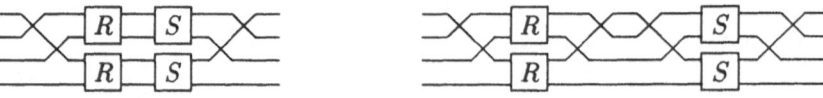

Figure 2: $\mathsf{vee}(R\,;S)$ and $\mathsf{vee}\,R\,;\mathsf{vee}\,S$

Figure 3: two vee R and vee two R

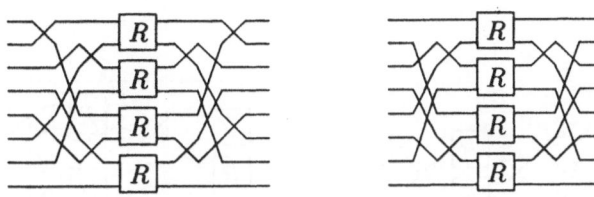

Figure 4: vee ilv R and ilv ilv R

because it swaps the first and last elements, second and second last, and so on. Similarly, **vee**^{n} *cmp* compares the first and last elements of a sequence, the second and second last, and so on. For example, the sequence $\langle 0, 4, 1, 5, 2, 6, 3, 7 \rangle$ is related by **vee**^{2} *cmp* to $\langle 0, 3, 1, 2, 5, 6, 4, 7 \rangle$. For $R : 2 \rightarrow 2$, the relations **vee**^{n} R and **ilv**^{n} R are related by

$$\textbf{vee}^n R \;=\; (\textbf{ilv}^n R) \setminus \textbf{one } rev \tag{7}$$

If you want to think about binary representations of indices, then ilv R divides elements of its domain and range (between instances of R) according to the least significant bit of the index, while **two** R divides according to the most significant bit. Amazingly enough, **vee** R divides according to the parity of the two least significant bits! It is best to stop thinking about bits as soon as possible.

The butterfly-like structure that arose in the discussion of the bitonic merger is defined by

$$\mathbb{W}_n R \;=\; \overset{n}{\underset{i=0}{\;;\;}} \textbf{vee}^{n-i} \textbf{ two}^i R$$

We read this as 'veefly R'. Because vee is so much like ilv the structure has a great many recursive decompositions like those of the butterfly, including

$$\mathbb{W}_{p+q+1} R \;=\; \mathbb{W}_p \textbf{vee}^{q+1} R \,;\, \mathbb{W}_q \textbf{two}^{p+1} R$$
$$=\; \textbf{vee}^{q+1} \mathbb{W}_p R \,;\, \textbf{two}^{p+1} \mathbb{W}_q R$$

and choosing p or q to be zero,

$$\mathbb{W}_{n+1} R \;=\; \textbf{vee}^{n+1} R \,;\, \mathbb{W}_n \textbf{two} R$$
$$=\; \textbf{vee}^{n+1} R \,;\, \textbf{two} \, \mathbb{W}_n R$$
$$=\; \mathbb{W}_n \textbf{vee} R \,;\, \textbf{two}^{n+1} R$$
$$=\; \textbf{vee} \, \mathbb{W}_n R \,;\, \textbf{two}^{n+1} R$$

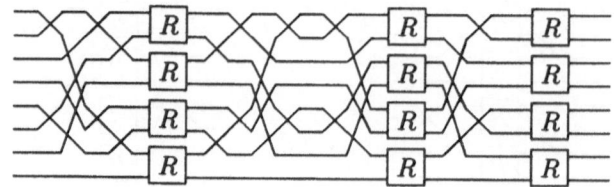

Figure 5: $\mathbb{W}_2\,R = \mathbf{vee}^2\,R$; $\mathbb{W}_1\,\mathbf{two}\,R = \mathbb{W}^2\,R$; $\mathbf{vee}\,\mathbf{two}\,R$; $\mathbb{W}_0\,\mathbf{two}^2\,R$

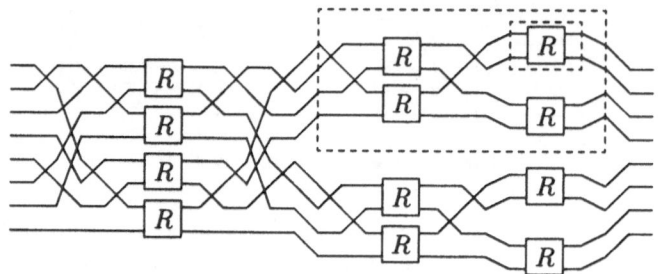

Figure 6: $\mathbb{W}_2\,R = \mathbf{vee}^2\,R$; $\mathbf{two}\,\mathbb{W}_1\,R = \mathbf{vee}^2\,R$; $\mathbf{two}(\mathbf{vee}^1\,R\,;\,\mathbf{two}\,\mathbb{W}_0\,R)$

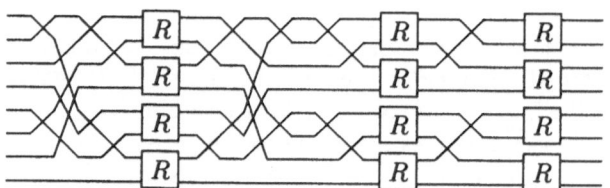

Figure 7: $\mathbb{W}_2\,R = \mathbb{W}_1\,\mathbf{vee}\,R$; $\mathbf{two}^2\,R = \mathbb{W}_0\,\mathbf{vee}^2\,R$; $\mathbf{two}\,\mathbf{vee}\,R$; $\mathbf{two}^2\,R$

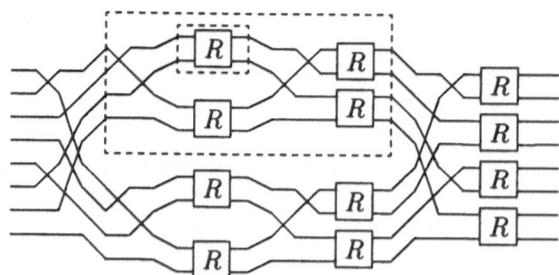

Figure 8: $\mathbb{W}_2\,R = \mathbf{vee}\,\mathbb{W}_1\,R$; $\mathbf{two}^2\,R = \mathbf{vee}(\mathbf{vee}\,\mathbb{W}_0\,R\,;\,\mathbf{two}\,R)$; $\mathbf{two}^2\,R$

each of which suggests a layout for the network. The four decompositions of $\mathbb{W}_3\,R$ for a component $R: 2 \to 2$ are shown in figures 5 to 8.

The wiring permutation $\overset{n-1}{\underset{i=0}{\text{\Large ;}}}$ vee^i alt_{n-i} that arose in the discussion of the bitonic merger is itself the inverse of a veefly.

$$\overset{n-1}{\underset{i=0}{\text{\Large ;}}} \text{vee}^i\, alt_{n-i} \;=\; \overset{n-1}{\underset{i=0}{\text{\Large ;}}} \text{vee}^i\, \text{two}^{n-1-i}\, \text{one}\, swp$$

$$= \; (\overset{n-1}{\underset{i=0}{\text{\Large ;}}} \text{vee}^{n-1-i}\, \text{two}^i\, \text{one}\, swp)^{-1}$$

$$= \; (\mathbb{W}_{n-1}\, \text{one}\, swp)^{-1}$$

It is also a butterfly. It can be shown by induction that

$$\overset{n-1}{\underset{i=0}{\text{\Large ;}}} \text{vee}^i\, alt_{n-i} \;=\; \overset{n-1}{\underset{i=0}{\text{\Large ;}}} \text{ilv}^{n-1-i}\, alt_{i+1}$$

$$= \; \overset{n-1}{\underset{i=0}{\text{\Large ;}}} \text{ilv}^{n-1-i}\, \text{two}^i\, \text{one}\, swp$$

$$= \; \bowtie_{n-1}\, \text{one}\, swp$$

We can conclude that

$$\mathcal{B}_n \;=\; (\mathbb{W}_{n-1}\, \text{one}\, swp)^{-1}\,;\, \mathbb{W}_n\, cmp$$

$$= \; \bowtie_{n-1}\, \text{one}\, swp\,;\, \mathbb{W}_n\, cmp$$

5   The balanced merger

In reference [3] the original designers of the balanced merger present it as a modification to the bitonic merger.

> We apply the permutation $(n/2 - 1, n/2 - 2, \ldots, 1, 0, n/2, n/2 + 1, \ldots, n - 2, n - 1)$ to the first phase of the bitonic merging network to obtain the new first phase comparing elements $x(0)$ with $x(n - 1)$, $x(1)$ with $x(n - 2)$, $\ldots$ $x(n/2 - 1)$ and $x(n/2)$, where x is the input vector, that is, comparing the first element with the last one, the second with the second to last, etc. Applying this permutation to the following phases of the bitonic merging network does not change those phases. Instead, we follow the bitonic merging network in assuming the partition of the elements into two halves of the smaller and the larger elements and applying in the second phase the same structure of the first phase for both halves. We continue recursively for the consecutive phases.

The authors write sequences of numbers $x = (x_0, \ldots, x_i, \ldots, x_{n-1})$ to name the permutation that takes i to x_i. They also number the sequences in their diagrams from top to bottom, so the permutation that they write as $(n/2 - 1, n/2 - 2, \ldots, 1, 0, n/2, n/2 + 1, \ldots, n - 2, n - 1)$ is written $n\,;\,\text{one}\, rev$ in our notation. It reverses the top half of a sequence of length n.

To construct the balanced merger from the bitonic merger, we transform the first rank of comparators from $\text{ilv}^{p+1}\, cmp$ to $\text{vee}^{p+1}\, cmp$ using the properties of the permutation **one** *rev* and the fact that *rev* is a left-identity of the bitonic merger.

$$\textbf{one}\ rev\ ;\ \mathcal{B}_{p+1}\ =\ \{\ \text{definition}\ \mathcal{B}\ \}$$
$$\textbf{one}\ rev\ ;\ \mathsf{ilv}^{p+1}\ cmp\ ;\ \textbf{two}\ \mathcal{B}_p$$
$$=\ \{\ \text{equation 7}\ \}$$
$$\mathsf{vee}^{p+1}\ cmp\ ;\ \textbf{one}\ rev\ ;\ \textbf{two}\ \mathcal{B}_p$$
$$=\ \{\ rev\ ;\ \mathcal{B}_p = \mathcal{B}_p\ \}$$
$$\mathsf{vee}^{p+1}\ cmp\ ;\ \textbf{two}\ \mathcal{B}_p$$

The relation $\mathsf{vee}^{p+1}\ cmp$ compares the first and last elements of a sequence, the second and second last elements, and so on, as required.

We also want to replace each of the recursive calls of $\mathcal{B}_p$ by **one** *rev* ; $\mathcal{B}_p$ in the same way, and so on recursively. It can be shown by induction that

$$\left(\ \overset{p}{\underset{i=0}{\text{\Large ;}}}\ \textbf{two}^i\ \textbf{one}\ rev\right)\ ;\ \mathcal{B}_{p+1}\ =\ \overset{p+1}{\underset{i=0}{\text{\Large ;}}}\ \mathsf{vee}^{p+1-i}\ \textbf{two}^i\ cmp$$
$$=\ \mathbb{W}_{p+1}\ cmp$$

So the balanced merger, $\mathcal{M}_{p+1}$, is just the network $\mathbb{W}_{p+1}\ cmp$ that we have already seen, and it is related to the bitonic merger by

$$\mathcal{M}_{p+1} = \left(\ \overset{p}{\underset{i=0}{\text{\Large ;}}}\ \textbf{two}^i\ \textbf{one}\ rev\right)\ ;\ \mathcal{B}_{p+1}$$

The wiring permutation $\overset{p}{\underset{i=0}{;}}\ \textbf{two}^i\ \textbf{one}\ rev$, when it operates on sequences of length 2^{p+2} as it does here, is $\mathbb{W}_p\ \textbf{one}\ swp$, which we saw above.

$$\overset{p}{\underset{i=0}{\text{\Large ;}}}\ \textbf{two}^i\ \textbf{one}\ rev\ ;\ 2^{p+2}\ =\ \{\ rev\ ;\ 2^{j+1} = \mathsf{vee}^j\ swp\ \}$$
$$\overset{p}{\underset{i=0}{\text{\Large ;}}}\ \textbf{two}^i\ \textbf{one}\ \mathsf{vee}^{p-i}\ swp$$
$$=\ \{\ \textbf{one}\ \mathsf{vee}\ R = \mathsf{vee}\ \textbf{one}\ R\ \}$$
$$\overset{p}{\underset{i=0}{\text{\Large ;}}}\ \textbf{two}^i\ \mathsf{vee}^{p-i}\ \textbf{one}\ swp$$
$$=\ \{\ \text{definition}\ \mathbb{W}\ \}$$
$$\mathbb{W}_p\ \textbf{one}\ swp$$

This is the permutation τ that appears mysteriously in reference [2] when the balanced merger is discussed. The natural language description of the balanced merger quoted above is typical of the way in which networks are described in the literature. Our formal description is much more precise, and it captures the designers' intuition in a satisfying way.

Knowing that the balanced merger is a veefly of comparators gives us numerous recursive decompositions of that network. In particular,

$$\mathcal{M}_0\ =\ cmp$$
$$\mathcal{M}_{n+1}\ =\ \mathsf{vee}^{n+1}\ \mathcal{M}_0\ ;\ \textbf{two}\ \mathcal{M}_n$$
$$=\ \mathsf{vee}\ \mathcal{M}_n\ ;\ \textbf{two}^{n+1}\ \mathcal{M}_0$$

The designers of the periodic balanced sorter show [3] that

$$\text{ilv } inc \,;\, \mathcal{M}_n \;=\; \text{ilv } inc \,;\, \mathcal{M}_n \,;\, inc \tag{8}$$

That is, the balanced merger sorts a sequence consisting of two interleaved sorted sequences. Applying the function ilv^k to each side of equation 8 gives

$$\text{ilv}^{k+1} inc \,;\, \text{ilv}^k \mathcal{M}_n \;=\; \text{ilv}^{k+1} inc \,;\, \text{ilv}^k \mathcal{M}_n \,;\, \text{ilv}^k inc \tag{9}$$

To build a sorter for sequences of length 2^{n+1}, we need to relate an unsorted sequence (which satisfies $\text{ilv}^{n+1} inc$) to its sorted permutation (which satisfies $\text{ilv}^0 inc$). We can do this by progressing through permutations that obey $\text{ilv}^n inc$, $\text{ilv}^{n-1} inc$ and so on. The network

$$\mathcal{S}_n \;=\; \overset{n}{\underset{i=0}{\,\vdots\,}} \; \text{ilv}^{n-i}\,\mathcal{M}_i \tag{10}$$

sorts in this way. The proof that it is a sorter is by induction on n, using equation 9. For a given size of input, $\mathcal{S}_n$ has the same number of comparators as the bitonic sorter.

6   The periodic balanced sorting network

What makes the balanced merger interesting is that the composition of $n+1$ copies of $\mathcal{M}_n$, that is $\mathcal{M}_n^{n+1}$, is also a sorter. For a VLSI implementation, the resulting periodic circuit is attractive because only one copy of $\mathcal{M}_n$ need actually be laid out and its outputs can be fed back to its inputs. Thus space, a scarce resource, is traded off against time.

To prove the periodic sorter correct, we need to show that (for $0 \leq k \leq n$)

$$\text{ilv}^{k+1} inc \,;\, \mathcal{M}_n \;=\; \text{ilv}^{k+1} inc \,;\, \mathcal{M}_n \,;\, \text{ilv}^k inc \tag{11}$$

because then an induction, and the fact that $\text{ilv}^{n+1} inc$ is the identity on sequences of length 2^{n+1}, gives

$$\mathcal{M}_n^{n+1} \;=\; \mathcal{M}_n^{n+1} \,;\, inc$$

which is the desired result.

The proof of equation 11 is by induction. The base case is equation 8, which is proved in reference [3]; we will not prove it here. For the step:

$\text{ilv}^{k+2} inc \,;\, \mathcal{M}_{n+1}$

$\quad = \{\, \text{ilv}^2\, R = \text{vee ilv}\, R \text{ and definition } \mathcal{M} \,\}$

$\qquad \text{vee ilv}^{k+1} inc \,;\, \text{vee}\, \mathcal{M}_n \,;\, \text{two}^{n+1} cmp$

$\quad = \{\, \text{homogeneity} \,\}$

$\qquad \text{vee}(\text{ilv}^{k+1} inc \,;\, \mathcal{M}_n) \,;\, \text{two}^{n+1} cmp$

$\quad = \{\, \text{inductive hypothesis} \,\}$

$\qquad \text{vee}(\text{ilv}^{k+1} inc \,;\, \mathcal{M}_n \,;\, \text{ilv}^k inc) \,;\, \text{two}^{n+1} cmp$

$\quad = \{\, \text{homogeneity and equation 6} \,\}$

$\qquad \text{vee}(\text{ilv}^{k+1} inc \,;\, \mathcal{M}_n) \,;\, \text{vee ilv}^k inc \,;\, \text{two}^{n+1} cmp \,;\, \text{ilv}^{k+1} inc$

$\quad = \{\, \text{reversing the steps in the above calculation} \,\}$

$\qquad \text{ilv}^{k+2} inc \,;\, \mathcal{M}_{n+1} \,;\, \text{ilv}^{k+1} inc$

This demonstrates the correctness of the periodic sorter.

To compare the sizes of $\mathcal{S}_n$ and the periodic sorter, note that we have replaced each $\text{ilv}^{n-i}\,\mathcal{M}_i$ in equation 10 by the larger $\mathcal{M}_n$. In $\mathcal{S}_n$, the ith column of mergers has $2^{n-i}(i+1)2^i = (i+1)2^n$ comparators while in the periodic sorter, each column of mergers has $(n+1)2^n$ comparators. This means that the complete periodic sorter has roughly twice as many comparators. For such a small constant factor, one might consider laying out the complete periodic network on silicon, instead of the smaller but less regular $\mathcal{S}_n$.

7 Conclusion

The work on permutation and comparator networks is only just starting. The approach looks promising, especially when compared with standard methods, which tend to make obscure appeals to the binary representations of indices. Our proof of the periodic sorter is appealingly simple, largely because we were able to use exactly the right recursive decomposition of the balanced merger. Our first attempt at the proof had the same structure as the original proof in reference [3]. It used an inappropriate recursive decomposition of the merger, and so was long and complicated. The fact that we can express alternative recursive decompositions easily is an important advantage of our use of structuring functions. It is to be hoped that it will also be useful in the mapping of algorithms onto structured networks.

There is clearly a whole family of structuring functions like **vee** waiting to be investigated; in particular, there is the structuring function that matches **vee** in the same way that **two** matches **ilv**. This will lead to a family of butterfly-like networks for different forms of divide-and-conquer algorithms.

Acknowledgements Thanks to Geraint Jones, David Murphy and Lars Rossen for comments and suggestions.

References

[1] K. E. Batcher, *Sorting networks and their applications*, in Proc. AFIPS Spring Joint Comput. Conf., Vol. 32, April 1968.

[2] G. Bilardi, *Merging and Sorting Networks with the Topology of the Omega Network*, IEEE Transactions on Computers, Vol. 38, No. 10, October 1989.

[3] M. Dowd, Y. Perl, L. Rudolph and M. Saks, *The Periodic Balanced Sorting Network*, Journal of the ACM, Vol. 36, No. 4, October 1989.

[4] G. Jones and M. Sheeran, *The study of butterflies*, in this volume.

[5] T. Nakatani, S.-T. Huang, B. W. Arden and S. T. Tripathi, *K-Way Bitonic Sort*, IEEE Transactions on Computers, Vol. 38, No. 2, February 1989.

[6] H. S. Stone, *Parallel processing with the perfect shuffle*, IEEE Transactions on Computers, Vol. C-20, No. 2, February 1971.

A fast flutter by the Fourier transform

Geraint Jones
Programming Research Group
Oxford University Computing Laboratory
11 Keble Road
Oxford OX1 3QD
England
Geraint.Jones@comlab.oxford.ac.uk

Abstract

This paper explains some familiar but intricate circuit forms that are used to implement the fast Fourier transform. They are shown to be solutions to a recursion equation that defines the transform. An earlier paper [6] showed that the essence of the fast Fourier transform is captured by an equation characteristic of divide-and-conquer algorithms. Butterfly circuits have been shown [8] to be solutions to such equations, and in this paper solutions are derived to the particular equation defining the fast Fourier transform.

1 Introduction

Twenty-five years ago Cooley and Tukey rediscovered an optimising technique usually attributed to Gauss, who used it in hand calculation. They applied the technique to the discrete Fourier transform, reducing an apparently $O(n^2)$ problem to the almost instantly ubiquitous $O(n \log n)$ 'fast Fourier transform' [3]. The fast Fourier transform is not of course a different transform, but a fast implementation of the discrete transform.

Its greatest virtue lies in that it can be executed in $O(\log n)$ time on $O(n)$ processors in a uniform way – which is to say that it lends itself to a low-latency high-throughput pipelined hardware implementation. Indeed, a footnote to the Cooley–Tukey paper records that a hardware implementation was underway as the paper was published, specifically that a component for evaluating a four-point transform had been 'designed by R. E. Miller and S. Winograd of the IBM Watson Research Centre'.

The unfortunate disadvantage of the fast algorithm is that although the fundamental idea is simple, the detail of its efficient implementation is very hard to understand. That efficiency depends on intricate permutations which rearrange data to maximise the sharing of work done in calculating intermediate results. Presentations of the algorithm abound in mysterious artefacts like the reversal of bits in subscripts [1], and the translation of parts of subscripts from time space to frequency space [9]. More recent descriptions of implementations seem to gloss over the problem, either referring the reader back to older presentations [11], or apparently assuming that the algorithm – because it is well known – must be well understood [2].

An earlier paper [6] reports the derivation of the Cooley–Tukey fast Fourier algorithm from the specification of the discrete Fourier transform. A functional programming notation was used to express the discrete transform, and an equation describing the fast algorithm calculated from it. That recursion equation shows that the 'fast transform' is an application of a divide-and-conquer strategy. In this paper we take the derivation further by finding a solution to the recursion equation, a solution which is the well-known butterfly circuit.

2 The discrete Fourier transform

The discrete Fourier transform is defined in terms of the arithmetic on an integral domain. You can think of arithmetic on complex numbers, for a definite example, although there are applications where finite fields or vector spaces over integral domains are appropriate. The derivation depends only on the algebraic properties of the arithmetic, not on the underlying arithmetic itself, so everything said here about the algorithm will be true for finite fields and vector spaces as well.

The discrete Fourier transform of a vector x of length n is a vector y of the same length for which

$$y_j = \sum_{k:0 \leq k < n} \omega^{j \times k} \times x_k$$

where ω is a principal n-th root of unity. (In the example of complex numbers, you can think of $\omega = e^{2\pi i/n}$.) The result, y, is sometimes called the 'frequency spectrum' of the sample x.

Even if the powers of ω are pre-calculated, it would appear that $O(n^2)$ multiplications are required to evaluate the whole of y for any x. The fast algorithm avoids many of these by making use of the fact that $\omega^n = 1$. The discovery made by Cooley and Tukey was that if n is composite, the calculation can be divided into what amounts to a number of smaller Fourier transforms. Suppose $n = p \times q$, then by a change of variables

$$
\begin{aligned}
y_{pa+b} &= \sum_{c:0\leq c<p} \sum_{d:0\leq d<q} \omega^{(pa+b)(qc+d)} x_{qc+d} \\
&= \sum_{c:0\leq c<p} \sum_{d:0\leq d<q} (\omega^{pq})^{ac}(\omega^p)^{ad}(\omega^q)^{bc}\omega^{bd} x_{qc+d} \\
&= \sum_{d:0\leq d<q} (\omega^p)^{ad}\omega^{bd} \sum_{c:0\leq c<p} (\omega^q)^{bc} x_{qc+d}
\end{aligned}
$$

Since ω^q is a p-th root of unity, and ω^p is a q-th root of unity, it is not surprising that the above calculation leads to an implementation in which p-sized and q-sized transforms appear.

In particular, if $p = 2$ there is an implementation involving only transforms of size 2 – which are particularly simple – and a pair of transforms of size $n/2$. Repeated division by two permits of an implementation consisting solely of transforms of size two, for any transform which has a width that is a power of two. It is however rather difficult to see from the above calculations what these implementations might be.

In reference [6] the divide-and-conquer strategy is revealed by a calculation in which the expressions are algorithms, rather than data values. For this we will need the notation from a companion paper [8] and a small amount of extra notation specific to this problem.

3 Triangles

With the constructors introduced in reference [8], any path from the domain to the range has to go through the same number of components. In order to deal with a wider class of circuits we introduce

$$\text{one } R = [id, R] \setminus halve^{-1}$$

where id is the identity relation, the unit of sequential composition. This constructor behaves very like **two**, for example, remembering that the variables range over only

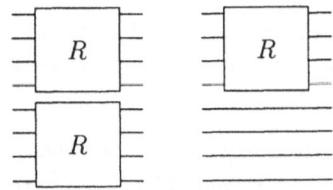

Figure 1: circuit arrangements for **two** R and **one** R

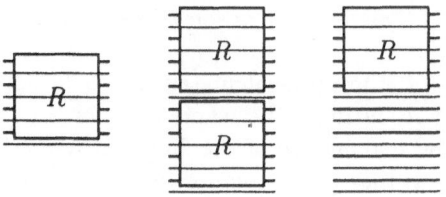

Figure 2: thw R, two thw R = thw two R, and one thw R = thw one R

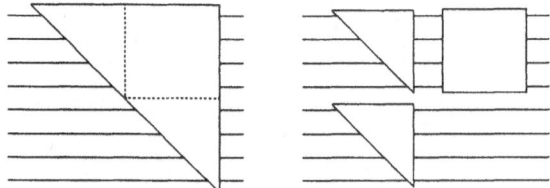

Figure 3: $\text{tri}_{n+1} R = \text{two tri}_n R \,;\, \text{one block}_n R$

length-homogeneous relations

$$\begin{aligned} \text{one}(R\,;\,S) &= \text{one}\,R\,;\,\text{one}\,S \\ \text{ilv one}\,R &= \text{one ilv}\,R \end{aligned}$$

but be careful because two one $R \neq$ one two R.

Of course, you can riffle together the two halves of a one R. Define

$$\text{thw}\,R = (\text{one}\,R) \setminus \textit{riffle}$$

for 'through-wire', and it should come as no surprise that

$$\begin{aligned} \text{thw one}\,R &= \text{one thw}\,R \\ \text{thw two}\,R &= \text{two thw}\,R \end{aligned}$$

although in general thw ilv $R \neq$ ilv thw R.

There are two families of these constructors, the *straight* ones: one and two, and the *shuffled* ones: ilv and thw. Just as before we were able to say that the only thing that mattered in a term made by applying ilv and two was the number of each, so now we can say that the term is determined by the number and order of the straight constructors, and the number and order of the shuffled ones. The order of the constructors matters within a family, but not the way in which the constructors from the two families are interleaved. The shuffled constructors pass through the straight ones like ghosts though walls, but behave quite reasonably with respect to each other.

You can think of one R as a small triangular-shaped circuit, and figure 3 suggests that larger triangular-shaped circuits can be made by a recursion similar to that for butterflies.

$$\begin{aligned} \text{tri}_{n+1} R &= \text{two tri}_n R \,;\, \text{one block}_n R \\ &= \text{one block}_n R \,;\, \text{two tri}_n R \\ &\text{where }\ \text{block}_n = \text{two}^n R^{2^n} \end{aligned}$$

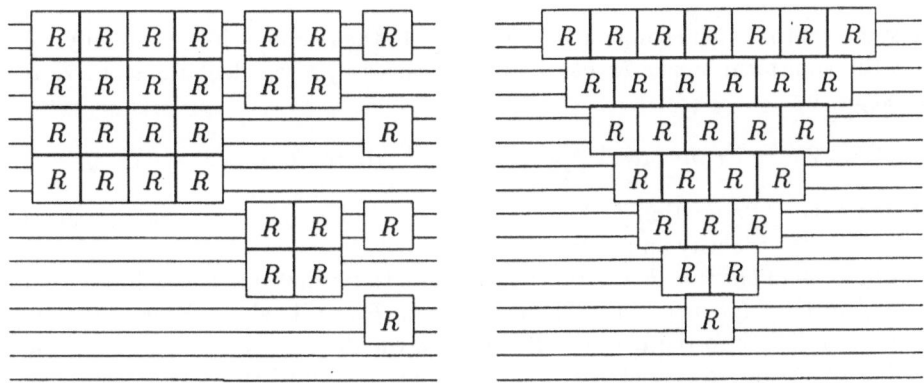

Figure 4: $\text{tri}_3\, R = \text{one two}^2\, R^4\,;\, \text{two one two}\, R^2\,;\, \text{two}^2\, \text{one}\, R$

where this time $\text{tri}_0\, R = id$ is the identity relation, $\text{tri}_1\, R = \text{one}\, R$, and so on. You can define a tri of general width and depth by

$$\text{tri}\, R \;=\; \sum_{i=0}^{\infty} \text{tri}_i\, R$$

which is again a disjoint sum in case R has a fixed width.

An iterative solution to the recursion for triangle is given by

$$\text{tri}_n\, R \;=\; \overset{n}{\underset{i=1}{\text{\Large ;}}}\, \text{two}^{i-1}\, \text{one two}^{n-i}\, R^{2^{n-i}}$$

and a layout suggested by this equation is shown in figure 4. Because each of the constructors in a triangle is straight, it follows that $\text{ilv tri}\, R = \text{tri ilv}\, R$ so triangle itself has straight properties. The proof goes like

$$
\begin{aligned}
\text{ilv tri}\, R \;&=\; \text{ilv} \sum_{i=0}^{\infty} \overset{i}{\underset{j=1}{\text{\Large ;}}}\, \text{two}^{j-1}\, \text{one two}^{i-j}\, R^{2^{i-j}} \\
&=\; \sum_{i=0}^{\infty} \overset{i}{\underset{j=1}{\text{\Large ;}}}\, \text{two}^{j-1}\, \text{one two}^{i-j}\, \text{ilv}\, R^{2^{i-j}} \\
&=\; \sum_{i=0}^{\infty} \overset{i}{\underset{j=1}{\text{\Large ;}}}\, \text{two}^{j-1}\, \text{one two}^{i-j}\, (\text{ilv}\, R)^{2^{i-j}} \\
&=\; \text{tri ilv}\, R
\end{aligned}
$$

and similarly $\text{thw tri}\, R = \text{tri thw}\, R$.

(If you are comparing this paper with earlier presentations such as that in reference [7], beware that this is not quite the same definition of triangle: that paper defines a triangular constructor which assumes that the component is $R : 1 \to 1$.)

4   The fast Fourier transform

At the end of reference [6] it is suggested that, at least for certain factorisations, the algorithm admits of an implementation which is like a butterfly network. The substance of that claim can now be explained. In the reference it is eventually shown that the transform of size $2n$ can be implemented by two calculations of size n by the algorithm

$$\mathcal{F}_f ; 2n = riffle ; \mathsf{two}^n(\mathcal{F}_{f^n} ; 2) ; riffle^{-1} ; \mathsf{tri}_1 \, \mathsf{tri}_n \, f ; \mathsf{two}(\mathcal{F}_{f^2} ; n) ; riffle$$

where the kernel operation $f : 1 \to 1$, multiplication by a $2n$-th root of unity, is such that f^{2n} is the identity on singletons.

The component $\varphi = \mathcal{F}_{f^n} ; 2$ takes two inputs to two outputs and will be assumed to be directly implementable. The other part, $\mathcal{F}_{f^2} ; n$ is also a Fourier transform because $(f^2)^n$ is also the identity. If n is even the division can be repeated, and in particular if n is a power of two it can be continued until the only $\mathcal{F}$ components are all φ.

Let $\Phi_n = \mathcal{F}_{f_n} ; 2^n$ where for each n the operation f_n is such that $f_n{}^{2^n}$ is the identity, and $f_n = f_{n+1}^2$. Then at least for $n > 1$

$$\begin{aligned}
\Phi_n &= riffle ; \mathsf{two}^{n-1} \, \varphi ; riffle^{-1} ; \mathsf{tri}_1 \, \mathsf{tri}_{n-1} \, f_{n-1} ; \mathsf{two} \, \Phi_{n-1} ; riffle \\
&= \{ \, riffle^n \text{ can be cancelled on } 2^n \, \} \\
&\quad riffle^{-(n-1)} ; \mathsf{two}^{n-1} \, \varphi ; riffle^{n-1} ; \mathsf{tri}_1 \, \mathsf{tri}_{n-1} \, f_{n-1} ; \mathsf{two} \, \Phi_{n-1} ; riffle \\
&= \{ \, \mathsf{two} \, R \setminus riffle = \mathsf{ilv} \, R \text{ and } \mathsf{two} \, \mathsf{ilv} \, R = \mathsf{ilv} \, \mathsf{two} \, R \text{ and then by induction} \, \} \\
&\quad \mathsf{ilv}^{n-1} \, \varphi ; \mathsf{tri}_1 \, \mathsf{tri}_{n-1} \, f_{n-1} ; \mathsf{two} \, \Phi_{n-1} ; riffle \\
&= \{ \, \text{unwinding the recursion, then by induction} \, \} \\
&\quad \overset{n-1}{\underset{i=1}{\vdots}} \; \mathsf{two}^{i-1}(\mathsf{ilv}^{n-i} \, \varphi ; \mathsf{tri}_1 \, \mathsf{tri}_{n-i} \, f_{n-i}) \; ; \; \mathsf{two}^{n-1} \, \varphi \; ; \; \overset{n}{\underset{i=2}{\vdots}} \; \mathsf{two}^{n-i} \, riffle
\end{aligned}$$

The term in the middle can be written, rather perversely, as

$$\mathsf{two}^{n-1} \, \varphi = \mathsf{two}^{n-1}(\mathsf{ilv}^0 \, \varphi ; \mathsf{tri}_1 \, \mathsf{tri}_0 \, f_0) ; \mathsf{two}^{n-1} \, riffle$$

by adding in some extra terms that happen to be identities, so

$$\Phi_n = \mathcal{B}_n ; \mathcal{R}_n$$

where

$$\mathcal{B}_n = \overset{n}{\underset{i=1}{\vdots}} \; \mathsf{two}^{i-1}(\mathsf{ilv}^{n-i} \, \varphi ; \mathsf{tri}_1 \, \mathsf{tri}_{n-i} \, f_{n-i}) \tag{1}$$

$$\mathcal{R}_n = \overset{n}{\underset{i=1}{\vdots}} \; \mathsf{two}^{n-i}(2^i ; riffle)$$

As in the decompositions of the butterfly, the $\mathcal{B}$ and $\mathcal{R}$ terms can be summed separately, since $\mathcal{B}_i ; \mathcal{R}_j$ is empty unless $i = j$. Let $\mathcal{B} = \sum_{i=0}^{\infty} \mathcal{B}_i$ and $\mathcal{R} = \sum_{i=0}^{\infty} \mathcal{R}_i$ then $\Phi = \sum_{i=0}^{\infty} \Phi_i = \mathcal{B} ; \mathcal{R}$. It is normal to implement the required part of $\mathcal{B}$ in a machine, and to leave the corresponding part of $\mathcal{R}$ to the way that the machine is connected to the outside world.

5   The butterfly

The part of the decomposition of Φ_n that looks like a butterfly circuit is $\mathcal{B}_n$, which is like a butterfly – specifically, like $\bowtie_{n-1} \varphi$ – in which to each column $\mathsf{two}^{i-1} \, \mathsf{ilv}^{n-i} \, \varphi$ has been added a term $\mathsf{two}^{i-1}\,\mathsf{tri}_1\,\mathsf{tri}_{n-i}\,f_{n-i}$. This is made with only straight constructors and powers of the kernel operation: in implementations it would be turned into a single column of multipliers.

For example, following the development of the shuffle network for a butterfly given in the companion paper [8], there is a shuffle network for the Fourier transform. Each column of $\mathcal{B}_n$ in equation 1 has the form

$$
\begin{aligned}
\mathsf{two}^{i-1}&(\mathsf{ilv}^{n-i}\,\varphi\,;\,\mathsf{tri}_1\,\mathsf{tri}_{n-i}\,f_{n-i}) \\
=\;& \mathsf{two}^{i-1}\,\mathsf{ilv}^{n-i}\,\varphi\,;\,\mathsf{two}^{i-1}\,\mathsf{tri}_1\,\mathsf{tri}_{n-i}\,f_{n-i} \\
=\;& \{\,\text{unriffling the } \mathsf{ilv}^{n-i}\,\varphi\,\} \\
& \mathit{riffle}^{-(n-i)}\,;\,\mathsf{two}^{n-1}\,\varphi\,;\,\mathit{riffle}^{n-i}\,;\,\mathsf{two}^{i-1}\,\mathsf{one}\,\mathsf{tri}_{n-i}\,f_{n-i} \\
=\;& \{\,\text{riffling the } \mathsf{two}^{i-1}\,\mathsf{one}\,R\,\} \\
& \mathit{riffle}^{-(n-i)}\,;\,\mathsf{two}^{n-1}\,\varphi\,;\,\mathit{riffle}^{n}\,;\,\mathsf{ilv}^{i-1}\,\mathsf{thw}\,\mathsf{tri}_{n-i}\,f_{n-i}\,;\,\mathit{riffle}^{n-i} \\
=\;& \{\,\mathit{riffle}^{n} \text{ can be cancelled on } 2^n\text{-lists, promoting straight operators}\,\} \\
& \mathit{riffle}^{-(n-i)}\,;\,\mathsf{two}^{n-1}\,\varphi\,;\,\mathsf{tri}_{n-i}\,\mathsf{ilv}^{i-1}\,\mathsf{thw}\,f_{n-i}\,;\,\mathit{riffle}^{n-i}
\end{aligned}
$$

but the term in the triangle

$$
\begin{aligned}
\mathsf{ilv}^{i-1}\,\mathsf{thw}\,f_{n-i}\;=\;& \{\,\text{unriffling}\,\} \\
& (\mathsf{two}^{i-1}\,\mathsf{one}\,f_{n-i}) \setminus \mathit{riffle}^{i} \\
=\;& \{\,\mathit{riffle}^{i} \text{ can be cancelled on } 2^i\text{-lists}\,\} \\
& \mathsf{two}^{i-1}\,\mathsf{one}\,f_{n-i}
\end{aligned}
$$

Re-assembling these columns in equation 1 and cancelling,

$$
\begin{aligned}
\mathcal{B}_n \;=\;& \overset{n}{\underset{i=1}{\text{\scalebox{1.5}{;}}}} \mathsf{two}^{i-1}(\mathsf{ilv}^{n-i}\,\varphi\,;\,\mathsf{tri}_1\,\mathsf{tri}_{n-i}\,f_{n-i}) \\
=\;& \overset{n}{\underset{i=1}{\text{\scalebox{1.5}{;}}}} (\mathit{riffle}^{-(n-i)}\,;\,\mathsf{two}^{n-1}\,\varphi\,;\,\mathsf{tri}_{n-i}\,\mathsf{two}^{i-1}\,\mathsf{one}\,f_{n-i}\,;\,\mathit{riffle}^{n-i}) \\
=\;& \mathit{riffle}^{-n}\,;\,\overset{n}{\underset{i=1}{\text{\scalebox{1.5}{;}}}} (\mathit{riffle}\,;\,\mathsf{two}^{n-1}\,\varphi\,;\,\mathsf{tri}_{n-i}\,\mathsf{two}^{i-1}\,\mathsf{one}\,f_{n-i})
\end{aligned}
$$

Now the term in the triangle is entirely straight, in fact it is

$$
\begin{aligned}
\mathsf{tri}_{n-i}\,&\mathsf{two}^{i-1}\,\mathsf{one}\,f_{n-i} \\
=\;& \overset{n-i}{\underset{j=1}{\text{\scalebox{1.5}{;}}}} \mathsf{two}^{j-1}\,\mathsf{one}\,\mathsf{two}^{n-(i+j)}(\mathsf{two}^{i-1}\,\mathsf{one}\,f_{n-i})^{2^{n-(i+j)}} \\
=\;& \overset{n-i}{\underset{j=1}{\text{\scalebox{1.5}{;}}}} \mathsf{two}^{j-1}\,\mathsf{one}\,\mathsf{two}^{(n-j)-1}\,\mathsf{one}\,f_j
\end{aligned}
$$

so

$$
\mathcal{B}_n \;=\; \overset{n}{\underset{i=1}{\text{\scalebox{1.5}{;}}}} (\mathit{riffle}\,;\,\mathcal{C}_i)
$$

$$
\text{where } \mathcal{C}_i = \mathsf{two}^{n-1}\,\varphi\,;\,\overset{n-i}{\underset{j=1}{\text{\scalebox{1.5}{;}}}} \mathsf{two}^{j-1}\,\mathsf{one}\,\mathsf{two}^{(n-j)-1}\,\mathsf{one}\,f_j
$$

The column $\mathcal{C}_i$ is a group of 2^{n-1} independent circuits, each of which is $\varphi\,;\,\mathsf{one}\,f^k_{n-i}$ for some k. It would be nice to conclude by showing this, but we have not yet found an elegant and convincing way of doing this within the notation.

6 The shuffle

Returning to the remaining part of the algorithm, an induction from $\mathbf{two}\,R\,;\mathit{riffle} = \mathit{riffle}\,;\mathsf{ilv}\,R$ will show that

$$\mathcal{R}_n \;=\; 2^n\,;\; \overset{n}{\underset{i=1}{\overset{\circ}{\circ}}}\;\mathbf{two}^{n-i}\,\mathit{riffle} \;=\; 2^n\,;\; \overset{n-1}{\underset{i=0}{\overset{\circ}{\circ}}}\;\mathsf{ilv}^i\,\mathit{riffle}$$

This is just a permutation on lists of length 2^n. It is that very thorough shuffle that appears mysteriously in many presentations of this algorithm: $x\,\mathcal{R}_n\,y$ if and only if x and y are both of length 2^n and $x_i = y_j$ where the (n-bit long) binary representations of i and of j are each the reverse of the other.

It is its own inverse, and is closely related to the butterfly since if $R : 2^k \to 2^k$ then $(\mathsf{ilv}\,R) \setminus \mathcal{R}_{k+1} = \mathbf{two}(R \setminus \mathcal{R}_k)$ and $(\mathbf{two}\,R) \setminus \mathcal{R}_{k+1} = \mathsf{ilv}(R \setminus \mathcal{R}_k)$, and so also $(\bowtie_n(R \setminus \mathcal{R}_k)) \setminus \mathcal{R}_{n+k} = (\bowtie_n(R^{-1}))^{-1}$. Proofs of these, and the discovery of many other pleasant properties are left for the reader's idle moments.

References

[1] A. V. Aho, J. E. Hopcroft and J. D. Ullman, *The design and analysis of computer algorithms*, Addison–Wesley, 1974.

[2] K. M. Chandy and J. Misra, *Parallel program design – a foundation*, Addison–Wesley, 1988.

[3] J. W. Cooley and J. W. Tukey, *An algorithm for the machine computation of complex Fourier series*, Mathematics of Computation, **19**, pp. 297–301, 1965.

[4] K. Davis and J. Hughes (eds.), *Functional programming, Glasgow 1989*, Springer Workshops in Computing, 1990.

[5] P. Denyer and D. Renshaw, *VLSI signal processing; a bit-serial approach*, Addison–Wesley, 1985.

[6] G. Jones, *Deriving the fast Fourier algorithm by calculation*, in [4]. (Programming Research Group technical report PRG–TR–4–89)

[7] G. Jones and M. Sheeran, *Circuit design in Ruby*, in [10].

[8] G. Jones and M. Sheeran, *The study of butterflies*, in this volume.

[9] S. G. Smith, *Fourier transform machines*, pp. 147–199 in [5].

[10] Jørgen Staunstrup (ed.), *Formal methods for VLSI design*, North-Holland, 1990.

[11] J. D. Ullman, *Computational aspects of VLSI*, Computer Science Press, 1984.

Parallel Computations
and Delay-Insensitive Circuits

Jo C. Ebergen *

Computer Science Department
University of Waterloo
Waterloo, Ontario, Canada N2L 3G1

jebergen@maytag.waterloo.edu

Abstract

Delay-insensitive circuits are attractive implementations for parallel computations. A delay-insensitive circuit is a special type of asynchronous circuit and can informally be characterised as a network of components of which the correctness is insensitive to delays in basic components and connection wires. The principles underlying the design of delay-insensitive circuits are explained. By means of a few examples we illustrate how parallel computations can be expressed conveniently in a simple program notation. In particular the design of the proper synchronisation among the subcomputations is illustrated. Subsequently, we show how such a program can be transformed into a delay-insensitive circuit and how timing problems can be avoided in implementing the synchronisations.

---

*This work was supported by the Natural Sciences and Engineering Research Council of Canada under grant OGP0041920.

1   Introduction

The purpose of this paper is to present some formal techniques for the design and implementation of a parallel computation. The techniques are illustrated by the design of various hardware solutions for the producer-consumer problem.

A major task in the design of parallel computations is the development of a program notation that assists designers in the specification of and reasoning about a parallel computation. With relative ease designers should be able to convince themselves and their colleagues that the parallel program they have designed does indeed satisfy the specification. Moreover, since we are interested in implementing the parallel programs as integrated circuits, the program notation should also assist designers in finding a decomposition of a program into a network of primitive circuit elements. We present a simple program notation, inspired by Hoare's CSP [8], and investigate whether it meets these objectives.

The avoidance of timing problems is one of the difficulties a designer faces in implementing a parallel computation by an integrated circuit. Synchronisation failure [2, 13], for example, is a notoriously difficult problem that may occur, when a computation is implemented by a synchronous circuit. The avoidance of such timing problems is one of the reasons why we have chosen to study *delay-insensitive circuits* for the implementation of parallel computations. A delay-insensitive circuit can be characterised informally as a network of primitive circuit elements of which the correctness is insensitive to any delays in the elements and connection wires. The advantages of these types of circuits are discussed and demonstrated in [6, 9, 10, 13, 14, 16, 17], for example. We briefly present a formalisation of a delay-insensitive circuit and illustrate how such a circuit can be used in the design of a micropipeline [14].

2   Producers and Consumers: Encore

We are asked to design a controller for an n-place buffer, $n > 0$. Input into the buffer is done by a so-called *producer* and output from the buffer is done by a so-called *consumer*. There may be multiple producers and multiple consumers, and they may all operate concurrently.

Software solutions for the bounded buffer, with various kinds of synchronisation primitives, abound in the literature. This time, however, we do *not* ask for a software solution, but for a hardware solution: we have to design a network of primitive circuit elements that does the job. We assume that the communication between a producer and the controller is as follows. Each producer and each consumer is connected to the controller with a pair of request and acknowledgement wires. A producer requests to put an item into the buffer by sending a signal on the request wire. If the buffer is not full, the put action is performed, and the controller responds by sending a signal on the acknowledgement wire indicating the completion of the put action. A consumer also communicates with the controller through a pair of request and acknowledgement wires. A consumer can get an item from the buffer by sending a request to the controller; if the buffer is not empty, the get action is performed and, subsequently, the controller responds with sending an acknowledgement indicating the completion of the get action. Requests and acknowledgements alternate. The controller for two producers and two consumers is illustrated in Figure 1.

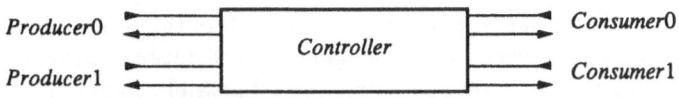

Figure 1: A controller for two producers and two consumers

The put and get actions for the buffer take place between a request and subsequent acknowledgement. For the moment, we are not interested in what type of items are stored in the buffer; we are only interested in the ordering of the communication actions that may take place on the request and acknowledgement wires. The controller should be designed in such a way that at any time the number of items contained in the buffer is at most n and at least 0.

The circuit for the n-place buffer controller for k producers and k consumers, $k > 0$, can be used as an implementation of a n-ary semaphore for k processes. Each P operation by a process can be seen as a put action, and each V operation can be seen as a get action. When a process arrives at a P operation, it sends a request to the controller. If the process receives an acknowledgement, then the P operation has been granted to the process. A similar reasoning holds when a process arrives at a V operation. Notice that, since P and V operations can both be performed by one process, a producer and consumer are thus combined in one process. In the original phrasing of the problem, producers and consumers are independent of one another and may operate concurrently.

3 A Program Notation

In order to specify the communication behaviour of the controller and of the primitive components, we introduce a program notation called *commands*. As a simple example of a command, we can specify the communication behaviour between the controller and one producer by

$$\textbf{pref } *[req\_put?; ack\_put!].$$

Here, $req\_put?$ denotes a receipt by the controller of a request to do a put action and $ack\_put!$ denotes the sending of an acknowledgement by the controller to the producer. The notation ';' denotes concatenation, '*[ ]' denotes repetition of the enclosed, and **pref** denotes prefix-closure. The prefix-closure stipulates that any prefix of a specified communication behaviour may also occur. The command expresses that requests and acknowledgements for put actions alternate and, if there is any communication action, start with a request. The communication behaviour of the controller with respect to one consumer is specified similarly by

$$\textbf{pref } *[req\_get?; ack\_get!].$$

We first present a formal definition of the semantics of the notation. In the next section we give an operational interpretation. Communication behaviours are represented by sets of *traces*, i.e., sets of finite sequences of symbols. The empty trace is denoted by ε. A complete behavioural specification of a component is given by a *directed trace structure*; it is a triple $\langle I, O, T \rangle$. The set I is called the *input alphabet* and consists of all the names of the input terminals of the component; O is called the *output alphabet* and consists of all the names of the output terminals of the component; T is called the *trace set* and represents all possible communication behaviours between a component and its environment. Every trace in T is constructed from symbols in $I \cup O$.

Instead of listing all traces of a directed trace structure, we represent a directed trace structure by means of a directed command similar to a regular expression. (Since we use directed commands and directed trace structures only, we drop the adjective 'directed' from now on.) The characters $\varepsilon, b?, b!$, and $!b?$ are *atomic commands* and represent the trace structures $\langle \emptyset, \emptyset, \{\varepsilon\}\rangle, \langle\{b\}, \emptyset, \{b\}\rangle, \langle \emptyset, \{b\}, \{b\}\rangle$, and $\langle\{b\}, \{b\}, \{b\}\rangle$ respectively.

From the atomic commands we can construct other commands as follows. Let commands be denoted by capital E's and let iE, oE, and tE denote the input alphabet, output alphabet, and trace set of the trace structure represented by E respectively. The alphabet of E is denoted by $\mathbf{a}E$ and given by $\mathbf{a}E = iE \cup oE$. The *concatenation, union, repetition, prefix-closure*, and *projection* of trace structures are defined as follows.

$$
\begin{aligned}
E0; E1 &= \langle iE0 \cup iE1, \ oE0 \cup oE1, \ (tE0)(tE1)\rangle \\
E0 \mid E1 &= \langle iE0 \cup iE1, \ oE0 \cup oE1, \ tE0 \cup tE1\rangle \\
*[E] &= \langle iE, oE, (tE)^*\rangle \\
\mathbf{pref}\,E &= \langle iE, \ oE, \ \{t_0 \mid (\exists t_1 :: t_0 t_1 \in tE)\}\rangle \\
E \downarrow B &= \langle iE \cap B, \ oE \cap B, \ \{t \downarrow B \mid t \in tE\}\rangle,
\end{aligned}
$$

where $t \downarrow B$ denotes the trace t projected on alphabet B, i.e., the trace t from which all symbols not in B have been deleted. Concatenation of sets is denoted by juxtaposition, and $(tE)^*$ denotes the set of all finite-length concatenations of traces in tE. For reasons of brevity, we use the same notation for commands and the trace structure represented by commands. Equality between commands denotes equality of the trace structures represented by the commands.

Projection is used to abstract away from so-called internal symbols. For example, we can represent a put action by the symbol *put* and express the communication behaviour between a producer and the controller, including the put actions, by the command E given by

$$E = \mathbf{pref} *[req\_put?; !put?; ack\_put!].$$

The symbol *put* is called an *internal symbol* of E and is denoted in a command by $!put?$. Although *put* is both an input and an output symbol of E, it does not belong to the alphabet of (external) communication symbols of the controller. The alphabet of the controller in case of one producer and one consumer is given by

$$B = \{req\_put, ack\_put, req\_get, ack\_get\}.$$

In order to obtain the (external) communication behaviour between the controller and a producer, internal symbols should be projected away. Thus, we get

$$E \downarrow \{req\_put, ack\_put\} = \mathbf{pref} *[req\_put?; ack\_put!].$$

Communication behaviours of components are specified by prefix-closed, non-empty trace structures with disjoint input and output alphabet. A trace structure E is called *prefix-closed*, if $\mathbf{pref}\,E = E$. Accordingly, by means of the **pref** operation we can construct prefix-closed trace structures. The condition that a trace structure must be prefix-closed is operationally justified by the argument that if a component can exhibit behaviour t, then it can also exhibit any behaviour that is a prefix of t. The condition that a trace structure must be non-empty is operationally justified by the argument that the initial state of any component is represented by the empty trace ε. (A trace structure is non-empty if $\mathbf{t}E \neq \emptyset$.) Consequently, for a component specified by command E, we always have $\varepsilon \in \mathbf{t}E$ and $\mathbf{i}E \cap \mathbf{o}E = \emptyset$. The set of prefix-closed, non-empty trace structures is one of the simplest semantic domains in which one can represent communication behaviours of components [8].

4   Some Basic Components

To illustrate the program notation, we specify the communication behaviour of three basic components. The specifications of the WIRE, IWIRE, and MERGE are given in Figure 2. First, we give an abstract mechanistic interpretation of the communication behaviour of these components; later, we discuss a physical interpretation.

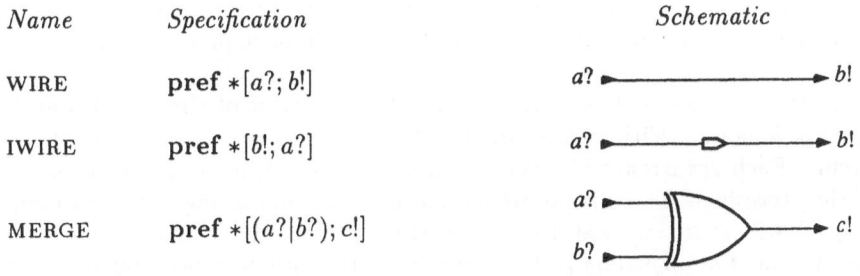

Figure 2: Specifications of WIRE, IWIRE, and MERGE.

A specification prescribes all possible communication behaviours at the interface between component and environment. The environment is the composite of the other components to which the component is connected. Furthermore, we stipulate that inputs are produced by the environment and outputs are produced by the component. This mechanistic interpretation of a communication between components differs from the CSP interpretation of a communication between sequential processes [8]. In the traditional CSP interpretation, a communication action between two processes takes place if both processes can engage in the communication action. In our mechanistic interpretation, a communication action is initiated by the component for which the action is an output. It is our obligation to ensure that the receiving component is ready to engage in the communication. If the receiving component is not ready to engage in the communication action, we say that there is *computation interference* [17]. The reason for adopting this different interpretation of a communication is that we wish to view components as abstractions of circuits and that our interpretation has a closer correspondence with the communications that take place between circuit elements.

With this mechanistic interpretation in mind, the specification for the WIRE prescribes that the component may produce an output b after each receipt of an input a. The environment of the WIRE may produce an input a initially and after each output b. Notice that the environment is not allowed to produce two inputs a in a row, since this would cause computation interference.

The IWIRE is like an 'initialised' WIRE. Here, the component may start with producing an output b, and then the same behaviour as for the WIRE evolves. (Notice that $\mathbf{pref} * [b!; a?] = \mathbf{pref}(b!; *[a?; b!])$.) The specification for the MERGE prescribes that the environment produces either an input a or an input b. It may do so initially and after each output c. The component may produce an output c after each receipt of either a or b.

In the above, we have used the words 'may produce' several times. For the moment, these words should be interpreted as 'every communication behaviour specified is possible to occur, but, due to non-deterministic behaviour, is not guaranteed to occur'. Later, we shall give a precise formulation of this interpretation.

The mechanistic interpretation of a specification can also be phrased informally as 'if the environment provides the inputs as specified, then the component may provide the outputs as specified'. Accordingly, on the one hand a specification can be used by an 'implementer' of the component who has to realise the component prescriptions. On the other hand, a specification can be used by a 'user' of the component who has to take care that the environment prescriptions are complied with.

A physical interpretation of a specification in terms of circuit behaviour can be given as follows. With each symbol in the alphabet, we associate a terminal of a circuit. Each occurrence of a symbol in a trace corresponds to a voltage transition at that terminal. There is no distinction between high-going and low-going transitions: both transitions are denoted by the same symbol. This type of signaling is called *transition signaling* [14]. Outputs are transitions caused by the circuit and inputs are transitions caused by the environment. If we assume that initially the voltage levels at the terminals are low, then the WIRE corresponds to a physical wire and the MERGE corresponds to a XOR gate. We shall not discuss any electrical implementations of other basic components in this paper, but instead concentrate on the abstract mechanistic interpretations.

5 Parallelism

The program notation we defined so far is rather inconvenient to express the parallel behaviour of a component. For this reason, we introduce a new programming primitive called *weaving*. Weaving is an operation defined on trace structures and expresses a parallel composition with synchronisation on common symbols. Formally, the weave $E0\|E1$ of two trace structures $E0$ and $E1$ is defined by

$$
\begin{aligned}
E0\|E1 \;=\; \langle\; &\mathbf{i}E0 \cup \mathbf{i}E1 \\
,\; &\mathbf{o}E0 \cup \mathbf{o}E1 \\
,\; &\{t \in (\mathbf{a}E0 \cup \mathbf{a}E1)^* \mid t{\downarrow}\mathbf{a}E0 \in \mathbf{t}E0 \;\wedge\; t{\downarrow}\mathbf{a}E1 \in \mathbf{t}E1\} \\
&\rangle.
\end{aligned}
$$

The weave $E0\|E1$ consists of all traces that are in accordance with the traces of $E0$ *and* of $E1$. For this reason, weaving can be considered as the *conjunction* of the subbehaviours expressed in $E0$ and $E1$. The correspondence between a weave of commands and a conjunction of subbehaviours is illustrated several times in the following.

There are two special cases of weaving. If $\mathbf{a}E0 \cap \mathbf{a}E1 = \emptyset$, then weaving $E0$ and $E1$ amounts to the interleaving of the traces of $E0$ and $E1$. If $\mathbf{a}E0 = \mathbf{a}E1$, then weaving $E0$ and $E1$ amounts to taking the intersection of the traces of $E0$ and $E1$.

We stipulate that weaving has highest priority of the binary operators, then concatenation, and then union.

A first component whose communication behaviour can be expressed by the weave is the primitive component called C-ELEMENT. Its specification is given in Figure 3. The mechanistic interpretation is that the C-ELEMENT may produce a c,

C-ELEMENT   **pref** $*[a?\|b?\,;c!]$

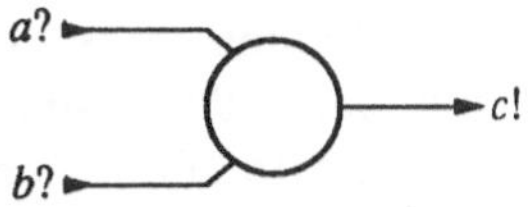

Figure 3: Specification of C-ELEMENT

each time when a *and* b have been received. The environment may produce inputs a and b initially and each time when a c has been produced.

The specification for the C-ELEMENT may be rewritten as follows.

$\quad$ **pref** $*[a?\|b?\,;c!]$

$=$ $\qquad$ { def. of weaving }

$\quad$ **pref** $*[a?;c!]$ $\|$ **pref** $*[b?;c!]$.

The last command can be interpreted as a conjunction of two subbehaviours: one behaviour where a and c alternate and one behaviour where b and c alternate. Output symbol c is a common symbol of the two behaviours and thus serves as a synchronisation symbol. Accordingly, the C-ELEMENT can be considered as a primitive component realising a synchronisation with respect to an output symbol.

At first sight, the specification of a C-ELEMENT as a weave of two commands that correspond to WIRE behaviours may be confusing. It may give the false impression that the C-ELEMENT can be realised by a connection of two WIREs. In general, a weave of commands should not be interpreted as representing the communication behaviour of a connection of components, where each component corresponds to a 'weavand'. Rather, weaving should be viewed as a programming primitive to express the parallel behaviour of *one* component. Consequently, weavands in a command do not necessarily have to represent the subcomponents in which a component can be decomposed. In fact, many primitive components with parallel behaviour are expressed by means of weaving, like the C-ELEMENT above. The rules for what constitutes a decomposition of a component are discussed later.

6 Mutual Exclusion

A primitive component with which mutual exclusion can be realised is the SE-QUENCER. The SEQUENCER sequences requests of a number of concurrent components. For example, the SEQUENCER of Figure 4 sequences requests of two com-

pref $*[r0?; g0!]$

|| pref $*[r1?; g1!]$

|| pref $*[n?; (g0!|g1!)]$

Figure 4: A SEQUENCER

ponents. The following meaning can be associated with the symbols occurring in Figure 4. Symbol $r0$ represents a request of component 0, and $g0$ represents a grant for component 0. A similar reasoning holds for the symbols $r1$ and $g1$, but now with respect to component 1. The symbol n indicates when a next grant may be produced.

The communication behaviour for the SEQUENCER is a conjunction of three sub-behaviours. The first line of the command in Figure 4 expresses the condition that requests of and grants for component 0 alternate. A similar reasoning holds for the second line in Figure 4, but now with respect to component 1. The last line of the command expresses the mutual exclusion condition with respect to granting requests: after each receipt of input n, either $g0$ or $g1$ may be produced. The conditions expressed in the three lines of the command are the only conditions that have to be satisfied with respect to the communication behaviour of the SEQUENCER. Accordingly, the communication behaviour for the SEQUENCER is conveniently expressed by the weave of the commands in the three lines. Notice that a grant $g0$ may be produced only when a request $r0$ *and* an input n have been received.

The SEQUENCER of Figure 4 sequences requests of 2 components only. A specification for a SEQUENCER that sequences requests of $k, k > 2$, concurrent components can be constructed similarly.

The SEQUENCER is one of many primitive components that realise mutual exclusion. Other primitive components for realising mutual exclusion are discussed in [4, 6, 9, 13, 14], for example.

7 A Command for the Controller

The weave is a very convenient programming primitive for specifying communication behaviours of a component with a high degree of parallelism. Some examples of this convenience are given in the previous sections, where we specified a SEQUENCER and a C-ELEMENT. In this section we give another example by deriving a specification for the three-place buffer controller, first in the special case of only one producer and one consumer, and then in the case of multiple consumers and producers.

Our first design decision is to think of the buffer controller as a FIFO consisting of three cells: cell 0, 1, and 2. We stipulate that each cell can contain at least zero and at most one item. Consequently, at any time the buffer contains at least zero and at most three items. Each item is first put in cell 0, then transferred to cell 1, subsequently transferred to cell 2, and finally output.

In order to specify the communication behaviour of the controller using this idea, we introduce some internal symbols to represent the transfers among the cells. The internal symbols and their associated meanings are given below.

put	put item of producer into cell 0;
*trans*0	transfer item from cell 0 to cell 1;
*trans*1	transfer item from cell 1 to cell 2;
get	consumer gets item from cell 2.

As before, *req_put* denotes a request by the producer for a put action; *ack_put* denotes the acknowledgement of a put action; *req_get* denotes a request by the consumer for a get action; and *ack_get* denotes an acknowledgement of a get action.

The communication behaviour of the controller, including the internal symbols, can be expressed as the conjunction of five subbehaviours: the behaviour with respect to the producer; the behaviour with respect to cell 0; the behaviour with respect to cell 1; the behaviour with respect to cell 2; and the behaviour with respect to the consumer.

All communication behaviours that may take place with respect to the producer are conveniently expressed by

$$\mathbf{pref} *[req\_put?; !put?; ack\_put!].$$

This command expresses that requests and acknowledgements alternate and that between a request and an acknowledgement an item from the producer is put into cell 0.

Since each cell may contain at least zero and at most one item, filling and emptying of a cell should alternate. We assume that initially the cells are empty. For cell 0, this condition is conveniently expressed by

$$\mathbf{pref} *[!put?; !trans0?].$$

Similarly, for cell 1 and cell 2 we derive the commands

$$\mathbf{pref} *[!trans0?; !trans1?] \quad \text{and} \quad \mathbf{pref} *[!trans1?; !get?],$$

respectively. Notice that *trans*0 denotes the emptying of cell 0, but also the filling of cell 1. A similar reasoning holds for *trans*1.

The conditions with respect to the consumer are that requests and acknowledgements alternate and that between a request and an acknowledgement the consumer gets an item from the buffer. This condition is expressed by

$$\mathbf{pref} *[req\_get?; !get?; ack\_get!].$$

These are all conditions that have to be satisfied. Consequently, the complete specification of the controller, including the internal symbols, is conveniently expressed by their conjunction, i.e., the weave of the five commands. Subsequently, since the internal symbols do not belong to the alphabet of the controller, we delete them by projecting on the alphabet of the controller. Thus, we obtain our final command, which we call *Controller*0 for later reference.

$Controller0$

=   { by definition}

(**pref** $*[req\_put?; !put?; ack\_put!]$ behaviour for producer

|| **pref** $*[!put?; !trans0?]$ for cell 0

|| **pref** $*[!trans0?; !trans1?]$ for cell 1

|| **pref** $*[!trans1?; !get?]$ for cell 2

|| **pref** $*[req\_get?; !get?; ack\_get!]$ for consumer

) $\downarrow \{req\_put, ack\_put$ alphabet producer

, req_get, ack_get alphabet consumer

}.

A generalisation of this command to a command for an n-place controller, $n > 0$, is constructed similarly.

A command for the controller in the case of multiple producers and consumers can be derived in much the same way. For reasons of simplicity, we assume that there are two producers and two consumers. A request for and an acknowledgement of a put action by producer 0 is denoted by req_put0 and ack_put0 respectively. Putting an item from producer 0 into cell 0 is denoted by $put0$. Similar meanings are associated with the symbols req_put1, ack_put1, and $put1$, but now with respect to producer 1. For a get action we have the following symbols. A request by and an acknowledgement for consumer 0 for a get action is denoted by req_get0 and ack_get0 respectively. Outputting an item from cell 2 to consumer 0 is denoted by $get0$. Similar symbols and meanings are used for the communication with respect to consumer 1.

Applying the same approach as for the problem with one producer and one consumer, we derive the following command for the controller.

$Controller1$

=   { by definition }

(**pref** $*[req\_put0?; !put0?; ack\_put0!]$ for producer 0

|| **pref** $*[req\_put1?; !put1?; ack\_put1!]$ for producer 1

|| **pref** $*[(!put0?|!put1?); !trans0?]$ for cell 0

|| **pref** $*[!trans0?; !trans1?]$ for cell 1

|| **pref** $*[!trans1?; (!get0?|!get1?)]$ for cell 2

|| **pref** $*[req\_get0?; !get0?; ack\_get0!]$ for consumer 0

|| **pref** $*[req\_get1?; !get1?; ack\_get1!]$ for consumer 1

) $\downarrow$ $\{req\_put0, req\_put1, ack\_put0, ack\_put1$ alphabet producers

, $req\_get0, req\_get1, ack\_get0, ack\_get1$ alphabet consumers

}.

The subbehaviour for cell 0 now reads as follows. Either producer 0 or producer 1 puts an item into cell 0, and, subsequently, cell 0 is emptied by a transfer to cell 1.

For cell 2, we have a similar reasoning: after an item is transferred into cell 2, either consumer 0 or consumer 1 gets the item.

A generalisation of this solution to the case of k, with $k > 0$, producers and l, with $l > 0$, consumers is done similarly.

8 Decomposition

After having given a command for the controller, our next task is to find a decomposition into primitive components. In order to do so, we first have to define what a decomposition is. Informally, a network of components is said to be a decomposition of a component E, if 'the network can produce the outputs as specified in E, provided the environment of the network produces the inputs as specified in E'. In this section we formalise this definition by stipulating four conditions that have to hold for a decomposition of a component into a network of components. In the next section we give some examples.

We consider a network consisting of components E_1, E_2, and E_3. This network is denoted by (E_1, E_2, E_3). The property that E can be decomposed into the network consisting of E_1, E_2, and E_3 is denoted by $E \rightarrow (E_1, E_2, E_3)$. We first assume that the environment of the network produces the inputs as specified in E. This environment is taken into account by stipulating a fourth component for the network. For this purpose we consider the *reflection* of E, which is denoted by $\overline{E}$ and defined by $\overline{E} = \langle \mathbf{o}E, \mathbf{i}E, \mathbf{t}E \rangle$. By reflecting E, we interchanged the role of component and environment by interchanging inputs and outputs. Instead of considering environment $\overline{E}$ and network (E_1, E_2, E_3), we now consider the network (E_0, E_1, E_2, E_3), where $E_0 = \overline{E}$.

In order for E to be decomposable into the network (E_1, E_2, E_3), four conditions have to hold for the network (E_0, E_1, E_2, E_3). The first two conditions concern the so-called *structure* of the network and are formulated in terms of the alphabets of the trace structures. They are

$$(\cup i : 0 \leq i < 4 : \mathbf{o}E_i) = (\cup i : 0 \leq i < 4 : \mathbf{i}E_i) \quad \text{and} \tag{1}$$

$$\mathbf{o}E_i \cap \mathbf{o}E_j = \emptyset \quad \text{for all } i, j : 0 \leq i, j < 4 \wedge i \neq j. \tag{2}$$

Condition (1) stipulates that every input is connected to an output and every output is connected to an input, i.e., there are no dangling inputs and outputs. If (1) holds, we say that the network (E_0, E_1, E_2, E_3) is *closed*.

The second condition stipulates that outputs of distinct components are not connected to each other. (Notice, however, that inputs may be connected to each other.) If (2) holds we say that the network is *free of output interference*. Condition (1) and (2) together guarantee that each symbol is an output of exactly one component and an input of at least one component.

The next two conditions are conditions on the *behaviour* of the network; they are phrased in terms of the trace sets and the alphabets. They are

$$\text{The network is free of computation interference,} \quad \text{and} \tag{3}$$

$$\mathbf{t}(E_0 \| E_1 \| E_2 \| E_3) \downarrow \mathbf{a}E = \mathbf{t}E. \tag{4}$$

The third condition prescribes that the environment prescription for any component in the network may not be violated. This condition can be verified as follows.

We can simulate the joint behaviour of all components in the network by generating traces of symbols. Formally, we construct the trace set X of all joint behaviours in the following way. Initially, $X = \{\varepsilon\}$. Choose a trace t, symbol z, and index i, where $0 \leq i < 4$, such that after joint behaviour t, component E_i can produce output z: in formula, we have

$$t \in X \wedge z \in \mathbf{o}E_i \wedge tz \downarrow \mathbf{a}E_i \in \mathbf{t}E_i .$$

If for all j, where $0 \leq j < 4$, component E_j can accept z, i.e., its environment prescription is not violated, then we add tz to X. In formula, we must have $tz \downarrow \mathbf{a}E_j \in \mathbf{t}E_j$. If some component can not accept z, we stop the simulation and conclude that the network has *computation interference*. When no computation interference occurs, X represents the joint behaviour of the network (E_0, E_1, E_2, E_3).

The fourth condition is that every trace of the component specified may also occur in the simulation. When no computation interference occurs, the joint behaviour of the network can be represented by $X = \mathbf{t}(E_0 \| E_1 \| E_2 \| E_3)$. Consequently, the fourth condition can be formulated as $X \downarrow \mathbf{a}E = \mathbf{t}E$, i.e., the behaviour of the network with respect to the alphabet of E is exactly the trace set of E. If (4) is satisfied we say that the network behaves as specified.

Condition (4) does not require that after a certain trace an output is guaranteed to occur. It only requires that each trace in $\mathbf{t}E$ *may* occur in the simulation. The actual occurrence of a trace in a simulation depends on the non-deterministic choices made by the components. Consequently, conditions (1) through (4) do not guarantee, for example, fairness nor absence of deadlock or livelock. If such additional conditions are required for a decomposition, they will have to be formulated. This is still a topic of further research. In other works on delay-insensitive circuits ([3, 4, 11]) condition (4) is not required to hold.

In the present paper, we take the above four conditions as our correctness criteria for a decomposition. They can be generalised naturally to any network of components. Furthermore, the conditions are simple to verify. Indeed, they are so simple that an automatic verifier for conditions (1) through (3) has been designed and is described in [4]. The time complexity of a straightforward verification algorithm, however, can be exponential in n, where n is the number of components in the network. Theorems that assist the designer in verifying or finding a decomposition in a possibly more efficient way are given in [4, 6]. We briefly discuss some of these theorems in the next section.

9   Some Decomposition Examples

In order to illustrate the four conditions, we verify some simple decompositions. For the first decomposition, we verify whether $E \to (E_1, E_2)$, where

$$E \;\; = \;\; \mathbf{pref} * [a?; c!] \;\; \| \;\; \mathbf{pref} * [c!; b?],$$

$$E_1 \;\; = \;\; \mathbf{pref} * [a?; c!] \;\; \| \;\; \mathbf{pref} * [y?; c!],$$

$$E_2 \;\; = \;\; \mathbf{pref} * [y!; b?].$$

Component E_1 is a C-ELEMENT and E_2 is an IWIRE. Command E can be rewritten as $\mathbf{pref}(a?; c!; *[a? \| b?; c!])$. This command is very similar to the command for the

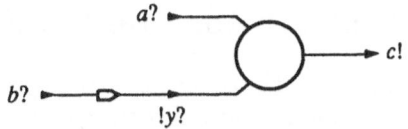

Figure 5: Decomposition of E

C-ELEMENT. In fact, E has the same behaviour as the C-ELEMENT, except that initially only an input a is needed for producing the first output c. Accordingly, component E can be viewed as an 'initialised' C-ELEMENT. The decomposition is illustrated in Figure 5.

The reflection of E is given by

$$\overline{E} = \mathbf{pref} * [a!; c?] \parallel \mathbf{pref} * [c?; b!].$$

It is readily verified that network (E_0, E_1, E_2), where $E_0 = \overline{E}$, is closed and free of output interference. When simulating the network's behaviour, we find that the joint behaviour X can be represented by

$$X = \mathbf{t}(\mathbf{pref} * [!a?; !c?] \parallel \mathbf{pref} * [!y?; !c?; !b?]),$$

and that no computation interference occurs. Furthermore,

$$X \downarrow \{a, b, c\} = \mathbf{t}E,$$

i.e., the network may exhibit any trace that is specified. Consequently, all four conditions hold for the decomposition $E \rightarrow (E_1, E_2)$.

In a similar way one can verify that an initialised SEQUENCER can be decomposed into an IWIRE and a SEQUENCER. This decomposition can be formulated as $E \rightarrow (E_1, E_2)$, where this time

$$
\begin{aligned}
E &= \mathbf{pref} * [r0?; g0!] \parallel \mathbf{pref} * [r1?; g1!] \parallel \mathbf{pref} * [(g0!|g1!); n?], \\
E_1 &= \mathbf{pref} * [r0?; g0!] \parallel \mathbf{pref} * [r1?; g1!] \parallel \mathbf{pref} * [y?; (g0!|g1!)], \\
E_2 &= \mathbf{pref} * [y!; n?].
\end{aligned}
$$

There are two theorems that can be helpful in finding a decomposition. Although a detailed discussion of these theorems is outside the scope of this paper, we mention them briefly.

The first theorem is called the Substitution Theorem. It allows us to decompose components by stepwise refinement. In short, the Substitution Theorem states that if we encounter in a decomposition a subcomponent for which we can find a decomposition in isolation, we may substitute that subcomponent by its decomposition. For example, if we encounter an initialised C-ELEMENT in a decomposition, we may simply substitute this initialised C-ELEMENT by its decomposition into an IWIRE and a C-ELEMENT.

The second theorem is the Separation Theorem. It allows us to decompose components by partwise refinement. In short, the Separation Theorem states that we can find a decomposition of a component by first finding decompositions for parts of its behaviour and then combining these decompositions in a specific way. The Separation Theorem is usually applied to specifications that are expressed as a weave of a number of commands, like the specifications of the initialised C-ELEMENT, the initialised SEQUENCER, and both controller specifications. A detailed explanation of both theorems can be found in [7].

98

10   A Decomposition for the Controller

A decomposition for the 3-place buffer controller for one producer and one consumer can be derived with the Separation and Substitution Theorem. Since we have not discussed these theorems in detail, we just list the decompositions without doing a formal verification.

The first step yields the following decomposition.

Controller0

$\rightarrow$ {decomposition}

(**pref** $*[req\_put?; put!]$ $\|$ **pref** $*[put!; trans0?]$ initialised C-ELEMENT

, **pref** $*[put?; ack\_put!]$ WIRE

, **pref** $*[put?; trans0!]$ $\|$ **pref** $*[trans0!; trans1?]$ initialised C-ELEMENT

, **pref** $*[trans0?; trans1!]$ $\|$ **pref** $*[trans1!; get?]$ initialised C-ELEMENT

, **pref** $*[req\_get?; get!]$ $\|$ **pref** $*[trans1?; get!]$ C-ELEMENT

, **pref** $*[get?; ack\_get!]$ WIRE

).

Remark. Verifying the correctness of this decomposition without applying the Separation Theorem would be a tedious task, since this is a decomposition where the simulation indeed takes time exponential in the number of components. □

The second, fifth, and sixth component in the above list are the primitive components WIRE, C-ELEMENT, and WIRE respectively. Each of the other components is an initialised C-ELEMENT and can be decomposed further into a C-ELEMENT and

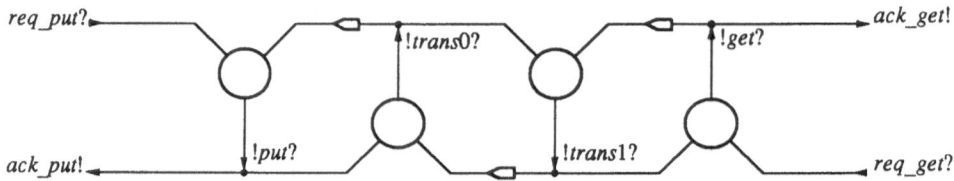

Figure 6: Decomposition of controller for 1 producer and 1 consumer

an IWIRE, as we have seen in the previous section. Accordingly, by the Substitution Theorem, the controller can be decomposed into the following primitive components: four C-ELEMENTs, three IWIREs, and two WIREs. There is one C-ELEMENT for realising the synchronisation with respect to symbol *put*, one for symbol *trans0*, one for symbol *trans1*, and one for symbol *get*. The IWIREs are needed for the proper initialisation. The complete decomposition is illustrated in Figure 6.

The decomposition for the 3-place buffer controller with two producers and two consumers can also be obtained by application of the Separation Theorem and the Substitution Theorem. Without proof we give the first step of the decomposition below.

*Controller*1

→ {decomposition}

(**pref** *[*req_put0?; put0!*]   initialised

|| **pref** *[*req_put1?; put1!*]   SEQUENCER

|| **pref** *[(put0!|put1!); trans0?*]

, **pref** *[*put0?; ack_put0!*]   WIRE

, **pref** *[*put1?; ack_put1!*]   WIRE

, **pref** *[(put0?|put1?); put!*]   MERGE

, **pref** *[*put?; trans0!*] || **pref** *[*trans0!; trans1?*]   initialised C-ELEMENT

, **pref** *[*trans0?; trans1!*] || **pref** *[*trans1!; get?*]   initialised C-ELEMENT

, **pref** *[(get0?|get1?); get!*]   MERGE

,   **pref** *[*req_get0?; get0!*]

|| **pref** *[*req_get1?; get1!*]   SEQUENCER

|| **pref** *[*trans0?; (get0!|get1!)*]

, **pref** *[*get0?; ack_get0!*]   WIRE

, **pref** *[*get1?; ack_get1!*]   WIRE

).

By application of the Substitution Theorem, we can replace the initialised C-ELEMENTs by C-ELEMENTs andIWIREs, and the initialised SEQUENCER by a SEQUENCER and an IWIRE. The complete decomposition is depicted in Figure 7.

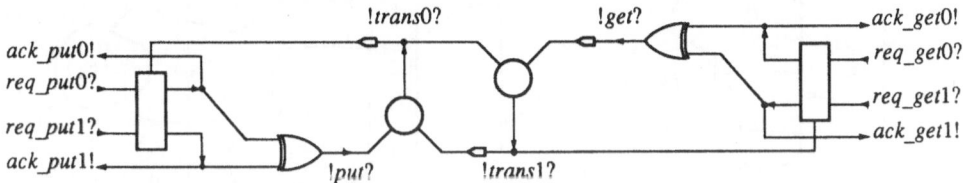

Figure 7: Decomposition of controller for multiple producers and consumers

Notice that in comparison to Figure 6 two C-ELEMENTs have been replaced by SEQUENCERs, and two MERGEs and WIREs have been introduced. The reason that we obtain SEQUENCERs instead of C-ELEMENTs is that, in the case of multiple producers and consumers, not only synchronisation but also mutual exclusion needs to be realised.

A generalisation of this decomposition to k producers, $k > 0$, and l consumers, $l > 0$, is done similarly. The only change in the decomposition is the replacement of the 2-input SEQUENCERs by a k-input SEQUENCER and an l-input SEQUENCER respectively. The k-input SEQUENCER, however, is not a primitive component for $k > 2$. (For $k = 1$, it is a C-ELEMENT.) So we have to find a decomposition for the k-input SEQUENCER into primitive components. This is a non-trivial, but nice, problem. We leave it as an exercise for the reader. A solution can be found in [6] or for a similar problem in [7].

11 DI Decomposition

In Section 8 we gave a formal definition of decomposition based on our mechanistic interpretation of a component's behaviour. The physical interpretation of decomposition is intended to correspond to the realisation of a circuit by a network of subcircuits. These subcircuits may have arbitrary, nonnegative response times. The communications between the subcircuits, however, are assumed to be instantaneous. Thus, a circuit obtained by means of decomposition can be called a *speed-independent circuit*, i.e., its correctness is independent of any delays in the response times of the components.

In practice, the subcircuits are connected to each other by means of wires that may have unspecified delays. Such delays may affect the correctness of the circuit. If the correctness of the circuit is independent of any delays in the response times of components *and* connection wires, then we call such a circuit a *delay-insensitive circuit*.

While a speed-independent circuit is formally described by means of a decomposition, a delay-insensitive circuit is formally described by means of a *DI decomposition*. A DI decomposition is a decomposition in which all connection wires between the components are taken into account. Formally, these connection wires are represented by WIREs and connect components with each other through an intermediate boundary as exemplified in Figure 8.

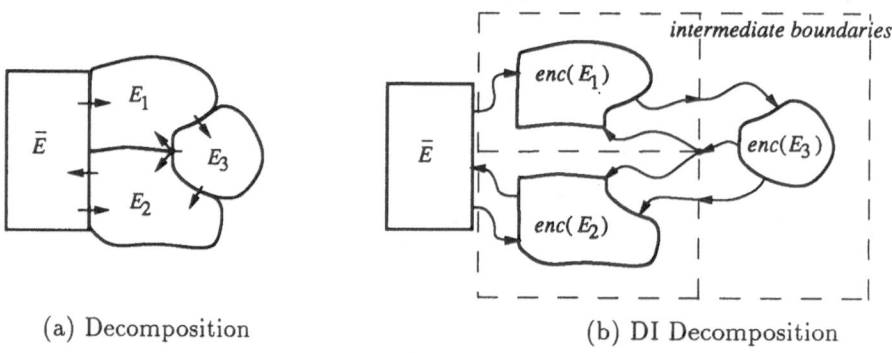

(a) Decomposition (b) DI Decomposition

Figure 8:

Here is a brief formalisation of 'realising a component E by means of a delay-insensitive circuit (E_1, E_2, E_3).' First, we define the *enclosure* $enc(E_1)$, i.e., the component enclosed by the intermediate boundary, by renaming the symbols in the command E_1 to their 'localised' versions. The collection of WIRE components connecting the enclosure $enc(E_1)$ with its intermediate boundary is denoted by $Wires(E_1)$. E_2 and E_3 are treated similarly. We say that the components E_1, E_2, and E_3 form a DI decomposition of component E, denoted by $E \xrightarrow{DI} (E_1, E_2, E_3)$ if and only if

$$E \rightarrow (enc(E_1), Wires(E_1), enc(E_2), Wires(E_2), enc(E_3), Wires(E_3)).$$

In general, DI decompositions are more difficult to derive and verify than de-compositions, because of all the (connection) WIREs. It becomes easier, however, if all the constituent components of a decomposition are so-called DI components. A component E is called a DI component, if

$$E \rightarrow (\mathit{enc}(E), \mathit{Wires}(E)).$$

By means of the Substitution Theorem, it follows that a decomposition is a DI decomposition, if all constituent components are DI components.

The DI property formalises that the communication behaviour between compo-nent and environment is insensitive to wire delays. Formally speaking, we say that specification E is invariant under any extension with WIREs. All basic components we have discussed in this paper, like the WIRE, IWIRE, MERGE, C-ELEMENT, and SEQUENCER, are DI components. Since all basic components of the decomposition of Figure 7 are DI components, this decomposition is a DI decomposition. Ac-cordingly, the circuit of Figure 7 represents a delay-insensitive circuit. The same reasoning holds for Figure 6.

The idea of formalising delay-insensitivity using a characterisation of a DI compo-nent originates from Molnar [10]. Udding was the first to give a rigorous formulation of the DI property in terms of directed trace structures[15].

12 Control Flow and Data Flow

A nice illustration of the use of a delay-insensitive circuit is given by I. Sutherland in his Turing Award lecture [14]. In this lecture, Sutherland demonstrates how a so-called micropipeline can be constructed using the circuit of Figure 6, where there is only one producer and one consumer. For this purpose, the circuit of Figure 6 is viewed as the control part that dictates the data flow through the pipeline. The data part is formed by a number of registers that store the contents of each cell and, if desired, combinational logic. The put, get, and $trans$ signals of the control circuit are inputs to these registers and dictate the register transfers in accordance with their associated meanings. Thus, the command $Controller0$ can be seen as a register transfer program.

We assume that the data flow is implemented using a *data bundling scheme* [14]. In this encoding scheme, the data is encoded on a set of data wires using a traditional level encoding and the validness of the data is signaled on a data valid wire. The data bundling constraint stipulates that at a component's boundary the signal on the data valid wire always arrives after the data on the data wires have become valid. In order to meet this data bundling constraint, specific delays have to be inserted in data valid wires. These delays may vary and depend on the operations that are performed on the data. If the control circuit is a delay-insensitive circuit, however, its correct operation is insensitive to the insertion of any delays anywhere in the circuit. For this reason, delay-insensitive circuits are attractive to use as control circuits for the implementation of the data flow.

In Figure 9 we have illustrated the complete circuit, where the control part and the data part are combined. Dashed lines represent the data part and solid lines represent the control part. If a wire in the control part is the data valid wire for a set of data wires, this relation is depicted by encircling the data valid wire and the

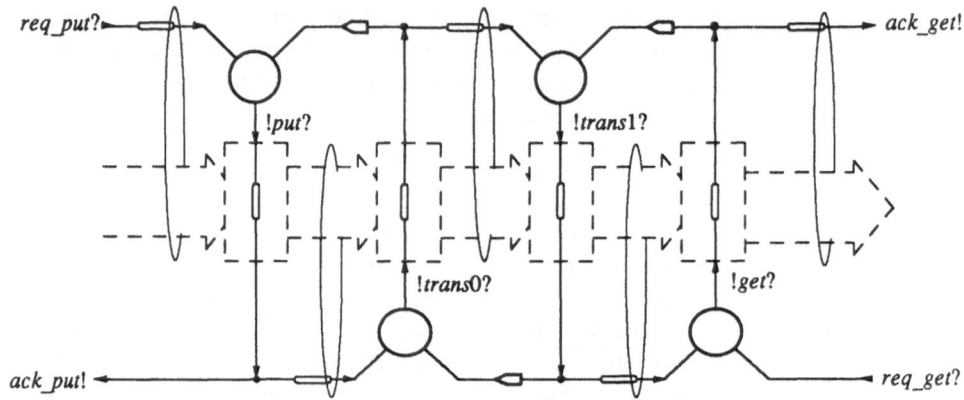

Figure 9: Combining Data flow and Control Flow

data wires. Small ovals represent specific delays inserted in the control part in order to comply with the data bundling constraint or to account for the delay incurred in the registers.

Remark. Depending on what data items are considered to be stored in the buffer, the circuit of Figure 9 can be viewed also as a four-place buffer [14] or a five-place buffer [6]. For the four-place buffer, the contents of the last register is considered being part of the buffer as well. For the five-place buffer, the data of the last register and the data present before the first register is considered to be part of the buffer as well. □

13 Concluding Remarks

We have discussed an approach to the design and implementation of a parallel computation. The approach was illustrated by the design of a non-trivial and useful component, viz., a controller for a bounded buffer.

As our programming notation we have used so-called commands. We have demonstrated through various examples that weaving is a very convenient programming primitive for expressing parallel communication behaviours of components. The examples included the specification of primitive components that realise synchronisation and mutual exclusion, and the specification of various controllers for bounded buffers.

We have used the same formalism and program notation for the specification and decomposition of a component. This formalism allowed us to reason about and formulate conditions for a decomposition in a rigorous way. Thus, we have been able to discuss the benefits and deficiencies of our conditions for a decomposition. Furthermore, we indicated that the command notation may assist the designer not only in finding a command expressing the component's behaviour, but also in finding a decomposition into primitive components.

A simplified version of the bounded buffer has been presented in [1]. That work also contains a discussion of the differences between the classical asynchronous design techniques and the technique presented in this note. A different solution for the producer and consumer problem is given in [14] and verified in [5]. In these articles the communication behaviour of the controller is specified by means of Petri-Nets.

After having gone through this exercise we may wonder whether we have designed a software solution or a hardware solution for the controller of the bounded buffer. After all, almost every specification in this paper was given in a specific program notation. Perhaps, we may reach the conclusion that, to a large extent, we have reduced circuit design to program design.

Acknowledgements

Acknowledgements are due to the Eindhoven VLSI Club and Charles Molnar for their comments on earlier presentations of this material.

References

[1] J.A. Brzozowski and J.C. Ebergen, Recent Developments in the Design of Asynchronous Circuits, Proc. *Fundamentals of Computation Theory - FCT'89*, J. Csirik, J. Demetrovics, F. Gecség (eds), Lecture Notes in Computer Science, vol. 380, (Springer-Verlag, Berlin, 1989), 78–95.

[2] T.J. Chaney and C.E. Molnar, Anomalous Behavior of Synchronizer and Arbiter Circuits, *IEEE Transactions on Computers*, (C-22), (1973), 421-422.

[3] W. Chen, J.T. Udding, and T. Verhoeff, Networks of Communicating Processes and Their (De-)Composition, in: J.L.A. van de Snepscheut (ed), *Mathematics of Program Construction*, Lecture Notes in Computer Science 375, (Springer-Verlag, 1989), 174-196.

[4] D.L. Dill, *Trace Theory for Automatic Hierarchical Verification of Speed-Independent Circuits*, (MIT Press, 1989).

[5] David L. Dill, Steven M. Nowick, and Robert F. Sproull, Automatic Verification of Speed-independent Circuits with Petri Net Specifications, Proc. *1989 IEEE International Conference on Computer Design: VLSI in Computers and Processors*, (IEEE Computer Society, 1989), 212–216.

[6] Jo C. Ebergen, *Translating Programs into Delay-Insensitive Circuits*, CWI Tract 56, (Centre for Mathematics and Computing Science, Amsterdam, 1989).

[7] Jo C. Ebergen, *Arbiters: An Exercise in Specifying and Decomposing Asynchronously Communicating Components*, Technical Report CS-90-29, Department of Computer Science, University of Waterloo, (1990).

[8] C.A.R. Hoare, *Communicating Sequential Processes*, (Prentice-Hall, 1985).

[9] A.J. Martin, Programming in VLSI: From Communicating Processes to Delay-Insensitive Circuits, in: C.A.R. Hoare (ed), *UT Year of Programming Institute on Concurrent Programming*, (Addison-Wesley, 1989).

[10] C.E. Molnar, T.P. Fang and F.U. Rosenberger, Synthesis of Delay-Insensitive Modules, in: H. Fuchs (ed), *Proceedings 1985 Chapel Hill Conference on VLSI*, (Computer Science Press, 1985), 67-86.

[11] M. Rem, The Nature of Delay-Insensitive Computing, in these proceedings.

[12] M. Rem, Trace Theory and Systolic Computations, in: J.W. de Bakker, A.J. Nijman and P.C. Treleaven (eds), *Proceedings PARLE, Parallel Architectures and Languages Europe*, Vol. 1, (Springer-Verlag, 1987), 14-34.

[13] C.L. Seitz, System Timing, in: Carver Mead and Lynn Conway (eds), *Introduction to VLSI Systems*, (Addison-Wesley, 1980), 218-262.

[14] I.E. Sutherland, Micropipelines, *Communications of the ACM*, (32) 6, (1989), 720-738.

[15] J.T. Udding, A Formal Model for Defining and Classifying Delay-Insensitive Circuits and Systems, *Distributed Computing*, (1), (1986), 197-204.

[16] C. van Berkel, C. Niessen, M. Rem, and R. Saeijs, VLSI Programming and Silicon Compilation: a Novel Approach from Philips Research, in: *Proceedings of IEEE International Conference on Computer Design 1988*, (1988).

[17] J.L.A. van de Snepscheut, *Trace Theory and VLSI Design*, Lecture Notes in Computer Science 200, (Springer-Verlag, 1985).

The Nature of Delay-Insensitive Computing

Martin Rem

Department of Mathematics and Computing Science
Eindhoven University of Technology
P.O. Box 513, 5600 MB Eindhoven
The Netherlands

wsinrem@win.tue.nl

Abstract

Delay-insensitive systems are systems whose correct functioning does not depend on delay assumptions. In this paper a gradual introduction to delay-insensitivity is given, illustrated by many examples. Precise definitions are given of delay-insensitivity, decomposition (or refinement), and speed-independence. Recent results of the associated theory are touched upon.

1 Introduction

Almost all digital circuits contain clocks; not the types of clock that tell the time, but rather more like metronomes: in its simplest form a clock produces a periodic signal that alternates between a low and a high voltage level. Its high and low going transitions are used to synchronize different parts of the circuit.

Now imagine that the circuit has an input wire whose voltage level is sensed during the period when the clock is high, i.e. from a high going to the next low going transition. This sensing is done by producing the logical conjunction of the levels of the input wire and the clock. The result is stored in a flip-flop. A flip-flop is a device with two stable states; it enters one of these states depending on the level of the voltage it is offered.

If the input wire that is sensed happens to make a high going transition towards the end of the clock period, the voltage produced may be just a small 'runt' pulse, cf. Fig. 1. If the flip-flop is offered such a marginal pulse, it may linger for a while in a metastable state before entering one of its stable states. Unfortunately, there is no upper bound for the time the flip-flop may stay in the metastable state. This phenomenon is known as the *metastability phenomenon*[3,13]. It is sometimes referred to as the glitch phenomenon.

It is essential for clocked circuits that the clock period be chosen sufficiently long to guarantee that all parts of the circuit stabilize within the clock period. The metastability phenomenon obviously conflicts with this timing constraint.

The example above exhibits metastability in the presence of asynchronous inputs, but metastability also arises in arbitration and synchronization. An arbiter is a device that is used to establish mutual exclusion among asynchronous requests. A synchronizer is a device that delays an asynchronous input in such a way that it is synchronized with another signal. The latter is usually the clock. Both arbiters and synchronizers can be realized only if we impose no upper bound on the time they take to produce their outputs. In essence, they do not produce their outputs until they have left the metastable states they possess.

In delay-insensitive systems we accept the fact that the durations of subcomputations may be unbounded. We, therefore, do not use an autonomous clock to synchronize the parts, but we have the different components of the system signal their completion explicitly[1]. We are aware that it may take quite some time before

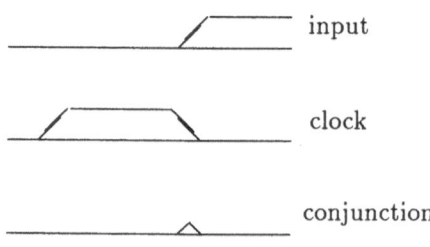

Figure 1: A 'runt' pulse

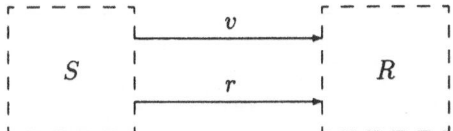

Figure 2: Communication with a data valid signal

completions are signaled, but we cater to this by designing the system in such a way that its correct functioning does not depend on these delays.

A system consists of components and connecting wires. It is called *delay-insensitive* if it functions correctly under arbitrary and possibly varying delays in components and wires. Of course, the delays will affect the operating speed of the system, but this is not considered part of the 'correct functioning'. The type of correctness we do have in mind will be made precise in the sequel.

2 Communicating data

In order to acquire an operational appreciation of delay-insensitivity, we discuss the problem of delay-insensitively communicating data from one component to another. The problem is to send one bit of information from component S to component R, cf. Fig. 2.

As a first try, we connect the components by two wires: wire v to convey the bit, and wire r to signal that the data have been sent. The latter is known as a 'data valid' signal. Initially both wires are low. Component S first gives wire v the value of the bit to be communicated; after that it makes wire r high. Component R waits until wire r is high, after which it copies (for instance, into a flip-flop) the value of wire v.

The above scheme will solve the problem only if we know that the delay in wire v does not exceed that in wire r. Such a delay assumption, known as a 'bundling constraint' can, of course, not be made if we want the communication to be delay-insensitive.

The solution is to code the bit to be communicated in such a way that R can detect its arrival[20]. This requires at least two wires to convey the bit: one wire can only have two states (low and high), but we need a third state to indicate the absence of a value. *Dual-rail encoding* is a technique that uses two wires per bit, cf. Fig. 3. The absence of a value is coded by two low wires. Value 0 is sent by making wire $v0$ high, and value 1 by making wire $v1$ high. The two wires are never high simultaneously.

The above scheme is not very useful if more bits have to be communicated successively: when may we decide that S can again send a bit? The only way out is to have R acknowledge that the bit has been received, cf. Fig. 4. Again, all wires are low initially. A complete cycle of sending one bit and acknowledging its receipt is now:

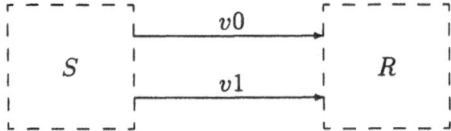

Figure 3: Dual rail communication

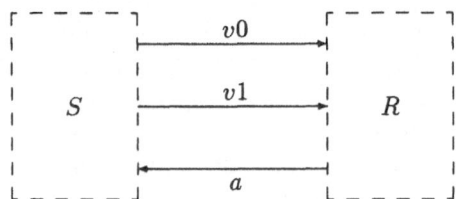

Figure 4: Communication with acknowledgement

S : $vi\uparrow\,;[a]\,;vi\downarrow\,;[\neg a]$

R : $[v0 \vee v1]\,;a\uparrow\,;[\neg v0 \wedge \neg v1]\,;a\downarrow$

Statement $vi\uparrow$ stands for 'make wire vi ($i = 0$ or $i = 1$) high' and, similarly, $vi\downarrow$ stands for 'make vi low'. Statement $[a]$ stands for 'wait until a holds', where high and low are interpreted as *true* and *false*, respectively. In the above patterns we have not coded how S determines (at the beginning of its cycle) i, nor how R copies (at the first semicolon of its cycle) the value received. Notice that after a complete cycle all wires are low again. This form of signaling is known as *four-phase signaling*. Component R can generate signal a by using an OR-gate, cf. Fig. 5.

Component S initiates the communication by making wire vi high; S is the active partner in the communication. Component R starts with waiting for $v0$ or $v1$ to become high; this is the passive partner. In this case the distinction active/passive coincides with that of sender/receiver. This is not necessary: we can equally well have the sender be passive and the receiver active. A complete cycle then consists of

S : $[a]\,;vi\uparrow\,;[\neg a]\,;vi\downarrow$

R : $a\uparrow\,;[v0 \vee v1]\,;a\downarrow\,;[\neg v0 \wedge \neg v1]$

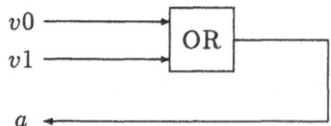

Figure 5: Generation of acknowledgement

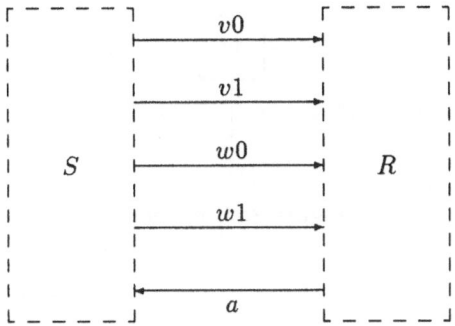

Figure 6: A 2-bit message

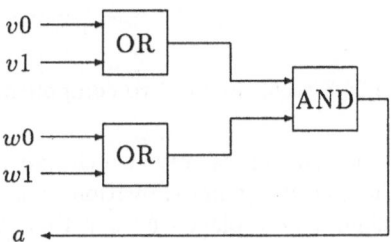

Figure 7: Erroneous implementation of acknowledgement

Now the receiver is the one that initiates the communication, viz. by making (request) wire a high. The sender does not start sending the bit until it has received this request. The schemes of active and passive sending are also known as data driven and demand driven, respectively.

3 C-element

The communication protocols developed above can easily be adapted for sending multiple-bit messages. We employ two wires per bit and extend the protocols straightforwardly, cf. Fig. 6. Since R acknowledges complete messages only, one acknowledge wire suffices.

We have seen that 1-bit messages can be acknowledged by means of an OR-gate. An interesting question is what mechanism we need for 2-bit messages. Consider the case that S is active. One may be tempted to generate signal a as the conjunction of $v0 \vee v1$ and $w0 \vee w1$, cf. Fig. 7.

This implementation, however, is erroneous. A possible sequence of events is

$$v0\uparrow;w0\uparrow;a\uparrow;v0\downarrow;a\downarrow$$

At this point the sender is allowed to transmit another message. However, the

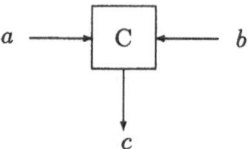

Figure 8: C-element

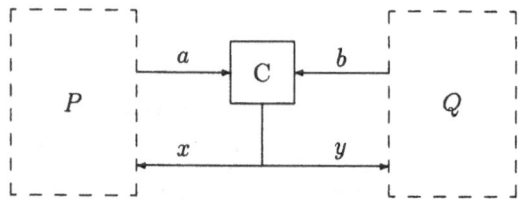

Figure 9: Synchronizing two components

low going transition on $w0$ is still on its way, which can interfere with the next message. The problem is that the low going transition on a is generated too earley. Obviously, the AND-gate should be replaced by one that does not produce a low going transition on its outputs until both inputs have gone low.

Such an element is known as a Muller C-element, or simply C-element, cf. Fig. 8. It is sometimes called a last-of or a rendezvous element. If both inputs a and b have equal values, this value is also produced at output c; otherwise c remains what it was. This is a state-holding element: if the values at a and b differ, the value at c equals the last common value of the inputs.

A C-element is often used to synchronize different components, cf. Fig. 9. Components P and Q have to be synchronized to accomplish 'mutual inclusion', i.e., they each have a synchronization point at which they must wait for the other component to reach its synchronization point. This can be realized by the following protocol for P:

$$a\uparrow\, ;[x]\, ;S\, ;a\downarrow\, ;[\neg x]$$

and similarly for Q. Statement S represents the part that is executed in mutual inclusion with component Q.

4 Think transitions

Above we have tried to give a conventional description of a C-element, viz. by giving how the output values depend on the input values. Such descriptions, however, are not very adequate for use in delay-insensitive systems. In delay-insensitive systems the transitions are the important events, and what should be specified are the possible orders in which these events may take place[15]. For the C-element these possible orders may be specified by the following behavioral expression:

$$(a\uparrow, b\uparrow ; c\uparrow ; a\downarrow, b\downarrow ; c\downarrow)^*$$

It expresses that first input wires a and b go high (the comma, which takes priority over the semicolon, expresses concurrency), after which output wire c goes high (the semicolon expresses order), which is followed by a and b going low, after which c goes low. From then on it starts all over again (the asterisk expresses repetition). The assumption is again that initially all wires are low. If we neglect the directions of the transitions the above expression may be written as

$$(a, b ; c)^*$$

We draw a scheme that shows how the values on the output wires depend on those on the input wires, writing 'low' as 0 and 'high' as 1:

a	b	c
0	0	0
1	0	0
0	1	0
1	1	1
0	1	1
1	0	1

The fact that we have different output values for the same input combination shows that C-elements are indeed sequential (or state-holding) elements.

A behavioral expression specifies an interface between a component and its environment. It specifies when the component may produce output transitions, but it also specifies when its environment may offer input transitions: input transitions are not allowed to arrive at 'wrong moments'. If an input transition arrives 'out of order' this is called *computation interference*. Now it is becoming clear what we mean by 'correct functioning' of a system. A system consists of components, each specified by the possible orders in which the transitions may occur. The components should be such that the system cannot exhibit computation interference.

In delay-insensitive systems one usually discerns a second correctness requirement, besides absence of computation interference, and that is absence of transmission interference. We speak of *transmission interference* if there is a connecting wire at which there are at least two transitions simultaneously present. We can phrase transmission interference as a form of computation interference by saying that each wire from point a to point b is a component with

$$(a\uparrow ; b\uparrow ; a\downarrow ; b\downarrow)^*$$

or simply $(a ; b)^*$, as its behavioral expression.

The behavioral expression does not give a complete description of what a component 'can do'. Consider, for example, the following expression:

$$(a? ; c! ; b? ; d!)^*$$

Symbols '?' and '!' specify that a and c are inputs and b and d outputs. We have not mentioned the directions of the transitions. This component can be implemented by just two wires that connect a with c and b with d. The same two wires would, however, also implement, for example,

$$(a? ; c! ; a? ; c! \mid b? ; d! ; b? ; d!)^*$$

where the bar denotes the choice-operator, similar to the plus in regular expressions. The bar has a lower priority than the comma and the semicolon.

Next replace in the above expression d by c, so that only one output remains:

$$(a? ; c! ; a? ; c! \mid b? ; c! ; b? ; c!)^*$$

This component may be implemented by an OR-gate, as the following table shows:

a	b	c
0	0	0
1	0	1
0	1	1

In contrast to that of the C-element, this table exhibits exactly one output value per input combination. Such processes are called *combinational*.

5 Formal definition of processes and systems

Before giving a formal (operational) definition of delay-insensitivity, we must first define what processes and systems are. We use a simple trace-theoretic model for processes:

A *process* T, sometimes referred to as a directed process, is a triple $\langle I, O, T \rangle$ such that

$$I \cap O = \emptyset$$
$$T \subseteq (I \cup O)^*$$
$$T \neq \emptyset$$
$$T \text{ prefix-closed}$$

Set I is the set of input symbols and O the set of output symbols. The elements of T are finite-length sequences, known as *traces*, of elements in $I \cup O$. Trace set T is called *prefix-closed* if $sa \in T \Rightarrow s \in T$ for $a \in I \cup O$.

Example 1 Consider process $\langle I, O, T \rangle$ with

$$I = \{a, b\}$$
$$O = \{c\}$$
$$T = \{\varepsilon, a, b, ab, ba, abc, bac, abca, baca, \cdots\}$$

where ε denotes the empty trace. This process is a C-element. We usually specify it by the behavioral expression

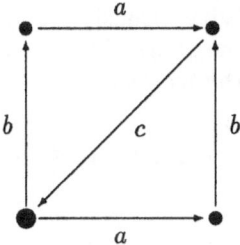

Figure 10: State graph of a C-element

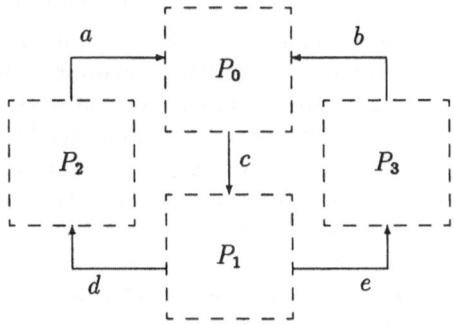

Figure 11: A system of four processes

$$(a?, b? \,; c!)^*$$

Its trace set consists of all sequences of symbols one encounters when traversing the graph of Fig. 10, starting in the lower left-hand corner.

A *system* is a set of processes, such that each symbol of a process occurs in exactly one process as input symbol and in exactly one process as output symbol. The connecting wires are not modeled explicitly; each symbol represents a wire, running from the process of which it is an output symbol to the process of which it is an input symbol. Thus we have defined what is known as a closed system (no dangling inputs or outputs) with point-to-point connections. Both conditions may be weakened, but the restricted definition suffices for our purposes.

Example 2 Consider the system consisting of four processes specified by

P_0 :	$(a?, b? \,; c!)^*$
P_1 :	$(d! \,; e! \,; c?)^*$
P_2 :	$(d? \,; a!)^*$
P_3 :	$(e? \,; b!)^*$

Process P_0 is a C-element. A pictorial impression of the system is shown in Fig. 11.

Definition of delay-insensitivity Consider a system of n processes: $P_0, P_1, \cdots$, P_{n-1}, where $P_i = \langle I_i, O_i, T_i \rangle$. The *states* of the system are n-tuples $\langle t_0, t_1, \cdots, t_{n-1} \rangle$ with $t_i \in (I_i \cup O_i)^*$. We define the *reachable states* of the system as follows:

1) $\langle \varepsilon, \varepsilon, \cdots, \varepsilon \rangle$ is reachable

2)   if $\langle t_0, \cdots, t_i, \cdots, t_{n-1} \rangle$ is reachable $(0 \leq i < n)$ and

   $\quad a \in O_i \ \wedge \ t_i a \in T_i$

   or

   $\quad a \in I_i \cap O_j \ \wedge \ a\#t_j > a\#t_i$

   then $\langle t_0, \cdots, t_i a, \cdots, t_{n-1} \rangle$ is reachable

3)   no other states are reachable

where $a\#t$ denotes the number of occurrences of symbol a in trace t.

The idea behind the above definition is that in state $\langle t_0, t_1, \cdots, t_{n-1} \rangle$ trace t_i is the current trace of process P_i. Condition 1) expresses that the initial state is reachable. In the course of a computation current traces are extended only. They can be extended with output symbols and with input symbols. The rule governing these extensions distinguishes output and input. Condition 2) expresses that the current trace of a process may be extended with an output symbol if the extended trace belongs to the trace set of the process. Notice that the prefix-closedness implies that then the current trace was in the trace set as well. The second part of 2) expresses that the current trace may be extended with an input symbol if that symbol happens to be 'on its way', i.e. if it has been output more often than it has been received. This extension may lead to a current trace that is not in the trace set of the process. The reception of an input is actually the only way to bring the current trace outside the trace set. The model captures that processes do control (by their trace sets) the sending of outputs but not the reception of inputs.

Examples of reachable states for the system of Example 2 are

$$\langle \varepsilon, \varepsilon, \varepsilon, \varepsilon \rangle$$
$$\langle \varepsilon, d, \varepsilon, \varepsilon \rangle$$
$$\langle \varepsilon, de, \varepsilon, \varepsilon \rangle$$
$$\langle \varepsilon, de, \varepsilon, e \rangle$$
$$\langle \varepsilon, de, \varepsilon, eb \rangle$$
$$\langle b, de, \varepsilon, eb \rangle$$

We have now all ingredients to define delay-insensitivity for systems. State $\langle t_0, t_1, \cdots, t_{n-1} \rangle$ is called *safe* if

$$(\forall j : 0 \leq j < n : t_j \in T_j)$$

$$\wedge$$

$$(\forall a, i, j : a \in I_i \cap O_j : a\#t_j \leq a\#t_i + 1)$$

The first condition expresses the absence of computation interference and the second one the absence of transmission interference. A system is called *delay-insensitive* if all its reachable states are safe.

The system of Example 2 is an example of a delay-insensitive system. The following example is not delay-insensitive. Process $\tilde{P}$ denotes the *reflection* of process P, i.e. if $P = \langle I, O, T \rangle$ then $\tilde{P} = \langle O, I, T \rangle$.

Example 3 Consider the system consisting of process P_1 of Example 2 and its reflection:

P_1 : $(d! \, ; e! \, ; c?)^*$
$\tilde{P}_1$: $(d? \, ; e? \, ; c!)^*$

Reachable states are

$$\langle \varepsilon, \varepsilon \rangle$$
$$\langle d, \varepsilon \rangle$$
$$\langle de, \varepsilon \rangle$$
$$\langle de, e \rangle$$

However, the latter state is not safe; computation interference has occurred: e is not a trace of proces $\tilde{P}_1$. The system is, consequently, not delay-insensitive.

Example 4 An example of a system with transmission interference is $\{P_0, P_1\}$:

P_0 : $(a!, b?)^*$
P_1 : $(a?, b!)^*$

The following table shows some reachable states of this system:

P_0	a		b	a	...
P_1		b			

The vertical lines correspond to reachable states, viz. from left to right: $\langle \varepsilon, \varepsilon \rangle$, $\langle a, \varepsilon \rangle$, $\langle a, b \rangle$, $\langle ab, b \rangle$, $\langle aba, b \rangle$, i.e. time goes to the right and the rows of symbols represent current traces of the processes listed in the first column. Since $a\#aba > a\#b + 1$, the latter state exhibits transmission interference.

6   Decomposition

Suppose a computation is specified as a process and we have to design a delay-insensitive implementation for it. In other words, we have to find a set of processes into which the specified process can be decomposed [21,12,11,8,18].

Let P be a process and let X be a set of processes such that $\tilde{P} \notin X$. We define set X to be a *decomposition* of process P if set $X \cup \{\tilde{P}\}$ is a delay-insensitive system.

Example 5 As a first example of a decomposition we consider set $\{P_0, P_1\}$:

P_0 : $(a? \, ; b!)^*$
P_1 : $(b? \, ; c!)^*$

This is a decomposition of

Q : $(a? \, ; c!)^*$

Consider the system consisting of processes P_0, P_1, and $\tilde{Q}$. Its reachable states are given by the following table:

P_0		a	b					a	
P_1				b	c				$\cdots$
$\tilde{Q}$	a	a				c	a		

where $\tilde{Q}$ is the process given by $(a!\,;c?)^*$. All reachable states are safe. The example shows that a wire may be decomposed into two connected wires.

Example 6 Next we consider two unconnected wires. Let processes P_0 and P_1 be given by

P_0 : $\qquad (a?\,;c!)^*$

P_1 : $\qquad (b?\,;d!)^*$

Set $\{P_0, P_1\}$ is a decomposition of

Q : $\qquad (a?\,;c!\,;b?\,;d!)^*$

as the following table of reachable states shows:

P_0		a	c						
P_1					b	d			$\cdots$
$\tilde{Q}$	a			c	b		d	a	

where $\tilde{Q}$ is the process given by $(a!\,;c?\,;b!\,;d?)^*$. It is, however, also a decomposition of, for example,

$$(a?\,;c!\,;a?\,;c! \ | \ b?\,;d!\,;b?\,;d!)^*$$

as can be easily checked. This proves the claim made in Section 4. It also shows that composition cannot simply be the inverse of decomposition. A suitable definition of composition can be found in [17,4].

Example 7 A 3-input C-element can be decomposed into two 2-input C-elements:

Q : $\qquad (a?,b?,c?\,;e!)^*$

P_0 : $\qquad (a?,b?\,;d!)^*$

P_1 : $\qquad (c?,d?\,;e!)^*$

Now Q decomposes into $\{P_0, P_1\}$, as can be checked easily.

A decomposition rule is useful only if it satisfies the *substitution property*. This property states that if process P decomposes into $X \cup \{Q\}$ and process Q decomposes into Y then P decomposes into $X \cup Y$. Our decomposition rule indeed satisfies the substitution property, provided that distinct names are used for the internal wires in X and Y.

Example 8 In this example a process is decomposed into a set of just one process. In other words, the latter process implements, or 'refines', the other process.

Consider process P, given by

$$P: \qquad (a? \,;(b! \mid c!))^*$$

and process $Q = \langle I, O, T \rangle$ with $I = \{a\}$, $O = \{b, c\}$, and T given by

$$(a? \,; b!)^*$$

Process Q differs from process P in that it does not produce output c. Process P can be decomposed into process Q, as the following table shows:

P		a	b			$\ldots$
$\tilde{Q}$	a			b	a	

This example demonstrates that in the choice between outputs the designer is allowed to make an a priori choice. The word 'allowed' means here, of course: without running the risk of causing computation or transmission interference, since these are the only correctness concerns we have introduced. In particular have we not considered progress requirements.

A designer is not allowed to make an a priori choice between inputs. For example, process $\tilde{P}$ does not decompose into $\tilde{Q}$:

$\tilde{Q}$	a			c	$\ldots$
P		a	c		

Here we have computation interference: ac is not a trace of $\tilde{Q}$. As an aside we mention that $\tilde{Q}$ does decompose into $\tilde{P}$.

An interesting question is whether a process decomposes into itself. This is in general not the case. Process P_1 of Example 2 is a process that does not decompose into itself, as we observed in Example 4.

Processes that decompose into themselves are known as *delay-insensitive* processes. The C-element is an example of a delay-insensitive process. There are several characterizations of delay-insensitive processes, the oldest of which was given by J.T. Udding[16]. As we have seen in Example 2, processes that are not delay-insensitive can very well be used to construct delay-insensitive systems.

7 Building blocks

The typical way of designing an inverter in CMOS is shown in Fig. 12. The input is forked to two transistors. This is clearly not a delay-insensitive decomposition of an inverter into two transistors: if one of the two branches of the fork is exceptionally slow a conveying connection between power and ground is maintained, a situation that is more commonly known as a short circuit.

Individual transistors are simply too primitive to be used as building blocks for delay-insensitive compositions. Delay-insensitive systems require building blocks of a higher aggregation level. Ebergen[5] has outlined a finite set of building blocks

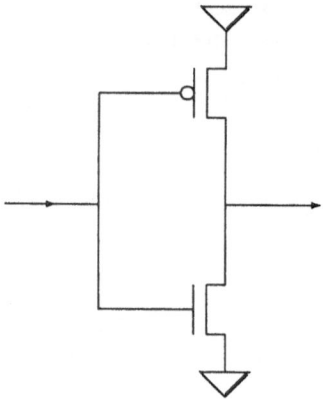

Figure 12: A CMOS inverter

into which all delay-insensitive processes can be decomposed. This set consists of two types of C-elements, a fork, an exclusive OR, a toggle, and an arbiter. Internally such building blocks will not be delay-insensitive. They correspond to what Seitz[14] has termed *equipotential regions*.

As mentioned in Section 4, combinational processes are processes that have exactly one output combination for each combination of input values. An example of a combinational process is

$$M: \qquad (a?, b? \,; d! \,; c? \,; e!)^*$$

as the following table of input values and corresponding output values shows:

a	b	c	d	e
0	0	0	0	0
1	0	0	0	0
0	1	0	0	0
1	1	0	1	0
1	1	1	1	1
0	1	1	1	1
1	0	1	1	1
0	0	1	0	1

M is a process with two outputs. According to the table above, output d is the majority of the input values and output e is a copy of input c. Let process P be specified by $(d? \,; c!)^*$. Then C-element $(a?, b? \,; e!)^*$ can be decomposed into $\{M, P\}$:

M			a	b	d			c	e				...
P						d	c						
$\tilde{C}$	a	b								e	a	b	

Thus we have exhibited a delay-insensitive decomposition of a sequential process into two combinational processes.

Brzozowski and Ebergen[2] have shown that sequential processes cannot be decomposed into sets that contain only forks, i.e. processes of the form $(a?\,; b!, c!)^*$, and single-output combinational processes. Martin[9] shows that extending these sets with C-elements does not help very much. Essentially, the only sequential processes that can then be built are various forms of C-elements.

8   Speed-independent

In the speed-independent computing model, which is older than the delay-insensitive one[10], all delays are assumed to be in the components. The wires do not exhibit delay, which makes transmission interference not an issue.

In order to define speed-independence more precisely, we need to change our definition of reachable states (which models asynchronous communication) into one that is based on synchronous communication. For *synchronously reachable* the second condition in the definition of reachable reads:

2)   if $\langle t_0, \cdots, t_i, \cdots, t_j, \cdots, t_{n-1} \rangle$ is reachable and
   $$a \in O_i \cap I_j \ \wedge \ t_i a \in T_i$$
   then $\langle t_0, \cdots, t_i a, \cdots, t_j a, \cdots, t_{n-1} \rangle$ is reachable

A state $\langle t_0, t_1, \cdots, t_{n-1} \rangle$ is called *safe* if

$$(\forall j : 0 \le j < n : t_j \in T_j)$$

A system is called *speed-independent* if all states that are synchronously reachable are safe.

The reachable states under synchronous communication form a subset of those that are reachable under asynchronous communication. Delay-insensitive systems are, consequently, also speed-independent. The inverse is not true.

We show that a C-element can speed-independently be decomposed into a single-output combinational process P_0 and a fork P_1[6]:

P_0 : $(a?, b?\,; d!\,; e?)^*$
P_1 : $(d?\,; e!\,; c!)^*$

Process P_0 is combinational, as the following table shows:

a	b	e	d
0	0	0	0
1	0	0	0
0	1	0	0
1	1	0	1
1	1	1	1
1	0	1	1
0	1	1	1
0	0	1	0

Process P_1 is a kind of fork that is (in speed-independent settings) often referred to as an *isochronic fork*. In order to demonstrate that C-element

$$C: \qquad (a?, b?\,; c!)^*$$

can speed-independently be decomposed into $\{P_0, P_1\}$, we investigate system $\{P_0, P_1, \tilde{C}\}$, with $\tilde{C}$ given by $(a!, b!\,; c?)^*$. This system is indeed speed-independent:

P_0	a	b	d	e		a	
P_1			d	e	c		...
$\tilde{C}$	a	b			c	a	

System $\{P_0, P_1, \tilde{C}\}$ is not delay-insensitive. An important difference between speed-independence and delay-insensitivity is that in the speed-independent model we can realize forks that guarantee that one of its outputs arrives earlier at a component than the other one does.

9 Conclusion

Starting with the problem of communicating data, we have gradually found our way to an operational, but precise, definition of delay-insensitivity. The virtue of this operational model is not only its relative simplicity, but also its clear relation with computing media in general and VLSI circuitry in particular. We have used trace theory[19,7] to formulate these definitions, since traces are very well-suited to express nontemporal relations between events. Our treatment exhibits a clear separation between the *communication model*, which captures the types of delays we want the correctness of the system to be independent of, and the *correctness concerns*. We have discussed two communication models: one in which the delays are both in the components and in the wires, and one in which the delays are just in the wires. With respect to correctness we have, throughout the paper, sticked to just one correctness concern: absence of interference.

Design is nothing else than decomposing large problems into smaller ones, until the latter problems either are trivial or have been solved before. Therefore, we have extensively addressed the concept of decomposition, interleaved with many examples. There is a limit to delay-insensitivity: one ends up with primitive building blocks of one kind or another. We have briefly discussed the nature of these blocks.

10 Acknowledgements

I am indebted to Tom Verhoeff, who is the inspirator behind the operational model in this paper. Ivan Sutherland coined the title of Section 4. Acknowledgements are also due to Kees van Berkel and the members of the Eindhoven VLSI Club for numerous discussions on the ins and outs of delay-insensitivity.

References

[1] Clifford Barney. Logic designers toss out the clock. *Electronics*, Dec. 9, 1985, 42–45

[2] J.A. Brzozowski and J.C. Ebergen. *On the Delay-Sensitivity of Gate Networks.* Computing Science Note 90/5, TU Eindhoven, 1990

[3] T.J. Chaney and C.E. Molnar. Anomalous behavior of synchronizer and arbiter circuits. *IEEE Transactions on Computers*, Vol. C-22, 1973, 421–422

[4] W. Chen, J.T. Udding, and T. Verhoeff. Networks of communicating processes and their (de)-composition in *The Mathematics of Program Construction* (J.L.A. van de Snepscheut, ed.). LNCS 375, Springer-Verlag, 1989, 174–176

[5] J.C. Ebergen. *Translating Programs into Delay-Insensitive Circuits.* CWI Tract 56, CWI, Amsterdam, 1989

[6] Mark B. Josephs. *Receptive Process Theory.* Computing Science Note 90/8, TU Eindhoven, 1990

[7] Anne Kaldewaij. *A Formalism for Concurrent Processes.* Ph.D. Thesis, TU Eindhoven, 1986

[8] Alain J. Martin. Compiling communicating processes into delay-insensitive circuits. *Distributed Computing*, 1, 1986, 247–260

[9] Alain J. Martin. The limitations of delay-insensitivity in asynchronous circuits in *Beauty Is Our Business* (W.H.J. Feijen et al., eds.) Springer-Verlag, 1990, 302–311

[10] R.E. Miller. *Switching Theory*, Vol. 2, Wiley, 1965

[11] Charles E. Molnar, Ting-Pien Fang and Frederick U. Rosenberger. Synthesis of delay-insensitive modules in *1985 Chapel Hill Conference on Very Large Scale Integration* (Henry Fuchs, ed.) Computer Science Press, 1985, 67–86

[12] Martin Rem. Concurrent computations and VLSI circuits in *Control Flow and Data Flow* (M. Broy, ed.) Springer-Verlag, 1985, 399–437

[13] Science and the citizen. *Scientific American*, **228**, April 1973, 43–44

[14] C.L. Seitz. System timing in Carver Mead and Lynn Conway, *Introduction to VLSI Systems.* Addison-Wesley, 1980, 218–262

[15] I.E. Sutherland. Micropipelines. *Commun. ACM*, **32**, 1989, 720–738

[16] Jan Tijmen Udding. A formal model for defining and classifying delay-insensitive circuits and systems. *Distributed Computing*, 1, 1986, 197–204

[17] Jan Tijmen Udding and Tom Verhoeff. *The Mathematics of Directed Specifications.* Technical Report WUCS 88-20, Washington University, 1988

[18] C.H. (Kees) van Berkel and Ronald W.J.J. Saeijs. Compilation of communicating processes into delay-insensitive circuits in *1988 IEEE Int. Conf. on Computer Design*, IEEE Computer Society Press, 1988, 157–162

[19] Jan L.A. van de Snepscheut. *Trace Theory and VLSI Design.* LNCS 200, Springer-Verlag, 1985

[20] Tom Verhoeff. Delay-insensitive codes—an overview. *Distributed Computing*, **3**, 1988, 1–8

[21] Alexandre Yakovlev. Designing self-timed systems. *VLSI Systems Design*, September 1985, 70–90

A Higher Order Logic Mechanization of the CSP Failure-Divergence Semantics

Albert J. Camilleri

Hewlett-Packard Laboratories
Filton Road, Stoke Gifford
Bristol BS12 6QZ
England

ac@hplb.hpl.hp.com

Abstract

Reasoning using process algebras often involves doing complex proofs, and computer-based support to facilitate the task is therefore desirable. In this paper we show how a general-purpose theorem prover based on higher order logic provides a natural framework for mechanizing the process algebra CSP. This is done by defining the semantics of the CSP operators in the logic and proving the high-level algebraic laws from the definitions as theorems. We mechanize a variation on the failure-divergence semantics that does not use alphabets at the syntactic level, but embeds them in the semantics. Our approach abstracts further from the explicit use of alphabets by modelling them as type variables. The result is a mechanized theory for a polymorphic formalization of CSP.

1   Introduction

This paper discusses pragmatic and theoretical issues involved in mechanizing the process algebra CSP [16] in higher order logic. Our choice of this formalism for mechanizing CSP is largely influenced by the availability of the HOL theorem prover [12] for higher order logic and Gordon's previous work using HOL [13], which shows the suitability of higher order logic for expressing other formalisms such as temporal and modal logics, VDM style specifications, and Dijkstra's weakest preconditions. Furthermore, reasoning in the semantics of CSP often involves extensive use of non-trivial mathematics; so to express both the process algebra and its underlying mathematical framework, a logical system at least as powerful as set theory or type theory is required [15].

Since several variants of CSP exist, one of our goals is to provide a single environment which supports reasoning in alternative models of the language, thus allowing formal comparisons to be carried out between specifications written using different semantics. For this purpose, a general-purpose theorem prover like HOL is ideal, since several theories for CSP can be supported, and theories can be soundly extended when additional concepts need to be mechanized.

The use of HOL for supporting formal proof in the *trace* semantics of CSP [16] is already described in detail in [3]; and the use of the resulting mechanization is illustrated in [4], where it is shown how standard CSP laws can be mechanically proved from their semantics. In this paper we describe the mechanization of a more powerful and descriptive semantics than trace semantics, namely a variation on the *failure–divergence* semantics [2] proposed by Roscoe in [18].

One major difference between the semantics discussed in [2, 18] and that in [16] lies in the treatment of *alphabets* (the sets of events which processes are allowed to engage in). In [16], alphabets are explicit in the syntax of processes, so that each process has its own particular alphabet. In [2], however, the notion of alphabets is embedded in the semantics by means of a universal alphabet, so that all processes share the same alphabet. In this paper we show that the mechanization of processes using the notion of a universal alphabet is much more elegant than the mechanization using explicit, individual alphabets described in [3] since the latter often gives rise to partially defined operators that make reasoning cumbersome.

The subset of the CSP language dealt with in this paper has the following syntax:

$$\text{STOP} \mid \text{SKIP} \mid a \longrightarrow P \mid P \sqcap Q \mid P \,\square\, Q \mid P \parallel Q \mid P \setminus a \mid \mu X.\, F(X)$$

STOP represents the deadlock process, and SKIP represents a successfully terminating process. The notation $a \longrightarrow P$ represents a process P prefixed by some event a, whereas $P \setminus a$ represents the hiding of all occurrences of event a from the observation of the behaviour of P. The two choice operators, non-deterministic and deterministic, are represented as $P \sqcap Q$ and $P \,\square\, Q$ respectively, and the parallel composition of two processes is represented as $P \parallel Q$. The notation $\mu X.\, F(X)$ represents a process recursive in F.

The definition of each of the above operators in HOL is described in Sections 4 and 6, and some properties which can be derived from their definitions are discussed in Section 5. The next section describes some intuitions behind the failure-divergence semantics and Section 3 gives a brief introduction to HOL. A summary of related work, and a discussion of our approach is given in Sections 7 and 8.

2 The Failure-Divergence Semantics

In the trace semantics model of CSP it is not possible to describe certain concepts that commonly arise when reasoning about concurrent systems. In particular, it is not possible to express non-determinism, or to distinguish deadlock from infinite internal activity. The failure-divergence model incorporates the information available in the trace semantics, and in addition introduces the notions of *refusals* and *divergence* to model such concepts. The following two examples illustrate this.

2.1 Example 1: Non-Determinism

Let a and b be any two events in some set of events Σ. The two processes

$$(a \longrightarrow \text{STOP}) \square (b \longrightarrow \text{STOP}) \tag{1}$$

and

$$(a \longrightarrow \text{STOP}) \sqcap (b \longrightarrow \text{STOP}) \tag{2}$$

cannot be distinguished under the trace semantics, in which both processes are capable of performing the same sequences of events, i.e. both have the same set of traces $\{\langle\rangle, \langle a\rangle, \langle b\rangle\}$. This is because both processes can either engage in a and then STOP, or engage in b and then STOP. We would, however, like to distinguish between a deterministic choice of a or b (1) and a non-deterministic choice of a or b (2).

This can be done by considering the events which a process can refuse to engage in when these events are offered by the environment. The deterministic process (1) must engage in either a or b as offered by the environment; it cannot refuse either, so we say its *maximal refusal set*[1] is the set containing all elements in Σ apart from a and b, written $\Sigma \setminus \{a, b\}$, i.e. it can refuse all elements in Σ other than a and b. In the case of the non-deterministic process (2), however, we wish to express that if the environment offers the event a say, the process can non-deterministically choose either to engage in a, or to refuse a and engage in b. Likewise, if the environment offers b, the process non-deterministically chooses either to engage in b, or to refuse it and engage in a. We say, therefore, that process (2) has two maximal refusal sets, $\Sigma \setminus \{a\}$ and $\Sigma \setminus \{b\}$, because it can refuse to engage in either a or b, but not both. The notion of refusal sets is in this way used to distinguish non-determinism from determinism.

---

[1] i.e. the largest refusal set.

2.2   Example 2: Infinite Internal Chatter

Consider the infinite process

$$\mu X . a \longrightarrow X$$

which performs an infinite stream of a's. If one now conceals the event a in this process by writing

$$(\mu X . a \longrightarrow X) \setminus a \qquad (3)$$

it no longer becomes possible to observe any behaviour of this process. In fact, it becomes impossible to distinguish the behaviour of this process from that of the deadlock process STOP. We would like to be able to make such a distinction, since the former process has clearly not stopped but is engaging in an unbounded sequence of internal actions invisible to the environment. We say the process has diverged, and introduce the notion of a *divergence set* to denote all sequences of events that will cause a process to diverge. Hence, the process STOP is assigned the divergence set $\varnothing$, since it cannot diverge, whereas the process (3) above diverges on any sequence of events since the process begins to diverge immediately, i.e. its divergence set is Σ^*, where Σ^* denotes the set of all sequences with elements in Σ. Divergence is undesirable and so it is essential to be able to express it to ensure that it is avoided.

2.3   The Semantics

In the model of CSP presented in [2] a process communicates with its environment by engaging in events drawn from some *alphabet* Σ. In the failure-divergence semantics a process is characterised by:

- its *failures*—these are sets of pairs (s, X), where s is a possible sequence of events a process can engage in (a *trace*), and X is the set of events that the process can refuse to engage in (the *refusals*) after having engaged in s,

- and its *divergences*—these are the traces that will cause the process to diverge if any of them are performed.

Processes are therefore represented by pairs (F, D), where F is a failure set and D is a divergence set.

The failures and divergences of a process must satisfy six well-definedness conditions [18]: (i) the initial trace of a process must be empty, (ii) the prefixes of all traces of a process are themselves traces of that process, i.e. traces are *prefix closed*, (iii) a process can refuse all subsets of a refusal set, (iv) all events which are impossible to perform on the next step can be included in a refusal set, (v) a divergence set is *suffix* closed, and (vi) once a process has diverged, it can engage in, or refuse, any sequence of events.

More formally, given a (possibly infinite) set of events Σ and sets F and D such that

$$F \subseteq \Sigma^* \times \mathbf{P}(\Sigma)$$
$$D \subseteq \Sigma^*$$

then using a set theory and predicate calculus notation similar to that adopted in [18], the above six well-definedness conditions for processes can be stated as:

$$(\langle\rangle, \varnothing) \in F \tag{4}$$

$$(st, \varnothing) \in F \supset (s, \varnothing) \in F \tag{5}$$

$$(s, X) \in F \wedge (Y \subseteq X) \supset (s, Y) \in F \tag{6}$$

$$(s, X) \in F \wedge (\forall c \in Y. ((s\langle c\rangle, \varnothing) \notin F)) \supset (s, X \cup Y) \in F \tag{7}$$

$$s \in D \supset st \in D \tag{8}$$

$$s \in D \supset (st, X) \in F \tag{9}$$

where $\langle\rangle$ denotes the empty trace, and the notation st is used to represent the concatenation of two traces s and t.

In the model originally presented in [2], the converse of (6) is also a well-definedness condition. This condition, which is shown formally below, states that a set is refusable if all its finite subsets are refusable.[2]

$$(\forall Y \in p(X). (s, Y) \in F) \supset (s, X) \in F \tag{10}$$

In [18], Roscoe explains that this condition can in fact be omitted from the definition of processes, but that if this is done, a coarser, more complex ordering on processes must be defined since the ordering presented in [2] is no longer a complete partial order if condition (10) is omitted from the definition of a process.

From a pragmatic point of view, it is arguably better to mechanize the version which omits condition (10) since including it would mean that an additional well-definedness condition has to be proved each time a new process operator is defined, whereas the proof that the new ordering on processes is a complete partial order, despite being more complex than that for the original ordering, needs to be done only once. Furthermore, condition (10) is often the hardest to prove when showing well-definedness of processes, and it sometimes requires fundamental set theoretic properties (such as the Compactness Theorem [1]) to do so.

Of course, there is no reason why both models cannot be supported as separate theories in the HOL system. We describe hereafter, however, only a mechanization of the semantics in which condition (10) is omitted. Before we describe this mechanization, we first introduce the HOL theorem proving system.

---

[2]The notation $p(X)$ denotes the set of all finite subsets of X.

3   The HOL System

The HOL system, developed by Gordon [12], is based directly on the LCF theorem prover [11], and the theorem proving methodology supported by HOL is inherited from that originally developed by Milner for LCF. The following sections provide a short introduction to the logic supported by HOL and the way in which it is manipulated to conduct proofs.

3.1   The HOL Logic

The HOL logic is a variety of higher order logic based on Church's formulation of type theory [6]. In the HOL logic, one uses standard predicate calculus notation: $P\,x$ to express the proposition that x has the property P, $R\,(x, y)$ to assert that the relation R holds between x and y, and the logical connectives $\neg$, $\wedge$, $\vee$, $\supset$ and $\equiv$ to express negation, conjunction, disjunction, implication and equivalence respectively. The conventional notation of universal and existential quantifiers for binding free variables is also used: $\forall x.\,P\,x$ to express the assertion that P holds for every value of x, and $\exists x.\,P\,x$ to express the assertion that P holds for at least one value of x. Additional notation includes $b \Rightarrow t_1 \mid t_2$, which is used to represent the conditional 'if b then t_1 else t_2'.

Higher order logic extends the notation of predicate calculus in three major ways:

- variables are allowed to range over functions, and the arguments of functions can themselves be functions (hence 'higher order'),

- functions can be written as λ-abstractions, and

- terms can be polymorphic, i.e. terms can have variable types (every term in the logic must be typed, to avoid Russell's paradox [12]).

In addition Hilbert's choice operator, ε, is included in the HOL logic. The ε operator is generally used to denote values which are known to exist but have no name. More precisely, if $t[x]$ is a boolean term containing a free variable x of type α, then the term $\varepsilon\,x.\,t[x]$ denotes some value of type α, a say, such that $t[a]$ is true. For example, the term $\varepsilon\,x.\,x > 5$ denotes an unspecified number greater than 5. If there is no value a such that $t[a]$ is true, then $\varepsilon\,x.\,t[x]$ denotes a fixed but unknown value of type α. For example, $\varepsilon\,n{:}num.\,\neg(n = n)$ denotes some unspecified natural number. The notation *term:type* is used within the HOL logic to explicitly specify the type of a term, in this case the type of natural numbers *num*. We show later that the ε operator is useful when writing partially defined specifications.

3.2   The HOL Theorem Prover

In HOL, the logic described above is embedded in the general purpose programming language ML [8]. Terms of the HOL logic are distinguished from other ML expressions by virtue of having the ML type *term*. Every expression of higher order logic must be well typed according to the typing rules of the logic before being accepted by ML as a value of type *term*.

The ML language is used to manipulate HOL logic terms. In particular, ML is used to prove that certain terms are *theorems*. Theorems proved in the system are distinguished from ordinary terms by being assigned another built-in ML type *thm*. A theorem is represented by a finite set of terms called *assumptions* and a term called a *conclusion*. Given a set of assumptions Γ and a conclusion t, we write $\Gamma \vdash t$ to represent the corresponding theorem or, if Γ is empty, $\vdash t$.

To introduce values of type *thm* into ML, they must either be postulated as *axioms*, or deduced from existing theorems by ML programs that correspond to *inference rules*, in a sequence of steps constituting a *proof*. These programs check that the *conclusion* of a proof follows logically from the *hypotheses*—in other words, that truth is preserved throughout the proof. For example, given the two theorems $\Gamma_1 \vdash t_1 \supset t_2$ and $\Gamma_2 \vdash t_1$, the inference rule for *modus ponens* would deduce the theorem $\Gamma_1 \cup \Gamma_2 \vdash t_2$. The core of the HOL system is made up of a small set of inference rules called *primitive inference rules* and a small number of definitions and axioms from which all the standard rules of logic (and indeed, all other theorems) are derived.

A collection of logical types, type operators, constants, definitions, axioms and theorems is called a *theory*. To make a definition, prove a theorem, or declare a new HOL type, one must first enter a theory and, if facts from other theories are to be used, the relevant existing theories must be declared as *parents*. For example, if one is working within a theory th_1, and an object from theory th_2 is required in th_1, then th_2 must be declared a parent of th_1. If th_2 is a parent of th_1 then all the objects available in th_2 are also available in th_1. Theories, therefore, enable a hierarchical organisation of facts. A library of commonly used theories is available in the HOL system to allow established and commonly used theorems to be reused. Later in the paper we discuss how the availability of such a library helped the task of mechanizing CSP.

3.3 Definitions in the HOL Logic

To understand the mechanization of CSP described in the following sections, it is first necessary to know how definitions are used in HOL. *Definitions* are axioms of the form $\vdash c = t$ where c is a constant not previously defined and t is a term containing no free variables. Ideally, all axioms should be of this definitional form, since the freedom to postulate arbitrary axioms allows one to introduce inconsistencies. It is safe to introduce definitional axioms, because they merely define abbreviations.

Axioms written in the form $f\,x_1 \ldots x_n = t$, where the free variables of t are included among $x_1 \ldots x_n$, are also regarded as definitions in HOL because they are equivalent to the term $f = \lambda\,x_1 \ldots x_n.\,t$. Functional definitions are also allowed to have tupled parameters, i.e. $f\,(x_1, \ldots, x_n) = t$, or to be *primitive recursive* since this restricted form of recursion uniquely defines functions that have an equivalent non-recursive definition [12].

A theory forms a sound extension to the logic (i.e. a *conservative* extension) if all the axioms present in it are definitions. For this reason, the HOL system distinguishes definitions from axioms. Before accepting a new definition, the system first checks that (a) the definition being made is of one of the forms described above, and (b) the constant being defined has not already been defined previously.

It can sometimes be inelegant, however, to write definitions in this restricted form, and an alternative way of making definitions is available in the HOL system. It is mostly used to define constants by specifying only some of their properties, and is somewhat analogous to the *loose specification* approach used for defining algebraic data types [19]. The method involves first proving the existence of a value which has the required properties, and then invoking the appropriate HOL definition mechanism to introduce a constant with those properties. The reason one must first prove that a value with the required properties exists before the definition of a constant is allowed is again to ensure a sound extension to the logic. In general, given a theorem

$$\vdash \exists\, x_1\, \ldots\, x_n.\, t[x_1, \ldots, x_n]$$

where $t[x_1, \ldots, x_n]$ represents some term t containing occurrences of $x_1 \ldots x_n$ as its only free variables, this definition mechanism can introduce constants $c_1 \ldots c_n$ say, satisfying

$$\vdash t[c_1, \ldots, c_n]$$

Another kind of conservative extension is that of type definitions. In HOL, a new data type can be conservatively added to the logic by defining a new type which is isomorphic to a non-empty subset of some existing type [17]. Briefly, if ty is an existing logical type and P is some predicate on values of type ty that defines a non-empty subset of the set denoted by ty, then a new type ty' can be defined to denote a set having identical properties to the subset defined by P. The HOL type definition mechanism checks that a theorem of the form $\vdash \exists x{:}ty.\, P\, x$ has been proved for a particular P before it allows the definition of some corresponding type ty'. Upon defining a new type ty', it also automatically defines an isomorphism REP_ty' to establish that the set denoted by ty' has the same properties as the subset of ty defined by P. Further details about type definitions are given in [17].

A theory containing definitions as the only form of axiom is called a *definitional theory*. The mechanization we describe is built only from definitional theories to ensure that the logic is conservatively extended.

4 Mechanizing CSP

The approach we adopt for mechanizing CSP is to first define the CSP operators in terms of the chosen semantic model, and then prove the laws which hold of these operators from their semantic definitions. Proving the high-level process algebra laws from the semantics, as opposed to axiomatizing them, not only supports the natural and high-level reasoning made available by the laws, but also guarantees that the laws relate directly to the semantics intended for CSP. This is especially important if different semantics for CSP are to be mechanized, since different laws hold for different semantics. We consider below a mechanization of the subset of CSP (described in Section 1) done in this manner; we first outline the representation of traces, refusals, failures, divergences and processes as high-level data types, and then consider the mechanization of some operators on processes.

4.1 Failure-Divergence Semantics in Higher Order Logic

The entire semantics, as introduced in Section 1, are centred around the notion of a universal alphabet Σ of events in which processes are allowed to engage. The semantics of the operators are given in terms of failure and divergence sets containing events drawn from Σ. For example, in [2, 18], the failure set of STOP is denotationally given as:

$$\mathcal{F}[\![\text{STOP}]\!]\rho = \{(\langle\rangle, X) \mid X \in \mathbf{P}(\Sigma)\} \tag{11}$$

This states that STOP engages in no events and refuses all events in Σ. From the above definition, it is obvious to see that Σ is not merely a variable; if it were, then it would need to be parameterised on the left hand side in the above definition of STOP, and this would result in a model of explicit alphabets as described in [16]. So Σ is a constant. But it is not a fixed constant, either, since the theory developed for CSP using this semantic model holds for any constant value of Σ. So in this sense, Σ is a variable, which must be instantiated to some constant value to define the behaviour of the CSP operators for a particular alphabet.

This immediately suggests an analogy to polymorphism in type theory, in which Σ can be viewed as a type variable. In this way, a polymorphic theory for CSP can be defined that can be instantiated to any constant type to define a specific theory. The only difference is that Σ is modelled as a type instead of a set. In the rest of the paper we show that this idea of representing Σ as a polymorphic type gives rise to a practical and elegant mechanization of CSP.

We begin in HOL by modelling Σ as a type variable; for clarity we also refer to this type variable as Σ. The notions of *events*, *traces*, *refusals*, *failures*, and *divergences* can now be represented directly in HOL using the type Σ, and the (polymorphic) types for lists and sets pre-defined in the HOL system, as shown in the table below.

CSP notions	Representing HOL types
traces	$(\Sigma)\ list$
refusal sets	$(\Sigma)\ set$
failure sets	$((\Sigma)\ list \times (\Sigma)\ set)\ set$
divergence sets	$((\Sigma)\ list)\ set$

Events are simply modelled as elements of type Σ. Traces can be denoted by lists of events, refusal sets by sets of events, failure sets by sets of pairs of traces and refusal sets and divergence sets by sets of traces.

We use pairs of failure sets and divergence sets to denote processes. But, as explained in Section 1, not all pairs of failure sets and divergence sets constitute well-defined processes. To express this, a predicate PROCESS_REP must be defined to state that a pair (F, D) represents a well-defined process according to the well-definedness conditions (4–9) as follows:

$$\vdash \text{PROCESS\_REP}(F, D) \equiv$$
$$([\,], \varnothing) \in F \,\wedge$$
$$(\forall s\, t.\, (s \wedge t, \varnothing) \in F \supset (s, \varnothing) \in F) \,\wedge$$
$$(\forall s\, X\, Y.\, (s, X) \in F \wedge (Y \subseteq X) \supset (s, Y) \in F) \,\wedge$$
$$(\forall s\, X\, Y.\, (s, X) \in F \wedge (\forall c.\, c \in Y \supset \neg((s \wedge [c], \varnothing) \in F)) \supset$$
$$(s, X \cup Y) \in F) \,\wedge$$
$$(\forall s.\, s \in D \supset \forall t.\, s \wedge t \in D) \,\wedge$$
$$(\forall s.\, s \in D \supset \forall t\, X.\, (s \wedge t, X) \in F)$$

where the square bracket notation is used in HOL to represent lists, and the infix operator $\wedge$ to represent the append function on lists.

To distinguish between reasoning about pairs of sets and reasoning about processes, an abstract data type for processes is defined which is isomorphic to the subset of pairs defined by PROCESS_REP. By using the appropriate HOL mechanism for defining logical types, such a type $(\Sigma)process$ can be defined, and an isomorphism introduced, that maps values of this type to values of the representing type of pairs. As explained in Section 3.3, it must first be shown that the representing type is non-empty, i.e. by proving that

$$\vdash \exists\, F\, D.\, \text{PROCESS\_REP}\, (F, D)$$

The pair of infinite sets $(\{x \mid \top\}, \{x \mid \top\})$ (where $\top$ represents the boolean value 'true') satisfies the well-definedness predicate PROCESS_REP, so the existence theorem above is straightforward to prove. Given this existence theorem, the new abstract type $(\Sigma)process$ can be defined to be isomorphic to the subset of pairs defined by PROCESS_REP by using the HOL mechanism for defining logical types. The isomorphism that maps values of the abstract type $(\Sigma)process$ to values of the representing type is automatically defined by the data type definition function and is called REP_process. This function REP_process, and the destructor functions on pairs FST and SND, can now be used to define two destructor functions on processes, FAILURES and DIVERGENCES, which represent the failures and divergences of a process respectively. Formally,

$$\vdash \forall P.\, \text{FAILURES}\, P = \text{FST}\, (\text{REP\_process}\, P)$$

$$\vdash \forall P.\, \text{DIVERGENCES}\, P = \text{SND}\, (\text{REP\_process}\, P)$$

When reasoning about processes, the above destructor functions can now be used to extract the relevant components of a process. Two further useful functions, defining the traces and refusals of a process, can also be defined:

$$\vdash \forall P.\, \text{TRACES}\, P = \{s \mid \exists X.\, (s, X) \in (\text{FAILURES}\, P)\}$$

$$\vdash \forall P.\, \text{REFUSALS}\, P = \{X \mid ([\,], X) \in (\text{FAILURES}\, P)\}$$

Theorems which state that the properties stipulated by the well-definedness conditions hold for all values of type $(\Sigma)process$ can now also be proved:

$\vdash \forall P{:}(\Sigma)process.\ ([\,],\varnothing) \in (\textsf{FAILURES } P)$

$\vdash \forall P{:}(\Sigma)process.\ \forall s\ t.\ (s \wedge t, \varnothing) \in (\textsf{FAILURES } P) \supset (s, \varnothing) \in (\textsf{FAILURES } P)$

$\vdash \forall P{:}(\Sigma)process.$
$\quad \forall s\ X\ Y.\ (s, X) \in (\textsf{FAILURES } P) \wedge (Y \subseteq X) \supset (s, Y) \in (\textsf{FAILURES } P)$

$\vdash \forall P{:}(\Sigma)process.$
$\quad \forall s\ X\ Y.\ (s, X) \in (\textsf{FAILURES } P) \wedge$
$\qquad\qquad (\forall c.\ c \in Y \supset \neg((s \wedge [c], \varnothing) \in (\textsf{FAILURES } P))) \supset$
$\qquad\qquad (s, X \cup Y) \in (\textsf{FAILURES } P)$

$\vdash \forall P{:}(\Sigma)process.$
$\quad \forall s.\ s \in (\textsf{DIVERGENCES } P) \supset \forall t.\ s \wedge t \in (\textsf{DIVERGENCES } P)$

$\vdash \forall P{:}(\Sigma)process.$
$\quad \forall s.\ s \in (\textsf{DIVERGENCES } P) \supset \forall t\ X.\ (s \wedge t, X) \in (\textsf{FAILURES } P)$

The theorem for stating that two processes are equal if and only if both their failures and their divergences are equal, follows naturally from this formalization.

$\vdash \forall P\ Q{:}(\Sigma)process.$
$\quad (P = Q) \equiv$
$\quad ((\textsf{FAILURES } P) = (\textsf{FAILURES } Q)) \wedge$
$\quad ((\textsf{DIVERGENCES } P) = (\textsf{DIVERGENCES } Q))$

The types defined above and the functions FAILURES, DIVERGENCES, REFUSALS, and TRACES are used to mechanize the CSP operators presented in Section 1. Below we outline the definitions of these operators as mechanized in HOL in [3].

4.1.1 STOP

The first process we consider is STOP which signifies a process that will never engage in any event. This means that it refuses all events in Σ, and that it cannot diverge. Its traces, therefore, consist solely of the empty trace [ ], its divergence set is empty, and its maximal refusal set is Σ.

There are several ways of defining this process as a conservative extension to the logic. One way (explained in Section 3.3) is to first prove the existence of a constant, c say, which has the required properties, i.e.

$\vdash \exists c.\ \textsf{FAILURES } c = \{(s, X) \mid s = [\,]\} \wedge \textsf{DIVERGENCES } c = \varnothing$

and then use the HOL primitive definition mechanism to define a constant Stop of type $(\Sigma)process$ with the above properties, i.e.

$\vdash \textsf{FAILURES } (\textsf{Stop}) = \{(s, X) \mid s = [\,]\} \wedge \textsf{DIVERGENCES } (\textsf{Stop}) = \varnothing$

It is interesting to note that the representation of Σ as a type has an advantage that it does not appear explicitly even in the semantic definition of the operator. The condition on the refusal set for STOP shown in equation (11), $X \in \mathsf{P}(\Sigma)$, is implicit in the type theory definition: by leaving the refusal set unconstrained, the only information available about the refusal set is that it is of type $(\Sigma)set$, i.e. it is any set of events.

Another interesting point is that in order to prove the existence theorem needed to define **Stop**, it is first necessary to prove that the pair $(\{(s, X) \mid s = [\,]\}, \varnothing)$ represents a well-defined process, i.e.

$$\vdash \text{PROCESS\_REP}\,(\{(s, X) \mid s = [\,]\}, \varnothing)$$

so the task of proving that a process representation is well-defined before being able to define the process is enforced, rather than merely left as good practice.

In fact, in the definitions of all the operators, two theorems routinely had to be proved: the well-definedness theorem for the chosen representation of the process, and the existence theorem for the process operator. From these, the process operators were defined as loose specifications stating the failures and the divergences of the process they constructed. In our presentation of the rest of the operators, the well-definedness and existence theorems are not presented.

4.1.2 SKIP

The term SKIP denotes a process which terminates successfully. To express this, we first define a special constant event $\sqrt{}$ to denote termination. The constant can be defined using the ε operator as shown below to denote some fixed but unspecified event:

$$\vdash \sqrt{} = \varepsilon x{:}\Sigma.\ \mathsf{T}$$

We do not wish to associate any special semantic meaning directly to this constant. We merely want to distinguish it from other events.

We can formally define a constant **Skip** such that:

$$\vdash \text{FAILURES (Skip)} = \{(s, X) \mid (s = [\,]) \wedge \neg(\sqrt{} \in X)\} \cup \{(s, X) \mid s = [\sqrt{}\,]\} \wedge$$
$$\text{DIVERGENCES (Skip)} = \varnothing$$

This states that **Skip** initially refuses to engage in all events apart from $\sqrt{}$, but once it engages in $\sqrt{}$, it refuses to engage in all events (i.e. it terminates). Like **Stop**, this process does not diverge.

4.1.3 Prefix

We next consider the prefix operator $\longrightarrow$. If P is a process and a is an event in Σ, then we write $a \longrightarrow P$ to denote a process which first engages in a and then behaves like P.

The semantics of the process $a \longrightarrow P$ are simple to deduce. The process initially engages in the empty trace and refuses to engage in any event but a. Thereafter the process performs an a followed by any trace possible for P, at each stage refusing to engage in any event refused by P. Likewise, after having performed the a, the process diverges on any trace that causes P to diverge.

In HOL, we define an infix operator Prefix with this behaviour as shown below, where the notation $a.t$ is used to mean the *cons* of an element a onto a list t.

$\vdash \forall\, a\, P\,.$
  FAILURES $(a\ \mathsf{Prefix}\ P)\ =$
    $\{(s, X) \mid (s = [\,]) \wedge \neg(a \in X)\} \cup$
    $\{(s, X) \mid \exists\, t\,.\, (s = a.t) \wedge (t, X) \in$ FAILURES $(P)\} \wedge$
  DIVERGENCES $(a\ \mathsf{Prefix}\ P)\ =$
    $\{s \mid \exists\, d\,.\, (s = a.d) \wedge d \in$ DIVERGENCES $(P)\}$

4.1.4 Choice

Non-deterministic choice is the easier of the two choice operators to define. Informally, $P \sqcap Q$ can do any trace of either P or Q, it can refuse to engage in any event that either P or Q can refuse, and it will diverge on any trace that will cause either P or Q to diverge. The operator is formally defined as an infix function Ndet as follows:

$\vdash \forall\, P\, Q\,.$
  FAILURES $(P\ \mathsf{Ndet}\ Q) =$ FAILURES $(P) \cup$ FAILURES $(Q) \wedge$
  DIVERGENCES $(P\ \mathsf{Ndet}\ Q) =$ DIVERGENCES $(P) \cup$ DIVERGENCES (Q)

Deterministic choice is slightly more complex. Initially, $P \square Q$ can refuse to engage in only those events which both processes (not either) can individually refuse. This is because if one process is ready to engage in an event, the other process cannot—as in the case of non-deterministic choice—over-ride the choice decision and refuse it in order to engage in something else. Once a choice is made, however, then the overall process will behave as the chosen process. The overall process can, of course, engage in any trace of events that will cause either process to diverge, and the overall process diverges when either of the two processes diverges. Formally, the definition of the deterministic choice operator Det goes as follows:

$\vdash \forall\, P\, Q\,.$
  FAILURES $(P\ \mathsf{Det}\ Q) =$
    $\{(s, X) \mid (s = [\,]) \wedge ([\,], X) \in$ FAILURES $(P) \cap$ FAILURES $(Q)\} \cup$
    $\{(s, X) \mid \neg(s = [\,]) \wedge (s, X) \in$ FAILURES $(P) \cup$ FAILURES $(Q)\} \cup$
    $\{(s, X) \mid s \in$ DIVERGENCES $(P\ \mathsf{Det}\ Q)\} \wedge$
  DIVERGENCES $(P\ \mathsf{Det}\ Q) =$ DIVERGENCES $(P) \cup$ DIVERGENCES (Q)

4.1.5 Parallel

Concurrent communication between two processes P and Q is expressed using the parallel operator $\|$, and is written as $P \| Q$. Two processes communicating in parallel can undertake traces of events that both can individually undertake, and will refuse all events that either can individually refuse. The process $P \| Q$ diverges on any trace that causes either P or Q to diverge, as long as both processes can engage in the trace. Once the process diverges, however, the cooperation of both processes will no longer be necessary, and the process will engage in any trace at all.

Formally, we define the parallel operator using an infix function **Par** as follows:

$\vdash \forall P\ Q.$
    FAILURES $(P$ Par $Q) =$
        $\{(s, X) \mid \exists Y\ Y'.\ (X = Y \cup Y') \wedge (s, Y) \in$ FAILURES $(P) \wedge$
                                  $(s, Y') \in$ FAILURES $(Q)\} \cup$
        $\{(s, X) \mid s \in$ DIVERGENCES $(P$ Par $Q)\} \wedge$
    DIVERGENCES $(P$ Par $Q) =$
        $\{s \mid \exists t\ u.\ (s = t \,^\wedge u) \wedge t \in ((\text{DIVERGENCES}\,(P) \cap \text{TRACES}\,(Q)) \cup$
                              $(\text{DIVERGENCES}\,(Q) \cap \text{TRACES}\,(P)))\}$

4.1.6 Hiding

Before defining the hiding operator we need two further functions on traces. The first is that of iteration; we wish to be able to write TRACE_ITER n a to represent a trace of n consecutive events a. The definition of this operator is done using primitive recursion as shown below.

$\vdash \forall a{:}\Sigma.\ \text{TRACE\_ITER } 0\ a = [\,] \wedge$
$\vdash \forall n\ a.\ \text{TRACE\_ITER } (n{+}1)\ a = (\text{TRACE\_ITER } n\ a)\,^\wedge[a]$

The second operator, TRACE_HIDE, performs a kind of hiding on traces; it eliminates from a trace all occurrences of a specified event, e.g. TRACE_HIDE$[a;\ b;\ c;\ b]b = [a;\ c]$. This operator is defined by primitive recursion on lists, as follows:

$\vdash \forall x{:}\Sigma.\ \text{TRACE\_HIDE } [\,]\ x = [\,] \wedge$
$\vdash \forall x\ a\ l.\ \text{TRACE\_HIDE } (a.l)\ x =$
                $(a = x) \Rightarrow (\text{TRACE\_HIDE } l\ x) \mid (a\ .\ (\text{TRACE\_HIDE } l\ x))$

The definition of the hiding operator can now be made using these two functions on traces. The process $P \setminus a$ conceals all occurrences of the event a from the behaviour of P. So $P \setminus a$ is seen to engage in the same traces as P, but with all the a events removed, and it is not seen to refuse to engage in the event a. Furthermore, traces that ordinarily cause P to diverge will also cause $P \setminus a$ to diverge, but again the a events are not observable in the divergent traces, and $P \setminus a$ also diverges if P is capable of engaging in an infinite sequence of a events. This behaviour of the hiding operator is formally described below as an infix function **Hide**.

$\vdash \forall a\ P.$
    FAILURES $(P$ Hide $a) =$
        $\{(s, X) \mid \exists s'.\ (s = \text{TRACE\_HIDE } s'\ a) \wedge (s', X \cup \{a\}) \in$ FAILURES $(P)\} \cup$
        $\{(s, X) \mid s \in$ DIVERGENCES $(P \setminus a)\} \wedge$
    DIVERGENCES $(P$ Hide $a) =$
        $\{s \mid \exists u\ t.\ (s = (\text{TRACE\_HIDE } u\ a)\,^\wedge t) \wedge$
                $(u \in$ DIVERGENCES $(P) \vee$
                    $\forall n.\ u\,^\wedge(\text{TRACE\_ITER } n\ a) \in$ TRACES $(P))\}$

4.2   Recursion

To express the semantics of the recursion operator μ, one requires a general theory for *fixed points* [20]. During the course of mechanizing the CSP language, such a theory was not available as part of the HOL system, so before mechanizing the μ operator a theory of fixed points had to be developed. In fact, the theory of fixed points was the only supporting theory required in the course of mechanization which was not yet available as part of the HOL library.

4.2.1   Fixed Point Theory in HOL

Before we present the formal description of the CSP recursion operator, we first present our mechanization of fixed point theory in HOL. Besides making the paper self-contained, this presentation shows that the flexibility and power of higher order logic are sufficient to allow the formalization of complex mathematics.

4.2.1.1   Partial Orders

We begin by defining the notion of a *partial order*. In mathematics, a partially ordered set is a pair $(D, \sqsubseteq)$ where D is a set and $\sqsubseteq$ is a *reflexive*, *transitive* and *anti-symmetric* binary relation on D. We could easily define partial orders in this way in higher order logic, but the explicit presence of the set D would unnecessarily clutter our definitions. As with our solution to representing alphabets, we propose to use a binary relation $\sqsubseteq$ ranging over a polymorphic type α, i.e. a relation of type $\alpha \rightarrow \alpha \rightarrow bool$. This approach might not be adequate for developing a full-scale domain theory; but for the purposes of our mechanization only a small subset of this theory is required, and for this, the approach of using types gives rise to an elegant theory for fixed points.

We begin by defining the notions of reflexivity, transitivity and anti-symmetry in the standard way.

$$\vdash \forall r.\ \mathsf{REFL}\ r \equiv \forall x{:}\alpha.\ r\ x\ x$$
$$\vdash \forall r.\ \mathsf{TRANS}\ r \equiv \forall x\ y\ z{:}\alpha.\ (r\ x\ y) \wedge (r\ y\ z) \supset (r\ x\ z)$$
$$\vdash \forall r.\ \mathsf{ANTISYM}\ r \equiv \forall x\ y{:}\alpha.\ (r\ x\ y) \wedge (r\ y\ x) \supset (x = y)$$

Any binary relation $r{:}\alpha \rightarrow \alpha \rightarrow bool$ is a partial order of α if it satisfies these three properties:

$$\vdash \forall r.\ \mathsf{PO}\ r \equiv (\mathsf{REFL}\ r) \wedge (\mathsf{TRANS}\ r) \wedge (\mathsf{ANTISYM}\ r)$$

4.2.1.2   Upper Bounds

An element of type α, b say, is said to be an *upper bound* of some set X (of elements of type α) ordered under a relation r if and only if r is a partial order and all elements in X are ordered below b:

$$\vdash \forall b\ X\ r.\ \mathsf{IS\_UB}\ b\ X\ r \equiv (\mathsf{PO}\ r) \wedge (\forall a{:}\alpha.\ (a \in X) \supset r\ a\ b)$$

An element b of type α is the *least upper bound* of a set X if and only if it is an upper bound of X and all other upper bounds are ordered above b:

$$\vdash \; \forall b \, X \, r.\; \text{IS\_LUB } b \, X \, r \equiv (\text{IS\_UB } b \, X \, r) \wedge (\forall c{:}\alpha.\; (\text{IS\_UB } c \, X \, r) \supset r \, b \, c)$$

Sometimes it is necessary to explicitly refer to the least upper bound of a set, so a direct definition is required. Of course, a least upper bound does not always exist, so it is convenient to use the ε operator to define it.

$$\vdash \; \forall X \, r.\; \text{LUB } X \, r = \varepsilon b{:}\alpha.\; (\text{IS\_LUB } b \, X \, r)$$

In this way, if the least upper bound of a set X does not exist for some r, then the value of $\text{LUB } X \, r$ remains undefined. If it exists, however, then its value is unique, and from the definitions above it is straightforward to show this by proving the following theorem:

$$\vdash \; \forall r \, X \, x.\; \text{IS\_LUB } x \, X \, r \supset \forall y.\; \text{IS\_LUB } y \, X \, r \supset (y = x)$$

4.2.1.3 Complete Partial Orders

To define the notion of a *complete partial order* (CPO), we first define the notion of a *directed* set. A non-empty set X is said to be directed on a partial order r if and only if any two elements in X can be ordered below some particular element in X. Formally we define:

$$\vdash \; \forall X \, r.\; \text{DIRECTED } X \, r \equiv$$
$$(\text{PO } r) \wedge$$
$$\neg(X = \varnothing) \wedge$$
$$\forall a \, b.\; (a \in X) \wedge (b \in X) \supset \exists c.\; (c \in X) \wedge (r \, a \, c) \wedge (r \, b \, c)$$

A relation $r{:}\alpha{\to}\alpha{\to}bool$ is a CPO if (1) it is a partial order, (2) there exists some bottom element in α which is ordered below all other elements in α, and (3) all directed subsets of α have a least upper bound.

$$\vdash \; \forall r.\; \text{CPO } r \equiv$$
$$(\text{PO } r) \wedge$$
$$\exists bot.\; \forall x.\; r \, bot \, x \wedge$$
$$\forall X.\; (\text{DIRECTED } X \, r) \supset \exists b.\; \text{IS\_LUB } b \, X \, r$$

4.2.1.4 Monotonicity and Continuity

Having defined the notion of a CPO, it is now possible to define *monotonicity* and *continuity*. Let $r_1{:}\alpha{\to}\alpha{\to}bool$ and $r_2{:}\beta{\to}\beta{\to}bool$ be any two CPOs, and $f{:}\alpha{\to}\beta$ be some function. We say that f is monotonic if and only if the application of f to any two values $p_1{:}\alpha$ and $p_2{:}\alpha$, ordered by r_1, produces two values correspondingly ordered by r_2.

$$\vdash \; \forall r_1 \, r_2.$$
$$((\text{CPO } r_1) \wedge (\text{CPO } r_2)) \supset$$
$$\forall f{:}\alpha{\to}\beta.\; (\text{MONOTONIC } f \, r_1 \, r_2) \equiv \forall p_1 \, p_2.\; (r_1 \, p_1 \, p_2) \supset (r_2 \, (f \, p_1) \, (f \, p_2))$$

Let X be a set directed over r_1 and Y be the set obtained by applying f to all the members of X, denoted by the expression IMAGE f X defined below:

$$\vdash \text{IMAGE } f \ X = \{y{:}\beta \mid \exists \ x{:}\alpha. \ (x \in X) \wedge (y = (f \ x))\}$$

We say that f is continuous with respect to r_1 and r_2 if Y is directed over r_2, and if the application of f to the least upper bound of X is equal to the least upper bound of Y. In HOL, we define this formally as follows:

$$
\begin{aligned}
&\vdash \ \forall r_1 \ r_2. \\
&\quad ((\text{CPO } r_1) \wedge (\text{CPO } r_2)) \ \supset \\
&\quad \forall f{:}\alpha{\rightarrow}\beta. \\
&\quad\quad (\text{CONTINUOUS } f \ r_1 \ r_2) \equiv \\
&\quad\quad \forall X. \ (\text{DIRECTED } X \ r_1) \ \supset \\
&\quad\quad\quad (\text{DIRECTED } (\text{IMAGE } f \ X) \ r_2) \wedge \\
&\quad\quad\quad (f \ (\text{LUB } X \ r_1) = (\text{LUB } (\text{IMAGE } f \ X) \ r_2))
\end{aligned}
$$

From the above definitions it is possible to prove that all continuous functions are monotonic:

$$
\begin{aligned}
&\vdash \ \forall r_1 \ r_2. \\
&\quad ((\text{CPO } r_1) \wedge (\text{CPO } r_2)) \ \supset \\
&\quad \forall (f{:}\alpha{\rightarrow}\beta). \ (\text{CONTINUOUS } f \ r_1 \ r_2) \ \supset \ (\text{MONOTONIC } f \ r_1 \ r_2)
\end{aligned}
$$

4.2.1.5 Least Fixed Points

We finally need to define the notion of a least fixed point. A value $x{:}\alpha$ is said to be a *fixed point* of some function $f{:}\alpha{\rightarrow}\alpha$ if the application of f to x results in x. The fixed point which is ordered below all other fixed points, using some relation r, is said to be the *least fixed point*. The notion of least fixed point is formalized below as a predicate IS_FIX.

$$\vdash \ \forall x \ f \ r. \ \text{IS\_FIX } x \ f \ r \equiv (f \ x = x) \wedge (\forall y. \ (f \ y = y) \ \supset \ r \ x \ y)$$

As with least upper bounds, it is often necessary to refer to the value of the least fixed point explicitly; so, again, this is defined using the ε operator.

$$\vdash \ \forall f \ r. \ \text{FIX } f \ r = \varepsilon x{:}\alpha. \ \text{IS\_FIX } x \ f \ r$$

It can be proved that for any partial order, if the least fixed point of a function exists, it is unique.

$$\vdash \ \forall r. \ (\text{PO } r) \ \supset \ \forall f \ x. \ \text{IS\_FIX } x \ f \ r \ \supset \ \forall y. \ \text{IS\_FIX } y \ f \ r \ \supset \ (y = x)$$

4.2.1.6 The Knaster-Tarski Theorem

We can now prove the Knaster-Tarski Recursion Theorem which can be used to define recursive functions. The theorem states that the least fixed point of any function which is continuous for some CPO r is equal to the least upper bound of the set of all iterative applications of the function f to the bottom element $\bot$ of the CPO, i.e. the set of processes $\{\bot, f(\bot), f(f(\bot)), f(f(f(\bot))), \ldots\}$.

To mechanize the notion of iteratively applying a function n times to a value, we define a primitive recursive function ITER as follows:

$$\vdash \text{ITER } 0 \, f \, x = x \, \wedge$$
$$\text{ITER } (n{+}1) \, f \, x = f \, (\text{ITER } n \, f \, x)$$

The set $\{\bot, f(\bot), f(f(\bot)), f(f(f(\bot))), \ldots\}$, therefore, can now be represented as the set $\{x \mid \exists n.\ x = \text{ITER } n \, f \, bot\}$ and the Knaster-Tarski Theorem, as proved in the HOL logic from the previous definitions, is written:

$$\vdash \forall f \, r.\, (\text{CPO } r \wedge \text{CONTINUOUS } f \, r \, r) \supset$$
$$\forall bot.\, (\forall x.\, r \, bot \, x) \supset \text{FIX } f \, r = \text{LUB } \{x \mid \exists \, n.\, x = \text{ITER } n \, f \, bot\} \, r$$

This theorem is the basis for defining the CSP recursion operator, as described in the next section.

4.2.2   Recursion in CSP

In Section 2 we mentioned that a consequence of omitting condition (10) from the definition of well-definedness is that a more complex ordering on processes must be used. The original ordering $\sqsubseteq$ presented in [2], which says that a process P is less defined than a process Q if the failures and divergences of Q are subsets of the failures and divergences of P respectively:

$$\vdash \forall P \, Q.$$
$$P \sqsubseteq Q =$$
$$(\text{FAILURES } Q) \subseteq (\text{FAILURES } P) \, \wedge$$
$$(\text{DIVERGENCES } Q) \subseteq (\text{DIVERGENCES } P)$$

is no longer a complete partial order under the chosen semantics.

A coarser ordering is required. This is described in detail in [18], where its relationship to the original ordering is explained. The ordering, $\leq$, can be formalized in logic as follows:

$$\vdash \forall P \, Q.$$
$$P \leq Q =$$
$$(\text{DIVERGENCES } Q) \subseteq (\text{DIVERGENCES } P) \, \wedge$$
$$\forall s.\, (s \notin (\text{DIVERGENCES } P)) \supset (\text{R } P \, s = \text{R } Q \, s) \, \wedge$$
$$(\text{MIN\_ELEMS } (\text{DIVERGENCES } P)) \subseteq (\text{TRACES } Q)$$

where $(\text{R } P \, s)$ denotes the set of refusal sets of a process P after engaging in a trace s, and $(\text{MIN\_ELEMS } X)$ denotes the set of traces in X with minimum length. The definitions of these auxiliary functions are shown below:

$$\vdash \text{R } P \, s = \{X \mid (s, X) \in (\text{FAILURES } P)\}$$

$$\vdash \text{MIN\_ELEMS } X = \{x \in X \mid \forall t.\, (t \in X) \supset \neg(t < x)\}$$

$$\vdash\ s < t \equiv (s \neq t) \wedge \exists\ u.\,(s \wedge u) = t$$

Intuitively, the new ordering states that a process Q improves a process P, that is $P \leq Q$ if and only if:

- Q diverges less often than P, i.e. (DIVERGENCES Q) $\subseteq$ (DIVERGENCES P),

- the shortest traces that cause process P to diverge can be avoided by process Q, i.e. (MIN_ELEMS (DIVERGENCES P)) $\subseteq$ (TRACES Q), and

- if a trace s does not cause P to diverge then P and Q can refuse to engage in exactly the same events after they both engage in s.

In our mechanization, both orderings were defined because the original ordering is still useful for conducting process refinement. From the definitions of the two orderings, it is routine to prove that the new ordering $\leq$ incorporates more detail than the original ordering $\sqsubseteq$.

$$\vdash\ \forall\ P\ Q.\ P \leq Q \supset P \sqsubseteq Q$$

4.2.2.1 CSP Ordering as a CPO

It remains to prove that the new ordering is a complete partial order. The first step is straightforward; we prove that it is at least a partial order.

$$\vdash\ \mathsf{PO} \leq$$

For the second step, we need to find a process which is $\leq$-ordered before all other processes, i.e. a bottom element of the ordering $\leq$. This process is the one with infinite failure and divergence sets, defined as follows:

$$\vdash\ \mathsf{FAILURES\,(BOT)} = \{p \mid \mathsf{T}\} \wedge \mathsf{DIVERGENCES\,(BOT)} = \{t \mid \mathsf{T}\}$$

From this definition it is also straightforward to show that this process is indeed the bottom process, by proving the theorem:

$$\vdash\ \forall P.\ \mathsf{BOT} \leq P$$

For the third and final step, we need to represent the least upper bound of all $\leq$-directed sets of processes. For any $\leq$-directed set X, the least upper bound happens to be the process whose failure set is the intersection of failure sets of all the processes in X, and whose divergence set is the intersection of divergence sets of all the processes in X. Hence we define such a process INT_PROC:

$$\vdash\ \mathsf{DIRECTED}\ X \leq\ \supset$$
$$\mathsf{FAILURES\,(INT\_PROC}\ X) = \mathsf{INTER\,(IMAGE\ FAILURES}\ X) \wedge$$
$$\mathsf{DIVERGENCES\,(INT\_PROC}\ X) = \mathsf{INTER\,(IMAGE\ DIVERGENCES}\ X)$$

where INTER represents the intersection operator on sets, defined as follows:

$$\vdash\ \forall X.\ \mathsf{INTER}\ X = \{x \mid \forall s.\ s \in X \supset x \in s\}$$

We now prove that the process INT_PROC is indeed a least upper bound:

$$\vdash \forall X. (\text{DIRECTED } X \leq) \supset (\text{IS\_LUB (INT\_PROC } X) X \leq)$$

and finally prove that $\leq$ is a complete partial order:

$$\vdash \text{CPO} \leq$$

4.2.2.2 Definition of CSP Recursion

We are now in a position to define the CSP recursion operator. For any continuous function on processes f, we define Mu f to be the least fixed point of f and $\leq$.

$$\vdash \forall f. (\text{CONT } f) \supset (\text{Mu } f = \text{FIX } f \leq)$$

where CONT f is an abbreviation for CONTINUOUS $f \leq \leq$. From the fact that $\leq$ is a complete partial order, and from the Knaster-Tarski theorem, we derive that Mu f is indeed equal to the least upper bound of the set of processes obtained by iteratively applying f to the bottom process BOT:

$$\vdash \forall f. (\text{CONT } f) \supset (\text{Mu } f = \text{LUB } \{x \mid \exists n.\, x = \text{ITER } n\, f\, \text{BOT}\} \leq)$$

The failure and divergence sets of the recursive process are therefore equal to the intersection of the failure and divergence sets (respectively) of the processes in the set $\{\text{BOT}, f(\text{BOT}), f(f\,\text{BOT}), \ldots\}$.

$$\vdash \forall f. (\text{CONT } f) \supset$$
$$\text{FAILURES (Mu } f) =$$
$$\text{INTER (IMAGE FAILURES } \{x \mid \exists n.\, x = \text{ITER } n\, f\, \text{BOT}\}) \wedge$$
$$\text{DIVERGENCES (Mu } f) =$$
$$\text{INTER (IMAGE DIVERGENCES } \{x \mid \exists n.\, x = \text{ITER } n\, f\, \text{BOT}\})$$

Of course, many other intermediate lemmas and theorems, which are not shown here, had to be proved to obtain this result. Ideally, the next interesting theorem to prove is that which says that all the CSP operators are continuous. This result, however, has not yet been proved in HOL.

5 Proving CSP Laws

In the previous section we presented the formal definitions of several CSP operators, in the form in which they were mechanized in the theorem prover.[3] Reasoning at this semantic level, however, can be tedious, so we derive high-level laws about the operators from their definitions. This provides a more natural framework for reasoning than the low-level semantic model.

Listed below are some of the several laws and lemmas that were proved in HOL from the process definitions. These show how the method of representing alphabets using

---

[3]Except for some non-ascii syntax.

a universal notion gives rise to equational laws.[4] The list of laws is not exhaustive, but simply is a sample to illustrate their nature.

$\vdash \forall P.\ P\ \mathsf{Det}\ \mathsf{Stop} = P$

$\vdash \forall P.\ P\ \mathsf{Det}\ \bot = \bot$

$\vdash \forall P.\ P\ \mathsf{Det}\ P = P$

$\vdash \forall P\ Q.\ P\ \mathsf{Det}\ Q = Q\ \mathsf{Det}\ P$

$\vdash \forall P\ Q\ R.\ P\ \mathsf{Det}\ (Q\ \mathsf{Det}\ R) = (P\ \mathsf{Det}\ Q)\ \mathsf{Det}\ R$

$\vdash \forall P\ Q\ R.\ P\ \mathsf{Det}\ (Q\ \mathsf{Ndet}\ R) = (P\ \mathsf{Det}\ Q)\ \mathsf{Ndet}\ (P\ \mathsf{Det}\ R)$

$\vdash \forall P\ Q\ R.\ P\ \mathsf{Ndet}\ (Q\ \mathsf{Det}\ R) = (P\ \mathsf{Ndet}\ Q)\ \mathsf{Det}\ (P\ \mathsf{Ndet}\ R)$

$\vdash \forall a\ P\ Q.\ a\ \mathsf{Prefix}\ (P\ \mathsf{Ndet}\ Q) = (a\ \mathsf{Prefix}\ P)\ \mathsf{Ndet}\ (a\ \mathsf{Prefix}\ Q)$

$\vdash \forall a\ P\ Q.\ (a\ \mathsf{Prefix}\ P)\ \mathsf{Det}\ (a\ \mathsf{Prefix}\ Q) = (a\ \mathsf{Prefix}\ P)\ \mathsf{Ndet}\ (a\ \mathsf{Prefix}\ Q)$

$\vdash \forall P.\ P\ \mathsf{Ndet}\ \bot = \bot$

$\vdash \forall P.\ P\ \mathsf{Ndet}\ P = P$

$\vdash \forall P\ Q.\ P\ \mathsf{Ndet}\ Q = Q\ \mathsf{Ndet}\ P$

$\vdash \forall P\ Q\ R.\ P\ \mathsf{Ndet}\ (Q\ \mathsf{Ndet}\ R) = (P\ \mathsf{Ndet}\ Q)\ \mathsf{Ndet}\ R$

$\vdash \forall P.\ P\ \mathsf{Par}\ \bot = \bot$

$\vdash \forall P.\ (P = \bot) \supset P\ \mathsf{Par}\ \mathsf{Stop} = \mathsf{Stop}$

$\vdash \forall P\ Q.\ P\ \mathsf{Par}\ Q = Q\ \mathsf{Par}\ P$

$\vdash \forall P\ Q\ R.\ P\ \mathsf{Par}\ (Q\ \mathsf{Par}\ R) = (P\ \mathsf{Par}\ Q)\ \mathsf{Par}\ R$

$\vdash \forall P\ Q\ R.\ P\ \mathsf{Par}\ (Q\ \mathsf{Ndet}\ R) = (P\ \mathsf{Par}\ Q)\ \mathsf{Ndet}\ (P\ \mathsf{Par}\ R)$

$\vdash \forall a\ b\ P\ Q.\ (a\ \mathsf{Prefix}\ P)\ \mathsf{Par}\ (a\ \mathsf{Prefix}\ Q) =$
$\qquad (a = b) \Rightarrow a\ \mathsf{Prefix}\ (P\ \mathsf{Par}\ Q)\ |\ \mathsf{Stop}$

The algebraic nature of the laws contrasts with the form of the laws proved in the mechanization described in [3], in which the individual, explicit treatment of alphabets often led to non-equational laws that were cumbersome to use. This difference in the nature of the laws is a direct result of the way in which the semantics depends on the treatment of alphabets. In the case of universal, implicit treatment, the behaviour of all the operators can be totally defined (as described earlier), and this leads to straightforward algebraic laws. In the case of explicit treatment, however, most operators have to be only partially defined because the presence of alphabets gives rise to various premises without which processes cannot be defined. The premises which stipulate this partiality often persist into the derived laws, and hence, these laws cannot be simple equations.

6   Separating Syntax from Semantics

In the previous sections, we have shown how a theory for a subset of CSP can be formally defined in higher order logic, and how this theory can form the basis for deriving laws to support natural reasoning in the language.

In the formalization presented above, constructs of CSP were defined directly in terms of the failure-divergence semantics. We mentioned in Section 1 that one of our goals was to develop a system that supports various semantic models, since several

---

[4]Any laws under the described model which are non-equational are not so as a consequence of the way alphabets are handled.

semantics for CSP have been defined, (e.g. [2, 16]), each with a different degree of complexity and expressiveness. It is therefore desirable to separate the syntactic definition of the language from its associated semantics, so as to allow the language to be defined using different semantics but the same syntax. A system which supports theories for different semantic definitions of the same syntax enables one to choose a semantics in which to work depending on the requirements. Moreover, it allows a comparison to be made between reasoning in different semantic frameworks.

6.1 Defining the Syntax

Separating the definition of the syntax of a language from its semantics in order to allow multiple semantic definitions for the same framework can be done rather neatly in HOL by using a package (due to Melham [17]) for automatically defining concrete recursive data types from their syntactic components. We represent the syntax of the adopted language by defining a concrete type CSP in terms of all its possible constructors. This syntax is described by the *signature* grammar of the operators, and is written in terms of existing types and recursive calls to the type being defined as follows:

$$
\begin{aligned}
CSP = \ &\textsf{STOP} \mid \\
&\textsf{SKIP} \mid \\
&\Sigma \longrightarrow CSP \mid \\
&CSP \sqcap CSP \mid \\
&CSP \,\square\, CSP \mid \\
&CSP \parallel CSP \mid \\
&CSP \setminus \Sigma \mid \\
&\mu \ string \ CSP \mid \\
&\textsf{var} \ string
\end{aligned}
$$

The HOL data type definition mechanism is used to define a type CSP representing the above syntax of CSP expressions. We introduce the notion of variables in the syntax because in our chosen approach, we are otherwise unable to incorporate the syntax of the recursion operator μ. It is not possible to define a type

$$CSP = \ldots \mid \mu \, (CSP {\rightarrow} CSP) \mid \ldots$$

because the function mapping defined by $\rightarrow$ is total, and so the set denoted by the type on the right hand side of this equation will be strictly larger than the set on the left hand side denoted by CSP (see Cantor's theorem [14]) and hence the two types will not be isomorphic. For this form of definition to be done without using variables, our entire approach would have to be changed to reinterpret CSP as a domain and $\rightarrow$ as continuous function space, as in Scott's domain theory [20]. Instead, we use the standard solution of solving this form of recursion by introducing variables, as described above.

We do not give further details here of the method we use for defining data types; it will suffice to say that the data types are defined by automatic proof of an isomorphism to a subset of an existing type, as explained earlier. For details of this see [17].

6.2 Defining the Semantics

The data type *CSP* defined above represents only the syntax of the CSP language. One now has to define semantics to give meaning to this syntax. The semantics we have chosen in this paper is that for failures and divergences, so we show how a function $\mathcal{FD}$ can be defined to give a denotational style semantics to the language based on the failure-divergence semantics already defined in the previous sections.

Before defining this function, we first need to define the notion of an environment, since we need to denote variable processes. An environment ρ can be represented by a function that assigns values to variables in a particular state. We require the environment to store values of processes, so we model it by a function of type: $string \rightarrow (\Sigma)process$ i.e. a function that maps variable names onto the values of type $(\Sigma)process$. The failure-divergence semantic function $\mathcal{FD}$ is therefore of type $CSP \rightarrow env \rightarrow (\Sigma)process$ (where *env* is an abbreviation for $string \rightarrow (\Sigma)process$), and is defined as follows:

$\vdash \mathcal{FD}\,(\mathsf{STOP})\,\rho = \mathsf{Stop}$
$\vdash \mathcal{FD}\,(\mathsf{SKIP})\,\rho = \mathsf{Skip}$
$\vdash \mathcal{FD}\,(a \longrightarrow P)\,\rho = a\,\mathsf{Prefix}\,(\mathcal{FD}\,P\,\rho)$
$\vdash \mathcal{FD}\,(P \sqcap Q)\,\rho = (\mathcal{FD}\,P\,\rho)\,\mathsf{Ndet}\,(\mathcal{FD}\,Q\,\rho)$
$\vdash \mathcal{FD}\,(P \,\square\, Q)\,\rho = (\mathcal{FD}\,P\,\rho)\,\mathsf{Det}\,(\mathcal{FD}\,Q\,\rho)$
$\vdash \mathcal{FD}\,(P \parallel Q)\,\rho = (\mathcal{FD}\,P\,\rho)\,\mathsf{Par}\,(\mathcal{FD}\,Q\,\rho)$
$\vdash \mathcal{FD}\,(P \setminus a)\,\rho = (\mathcal{FD}\,P\,\rho)\,\mathsf{Hide}\,a$
$\vdash \mathcal{FD}\,(\mu\,s\,P)\,\rho = \mathsf{Mu}\,(\lambda\,x{:}(\Sigma)process.\,\mathcal{FD}\,P\,(\mathsf{Bnd}\,s\,x\,\rho))$
$\vdash \mathcal{FD}\,(\mathsf{var}\,s)\,\rho = \rho\,s$

The term $\mathsf{Bnd}\,s\,x\,\rho$ is used to denote the environment ρ' which binds the variable name s to the value x, leaving all other variable bindings in ρ unchanged, i.e.

$\vdash \mathsf{Bnd}\,s\,x\,\rho = \lambda\,s'.\,(s' = s) \Rightarrow x \mid (\rho\,s')$

The definition of $\mathcal{FD}$ is recursive and makes use of the failure-divergence semantic definitions of the operators given earlier.

6.3 Definition of Equality

We can now define equality on processes for the failure-divergence semantics as follows:

$\vdash \forall\,P\,Q.\,P =_{\mathsf{FD}} Q \equiv \forall \rho.\,\mathcal{FD}\,P\,\rho = \mathcal{FD}\,Q\,\rho$

where two syntactic processes are said to be equal if and only if their failure-divergence semantics are equal.

Clearly, we now want to abstract the process algebra laws we proved to hold for our syntactic definition in terms of the failure-divergence equivalence operator above. This is particularly useful because we want to (a) abstract away from the details of the denotational semantics, and (b) distinguish between laws that hold for different semantic equivalences. Laws proved using the failure-divergence semantics need not hold for other semantics, so it is useful to associate equivalence to the respective semantics. In the earlier approach, for example, we proved that

$$\vdash \forall P\ Q.\ P\ \text{Par}\ Q = Q\ \text{Par}\ P$$

The standard equals operator could be used because the semantics of Par were implicit in its definition. If we now use a syntactic notion of a process, however, we need to reason using the equivalence operator defined on the chosen semantics, since the $\parallel$ operator alone has no meaning. Therefore we now prove the theorem:

$$\vdash \forall P\ Q.\ P \parallel Q =_{\text{FD}} Q \parallel P$$

from the definition of $\mathcal{FD}$ and the law $P\ \text{Par}\ Q = Q\ \text{Par}\ P$ proved in the HOL system as described earlier.

6.4   Comparing Different Semantics

Other semantics can, of course, be defined for the same syntactic data type CSP, together with their respective equivalence operators and derived laws [3]. These semantics can be formally compared, and properties of processes can be analysed in the different semantics, since they are all built on the same underlying logic. For example, the trace semantics of [16] and the failure semantics of [2] can be defined using two denotation functions $\mathcal{T}$ and $\mathcal{F}$. Their equivalence operators $=_{\text{TS}}$ and $=_{\text{FS}}$ can then be defined and the strictness of the equivalences compared using some partial order relation $\subset$ say, where one can prove that

$$=_{\text{FD}}\ \subset\ =_{\text{FS}}\ \subset\ =_{\text{TS}}$$

saying that $=_{\text{TS}}$ is least strict and $=_{\text{FD}}$ is most strict. Thus, showing that two processes are $=_{\text{FD}}$ implies that they are $=_{\text{TS}}$; but processes which have equivalent trace semantics need not have equivalent divergence semantics, so the laws proved for $=_{\text{TS}}$ need not hold for $=_{\text{FD}}$.

The above approach of separating the syntax of processes as a separate data type therefore brings about a generalised and flexible verification tool which can be further customised to particular requirements.

7   Related Work

Most computer-based tools for reasoning using process algebras concentrate on demonstrating properties of specifications by a method called *model checking*, in which labelled transition systems are generated, the possible state transitions are explored, and (with varying degrees of interaction) the transitions available at each stage are traversed to analyse the behaviour of the process. The advantage of such systems is that they are automatic. But the limitation is that, in practice, they can be used for reasoning about the behaviour of processes over only a finite number of state transitions, with a small number of branching transitions available at each stage. Our approach of using formal proof supports an alternative method of reasoning which can be used to prove a wider range of properties. Properties for processes with infinite state, for example, can be proved by using induction principles.

The idea of mechanically reasoning about process algebras via their algebraic laws, or of using a general purpose theorem prover to conduct the reasoning, is still relatively new. In [10], De Nicola et al. describe ongoing work on a system for manipulating and executing CCS specifications; in [7], Cleaveland and Panangaden describe an investigation into mechanizing CCS using the NUPRL *logical theory of types*; and in [9], Davies describes a proof tool for CSP developed using the B-tool. The general philosophy behind these approaches and ours is similar; but the resulting reasoning frameworks are different, and our investigations concentrate on emphasising different uses of the resulting tool. Research into mechanizing specialised formalisms using different embedding logics and proof systems is desired if one aims to discover mechanizations that are both natural and practical.

8   Conclusion

Research into reasoning with process algebras via a general purpose theorem prover is still in early stages and much work is still necessary to provide evidence of the practicality of this approach. In this section we draw some conclusions from our approach, and discuss some experiences gained.

A mechanization of a subset of CSP in higher order logic was undertaken with the aim of facilitating the process of reasoning about concurrently communicating systems. In the exercise, the well-definedness proofs which had to be done to define the CSP operators, and the derivation of the laws from these definitions, constituted the bulk of the work. The complexity of these proofs varied tremendously. The well-definedness of some operators, such as STOP and SKIP, is rather trivial to show. That of the hiding and parallel operators, however, is rather complex, as are the proofs of some of the their laws. In these more complex cases, fundamental mathematical results were at times needed, so both the expressive power of higher order logic, and the substantial library of mathematical theories available in the HOL system were found necessary to do the proofs.

In general, two issues predominantly influenced our approach: (a) in practice, when writing specifications and reasoning with formal languages, it is often the case that a large suite of notation is used—a mechanical system for formal verification solely geared towards supporting the CSP notation would be too restrictive, and (b) we would like to apply our tool to as general a problem domain as possible. Our approach, therefore, has been to obtain a framework which would allow for both automatic and interactive reasoning; one in which several notations can be formally supported and which can be extended to support further theoretical concepts as become necessary, in a way which preserves the soundness of the system.

The ability to express specifications in different notations and to soundly reason about them is one of the main advantages of our general approach. This is especially useful in cases where specification details due to different levels of abstraction are better expressed using different formalisms. For example, one might want to write high-level behavioural specifications in CSP, implementation descriptions in another logic, such as higher order logic or some mechanized temporal logic, and formally prove relationships between the two specifications written in the different notations. Without the common underlying formal framework, it is dangerous to reason with such a mixture of notations.

We also hope to support the specification of both data and process communication in the same underlying formalism. Process algebras like CSP and CCS do not allow the typing of data in specifications. Although it is often necessary to reason and abstract using data descriptions, this is not possible with most process algebras. LOTOS attempts to offer both kinds of specification, but its data specification language is separate from the control specification language, and there are no underlying formal semantics to connect the two. We hope that in our mechanization, the same data type definition capabilities available in the theorem prover for defining logical types can be used to define and incorporate types in CSP specifications.

Our experiences so far indicate that the technology of theorem provers is currently mature enough to be practically applied to the complex nature of the problems in question, and we hope to allow reasoning with process algebras using mathematical proof in a practical way. To ensure this we need to extend the mechanization of semantic models (as described in this paper) and their algebraic laws to support a higher level of reasoning via a variety of inference rules and tactics which allow proof to be conducted at a level which is natural to the process algebra. We have begun some research at developing such a proof infrastructure for CCS [5] but the work is still in early stages. The principles and pragmatic issues which arise in building such proof rules, such as efficiency and automation of high level reasoning steps, should be in general applicable to any process algebra.

Acknowledgements

I wish to thank several employees of Hewlett-Packard Laboratories for numerous inspiring discussions—in particular, Naiem Dathi and Mike Wray for their help with my understanding of the semantics of CSP, and Roger Fleming and Robin Gallimore for their support in carrying out this research. Thanks are also due to Mike Gordon and Tom Melham of the University of Cambridge for their advice on mechanization in HOL and to Glynn Winskel of the University of Århus for discussions on domain theory. Naiem Dathi, Tom Melham and Mike Wray made many constructive comments on earlier versions of this paper.

References

[1] Andrews P. B., *An Introduction to Mathematical Logic and Type Theory: To Truth through Proof*, Computer Science and Applied Mathematics Series, Aca-

demic Press Inc., 1986.

[2] Brookes S. D., and Roscoe A. W., 'An Improved Failures Model for Communicating Processes', in *Seminar on Concurrency*, Brookes S. D., Roscoe A. W., Winskel G. (eds.), Lecture Notes in Computer Science, Springer-Verlag, 1985, Vol. 197, pp. 281–305.

[3] Camilleri A. J., 'Mechanizing CSP Trace Theory in Higher Order Logic', *IEEE Transactions on Software Engineering*, 16 (9), pp. 993–1004, Special Issue on Formal Methods in Software Engineering, Leveson N. (ed.), September 1990.

[4] Camilleri A. J., 'Reasoning in CSP via the HOL Theorem Prover', in *Next Decade in Information Technology*, IEEE Computer Society Press, Los Alamitos, 1990, pp. 173–183, Proceedings of the 5th Jerusalem Conference on Information Technology, Jerusalem, Israel, 22–25 October 1990.

[5] Camilleri A. J., Inverardi P., and Nesi M., 'Combining Interaction and Automation in Process Algebra Verification', to appear in the proceedings of the Colloquium on Combining Paradigms for Software Development, TAPSOFT '91, Brighton, 8–12 April, 1991.

[6] Church A., 'A Formulation of the Simple Theory of Types', *The Journal of Symbolic Logic*, 1940, 5, pp. 56–68.

[7] Cleaveland R., and Panangaden P., 'Type Theory and Concurrency', *International Journal of Parallel Programming*, November 1988, 12 (2), pp. 153–206.

[8] Cousineau G., Huet G., and Paulson L., 'The ML Handbook', INRIA, 1986.

[9] Davies J., 'Assisted Proofs for Communicating Sequential Processes', M.Sc. Dissertation, Oxford University Computer Laboratory, Programming Research Group, September 1987.

[10] De Nicola R., Inverardi P., and Nesi M., 'Using Axiomatic Presentation of Behavioural Equivalences for Manipulating CCS Specifications', in *Automatic Verification Methods for Finite State Systems*, Sifakis J. (ed.), Lecture Notes in Computer Science, Springer-Verlag, 1990, Vol. 407, pp. 54–67.

[11] Gordon M. J., Milner A. J., and Wadsworth C. P., *Edinburgh LCF: A Mechanized Logic of Computation*, Lecture Notes in Computer Science, Springer-Verlag, 1979, Vol. 78.

[12] Gordon M. J. C., 'HOL—A Proof Generating System for Higher-Order Logic', in *VLSI Specification, Verification and Synthesis*, Birtwistle G. and Subrahmanyam P. A. (eds.), Kluwer Academic Publishers, Boston, 1988, pp. 73–128, Proceedings of the Hardware Verification Workshop, Calgary, Canada, 12–16 January 1987.

[13] Gordon M. J. C., 'Mechanizing Programming Logics in Higher Order Logic', in *Current Trends in Hardware Verification and Automated Theorem Proving*, Birtwistle G., Subrahmanyam P. (eds.), Springer-Verlag, 1989, pp. 387–439, Proceedings of the Banff Workshop on Hardware Verification, Banff, Canada, 1988.

[14] Halmos P. R., *Naive Set Theory*, Undergraduate Texts in Mathematics, Springer-Verlag, 1987 (5th impression).

[15] Hatcher W., *The Logical Foundations of Mathematics*, Pergamon Press, 1982.

[16] Hoare C. A. R., *Communicating Sequential Processes*, Prentice-Hall Int., 1985.

[17] Melham T. F., 'Automating Recursive Type Definitions in Higher Order Logic', in: *Current Trends in Hardware Verification and Automated Theorem Proving*, Birtwistle G., Subrahmanyam P. (eds.), Springer-Verlag, 1989, pp. 341–386, Proceedings of the Banff Workshop on Hardware Verification, Banff, Canada, 1988.

[18] Roscoe A. W., 'An Alternative Order for the Failures Model', in *Two Papers on* CSP, Technical Monograph PRG–67, Oxford University Computer Laboratory, Programming Research Group, July 1988.

[19] Sannella D., and Wirsing M., 'A Kernel Language for Algebraic Specification and Implementation', Technical Report CSR-131-83, University of Edinburgh, Department of Computer Science, September 1983.

[20] Stoy J. E., *Denotational Semantics: The Scott-Strachey Approach to Programming Language Theory*, MIT Press, 1977.

Partial Functions, Ordered Categories, Limits and Cartesian Closure

C. Barry Jay *

Department of Computer Science, University of Edinburgh
Department of Mathematics, University of Ottawa

cbj@lfcs.ed.ac.uk

Abstract

The natural order on partial functions should be preserved by all constructions. When this *Principle of Modularity* is observed then increasing the domain of definition of components, or modules of such a function merely enlarges its domain, without changing any of its existing values. Conversely, ignoring the principle will typically lead to the wrong concepts for pairing (products), function objects etc.

This principle arises naturally in *ordered categories*, where the homsets of the category are ordered, and composition (like all constructions there) is monotone. Then the desired products, general limits and function objects are all examples of *local* limits and adjoints, which differ from the corresponding elementary concepts in that some of the usual equations have been replaced by inequalities.

Without further constraints the properties of the resulting limits are rather weak, e.g. local products are not unique, even up to isomorphism. Their deficiencies can be removed by lifting the concept of *total function* from categories of partial functions to arbitrary ordered categories.

---

*The author is supported by SERC grants GR/E 78487 and GR/F 07866, and NSERC operating grant OGPIN 016.

1 Introduction

Partial maps are naturally ordered according to their extent of definition. Constructions on partial maps should preserve this order so that as a component or module in a construction (such as pairing or composition) becomes more defined then so does the construct as a whole, without changing any of its existing values. Yet despite the vast literature devoted to partial maps (e.g. [3, 6, 7, 16, 17]) this *Principle of Modularity* has not been given systematic attention. To do so the partial maps must be viewed as the morphisms of an ordered category, and the theory of limits, etc. developed in this context.

The usual limit theory is inadequate for ordered categories since even if the usual limits exist their constructions will typically violate the order. This can be rectified by the judicious replacement of equations by inequalities in the definition. It is expected that these results will be applicable not only to the study of partial maps, but to the many other computing situations in which ordered categories arise, such as rewrite theory, operational semantics, program transformation and refinement, domain theory etc.

The key technical idea is that total morphisms can be defined in an arbitrary ordered category, not just one of partial maps. Their presence allows one to constrain definitions by requiring that some inequalities become identities in the presence of total morphisms. Consequently, when restricted to the subcategory of total maps, the structures defined are just the usual ones (c.f. [5] for another application of this idea). Function objects (exponentials) require a slightly different treatment, as witnessed in **Sets** and ω-**Pos**, the category of ω-complete partial orders.

Some review of concepts well-established in the categorical literature, e.g. ordered categories (a special case of 2-categories), lax functors and transformations will be required. A more detailed presentation of the main concepts in this paper can be found in [12].

2 Partial Maps

Let $\mathcal{A}$ be a category. The partial maps in $\mathcal{A}$ are equivalence classes of spans (m, f) : $A \rightarrow B$ where m is a monomorphism

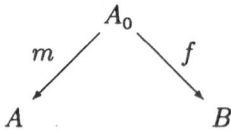

They are pre-ordered by $(m, f) \le (m', f') : A \rightarrow B$ iff there is a morphism p making the following diagram commute

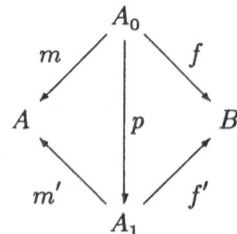

and are equivalent iff $(m, f) \leq (m', f') \leq (m, f)$ i.e. p is an isomorphism. Then m and m' represent the same subobject of A which is the *domain* of the partial map.

Composition of partial morphisms is just span composition

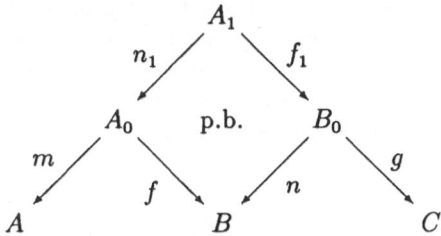

where the square in the diagram is a pullback: the composite is given by (mn_1, gf_1) : $A {\rightarrow} C$. Thus A_1 can be thought of as the largest subobject of A on which f is defined and takes values in the domain of g. Identities for composition are just $(id_A, id_A) : A {\rightarrow} A$.

Often it is appropriate to restrict the class of subobjects which are admitted as domains of partial maps to those which are computable in some sense, e.g. the r.e. subsets or opens in some topology [16, 17]. In order for composition of partial maps above to be well-defined the class $\mathcal{M}$ of monomorphisms that represent them must be a *realm* (a *dominion* in the sense of [16]) i.e. closed under: (i) composition; (ii) isomorphisms, and; (iii) pullbacks. This last condition is just the requirement that the pullback in the diagram above exists with $n_1 \in \mathcal{M}$. The corresponding subobjects are *admissible*. It follows that the admissible subobjects are closed under pairwise intersection. If they are closed under arbitrary intersection the the realm is *complete*. The resulting category of partial maps is called $\mathbf{Ptl}(\mathcal{A}, \mathcal{M})$ or just $\mathcal{A}_p$ when $\mathcal{M}$ is understood. The usual realm for **Sets** is of arbitrary subsets, and for ω-**Pos** is of open subsets in the Scott topology. There is a natural embedding $i : \mathcal{A} {\rightarrow} \mathcal{A}_p$ which is the identity on objects and maps $f : A {\rightarrow} B$ to the *total* partial map (id_A, f).

Composition of partial maps preserves the order, i.e. if $(m, f) \leq (m'f') : A {\rightarrow} B$ and $(n, g) \leq (n', g') : B {\rightarrow} C$ then

$$(n, g)(m, f) \leq (n', g')(m', f')$$

Definition 2.1 *An* ordered category *is a category $\mathcal{O}$ whose homsets are ordered, with monotone composition.* □

In general, the homsets may be pre-ordered, but it suffices below to consider partial orders. They are also known as *order-enriched* categories [15]. Examples include categories of partial maps, categories generated from typed rewrite systems with reduction as the order [18, 20], or from program refinement [9, 10], O-categories [19, 22] and categories of relations [1, 4].

In subsequent sections $(\mathcal{A}, \mathcal{M})$ and $(\mathcal{B}, \mathcal{N})$ will denote categories equipped with realms and $\mathcal{O}, \mathcal{O}'$ will denote ordered categories.

3   Total Limits

The usual notion of categorical limit is inadequate for ordered categories. Consider, for example, products in $\mathcal{A}_p$. Their existence doesn't follow from their existence in

154

$\mathcal{A}$; when they do exist they often differ from those of $\mathcal{A}$ and, most importantly; the operation of pairing may not be monotone, as we will now see.

The product of sets A and B in $\mathbf{Sets}_p$ is $A + (A \times B) + B$. A pair $\langle f, g \rangle_*$ takes values in the A-component if f is defined and g isn't, in the $A \times B$-component if they are both defined, etc. Now, replacing f by another partial map which is more defined will not merely increase the extent of definition of $\langle f, g \rangle_*$ but *change* its value, which would violate the Principle of Modularity. By contrast, consider the image in $\mathbf{Sets}_p$ of their set-theoretic product.

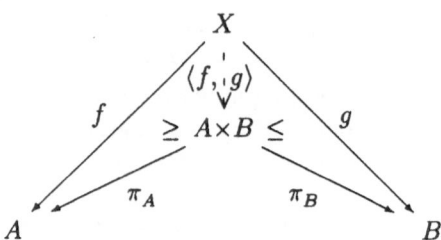

If $f = (m, f_0) : X \to A$ and $g = (n, g_0) : X \to B$ then $\langle f, g \rangle = (m \cap n, k)$ where $m \cap n$ is the diagonal of the pullback

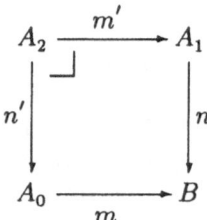

and k is the pairing of fn' and gm' in $\mathcal{A}$. In general $\langle f, g \rangle$ is less defined than either f or g, which forces the following inequalities

$$\pi_A \langle f, g \rangle \leq f \tag{1}$$
$$\pi_B \langle f, g \rangle \leq g \tag{2}$$

Further, $\langle f, g \rangle$ is maximal with this property, which implies that for any $h : X \to A \times B$ we have

$$h \leq \langle \pi_A h, \pi_B h \rangle \tag{3}$$

Motivated by this example, we generalise from products to arbitrary such limits.

Let I be a (directed multi-)graph and let $D : I \to \mathcal{O}$ be a diagram of type I in an ordered category $\mathcal{O}$. A *local limit* [11] of D is a *oplax cone* $\lambda : L \to D$ i.e.

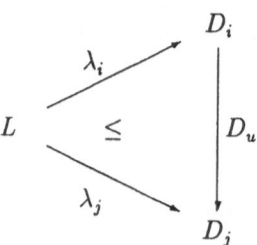

which is universal among such cones, in the following sense:

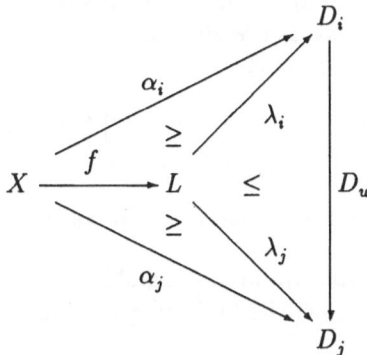

Given any other oplax cone $\alpha : X \to D$ there is a mediating morphism $f : X \to L$ such that for all vertices $i \in I$

$$\lambda_i f \le \alpha_i \qquad (4)$$

and f is the maximum such, i.e. if f' is any other morphism which satisfies (4) then $f' \le f$.

It follows that construction of the universal map is order-preserving since if $\beta : X \to D$ is another cone (with universal map g) such that $\alpha_i \le \beta_i$ for each i, then $f \le g$.

Note that local limits are not unique in any sense. For example, in $\mathbf{Sets}_p$ any subset of $A \times B$ is a local limit for A and B! To rectify this defect the definition of a local limit must be strengthened, by referring to the total morphisms, whose definition in an arbitrary ordered category is our next goal.

An endomorphism $\alpha : A \to A$ in $\mathcal{O}$ is a *deflation* if

$$\alpha^2 = \alpha \le id_A$$

An *embedding-projection pair* [19] in $\mathcal{O}$ consists of a pair of morphisms $m : A_0 \to A$ and $m_* : A \to A_0$ such that $m_* m = id_{A_0}$ and $m m_* \le 1_A$ whence $m m_*$ is a deflation.

Every admissible subobject $m : A_0 \to A$ in $\mathcal{A}$ yields an embedding $(1, m)$ in $\mathcal{A}_p$ with projection $(m, 1)$ and so generates a deflation $(m, m) : A \to A$. Conversely, every deflation in $\mathcal{A}_p$ is of this form. Thus deflations can play the role of subobjects in an arbitrary ordered category.

Definition 3.1 *A morphism $f : B \to A$ in $\mathcal{O}$ is* total *if for all morphism $g : C \to B$ and deflations $\gamma : C \to C$*

$$fg\gamma = fg \implies g\gamma = g$$

$\square$

This definition agrees with the usual one in $\mathcal{A}_p$ since pre-composition with γ is just restriction of the domain. To see this let $(m, f) : A \to B$ be a partial morphism of $\mathcal{A}$. Then $(m, f)(m, m) = (m, f)$. Hence if (m, f) is total in the above sense then $(m, m) = (id_A, id_A)$. The presence of the parameter g in the definition ensures that total morphisms are closed under composition, and so form an unordered subcategory $\mathcal{O}_t$ of $\mathcal{O}$, which contains all identities, and hence all objects.

Definition 3.2 *A local limit (L, λ) for a diagram $D : I \to \mathcal{O}$ is total (or simply, a total limit) if each of the components of λ is total and whenever $\alpha : \Delta X \to D$ is a lax cone over D whose components are all total then the mediating morphism $f : X \to L$ is total and $\lambda_i f = \alpha_i$ for all $i \in I$.* □

For example, Rosolini's p-categories [16, 17] (which include $\mathcal{A}_p$ when $\mathcal{A}$ has products) yield ordered categories with total products.

Lemma 3.3 *Total limits are unique up to isomorphism.* □

Note that if total morphisms are maximal in the order, as is the case in $\mathcal{A}_p$ then total limit cones are rigid, i.e. the limit diagram commutes.

Theorem 3.4 *Let $\mathcal{A}$ have all limits of type I. If I is finite or if the realm $\mathcal{M}$ is complete (as a category) then $\mathcal{A}_p$ has total limits of type I and the inclusion of $\mathcal{A}$ in $\mathcal{A}_p$ preserves them.*
Proof From a diagram $D : I \to \mathcal{O}$ we will build a diagram $D' : I \to \mathcal{A}$ whose limit will be the total limit of D. For each vertex i in I consider the paths beginning at i in which any loop that occurs is the whole path. Then D'_i is the intersection of the domains of these paths in D. If u is an edge in I then $D'u$ is the obvious restriction of Du. □

4 Total Lax Functors and Transformations

For ordinary (unordered) categories the existence of all limits of type I is equivalent (modulo some choice among isomorphic objects) to having a right adjoint to the diagonal functor. To express such a result for total limits requires some more machinery.

A functor $F : \mathcal{A} \to \mathcal{B}$ *defends the realm* if $m \in \mathcal{M}$ implies that $Fm \in \mathcal{N}$. Such a functor can be extended to $\mathbf{Ptl}(F) = F_p : \mathcal{A}_p \to \mathcal{B}_p$ having the same action on objects and satisfying

$$F(m, f) = (Fm, Ff) : FA \to FB$$

for $(m, f) : A \to B$. Clearly F_p preserves the ordering of partial morphisms and identities since F preserves commuting diagrams. It does not, however, preserve the composition unless F also preserves pullbacks. Given $(n, g) : B \to C$ we have instead

$$F_p((n, g)(m, f)) \leq F_p(n, g)F_p(m, f) \tag{5}$$

If, however, (n, g) is total, i.e. $n = id$, then the pullback is automatically preserved and both sides of (5) equal $(Fm, F(gf))$. Note too that F_p preserves total morphisms. This example leads us to the following

Definition 4.1 *A lax functor $F : \mathcal{O} \to \mathcal{O}'$ [2, 14] is given by a map (also called F) from the objects of $\mathcal{O}$ to those of $\mathcal{O}'$ and, for each pair A, B of objects of $\mathcal{O}$ an order-preserving function (also called F)*

$$\mathcal{O}(A, B) \longrightarrow \mathcal{O}'(FA, FB)$$

which together satisfy, for $f : A \to B$ and $g : B \to C$ in $\mathcal{O}$

$$Fg.Ff \;\leq\; F(gf) \qquad\qquad (6)$$
$$id_{FA} \;\leq\; Fid_A \qquad\qquad (7)$$

If the above inequalities are reversed then F is an oplax functor *while if they are equalities then F is a* rigid *(or sometimes* strict*) functor.*

F is a total lax (resp. oplax) functor if it is a lax (resp. oplax) functor such that whenever g is total in $\mathcal{O}$ then Fg is total and (6) is an equality. □

Where the key distinction to be made is between lax and rigid concepts then 'lax' may also refer to 'oplax' concepts. Also 'total lax' may be abbreviated to 'total'. Hence if F is a total functor then it restricts to a rigid functor $F_t : \mathcal{O}_t \to \mathcal{O}_t'$. For example, if $F : \mathcal{A} \to \mathcal{B}$ defends the realm then F_p is a total functor and $(F_p)_t = F$. Lax functors can also be used to model program behaviour [21].

Definition 4.2 *Let $F, G : \mathcal{O} \to \mathcal{O}'$ be lax functors (or, more generally, graph morphisms from some graph I into the underlying graph of $\mathcal{O}'$). An* oplax natural transformation *or* optransformation *$\beta : F \Rightarrow G : \mathcal{O} \to \mathcal{O}'$ is given by a family of morphisms $\beta_A : FA \to GA$ of $\mathcal{O}'$ indexed by the objects of $\mathcal{O}$ such that for every morphism $f : A \to B$ in $\mathcal{O}$ the following inequality holds*

$$
\begin{array}{ccc}
FA & \xrightarrow{\;\beta_A\;} & GA \\
\Big\downarrow{\scriptstyle Ff} & \leq & \Big\downarrow{\scriptstyle Gf} \\
FB & \xrightarrow[\;\beta_B\;]{} & GB
\end{array}
$$

If the squares all commute then β is a rigid transformation. *β is a* total optransformation *or* total transformation *if all of its components β_A are total, and whenever $f : A \to B$ is total then the square above commutes.* □

For example, if $\alpha : F \Rightarrow G : \mathcal{A} \to \mathcal{B}$ is a natural transformation between functors which defend the realm, then $\alpha_p : F_p \Rightarrow G_p$ given by $(\alpha_p)_A = \alpha_A$ is a total optransformation.

The natural context in which to define adjunctions is a 2-category, such as that of categories, functors and natural transformations. The ordered categories, lax functors and optransformations, however, fail to be one. The problem is that given an optransformation β as above and a lax functor $H : \mathcal{B} \to \mathcal{C}$ then the family $H\beta : HF \Rightarrow HG$ with components $H\beta_A$ is *not* in general an optransformation since for $f : A \to B$ in $\mathcal{O}$ we have

$$H\beta_B.HFf \geq H(\beta_A.Ff) \qquad\qquad (8)$$

Various attempts have been made to circumvent this problem [8, 11] with little success. However, if H and β are both total then (8) becomes an equality and $H\beta$ is a total optransformation. More precisely, the collection of ordered categories, total functors and total optransformations is a 2-category denoted **TOCat**.

Thus a *total lax adjunction* is given by total functors $F : \mathcal{O} \to \mathcal{O}'$ and $G : \mathcal{O}' \to \mathcal{O}$ with total optransformations $\eta : id \Rightarrow GF$ and $\varepsilon : FG \Rightarrow id$ (the unit and counit, respectively) which satisfy the triangle laws

$$G\varepsilon.\eta_G \ = \ id_G \tag{9}$$
$$\varepsilon_F.F\eta \ = \ id_F \tag{10}$$

This is an example of a *local adjunction* [11] since the usual isomorphisms of homsets have been replaced by adjunctions which are local to the homsets as orders (and hence categories)

$$\overline{F} \dashv \overline{G} : \mathcal{O}'(FA, B) \longrightarrow \mathcal{O}(A, GB)$$

where $\overline{F}f = \varepsilon.Ff$ and $\overline{G}g = Gg.\eta$.

Let $\mathcal{O}^I$ be the ordered category whose objects are diagrams $D : I \to \mathcal{O}$ (i.e. graph morphisms) and whose morphisms are total optransformations $\alpha : D \Rightarrow D'$ which are then ordered component-wise. Let $\Delta : \mathcal{O} \to \mathcal{O}^I$ be the (rigid) *diagonal functor* which maps an object A to the functor which is constantly A.

Theorem 4.3 *$\mathcal{O}$ has chosen total limits of type I iff $\Delta : \mathcal{O} \to \mathcal{O}^I$ has a total right adjoint lim, which is then a rigid functor. The total limit of $D : I \to \mathcal{O}$ is $(limD, \lambda_D)$ where λ is the counit of the adjunction.*

Proof Given the adjunction and a cone $\alpha : \Delta X \to D$ then the universal map is $lim\alpha.\eta : X \to limD$. Conversely, given the total limits then the action of the functor on diagram morphisms is given by the mediating morphisms between the limits. Rigidity of lim follows from totality (without which lim would be a mere oplax functor). $\square$

There is also a 2-category **RCat** of categories with realms, functors that defend them, and all their natural transformations.

Theorem 4.4 **Ptl** $= (-)_p : \mathbf{RCat} \to \mathbf{TOCat}$ *is a 2-functor. Hence it maps adjunctions to total adjunctions, and the total right adjoint is rigid.*

Proof For the last statement, note that if G is a right adjoint then it preserves all pullbacks, whence G_p is rigid. $\square$

Ptl can be viewed as a 2-functor $\mathbf{RCat} \to \mathbf{EOCat}_*$ where $\mathbf{EOCat}_*$ is a sub-2-category of **TOCat**[12]. It then has both a reflection and a coreflection which each yield a characterisations of ordered categories of partial maps.

5 Cartesian Closure

Proposition 5.1 *If $\mathcal{A}$ is cartesian closed and $\mathcal{M}$ is closed under exponentiation ($m \in \mathcal{M}$ implies $B \to m \in \mathcal{M}$ for each object B) then $(-) \times B : \mathcal{A}_p \to \mathcal{A}_p$ has a total right adjoint $(B \to (-))_p$ i.e. $\mathcal{A}_p$ has total exponentials (function objects).* $\square$

This proposition is another application of Theorem 4.4, but note that the premise is quite strong. The functor $B \to (-)$ preserves monomorphisms (since it is a right adjoint) and so the result holds for **Sets**$_p$. However, it fails for ω-**Pos**$_p$ which is not surprising since if $(B \to (-))_p$ exists then it picks out the total function space. Thus the partial function functor $B \to (-)$ must be handled separately. Consideration of this case, where partial maps can be represented by lifting, leads to the following

Definition 5.2 $\mathcal{O}$ *is partial cartesian closed if it has total products, and for each object* $B \in \mathcal{O}$ *the rigid functor* $(-) \times B$ *has a lax right adjoint* $B \rightarrow (-)$ *in the following sense:*

- $B \rightarrow (-)$ *is rigid*

- *the counit* $ev_p : (B \rightarrow -) \times B \Rightarrow id$ *is a rigid transformation*

- *the unit* $d : id \Rightarrow B \rightarrow (- \times B)$ *is a total optransformation*

- *the unit and counit satisfy the triangle equations*

- $B \rightarrow (-)$ *has image in* $\mathcal{O}_t$.

□

The definition forces $(-) \times B \dashv B \rightarrow (-) : \mathcal{O} \rightarrow \mathcal{O}_t$ as mere categories, which shows that the choice of $B \rightarrow (-)$ is unique up to isomorphism. Note that in **Sets**$_p$ the functor $(-) \times B$ has both kinds of lax right adjoint, i.e. total and partial function spaces. The differences between the two local adjoints can be highlighted by comparing the naturality squares for their evaluations, ev and ev_p respectively.

$$
\begin{array}{ccc}
(B \rightarrow C) \times B \xrightarrow{ev} C & \qquad & (B \rightarrow C) \times B \xrightarrow{ev_p} C \\
\Big\downarrow{\scriptstyle B \rightarrow h \times B} \quad \leq \quad \Big\downarrow{\scriptstyle h} & & \Big\downarrow{\scriptstyle B \rightarrow h \times B} \qquad \Big\downarrow{\scriptstyle h} \\
(B \rightarrow C') \times B \xrightarrow{ev} C' & & (B \rightarrow C') \times B \xrightarrow{ev_p} C'
\end{array}
$$

6 Further Work

The theory of colimits poses further difficulties that arise from the need for exactness conditions, e.g. if $\mathcal{M}$ is closed under sums then $\mathcal{A}_p$ has total sums (i.e. a left total adjoint to the diagonal). Together with the limits, these concepts should be applied to the study of partial algebras by developing partial algebraic theories in the style of Lawvere. As noted above, more than one notion of lax adjoint is required to describe total cartesian closure. Can these be better united? It remains to pursue the consequences for the study of computation, program transformation, etc.

References

[1] M. Barr, *Relational algebras*, in: *Reports of the Midwest Category Seminar*, Lecture Notes in Mathematics 47 (Springer, 1970) 39-55.

[2] J. Benabou, *Introduction to bicategories*, in: *Lecture Notes in Mathematics* 47, (Springer-Verlag, 1973) 1-77.

[3] A. Carboni, *Bicategories of partial maps*, Cah. de Top. et Géom. Diff. 28(2) (1987).

[4] A. Carboni, S. Kasangian and R. Street, *Bicategories of spans and relations*, J. Pure and Appl. Alg. 33 (1984) 259 – 267.

[5] A. Carboni, G.M. Kelly and R.J. Wood, *A 2-categorical approach to geometric morphisms, I*, Sydney Category Seminar Reports 89–19 (1989).

[6] P.L. Curien and A. Obtulowicz, *Partiality and cartesian closedness*, preprint (1986).

[7] R. diPaola and A. Heller, *Dominical categories: recursion theory without elements*, J. Symb. Log. 52 (1986) 594–635.

[8] J.W. Gray, *Formal category theory: adjointness for 2-categories*, Lecture Notes in Mathematics 391 (Springer-Verlag, 1974).

[9] C.A.R. Hoare and He, Jifeng, *Data refinement in a categorical setting*, Oxford University Computing Laboratory (1988).

[10] C.A.R. Hoare, He Jifeng and C.E. Martin, *Pre-adjunctions in order enriched categories*, Oxford University Computing Laboratory (1989).

[11] C.B. Jay, *Local adjunctions*, J. Pure and Appl. Alg. 53 (1988) 227–238.

[12] C.B. Jay, *Extendinging properties to categories of partial maps*, LFCS Tech. Rep. 90-107.

[13] C.B. Jay, *Fixpoint and loop constructions as colimits*, preprint.

[14] G.M. Kelly and R. Street, *Review of the elements of 2-categories*, in: *Category Seminar Sydney 1972/73*, Lecture Notes in Mathematics 240 (Springer,1974) 75–103.

[15] G.M. Kelly, *Basic Concepts of Enriched Category Theory*, London Mathematical Society Lecture Note Series 64 (Cambridge University Press, 1982).

[16] G. Rosolini, *Continuity and effectiveness in topoi*, D. Phil. thesis, University of Oxford, 1986.

[17] G. Rosolini and E. Robinson, *Categories of partial maps*, Inf. and Comp. 79(2) (1988) 95–130.

[18] D.E. Rydeheard and J.G. Stell, *Foundations of equational deduction: A categorical treatment of equational proofs and unification algorithms*, in: Pitt et al, (eds), *Category Theory and Computer Science*, Lecture Notes in Computer Science 283 (Springer, 1987) 114 – 139.

[19] M.B. Smyth and G.D. Plotkin, *The category-theoretic solution of recursive domain equations*, SIAM J. of Comp. 11 (1982).

[20] R.A.G. Seely, *Modelling computations: a 2-categorical framework*, in: *Proceedings of the Second Annual Symposium on Logic in Computer Science* (1987).

[21] B. Steffen, C.B. Jay and M. Mendler, *Compositional characterization of observable program properties*, Laboratory for Foundations of Computer Science, Report 89-99.

[22] M. Wand, *Fixed-point constructions in order-enriched categories*, Theoretical Computer Science 8 (1979) 13–30.

Evaluation Logic

Andrew M. Pitts*

University of Cambridge Computer Laboratory
Cambridge CB2 3QG England

Andrew.Pitts@cl.cam.ac.uk

Abstract

A new typed, higher-order logic is described which appears particularly well fitted to reasoning about forms of computation whose operational behaviour can be specified using the *Natural Semantics* style of structural operational semantics [5]. The logic's underlying type system is Moggi's *computational metalanguage* [11], which enforces a distinction between computations and values via the categorical structure of a strong monad. This is extended to a (constructive) predicate logic with modal formulas about evaluation of computations to values, called *evaluation modalities*. The categorical structure corresponding to this kind of logic is explained and a couple of examples of categorical models given.

As a first example of the naturalness and applicability of this new logic to program semantics, we investigate the translation of a (tiny) fragment of Standard ML into a theory over the logic, which is proved computationally adequate for ML's Natural Semantics [10]. Whilst it is tiny, the ML fragment does however contain both higher-order functional and imperative features, about which the logic allows us to reason without having to mention global states explicitly.

---

*Research supported by the CLICS project (ESPRIT BR Action nr 3003).

1 Introduction

Higher-order metalogics based on typed lambda calculi (such as Scott's LCF [20] and Plotkin's formalizations of domain-theoretic denotational semantics [19]) have been used to give semantics to programming languages via formal translations of programming language syntax into the types and terms of the metalogic. The basic features of such translations are their compositionality (i.e. the translation of a compound program expression depends only on the translations of its subexpressions) and that they adequately capture (via provability within the metalogic) the intended operational behaviour of program expressions. Armed with such a translation, amongst other things we can—at least in theory—use the metalogic to reason formally about program behaviours. The ease with which this can be done in practice depends partly on the 'naturalness' of the translation, which in turn depends on how well-fitted the logical forms of expression permitted by the metalogic are to programming language features and their operational semantics.

In this paper we will describe the core of a new metalogic, called *Evaluation Logic*, which appears particularly well fitted to reasoning about forms of computation that can be specified using a style of operational semantics known as *Natural Semantics*. The latter defines the behaviour of the phrases of a programming language via relations such as

$$State, Phrase \Rightarrow State', Value$$

which are inductively defined by rules reflecting the *structure* of program phrases. This style of operational semantics is a particular case of the structural approach of Plotkin [18]. It was developed independently in the context of intuitionistic type theory by P. Martin-Löf (see [15]), and has been further refined and developed by Milner, Kahn [5] and others. A large-scale example of Natural Semantics is provided by the official definition of the Standard ML language [10].

The starting point of the ideas described in this paper is the recent work by Moggi [11, 12, 13] making use of the categorical notion of a *strong monad* as a powerful organizing tool in the denotational semantics of programming languages. (See Gunter and Scott [4] and Mosses [14] for a survey of existing techniques in this area.) Roughly speaking, Moggi's viewpoint is that particular notions of computation can be modelled by various monads T on suitable categories of semantic domains: if datavalues of a particular type are modelled by a domain D, then the denotations of computations of data of that type lie in the domain $T(D)$. The efficacy of this viewpoint is borne out in Moggi's work not only by many concrete examples of monads, but also by the fact that these examples can be built up in a modular way by applying monad constructors corresponding to different features of computations. Instead of building new monads from old using monad constructors, one might consider *axiomatizing* extra, computation-related properties of a single strong monad within the framework of a suitable logic. It is the question of what is a suitable logic for doing this which is addressed in this paper.

There already exists an elegant equational logic of typed terms corresponding to the notion of strong monad (in the same way that the simply-typed lambda calculus corresponds to cartesian closedness). This is Moggi's *computational lambda calculus*, which we review in Section 2. As well as product and function types, this calculus contains *computation types*, $T\sigma$, with two associated term-forming operations capturing the structure of a strong monad. The first operation associates to a term M of type σ a term $[M]$ of type $T\sigma$, whose intended meaning is 'the computation which immediately evaluates to the value M'. The second operation associates to terms $E{:}T\sigma$ and $F(x){:}T\sigma'$ (the second depending upon a variable $x{:}\sigma$), a term

$$\text{let } x \Leftarrow E \text{ in } F(x)$$

of type $T\sigma'$, intended to denote a basic form of sequential composition: '*first* evaluate E, bind the result to the parameter x and *then* evaluate $F(x)$'.

Such informal statements about evaluation of computations—giving the intended interpretation of computation terms—are not captured directly in Moggi's computational lambda calculus, which instead gives certain basic *equations* between computations analogous to beta and eta conversion for lambda terms. In this paper we will extend the computational lambda calculus to a constructive predicate logic which permits the formulation of statements about *evaluation of computations to values*, and which accordingly we call *Evaluation Logic*. This is achieved by means of *evaluation modalities* which to each formula $\phi(x)$ containing a free variable $x{:}\sigma$, and to each term $E{:}T\sigma$, assign formulas

$$[x \Leftarrow E]\phi(x) \qquad \text{and} \qquad \langle x \Leftarrow E \rangle \phi(x)$$

in which x becomes a bound variable. The intended meaning of the first formula is 'if E evaluates to x, then necessarily $\phi(x)$ holds', whilst the intended meaning of the second is 'it is possible for E to evaluate to an x for which $\phi(x)$ holds'. These evaluation modalities have as derived forms predicates asserting evaluation of computations to values, and convergence and divergence of computations; they can also be used to formulate partial and total correctness statements in a natural way—see Remark 3.2.8.

The evaluation modalities and their rules of inference are described in Section 3. Their presence makes Evaluation Logic reminiscent of Dynamic Logic (see Kozen and Tiuryn [7] for a survey of the latter). Indeed the forms of modalities which appear in Dynamic Logic are the particular cases of evaluation modalities with σ the unit type 1 (the type containing a unique element up to equality). However, the motivation for formulating Evaluation Logic came more from the Natural Semantics style of operational semantics mentioned above. In Section 4 we give a simple example of translating programming language features into an Evaluation Logic *theory* adequately capturing operational behaviour specified in Natural Semantics. The example concerns a fragment of Standard ML containing both functional features (higher-order recursive function declarations) and imperative features (assignable global variables).

Metatheoretical conventions

Evaluation Logic, and the computational lambda calculus over which it is based, contain several unfamiliar variable-binding operations. We deal with these in a uniform way by adopting the increasingly common device (advocated by Aczel, Klop [6] and Martin-Löf [15] amongst others) of using a *higher-order* metalanguage to specify the syntax of object-language expressions. For our purposes here, it is sufficient to use a typed λ-calculus over a single ground type EXP (the type of object expressions), with meta-terms identified up to $\alpha\beta\eta$-conversion. Lambda abstraction in this metalanguage will be denoted by $(x)e$. Meta-application will be denoted by $e(e')$, with a multiple application such as $e(e')(e'')$ abbreviated to $e(e', e'')$. The result of substitution of a meta-term e for a meta-variable x throughout a meta-term e' will be denoted $e'(e/x)$.

In this way, the only variable binding takes place via lambda abstraction in the meta-language, and whilst object-language expressions may contain object-variables, no concept of a *free* object-variable is needed.

Acknowledgements

The work described here has benefited greatly from discussions with E. Moggi, upon whose work it builds, and also from discussions with the other members of the CLICS Project in Cambridge.

2 Computational Lambda Calculus

In this section we review, in a semi-formal style, Moggi's computational metalanguage [11, 13], which adds *computation types* to equational logic over the standard simply typed lambda calculus with unit type 1, product types $\sigma \times \sigma'$ and function types $\sigma \to \sigma'$.

In the calculus, the unique (up to provable equality) element of the unit type 1 will be denoted $\langle \rangle$. First and second projection from a product type will be denoted by *fst* and *snd*, and pairing denoted by $\langle \_, \_ \rangle$; surjective pairing axioms form part of the equational logic. Typed lambda abstraction will be denoted by $\lambda x{:}\sigma.F(x)$, and application by MM'; beta and eta conversion axioms form part of the equational logic. We omit further details and concentrate instead on the rules for computation types.

To formulate these, we will be a little more precise about the allowed forms of judgement in the computational lambda calculus, which are

$$x_1{:}\sigma_1, \ldots, x_n{:}\sigma_n \;\vdash\; M : \sigma$$
$$x_1{:}\sigma_1, \ldots, x_n{:}\sigma_n \;\vdash\; M = M' : \sigma$$

The intended meaning of these judgements is 'M is a term of type σ, given that the variables $x_1, \ldots, x_n$ have types $\sigma_1, \ldots, \sigma_n$ respectively' and 'M and M' are equal terms of type σ, given that the variables $x_1, \ldots, x_n$ have types $\sigma_1, \ldots, \sigma_n$ respectively'.

Remark 2.0.1 It will be a derived property of the systems we consider that for a given set of typing assumptions, a term has at most one type. Consequently we can abbreviate the second form of judgement to

$$x_1{:}\sigma_1, \ldots, x_n{:}\sigma_n \vdash M = M'$$

without ambiguity.

The finite list on the left-hand side of the '$\vdash$' symbol in the above judgements will be called a *context* and typically abbreviated to Γ. Only judgements satisfying the well-formedness conditions

- the variables $x_1, \ldots, x_n$ are distinct

- the variables occurring in M lie in the list $x_1, \ldots, x_n$

will be considered. In particular, in giving rule schemes for generating judgements we assume that both the hypotheses and conclusion are well-formed—this obviates the need for side-conditions in certain rules. We will denote by $\Gamma, x{:}\sigma$ a context Γ extended by assigning type σ to a variable x not occurring in Γ; similarly Γ, Γ' denotes juxtaposed contexts with disjoint sets of variables. We omit the standard rules relating to the structure of contexts and the usual properties of equality.

2.1 Computation types

If σ is a type, so is $T\sigma$. The term-forming rules are

$$\textbf{values} \qquad \frac{\Gamma \vdash M : \sigma}{\Gamma \vdash [M] : T\sigma}$$

$$\textbf{sequential composition} \qquad \frac{\Gamma \vdash E : T\sigma \quad \Gamma, x{:}\sigma \vdash F(x) : T\sigma'}{\Gamma \vdash let\, x{\Leftarrow}E\, in\, F(x) : T\sigma'}$$

Remark 2.1.1 Using the metatheoretical conventions mentioned in the Introduction, we should really write $let\, x{\Leftarrow}E\, in\, F(x)$ as $let(E, F)$—in other words, let is a meta-constant of type $\text{EXP}{\rightarrow}(\text{EXP}{\rightarrow}\text{EXP}){\rightarrow}\text{EXP}$. More trivially, a similar remark applies to value terms which, formally, make use of a meta-contant of type $\text{EXP}{\rightarrow}\text{EXP}$.

We think of terms of type $T\sigma$ as the (denotations of) 'computations of elements of type σ'. The intended meaning of the the value term $[M]$ is the trivial computation: 'immediately return the value M'. The intended meaning of the term $let\, x{\Leftarrow}E\, in\, F(x)$ is the following form of sequential composition of computations: 'first evaluate E, to x say, and then evaluate $F(x)$'. The reader may verify that the following equality rules respect these informal interpretations:

$$\frac{\Gamma \vdash M : \sigma \quad \Gamma, x{:}\sigma \vdash F(x) : T\sigma'}{\Gamma \vdash let\, x{\Leftarrow}[M]\, in\, F(x) = F(M)} \qquad \frac{}{e{:}T\sigma \vdash let\, x{\Leftarrow}e\, in\, [x] = e}$$

$$\frac{\Gamma \vdash E : T\sigma \quad \Gamma, x{:}\sigma \vdash F(x) : T\sigma' \quad \Gamma, x'{:}T\sigma' \vdash G(x') : T\sigma''}{\Gamma \vdash let\, x'{\Leftarrow}(let\, x{\Leftarrow}E\, in\, F(x))\, in\, G(x') = let\, x{\Leftarrow}E\, in\, (let\, x'{\Leftarrow}F(x)\, in\, G(x'))}$$

This completes our review of the computational lambda calculus. Note that it is a *higher-order* calculus not only in the usual sense of permitting the formation of functionals of higher types (iterating the function-type constructor), but also because it permits the formation of computations of computations, and so on (iterating the computation-type constructor).

2.2 Categorical models

The interpretation in a cartesian closed category of the unit, product and function types and their associated terms and equations is well known: see Lambek and Scott [8], for example. Here we merely recall the overall shape of this interpretation in one particular formulation. Using finite products and exponentials in the cartesian closed category $\mathcal{C}$, an object $[\![\sigma]\!]$ of $\mathcal{C}$ is assigned to each type σ by induction on its structure. Similarly, by induction on the structure of terms M, each derivable typing judgement $\Gamma \vdash M : \sigma$ gives rise to a morphism in $\mathcal{C}$

$$[\![\Gamma \vdash M : \sigma]\!] : [\![\Gamma]\!] \longrightarrow [\![\sigma]\!]$$

whose domain is by definition the finite product

$$[\![\Gamma]\!] \stackrel{\text{def}}{=} [\![\sigma_1]\!] \times \cdots \times [\![\sigma_n]\!]$$

when the context Γ is $x_1{:}\sigma_1, \ldots, x_n{:}\sigma_n$. The interpretation satisfies all provable equalities, in the sense that if $\Gamma \vdash M = M' : \sigma$ is derivable then $[\![\Gamma \vdash M : \sigma]\!]$ and $[\![\Gamma \vdash M' : \sigma]\!]$ are equal morphisms in $\mathcal{C}$.

Moggi has shown that to interpret computation types and their associated terms and equations in $\mathcal{C}$, one needs to give the extra structure of a *strong monad* on $\mathcal{C}$. This is a functor $T : \mathcal{C} \longrightarrow \mathcal{C}$ equipped with natural transformations

$$
\begin{array}{rcll}
\eta_X & : & X \longrightarrow T(X) & \text{(unit)} \\
\mu_X & : & T(T(X)) \longrightarrow T(X) & \text{(multiplication)} \\
t_{X,Y} & : & X \times T(Y) \longrightarrow T(X \times Y) & \text{(strength)}
\end{array}
$$

satisfying a number of commutative diagrams (seven, in fact)—see [11] for the full definition in this form. An equivalent definition, which is both simpler and closer to the syntax of computation types, is that of 'indexed Kleisli triple'. This is specified by a map on objects, sending X to $T(X)$, together with the following data

unit: for each object X, a morphism $\eta_X : X \longrightarrow T(X)$

lifting: for each morphism $f : X \times Y \longrightarrow T(Z)$, a morphism

$$f^* : X \times T(Y) \longrightarrow T(Z)$$

satisfying the following conditions, the first of which expresses naturality of lifting in the parameter X and the rest of which are parameterized versions of the usual axioms for a Kleisli triple (see [11, Definition 1.2]).

- given $f : X \longrightarrow X'$ and $g : X' \times Y \longrightarrow T(Z)$, then

$$(g \circ (f \times id_Y))^* = g^* \circ (f \times id_{T(Y)})$$

- given $f : X \times Y \longrightarrow T(Z)$, then $f^* \circ (id_X \times \eta_Y) = f$

- $(\eta_Y \circ \pi_2)^* = \pi_2 : X \times T(Y) \longrightarrow T(Y)$

- given $f : X \times Y \longrightarrow T(Z)$ and $g : X \times Z \longrightarrow T(W)$, then

$$(g^* \circ \langle \pi_1, f \rangle)^* = g^* \circ \langle \pi_1, f^* \rangle$$

(where the π_i are appropriate projection morphisms and $\langle,\rangle$ denotes pairing of morphisms).

Given such a structure on $\mathcal{C}$, we extend the interpretation of types as objects of $\mathcal{C}$ by defining

$$\llbracket T\sigma \rrbracket \overset{\text{def}}{=} T(\llbracket \sigma \rrbracket)$$

and extend the interpretation of terms by defining

$$\llbracket \Gamma \vdash [M] : T\sigma \rrbracket \overset{\text{def}}{=} \eta_{\llbracket \sigma \rrbracket} \circ \llbracket \Gamma \vdash M : \sigma \rrbracket$$

and

$$\llbracket \Gamma \vdash \text{let } x \!\Leftarrow\! E \text{ in } F(x) : T\sigma' \rrbracket \overset{\text{def}}{=} f^* \circ \langle id_{\llbracket \Gamma \rrbracket}, \llbracket \Gamma \vdash E : T\sigma \rrbracket \rangle$$

where f is $\llbracket \Gamma, x{:}\sigma \vdash F(x) : T\sigma' \rrbracket : \llbracket \Gamma \rrbracket \times \llbracket \sigma \rrbracket \longrightarrow T\llbracket \sigma' \rrbracket$. The conditions on unit and lifting given above ensure that this interpretation satisfies the equalities in 2.1.

3   Evaluation modalities

The informal interpretation of the value and sequential composition terms was given in Section 2.1 in terms of a relation of evaluation between computations and values (of a given type). In the computational lambda calculus, this intended meaning is only indirectly captured through its equational consequences. We are now going to embed the computational lambda calculus in a typed predicate logic containing not only atomic formulas for equality at each type, but also formulas expressing evaluation of computations to values. In fact evaluation will not be an atomic formula, but rather will be derived from 'modal quantifiers' which are really the key feature of the logic. The logic also contains propositional connectives: in this paper we will only consider conjunction and (intuitionistic) disjunction.

3.1   Formulas

To introduce the allowed formulas, we will give rules for deriving jugements of the form

$$\Gamma \vdash \phi \text{ prop}$$

where as in the previous section, $\Gamma = x_1{:}\sigma_1, \ldots, x_n{:}\sigma_n$ is a context assigning types to variables. To be well-formed, the above judgement must satisfy the condition that the variables occurring in ϕ lie in Γ. The intended meaning of the judgement is of course that 'ϕ is a well-formed proposition, given that the variables $x_1, \ldots, x_n$ have types $\sigma_1, \ldots, \sigma_n$ respectively'. The rules for deriving such judgements are:

Equality

$$\frac{\Gamma \vdash M : \sigma \quad \Gamma \vdash M' : \sigma}{\Gamma \vdash M = M' \text{ prop}}$$

Finite conjunction

$$\frac{}{\vdash true \text{ prop}} \qquad \frac{\Gamma \vdash \phi \text{ prop} \quad \Gamma \vdash \psi \text{ prop}}{\Gamma \vdash \phi \wedge \psi \text{ prop}}$$

Finite disjunction

$$\frac{}{\vdash \textit{false} \; \text{prop}} \qquad \frac{\Gamma \vdash \phi \; \text{prop} \quad \Gamma \vdash \psi \; \text{prop}}{\Gamma \vdash \phi \vee \psi \; \text{prop}}$$

Evaluation modalities

$$\frac{\Gamma \vdash E : T\sigma \quad \Gamma, x{:}\sigma \vdash \phi(x) \; \text{prop}}{\Gamma \vdash [x{\Leftarrow}E]\phi(x) \; \text{prop}} \qquad \frac{\Gamma \vdash E : T\sigma \quad \Gamma, x{:}\sigma \vdash \phi(x) \; \text{prop}}{\Gamma \vdash \langle x{\Leftarrow}E\rangle\phi(x) \; \text{prop}}$$

The intended meaning of $[x{\Leftarrow}E]\phi(x)$ is: 'if E evaluates to x, then necessarily $\phi(x)$ holds'. The intended meaning of $\langle x{\Leftarrow}E\rangle\phi(x)$ is: 'it is possible for E to evaluate to an x for which $\phi(x)$ holds'.

Remark 3.1.1 Just as in Remark 2.1.1, we note that the above notation is an informal one which has been adopted for readability. Thus $[x{\Leftarrow}E]\phi(x)$ and $\langle x{\Leftarrow}E\rangle\phi(x)$ stand for $\Box(E, \phi)$ and $\Diamond(E, \phi)$ respectively, where $\Box$ and $\Diamond$ are meta-constants of the higher type $\text{EXP}{\rightarrow}(\text{EXP}{\rightarrow}\text{EXP}){\rightarrow}\text{EXP}$.

3.2 Entailment

To specify the logical properties of the above formulas, we will give rules for deriving judgements of the form

$$\Gamma, \Phi \vdash \psi$$

where Γ is a context (as defined in Section 2), Φ is a finite set of formulas, ψ is a formula, and the variables occurring in Φ and ψ lie in Γ. The intended meaning of the judgement is an intuitionistic sequent asserting 'ψ is logically entailed by the hypotheses Φ'. As usual, if Φ is empty, a singleton $\{\phi\}$, or a union $\Phi_1 \cup \Phi_2$, we write $\Gamma, \Phi \vdash \psi$ as

$$\Gamma \vdash \psi, \qquad \Gamma, \phi \vdash \psi \quad \text{and} \quad \Gamma, \Phi_1, \Phi_2 \vdash \psi$$

respectively. Finally, we will write

$$\Gamma, \phi \dashv\vdash \psi$$

to indicate that both $\Gamma, \phi \vdash \psi$ and $\Gamma, \psi \vdash \phi$ are derivable.

The rules concerning the logical properties of equality, conjunction and disjunction are the standard rules for this fragment of intuitionistic predicate calculus (see Dummett [3]). Note that with the conventions mentioned in the previous paragraph, the equality judgement

$$\Gamma \vdash M = M'$$

used in Section 2 is now taken as the particular instance of the entailment judgement with no hypothesis formulas and conclusion formula $M = M'$. So we can use the rules of the computational lambda calculus concerning product, function and computation types to derive entailment judgements. Finally, the rules concerning evaluation modalities are as follows.

3.2.1 Evaluation modalities preserve entailment:

$$\frac{\Gamma \vdash E : T\sigma \quad \Gamma, x{:}\sigma, \phi(x) \vdash \psi(x)}{\Gamma, [x{\Leftarrow}E]\phi(x) \vdash [x{\Leftarrow}E]\psi(x)} \qquad \frac{\Gamma \vdash E : T\sigma \quad \Gamma, x{:}\sigma, \phi(x) \vdash \psi(x)}{\Gamma, \langle x{\Leftarrow}E\rangle\phi(x) \vdash \langle x{\Leftarrow}E\rangle\psi(x)}$$

3.2.2 Values:

$$\frac{\Gamma \vdash M : \sigma \quad \Gamma, x{:}\sigma \vdash \phi(x) \text{ prop}}{\Gamma, \phi(M) \dashv\vdash [x{\Leftarrow}[M]]\phi(x)} \qquad \frac{\Gamma \vdash M : \sigma \quad \Gamma, x{:}\sigma \vdash \phi(x) \text{ prop}}{\Gamma, \phi(M) \dashv\vdash \langle x{\Leftarrow}[M]\rangle\phi(x)}$$

3.2.3 Sequential composition:

$$\frac{\Gamma \vdash E : T\sigma \quad \Gamma, x{:}\sigma \vdash F(x) : T\sigma' \quad \Gamma, x'{:}T\sigma' \vdash \psi(x') \text{ prop}}{\Gamma, [x{\Leftarrow}E][x'{\Leftarrow}F(x)]\psi(x') \dashv\vdash [x'{\Leftarrow}(let\ x{\Leftarrow}E\ in\ F(x))]\psi(x')}$$

$$\frac{\Gamma \vdash E : T\sigma \quad \Gamma, x{:}\sigma \vdash F(x) : T\sigma' \quad \Gamma, x'{:}T\sigma' \vdash \psi(x') \text{ prop}}{\Gamma, \langle x{\Leftarrow}E\rangle\langle x'{\Leftarrow}F(x)\rangle\psi(x') \dashv\vdash \langle x'{\Leftarrow}(let\ x{\Leftarrow}E\ in\ F(x))\rangle\psi(x')}$$

3.2.4 Necessity modality preserves finite conjunctions:

$$\frac{}{x{:}\sigma, e{:}T\sigma \vdash [x{\Leftarrow}e]true}$$

$$\frac{\Gamma \vdash E : T\sigma \quad \Gamma, x{:}\sigma \vdash \phi(x) \text{ prop} \quad \Gamma, x{:}\sigma \vdash \psi(x) \text{ prop}}{\Gamma, [x{\Leftarrow}E]\phi(x), [x{\Leftarrow}E]\psi(x) \vdash [x{\Leftarrow}E](\phi(x) \wedge \psi(x))}$$

3.2.5 Possibility modality preserves finite disjunctions:

$$\frac{}{x{:}\sigma, e{:}T\sigma, \langle x{\Leftarrow}e\rangle false \vdash false}$$

$$\frac{\Gamma \vdash E : T\sigma \quad \Gamma, x{:}\sigma \vdash \phi(x) \text{ prop} \quad \Gamma, x{:}\sigma \vdash \psi(x) \text{ prop}}{\Gamma, \langle x{\Leftarrow}E\rangle(\phi(x) \vee \psi(x)) \vdash \langle x{\Leftarrow}E\rangle\phi(x) \vee \langle x{\Leftarrow}E\rangle\psi(x)}$$

3.2.6 Possibility and necessity:

$$\frac{\Gamma \vdash E : T\sigma \quad \Gamma, x{:}\sigma \vdash \phi(x) \text{ prop} \quad \Gamma, x{:}\sigma \vdash \psi(x) \text{ prop}}{\Gamma, [x{\Leftarrow}E]\phi(x), \langle x{\Leftarrow}E\rangle\psi(x) \vdash \langle x{\Leftarrow}E\rangle(\phi(x) \wedge \psi(x))}$$

3.2.7 Possibility and equality:

$$\frac{\Gamma \vdash E : T\sigma \quad \Gamma \vdash N : \sigma' \quad \Gamma \vdash N' : \sigma' \quad \Gamma, x{:}\sigma \vdash \phi(x) \text{ prop}}{\Gamma, N = N' \wedge \langle x{\Leftarrow}E\rangle\phi(x) \dashv\vdash \langle x{\Leftarrow}E\rangle(N = N' \wedge \phi(x))}$$

Remark 3.2.8 Using equality, truth and falsity, we get derived formulas asserting *evaluation* of computations to values, and *convergence* and *divergence* of computations:

$$E \Rightarrow M \overset{\text{def}}{=} \langle x{\Leftarrow}E\rangle(x = M) \quad \text{'}E \text{ can evaluate to } M\text{'}$$
$$E{\Downarrow} \overset{\text{def}}{=} \langle x{\Leftarrow}E\rangle true \quad \text{'}E \text{ can converge'}$$
$$E{\Uparrow} \overset{\text{def}}{=} [x{\Leftarrow}E]false \quad \text{'}E \text{ must diverge'}$$

One can also formulate partial and total correctness statements quite naturally in this language. Given a formula specifying an input-output relation from σ to σ'

$$\Gamma, x{:}\sigma, x'{:}\sigma' \vdash \psi(x, x') \text{ prop}$$

and a formula restricting the domain of admissible inputs

$$\Gamma, x{:}\sigma \vdash \phi(x) \text{ prop}$$

then we may say that a computation $\Gamma, x{:}\sigma \vdash F(x) : T\sigma'$ is partially correct for the specification if

$$\Gamma, x{:}\sigma, \phi(x) \vdash [x' {\Leftarrow} F(x)]\psi(x, x')$$

is derivable, and totally correct if

$$\Gamma, x{:}\sigma, \phi(x) \vdash [x' {\Leftarrow} F(x)]\psi(x, x') \wedge F(x){\Downarrow}$$

is derivable. Note that from rule 3.2.6, the conclusion of the second judgement entails $\langle x' {\Leftarrow} F(x)\rangle\psi(x, x')$.

We mention some simple consequences of the rules for evaluation modalities.

Proposition 3.2.9 *(i) Using the definition given in Remark 3.2.8 for the formula $E \Rightarrow M$, expressing evaluation of $E{:}T\sigma$ to $M{:}\sigma$, the following rules are derivable.*

$$\frac{\Gamma \vdash M : \sigma}{\Gamma \vdash [M] \Rightarrow M} \qquad \frac{\Gamma \vdash E \Rightarrow M \quad \Gamma \vdash F(E) \Rightarrow M'}{\Gamma \vdash (\text{let } x {\Leftarrow} E \text{ in } F(x)) \Rightarrow M'}$$

Thus in the logic we indeed get a formalization of the intended behaviour mentioned in Section 2.1 of value and sequential composition terms under evaluation

(ii) The judgement

$$x{:}\sigma, x'{:}\sigma, [x] = [x'] \vdash x = x'$$

is derivable. This expresses the 'mono condition' on the unit of the strong monad T —see [11].

□

Remark 3.2.10 We indicate briefly the relation between our evaluation modalities and the propositional modal operators of existing program logics, which take the form

$$[P]\phi \qquad \text{and} \qquad \langle P\rangle\phi$$

with P a program and ϕ a proposition. (See Kozen and Tiuryn [7] for a survey.)

The first point is that *we can interpret (the denotation of) programs as computations of unit type, i.e. as terms of type $T(1)$.* Termination of the program corresponds to evaluation of $P{:}T(1)$ to the unique value $\langle\rangle{:}1$. (This idea can be seen in practice in the language Standard ML [10], which combines higher-order functional and imperative features: see Section 4.)

Secondly, since every term of type 1 is provably equal to $\langle\rangle$, specifying a formula $\phi(x)$ depending on a variable $x{:}1$ amounts to specifying a formula $\phi(\langle\rangle)$ depending upon no variables, i.e. a proposition. Given $P{:}T(1)$ and a proposition ϕ, the evaluation modalities yield new propositions $[x{\Leftarrow}P]\phi$ and $\langle x{\Leftarrow}P\rangle\phi$ which we abbreviate to $[P]\phi$ and $\langle P\rangle\phi$ respectively.

Specializing the rules given above for evaluation modalities to the case $\sigma = 1$, we obtain some standard properties of the program modalities, such as:

$$
\begin{aligned}
[P]\phi \wedge \langle P\rangle\psi &\vdash \langle P\rangle(\phi \wedge \psi) \\
[skip]\phi &\dashv\vdash \phi \\
\phi &\dashv\vdash \langle skip\rangle\phi \\
[P;P']\phi &\dashv\vdash [P][P']\phi \\
\langle P;P'\rangle &\dashv\vdash \langle P\rangle\langle P'\rangle\phi
\end{aligned}
$$

where $skip$ stands for the value term $[\langle\,\rangle]$ and $P;P'$ for the sequential composition $let\ x{\Leftarrow}P\ in\ P'$ of two terms of type $T(1)$. Moreover, the equality rules for computation types in Section 2.1 imply associativity and unitary laws:

$$
\begin{aligned}
&\vdash\ (P;P');P'' = P;(P';P'') \\
&\vdash\ skip;P = P \\
&\vdash\ P;skip = P
\end{aligned}
$$

3.3   Categorical models

In Section 2.2 we reviewed how Moggi's computational lambda calculus is interpreted in a cartesian closed category, $\mathcal{C}$, equipped with a strong monad, T. To extend the interpretation to the predicate logic described above, we use the standard technique of categorical logic originating with Lawvere [9] of interpreting formulas in a suitable 'hyperdoctrine' over $\mathcal{C}$. Since here we are only considering provability rather than proofs, it is sufficient to consider the case of hyperdoctrines which are $\mathcal{C}$-*indexed meet semilattices*, $\mathcal{P}$, equipped with suitable extra structure appropriate to the particular logic under consideration. Thus $\mathcal{P}$ is at least a contravariant functor on $\mathcal{C}$ valued in the category meet semilattices (the category whose objects are posets possessing meets of all finite subsets (including the empty meet), and whose morphisms are functions which preserve finite meets). In other words, for each object X of $\mathcal{C}$ one has a meet semilattice $\mathcal{P}(X)$ of 'properties' of X; and for each morphism $f : X \longrightarrow Y$ in $\mathcal{C}$ one has a function $\mathcal{P}(f) : \mathcal{P}(Y) \longrightarrow \mathcal{P}(X)$ of 'substitution along f' which preserves finite meets. The action of $\mathcal{P}(f)$ on $B \in \mathcal{P}(Y)$ will be written $f^{-1}B$. Contravariant functoriality of $\mathcal{P}$ means that one has $id^{-1}B = B$ and $g^{-1}(f^{-1}B) = (f \circ g)^{-1}B$.

Given such a $\mathcal{P}$, we wish to interpret each derivable judgement $\Gamma \vdash \phi\ \text{prop}$ as an element

$$
[\![\Gamma \vdash \phi\ \text{prop}]\!] \in \mathcal{P}([\![\Gamma]\!])
$$

where as before, the object $[\![\Gamma]\!]$ in $\mathcal{C}$ is the finite product $[\![\sigma_1]\!] \times \cdots \times [\![\sigma_n]\!]$ when Γ is the context $x_1{:}\sigma_1, \ldots, x_n{:}\sigma_n$. We can then define the *satisfaction* of an entailment judgement $\Gamma, \Phi \vdash \psi$ to mean that

$$
\bigwedge_{\phi \in \Phi} [\![\Gamma \vdash \phi\ \text{prop}]\!] \leq [\![\Gamma \vdash \psi\ \text{prop}]\!]
$$

holds in the meet semilattice $\mathcal{P}(\llbracket \Gamma \rrbracket)$ (where $\wedge$ indicates finite meet and $\leq$ the partial order).

The definition of $\llbracket \Gamma \vdash \phi \; \text{prop} \rrbracket$ proceeds by induction on the structure of the formula ϕ, and each of the predicate formers in the logic requires some appropriate properties or extra structure on $\mathcal{P}$ to interpret it soundly. Soundness means that we should be able to prove for each rule of inference that the conclusion is satisfied when all of the hypotheses are.

The conditions on $\mathcal{P}$ needed to interpret finite conjunctions and disjunctions are quite standard: each $\mathcal{P}(X)$ should be a distributive lattice and each $f^{-1} : \mathcal{P}(Y) \longrightarrow \mathcal{P}(X)$ should, in addition to preserving finite meets, also preserve the finite joins as well. The property of $\mathcal{P}$ needed to soundly interpret equality is almost as well-known, except that in the absence of propositional implication certain subtleties arise which would otherwise be masked. Briefly, we require all the order-preserving functions

$$(\Delta_X \times id_Y)^{-1} : \mathcal{P}((X \times X) \times Y) \longrightarrow \mathcal{P}(X \times Y) \qquad (1)$$

(where Δ_X is the diagonal $\langle id_X, id_X \rangle$) to possess left adjoints, $\exists_{\Delta_X \times id_Y}$, and for these left adjoints to satisfy certain conditions termed by Lawvere [9] 'Beck-Chevalley' and 'Frobenius Reciprocity' conditions; moreover, equality of morphisms in $\mathcal{C}$ must be implied by satisfaction in $\mathcal{P}$ of the corresponding equality formula. Since we wish to concentrate here on describing the categorical semantics of the evaluation modalities, we merely refer the reader to [2] for more details.

Definition 3.3.1 (Cf. [12, Definition 4.8]) A *T-modality* on $\mathcal{P}$ is specified by a family of order-preserving functions

$$\Box_{X,Y} : \mathcal{P}(X \times Y) \longrightarrow \mathcal{P}(X \times T(Y))$$

one for each pair of objects X, Y in $\mathcal{C}$, satisfying the following three conditions relating to the formulation of the strong monad T as an 'indexed Kleisli triple' as in Section 2.2.

Naturality condition: given $f : X \longrightarrow X'$, then

$$
\begin{array}{ccc}
\mathcal{P}(X' \times Y) & \xrightarrow{(f \times id_Y)^{-1}} & \mathcal{P}(X \times Y) \\
{\scriptstyle \Box_{X',Y}} \downarrow & & \downarrow {\scriptstyle \Box_{X,Y}} \\
\mathcal{P}(X' \times T(Y)) & \xrightarrow[(f \times id_{T(Y)})^{-1}]{} & \mathcal{P}(X \times T(Y))
\end{array}
$$

commutes.

Unit condition: for all X and Y

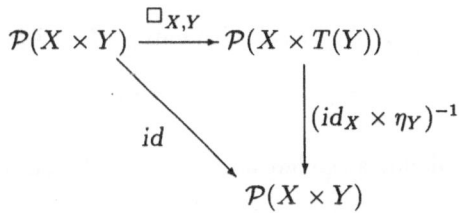

commutes.

174

Lifting condition: given $f : X \times Y \longrightarrow T(Z)$, then

$$
\begin{array}{ccc}
\mathcal{P}(X \times Z) \xrightarrow{\;\Box_{X,Z}\;} \mathcal{P}(X \times T(Z)) \xrightarrow{\;\langle \pi_1, f \rangle^{-1}\;} \mathcal{P}(X \times Y) \\[2mm]
\Big\downarrow{\scriptstyle \Box_{X,Z}} \qquad\qquad\qquad\qquad\qquad\qquad \Big\downarrow{\scriptstyle \Box_{X,Y}} \\[2mm]
\mathcal{P}(X \times T(Z)) \xrightarrow[\;\langle \pi_1, f^* \rangle^{-1}\;]{\hspace{5cm}} \mathcal{P}(X \times T(Y))
\end{array}
$$

commutes.

Given two such T-modalities on $\mathcal{P}$, $\Box$ and $\Diamond$, we can interpret the evaluation modalities as follows. Suppose, inductively, that we have

$$
\begin{aligned}
\llbracket \Gamma \rrbracket &= X \\
\llbracket \sigma \rrbracket &= Y \\
\llbracket \Gamma \vdash E : \sigma \rrbracket &= f : X \longrightarrow T(Y) \\
\llbracket \Gamma, x{:}\sigma \vdash \phi(x) \text{ prop} \rrbracket &= A \in \mathcal{P}(X \times Y)
\end{aligned}
$$

Then we define

$$
\begin{aligned}
\llbracket \Gamma \vdash [x{\Leftarrow}E]\phi(x) \text{ prop} \rrbracket &\overset{\text{def}}{=} \langle id_X, f \rangle^{-1}(\Box_{X,Y} A) \\
\llbracket \Gamma \vdash \langle x{\Leftarrow}E\rangle\phi(x) \text{ prop} \rrbracket &\overset{\text{def}}{=} \langle id_X, f \rangle^{-1}(\Diamond_{X,Y} A)
\end{aligned}
$$

The conditions imposed on $\Box$ and $\Diamond$ by Definition 3.3.1 ensure that the rules in 3.2.1, 3.2.2 and 3.2.3 are sound for this interpretation. To ensure soundness for the rules in 3.2.4, clearly we require

(i) each $\Box_{X,Y} : \mathcal{P}(X \times Y) \longrightarrow \mathcal{P}(X \times T(Y))$ preserves finite meets

whilst to ensure soundness for the rules in 3.2.5 we require

(ii) each $\Diamond_{X,Y} : \mathcal{P}(X \times Y) \longrightarrow \mathcal{P}(X \times T(Y))$ preserves finite joins.

Soundness for 3.2.6 requires

(iii) for all objects X, Y and all elements $A, B \in \mathcal{P}(X \times Y)$

$$
\Diamond_{X,Y}(A) \wedge \Box_{X,Y}(B) \leq \Diamond_{X,Y}(A \wedge B)
$$

Finally, soundness for 3.2.7 requires

(iv) for all objects X, Y and all elements $A, B \in \mathcal{P}(X \times Y)$

$$
\exists_{\Delta_X \times id_{T(Y)}}(\Diamond_{X,Y} A) = \Diamond_{X \times X, Y}(\exists_{\Delta_X \times id_Y} A)
$$

where $\exists_{\Delta_X \times id_Y}$ denotes the left adjoint to the function (1) mentioned above.

3.4 Examples

We give two examples of the categorical structure developed in the previous section. In fact, the underlying cartesian closed category in both examples is the same—namely the category of ω-cpo's (*without* least element) and ω-continuous functions, which we will denote by $\mathcal{C}po$. Thus the objects of $\mathcal{C}po$ are sets equipped with a partial order possessing least upper bounds of all countably infinite chains; the morphisms are functions preserving order and least upper bounds of countably infinite chains. Finite products in $\mathcal{C}po$ are created by the forgetful functor to the category of sets; an exponential $X{\to}Y$ in $\mathcal{C}po$ is given by the hom-set $\mathcal{C}po(X,Y)$ ordered pointwise from Y.

Of course $\mathcal{C}po$ (and its subcategories) has very much more structure than this, which is used in the traditional domain-theoretic approach to denotational semantics (see [4] for a survey). Moggi has noticed that the way in which this extra structure is actually used is via the construction of various strong monads reflecting various aspects of computation. From the many examples in [11, 13] we select those of *partiality* and *partiality with side-effects* and show how to extend them to models of our Evaluation Logic by giving suitable hyperdoctrines of properties equipped with modalities.

Example 3.4.1 (Partiality) For each ω-cpo X, recall that the *lifted* ω-cpo, $X_\perp$ is obtained by adjoining a least element to X. Specifically, to fix notation, define

$$X_\perp \stackrel{\text{def}}{=} \{[x] \mid x \in X\} \cup \{\perp\}$$

with partial order given by

> $e \sqsubseteq e'$ in $X_\perp$ iff for all $x \in X$, if $e = [x]$ then there is some $x' \in X$ with $e' = [x']$ and $x \sqsubseteq x'$ in X.

Then $X \mapsto X_\perp$ is the object part of a strong monad on $\mathcal{C}po$ whose unit functions $\eta_X : X \longrightarrow X_\perp$ are $x \mapsto [x]$, and whose lifting operation sends the ω-continuous function $f : X \times Y \longrightarrow Z_\perp$ to $f^* : X \times Y_\perp \longrightarrow Z_\perp$ where for all $x \in D$ and $e \in Y_\perp$

$$f^*(x,e) = \begin{cases} f(x,y) & \text{if } e = [y] \\ \perp & \text{if } e = \perp \end{cases}$$

In the resulting model of the computational lambda calculus, the only quality of computation modelled is non-termination ($\perp$). Computations of values in Y with a parameter in X, i.e. elements of the ω-cpo $X{\to}Y_\perp$, amount to partial continuous functions from X to Y.

To extend the model to formulas, we consider the $\mathcal{C}po$-indexed meet semilattice of *inclusive subsets*, $\mathcal{I}$. Its value, $\mathcal{I}(X)$, at an ω-cpo X is the set of all subsets $A \subseteq X$ which are closed under taking least upper bounds in X of countably infinite chains lying in A. For each ω-continuous function $f : X \longrightarrow Y$, $f^{-1} : \mathcal{I}(Y) \longrightarrow \mathcal{I}(X)$ sends an inclusive $B \in \mathcal{I}(Y)$ to the inverse image $f^{-1}B \stackrel{\text{def}}{=} \{x \in X \mid f(x) \in B\}$. Finite meets in $\mathcal{I}(X)$ are given by set-theoretic intersection.

It is not hard to see that the union of finitely many inclusive subsets of an ω-cpo is again inclusive. Consequently, each $\mathcal{I}(X)$ is a distributive lattice and each f^{-1} preserves finite joins in addition to finite meets. So $\mathcal{I}$ soundly models finite conjunction and disjunction. It also has the requisite properties to model equality formulas: this follows from the fact that the direct image of an inclusive $A \in \mathcal{I}(X \times Y)$ along the function $(x, y) \mapsto (x, x, y)$ is just $\{(x, x, y) \mid (x, y) \in A\}$, which is again inclusive. (It is not true in general that the image of an inclusive subset along an ω-continuous function is inclusive.)

Turning now to modelling the evaluation modalities, we define the following two modalities on $\mathcal{I}$ for the lifting monad:

$$\Box_{X,Y}(A) \stackrel{\text{def}}{=} \{(x, e) \in X \times Y_\perp \mid \forall y \in Y . e = [y] \supset (x, y) \in A\}$$

$$\Diamond_{X,Y}(A) \stackrel{\text{def}}{=} \{(x, e) \in X \times Y_\perp \mid \exists y \in Y . e = [y] \wedge (x, y) \in A\}$$

for all ω-cpo's X, Y and inclusive $A \in \mathcal{I}(X \times Y)$. The inclusivity of the right-hand sides in these definitions is not completely trivial, bearing in mind the fact that $\mathcal{I}$ is not a model of (intuitionistic) logic with either existential quantification or implication. Nevertheless the conditions in Definition 3.3.1 and conditions (i)–(iv) listed after that definition are all easily verified for these modalities. Indeed much more special properties hold of these particular modalities than we have required in our Evaluation Logic—namely $\Diamond_{X,Y}$ and $\Box_{X,Y}$ give respectively left and right adjoints to $(id_X \times \eta_Y)^{-1}$, and satisfy various Beck-Chevalley and Frobenius Reciprocity conditions. The categorical logic of this more special kind of modality is studied in [1, 2].

Example 3.4.2 (Side-effects) Let S be some fixed ω-cpo of 'states'. For example, if a state is completely specified by the contents of memory locations $\ell_1, \ell_2, \ldots$ each of which can contain a number, then S would be the set of finite partial functions from addresses to numbers (equipped with the discrete partial order of equality).

A computation of a value in X whose evaluation has some (unspecified) side-effects on the current state can be modelled in an extensional way by a (continuous) function $e : S \to (X \times S)_\perp$. Thus given any initial state $s \in S$, either $e(s) = \perp$, i.e. the computation does not terminate, or $e(s) = [(x, s')]$, i.e. the computation terminates yielding the value $x \in X$ and a new state $s' \in S$. Defining

$$T^S(X) \stackrel{\text{def}}{=} S \to (X \times S)_\perp$$

then $X \mapsto T^S(X)$ is the object part of a strong monad on $\mathcal{C}po$ whose unit functions are given by

$$\eta_X(x)(s) = [(x, s)]$$

and whose lifting operation sends $f : X \times Y \longrightarrow T^S(Z)$ to the function $f^* : X \times T^S(Y) \longrightarrow T^S(Z)$ given by

$$f^*(x, e)(s) = \begin{cases} f(x, y)(s') & \text{if } e(s) = [(y, s')] \\ \perp & \text{if } e(s) = \perp \end{cases}$$

Over $\mathcal{C}po$ equipped with this stong monad T^S we consider the following indexed meet semilattice, $\mathcal{I}^S$. The value of $\mathcal{I}^S$ at an ω-cpo X is the collection of inclusive subsets of the product $X \times S$, partially ordered by inclusion. In other words

$$\mathcal{I}^S(X) \stackrel{\text{def}}{=} \mathcal{I}(X \times S)$$

with $\mathcal{I}$ as in the previous example. Similarly, given $f : X \longrightarrow Y$ in $\mathcal{C}po$, then $f^{-1} : \mathcal{I}^S(Y) \longrightarrow \mathcal{I}^S(X)$ is defined to be the inverse image function $(f \times id_S)^{-1}$.

We will adopt the following notation when referring to elements of $\mathcal{I}^S(X)$: given $A \in \mathcal{I}^S(X)$, $s \in S$ and $x \in X$, we write

$$s \Vdash A(x)$$

to indicate that $(x, s) \in A$, and say 'in state s, x has property A'.

It follows immediately from the definition of $\mathcal{I}^S$ in terms of $\mathcal{I}$ that $\mathcal{I}^S$ inherits from the latter the properties needed to model equality formulas and finite conjunctions and disjunctions.

Turning now to modelling the evaluation modalities, we give two T^S-modalities, $\square^S$ and $\lozenge^S$, on $\mathcal{I}^S$. For each $A \in \mathcal{I}^S(X \times Y)$, define $\square^S_{X,Y}A$ and $\lozenge^S_{X,Y}A$ in $\mathcal{I}^S(X \times T^S(Y))$ by declaring that for all $s \in S$, $x \in X$ and $e \in T^S(Y)$

$$s \Vdash (\square^S_{X,Y}A)(x, e) \quad \text{iff} \quad \forall s' \in S . \forall y \in Y . e(s) = [(y, s')] \supset s' \Vdash A(x, y)$$
$$s \Vdash (\lozenge^S_{X,Y}A)(x, e) \quad \text{iff} \quad \exists s' \in S . \exists y \in Y . e(s) = [(y, s')] \land s' \Vdash A(x, y)$$

It is not hard to verify that these definitions do indeed yield inclusive subsets—either directly, or by noting that they can be expressed in terms of the modalities of Example 3.4.1:

$$\square^S_{X,Y}(A) \;=\; \{(x, e, s) \mid (x, e(s)) \in \square_{X,Y \times S}(A)\}$$
$$\lozenge^S_{X,Y}(A) \;=\; \{(x, e, s) \mid (x, e(s)) \in \lozenge_{X,Y \times S}(A)\}$$

Indeed this observation serves to show that $\square^S$ and $\lozenge^S$ inherit from the lifting-modalities $\square$ and $\lozenge$ the properties (i)–(iv) given after Definition 3.3.1. Finally it can be verified directly from the definition of the strong monad T^S that both $\square^S$ and $\lozenge^S$ satisfy the naturality, unit and lifting conditions required by Definition 3.3.1.

4 Translating Natural Semantics

In this section we will give an example of translating programming language features into suitable *theories* over Evaluation Logic. As discussed in the Introduction, the aim is to see how well fitted is this logic for capturing operational behaviour specified in terms of the 'Natural Semantics' style of operational semantics [18, 5].

An Evaluation Logic theory is specified by a *signature* of type- and term-constructors (and possibly formula-constructors, although we will not need these here), together with the *axioms* of the theory—which are a collection of judgements (involving expressions generated over the given signature). We will present such a theory for a fragment of the Standard ML language [10] containing both functional features (higher-order recursive function declarations) and imperative features (assignable global variables), and which we call TINY-ML. We begin by specifying the programming language syntax.

4.1 TINY-ML Types

These are the simple types over a ground types of integers, int, and a one-element ground type, unit:

$$\sigma ::= \text{int} \mid \text{unit} \mid \sigma_1 \rightarrow \sigma_2$$

$$\overline{\Gamma, x{:}\sigma, \Gamma' \vdash x : \sigma}$$

$$\overline{\Gamma \vdash () : \texttt{unit}} \qquad \overline{\Gamma \vdash \texttt{n} : \texttt{int}}$$

$$\frac{\Gamma \vdash \texttt{e}_1 : \texttt{int} \quad \Gamma \vdash \texttt{e}_2 : \texttt{int}}{\Gamma \vdash \texttt{op}(\texttt{e}_1, \texttt{e}_2) : \texttt{int}}$$

$$\frac{\Gamma \vdash \texttt{e}_1 : \texttt{int} \quad \Gamma \vdash \texttt{e}_2 : \sigma \quad \Gamma \vdash \texttt{e}_3 : \sigma}{\Gamma \vdash \texttt{if } \texttt{e}_1 = 0 \texttt{ then } \texttt{e}_2 \texttt{ else } \texttt{e}_3 : \sigma}$$

$$\frac{\Gamma, x{:}\sigma \vdash \texttt{e} : \sigma'}{\Gamma \vdash \texttt{fn } x{:}\sigma \Rightarrow \texttt{e} : \sigma \rightarrow \sigma'} \qquad \frac{\Gamma \vdash \texttt{e} : \sigma \rightarrow \sigma' \quad \Gamma \vdash \texttt{e}' : \sigma}{\Gamma \vdash \texttt{ee}' : \sigma'}$$

$$\frac{\Gamma, f{:}\sigma \rightarrow \sigma', x{:}\sigma \vdash \texttt{e}_1 : \sigma' \quad \Gamma \vdash \texttt{e}_2 : \sigma}{\Gamma \vdash \texttt{letrec } f(x) = \texttt{e}_1{:}\sigma' \texttt{ in } f(\texttt{e}_2) \texttt{ end} : \sigma'}$$

$$\frac{\Gamma \vdash \texttt{e} : \texttt{int}}{\Gamma \vdash \ell := \texttt{e} : \texttt{unit}} \qquad \overline{\vdash !\ell : \texttt{int}}$$

Table 1: Rules for the static semantics of TINY-ML

4.2 TINY-ML Expressions

These are given by the following grammar:

e	::=	x	variables
	|	()	unit value
	|	n	integer values
	|	$op(e_1, e_2)$	arithmetic operations
	|	if $e_1 = 0$ then e_2 else e_3	conditionals
	|	fn $x{:}\sigma \Rightarrow e$	λ-abstractions
	|	$e_1 e_2$	applications
	|	letrec $f(x) = e_1{:}\sigma$ in $f(e_2)$ end	recursive functions[1]
	|	$\ell := e$	assignment to ℓ
	|	$!\ell$	contents of ℓ

Here x ranges over a countably infinite set of variables, n ranges over the integers, op $\in \{+, -, *\}$, and ℓ ranges over a countably infinite set of global memory locations (constants of type int ref, in ML parlance). Recalling from the Introduction the metatheoretical treatment of variable-binding, we remark that the form fn $x{:}\sigma \Rightarrow e$ is in fact long-hand for the meta-expression $\text{fn}(\sigma, (x)e)$ with fn a meta-constant of type EXP$\rightarrow$(EXP$\rightarrow$EXP)$\rightarrow$EXP. Similarly, letrec $f(x) = e_1{:}\sigma$ in $f(e_2)$ end is long-hand for $\text{letrec}((f)(x)e_1, \sigma, e_2)$ with letrec a meta-constant of type (EXP$\rightarrow$EXP$\rightarrow$EXP)$\rightarrow$EXP$\rightarrow$EXP$\rightarrow$EXP.

Perhaps TINY-ML is not so tiny. Here are some derived forms of expression:

$$\text{let } x = e_1{:}\sigma \text{ in } e_2 \stackrel{\text{def}}{=} (\text{fn } x{:}\sigma \Rightarrow e_2)e_1$$

$$e_1; e_2 \stackrel{\text{def}}{=} \text{let } x = e_1{:}\text{unit in } e_2$$

$$\text{while } e_1 \neq 0 \text{ do } e_2 \stackrel{\text{def}}{=} \text{letrec } f(x) = (\text{if } e_1 = 0 \text{ then () else } e_2; x){:}\text{unit in } f(()) \text{ end}$$

4.3 Static Semantics of TINY-ML

Table 1 gives the rules for deriving type assignments, $\Gamma \vdash e : \sigma$, giving the TINY-ML type σ of a TINY-ML expression e in a context $\Gamma = x_1{:}\sigma_1, \ldots, x_n{:}\sigma_n$. Conventions about contexts are the same as those in Section 2 for the computational lambda calculus.

Remark 4.3.1 It is easy to see that *in a given context a* TINY-ML *expression has at most one type*: if $\Gamma \vdash e : \sigma$ and $\Gamma \vdash e : \sigma'$ are both derivable from the rules in Table 1 then $\sigma \equiv \sigma'$.

4.4 Dynamic Semantics of TINY-ML

4.4.1 Closed and canonical expressions

Let us call a TINY-ML expression e *closed* if there is some type σ for which $\vdash e : \sigma$ is derivable. Thus e contains no (free) variables, and by Remark 4.3.1 σ is uniquely determined by e.

---

[1]This should be regarded as an abbreviation for the legal Standard ML expression let val rec $f = $ fn $x \Rightarrow e_1{:}\sigma$ in $f(e_2)$ end.

$$\frac{}{c \twoheadrightarrow c} \quad (c \text{ canonical})$$

$$\frac{e_1 \twoheadrightarrow 0 \quad e_2 \twoheadrightarrow c}{\text{if } e_1 = 0 \text{ then } e_2 \text{ else } e_3 \twoheadrightarrow c} \qquad \frac{e_1 \twoheadrightarrow n \quad e_3 \twoheadrightarrow c}{\text{if } e_1 = 0 \text{ then } e_2 \text{ else } e_3 \twoheadrightarrow c} \quad (\text{if } n \neq 0)$$

$$\frac{e_1 \twoheadrightarrow n_1 \quad e_2 \twoheadrightarrow n_2}{\text{op}(e_1, e_2) \twoheadrightarrow n} \quad (\text{if } op(n_1, n_2) = n)$$

$$\frac{e_1 \twoheadrightarrow \text{fn } x{:}\sigma \Rightarrow e \quad e_2 \twoheadrightarrow c \quad e(c/x) \twoheadrightarrow c'}{e_1 e_2 \twoheadrightarrow c'}$$

$$\frac{e_2 \twoheadrightarrow c \quad e_1((\text{fn } x{:}\sigma \Rightarrow \text{letrec } f(x') = e_1{:}\sigma' \text{ in } f(x) \text{ end})/f, \, c/x) \twoheadrightarrow c'}{\text{letrec } f(x) = e_1{:}\sigma' \text{ in } f(e_2) \text{ end} \twoheadrightarrow c'}$$

$$\frac{s, e \twoheadrightarrow s', n}{s, \ell := e \twoheadrightarrow s'(\ell \mapsto n), \, ()} \qquad \frac{}{s, !\ell \twoheadrightarrow s, n} \quad (\text{if } n = s(\ell))$$

Table 2: Rules for the dynamic semantics of TINY-ML

Then the *canonical* TINY-ML expressions, c, comprise the subset of all closed TINY-ML expressions given by the following grammar:

$$c ::= () \mid n \mid fn\ x{:}\sigma \Rightarrow e$$

4.4.2 States

These are the finite functions, s, from the set of global memory locations to the set of integers. If s is a state with domain $\{\ell_1, \ldots, \ell_k\}$ and with $s(\ell_i) = n_i$, we will write s as

$$s = \{\ell_1 \mapsto n_1, \ldots, \ell_k \mapsto n_k\}$$

We write

$$s(\ell \mapsto n)$$

for the *updated* state which maps ℓ to n and otherwise acts like s.

4.4.3 The evaluation relation

This is a relation of the form

$$s, e \twoheadrightarrow s', c$$

where s and s' are states, e is a closed TINY-ML expression and c is a canonical one. The relation is inductively defined by the rules given in Table 2. In stating these rules we use the following simplifying convention from [10]:

'Sequentiality' convention.   A rule scheme of the form

$$\frac{e_1 \twoheadrightarrow c_1 \quad e_2 \twoheadrightarrow c_2 \quad \cdots \quad e_n \twoheadrightarrow c_n}{e \twoheadrightarrow c}$$

is an abbreviation for the rule scheme

$$\frac{s_1, e_1 \twoheadrightarrow s_2, c_1 \quad s_2, e_2 \twoheadrightarrow s_3, c_2 \quad \cdots \quad s_n, e_n \twoheadrightarrow s_{n+1}, c_n}{s_1, e \twoheadrightarrow s_{n+1}, c}$$

(Thus the order of hypotheses is significant when using this convention.)

Remark 4.4.1 It is not hard to see from the form of the rules in Table 2 that if $s, e \twoheadrightarrow s', c$ is derivable, then s and s' have the same domain, and e and c have the same type.

4.5   Translation of TINY-ML into Evaluation Logic

We begin by giving the theory over Evaluation Logic into which we will translate TINY-ML. As we said above, such a theory is specified by a signature and a collection of axioms.

$$\frac{}{\vdash n : Z} \qquad \frac{\Gamma \vdash M : Z \quad \Gamma \vdash M' : Z}{\Gamma \vdash op(M, M') : Z}$$

$$\frac{\Gamma \vdash M_1 : Z \quad \Gamma \vdash M_2 : \sigma \quad \Gamma \vdash M_3 : \sigma}{\Gamma \vdash cond(M_1, M_2, M_3) : \sigma}$$

$$\frac{\Gamma, f{:}\sigma{\rightarrow}T\sigma', x{:}\sigma \vdash E'(f, x) : T\sigma' \quad \Gamma \vdash M : \sigma}{\Gamma \vdash rec_{\sigma'}(E', M) : T\sigma'}$$

$$\frac{\Gamma \vdash M : Z}{\Gamma \vdash up_\ell(M) : T1} \qquad \frac{}{\vdash ct_\ell : TZ}$$

Table 3: The signature of the theory

4.5.1 Signature

The signature of the theory has a single ground type Z (type of integers) and meta-constants

$$
\begin{aligned}
n &: \text{EXP}\\
op &: \text{EXP}\!\to\!\text{EXP}\!\to\!\text{EXP}\\
cond &: \text{EXP}\!\to\!\text{EXP}\!\to\!\text{EXP}\!\to\!\text{EXP}\\
rec_\sigma &: (\text{EXP}\!\to\!\text{EXP}\!\to\!\text{EXP})\!\to\!\text{EXP}\!\to\!\text{EXP}\\
up_\ell &: \text{EXP}\!\to\!\text{EXP}\\
ct_\ell &: \text{EXP}
\end{aligned}
$$

where n ranges over the set of integers, op ranges over $\{+,-,*\}$, ℓ ranges over the set of global memory locations, and σ ranges over the set of types of the computational lambda calculus (see Section 2) generated from the ground type Z. The rules for introducing these meta-constants are given in Table 3. Note the difference between the last three rules in this table and the corresponding last three rules in Table 1.

4.5.2 Axioms

The intended meaning of the term $cond(M_1, M_2, M_3){:}\sigma$ is a conditional branching on whether $M_1{:}Z$ is equal to 0 or not. The intended meaning of the term $rec_{\sigma'}(E', M){:}T\sigma'$ is the computation of the value at $M{:}\sigma$ of the function recursively defined by the declaration

$$
f(x) \stackrel{\text{def}}{=} E'(f,x)
$$

(The type subscript on $rec_{\sigma'}$ is there to retain the uniqueness of type property mentioned in Remark 2.0.1.) The intended meaning of the term $up_\ell(M){:}T1$ is the 'program' (i.e. computation of unit type—cf. Remark 3.2.10) which assigns value $M{:}Z$ to location ℓ. The intended meaning of the term $ct_\ell{:}TZ$ is the computation which just returns the contents of location ℓ.

With these intended interpretations in mind, Table 4 formalizes certain expected properties: these are the axioms of the particular Evaluation Logic theory we wish to consider, and which are added to the rules for generating entailment judgements given in Sections 2 and 3. Some of the axioms employ a derived form of sequential composition

$$
E; E' \stackrel{\text{def}}{=} let\ x\!\Leftarrow\!E\ in\ E'
$$

in which the second computation is independent of the parameter x. Thus the derived rule of formation is

$$
\frac{\Gamma \vdash E : T\sigma \quad \Gamma \vdash E' : T\sigma'}{\Gamma \vdash E; E' : T\sigma'}
$$

and from the equational properties of let given in Section 2.1 one can derive

$$
\begin{aligned}
e{:}T\sigma, e'{:}T\sigma', e''{:}T\sigma'' &\vdash (e; e'); e'' = e; (e'; e'')\\
e{:}T\sigma &\vdash skip; e = e\\
e{:}T1 &\vdash e; skip = e
\end{aligned}
$$

where by definition, $skip$ is $[\langle\rangle]$.

$$x{:}\sigma, x'{:}\sigma \vdash cond(0, x, x') = x$$

$$\overline{x{:}\sigma, x'{:}\sigma \vdash cond(n, x, x') = x'} \quad (\text{if } n \neq 0)$$

$$\overline{\vdash op(n_1, n_2) = n} \quad (\text{if } op(n_1, n_2) = n)$$

$$\frac{\Gamma, f{:}\sigma{\rightarrow}T\sigma', x{:}\sigma \vdash E'(f, x) : T\sigma'}{\Gamma, x{:}\sigma \vdash rec_{\sigma'}(E', x) = E'(\lambda x{:}\sigma.rec_{\sigma'}(E', x), x)}$$

$$x{:}Z, x'{:}Z \vdash up_\ell(x); up_\ell(x') = up_\ell(x')$$

$$\overline{x{:}Z, x'{:}Z \vdash up_\ell(x); up_{\ell'}(x') = up_{\ell'}(x'); up_\ell(x)} \quad (\text{if } \ell \neq \ell')$$

$$x{:}Z \vdash up_\ell(x); ct_\ell = up_\ell(x); [x]$$

$$\overline{x{:}Z \vdash up_\ell(x); ct_{\ell'} = let\ x'{\Leftarrow}ct_{\ell'}\ in\ (up_\ell(x); [x'])} \quad (\text{if } \ell \neq \ell')$$

$$\vdash let\ x{\Leftarrow}ct_\ell\ in\ (let\ x'{\Leftarrow}ct_{\ell'}\ in\ [\langle x, x'\rangle]) = let\ x'{\Leftarrow}ct_{\ell'}\ in\ (let\ x{\Leftarrow}ct_\ell\ in\ [\langle x, x'\rangle])$$

$$x{:}Z \vdash up_\ell(x){\Downarrow}$$

Table 4: Theory axioms

4.5.3 Translation

The basic idea is that TINY-ML expressions $e{:}\sigma$ are translated into terms of *computation* type, $[\![e]\!]{:}T[\![\sigma]\!]$, in the computational lambda calculus. Furthermore, since the dynamic semantics of TINY-ML is strict ('call-by-value'), if e depends on some variables $x_1{:}\sigma_1,\ldots,x{:}\sigma_n$, then $[\![e]\!]$ should depend on variables ranging over the values of the translated types, $x_1{:}[\![\sigma_1]\!],\ldots,x_n{:}[\![\sigma_n]\!]$ (rather than on variables ranging over computations). Thus at the heart of the translation is Moggi's [11] call-by-value translation of lambda calculus into his computational lambda calculus (see also Plotkin [16]).

The translation is defined by induction on the structure of TINY-ML types and expressions by the clauses in Table 5. Note that for a canonical TINY-ML expression c (as defined in Section 4.4.1), the translation takes the form

$$[\![c]\!] = [|c|]$$

(where $|c|$ is of type $[\![\sigma]\!]$ when c is of type σ). Thus $|c|$ is the translation of the canonical term c as a *value* rather than as a computation.

4.6 Adequacy of the translation

The translation given by Table 5 is adequate for both the static and dynamic semantics of TINY-ML. For the static semantics this means

Proposition 4.6.1 (Static Adequacy) $x_1{:}\sigma_1,\ldots,x_n{:}\sigma_n \vdash e : \sigma$ *is derivable from the rules in Table 1 if and only if*

$$x_1{:}[\![\sigma_1]\!],\ldots,x_n{:}[\![\sigma_n]\!] \vdash [\![e]\!] : T[\![\sigma]\!]$$

is derivable from the type assignment rules of the computational lambda calculus augmented by the rules in Table 3.

The triviality of the type system of TINY-ML makes this proposition easy to prove by induction on the structure of e.

For the dynamic semantics, we first have to translate the operational evaluation relation

$$s, e \twoheadrightarrow s', c \tag{2}$$

into a corresponding judgement in Evaluation Logic. Taking into account Remark 4.4.1, we may suppose that e and c have the same type and that s and s' have equal domain. Supposing the states are

$$\begin{aligned} s &= \{\ell_1 \mapsto n_1,\ldots,\ell_k \mapsto n_k\} \\ s' &= \{\ell_1 \mapsto n_1',\ldots,\ell_k \mapsto n_k'\} \end{aligned}$$

then we will translate this instance of the evaluation relation into the Evaluation Logic judgement

$$\vdash \langle \vec{up}(\vec{n}) \rangle \langle x{\Leftarrow}[\![e]\!] \rangle \langle \vec{x'}{\Leftarrow}\vec{ct} \rangle \left(x = |c| \ \wedge \ \bigwedge_{i=1}^{k} x_i' = n_i' \right) \tag{3}$$

Types

$$[\![\texttt{int}]\!] \overset{\text{def}}{=} Z$$

$$[\![\texttt{unit}]\!] \overset{\text{def}}{=} 1$$

$$[\![\sigma \rightarrow \sigma']\!] \overset{\text{def}}{=} [\![\sigma]\!] \rightarrow T[\![\sigma']\!]$$

Expressions

$$[\![x]\!] \overset{\text{def}}{=} [x]$$

$$[\![()]\!] \overset{\text{def}}{=} [\langle \rangle]$$

$$[\![\texttt{n}]\!] \overset{\text{def}}{=} [n]$$

$$[\![\texttt{op}(\texttt{e}_1, \texttt{e}_2)]\!] \overset{\text{def}}{=} \textit{let } x_1 \Leftarrow [\![\texttt{e}_1]\!] \textit{ in}$$
$$(\textit{let } x_2 \Leftarrow [\![\texttt{e}_2]\!] \textit{ in } [op(x_1, x_2)])$$

$$[\![\texttt{if } \texttt{e}_1 = 0 \texttt{ then } \texttt{e}_2 \texttt{ else } \texttt{e}_3]\!] \overset{\text{def}}{=} \textit{let } x \Leftarrow [\![\texttt{e}_1]\!] \textit{ in } cond(x, [\![\texttt{e}_2]\!], [\![\texttt{e}_3]\!])$$

$$[\![\texttt{fn } x{:}\sigma \Rightarrow \texttt{e}]\!] \overset{\text{def}}{=} [\lambda x{:}[\![\sigma]\!].[\![\texttt{e}]\!]]$$

$$[\![\texttt{e}_1 \texttt{e}_2]\!] \overset{\text{def}}{=} \textit{let } f \Leftarrow [\![\texttt{e}_1]\!] \textit{ in } (\textit{let } x \Leftarrow [\![\texttt{e}_2]\!] \textit{ in } fx)$$

$$[\![\texttt{letrec } f(x) = \texttt{e}_1{:}\sigma' \texttt{ in } f(\texttt{e}_2) \texttt{ end}]\!] \overset{\text{def}}{=} \textit{let } x' \Leftarrow [\![\texttt{e}_2]\!] \textit{ in } rec_{[\![\sigma']\!]}((f)(x)[\![\texttt{e}_1]\!], x')$$

$$[\![\ell := \texttt{e}]\!] \overset{\text{def}}{=} \textit{let } x \Leftarrow [\![\texttt{e}]\!] \textit{ in } up_\ell(x)$$

$$[\![!\ell]\!] \overset{\text{def}}{=} ct_\ell$$

Table 5: Translation of Tiny-ML types and expressions

Here $\langle \vec{up}(\vec{n}) \rangle$ and $\langle \vec{x'} \!\Leftarrow\! \vec{ct} \rangle$ stand for iterated modalities, viz

$$\langle \vec{up}(\vec{n}) \rangle \ \stackrel{\text{def}}{=} \ \langle up_{\ell_1}(n_1) \rangle \cdots \langle up_{\ell_k}(n_k) \rangle$$
$$\langle \vec{x'} \!\Leftarrow\! \vec{ct} \rangle \ \stackrel{\text{def}}{=} \ \langle x'_1 \!\Leftarrow\! ct_{\ell_1} \rangle \cdots \langle x'_k \!\Leftarrow\! ct_{\ell_k} \rangle$$

where we are using the abbreviation mentioned in Remark 3.2.10 to write $\langle x \!\Leftarrow\! E \rangle \phi$ as

$$\langle E \rangle \phi$$

when E is a term of type $T1$ (such as $up_{\ell_i}(n_i)$) and ϕ does not depend upon x.

We hope the reader will agree that (modulo the unfamiliar formalism) the judgement (3) is a *natural* rendering of the operational evaluation relation into our logic, since it says something like: 'it is possible to make the assignments to $\ell_1, \dots, \ell_k$ to create the state s, then possible to evaluate $[\![e]\!]$ to a value equal to $|c|$ and have those locations contain the values of state s' as a result'. In any case, one can prove

Proposition 4.6.2 (Dynamic Adequacy) *If the evaluation relation (2) is derivable from the rules in Table 2, then the corresponding judgement (3) is derivable in Evaluation Logic from the theory described by Tables 3 and 4. The converse holds when c is of ground type (*int *or* unit*).*

Proof The proof of the first sentence is by induction on the derivation of (2). For the second sentence we use the fact that Example 3.4.2 yields a *model* of the Evaluation Logic theory we are considering. Since it is a model, derivability of (3) in the logic implies its satisfaction in the model. Assuming **e** is of (ground) type gnd, satisfaction in this model amount to requiring that

$$[\![e]\!](s) = (|c|, s') \in T^S([\![\text{gnd}]\!])$$

where now $[\![\_]\!]$ is essentially the standard domain-theoretic semantics of TINY-ML (see Mosses [14] for example)—from which it is known that we can recover the operational relation (2). $\square$

Concluding remarks

Evaluation Logic, we would claim, is a good medium in which to formulate logical principles reflecting the kind of operational behaviour expressible in Natural Semantics. The TINY-ML example we have given here is certainly too simple to really test this claim. However, note that even here the logic allows us to reason about the behaviour of expressions-with-state without having to specify a global state explicitly—unlike the traditional domain-theoretic approach (and its formalizations). This becomes much more important for forms of computation where a domain-theoretic modelling of global state is very complicated (or not known). Computation involving dynamically allocated resources is an example of this, and an appropriate Evaluation Logic is currently under development. (Of course, one still has to find concrete models of the logical theories which arise ...)

Another aspect of the over-simplicity of the TINY-ML example is that it is in fact possible to eliminate the use of evaluation modalities and give a version of the above 'dynamic adequacy' result purely within an equational theory over the computational lambda calculus. Indeed one can equate the evaluation relation (2) with satisfaction of the equation

$$\vdash (up_{\ell_1}(n_1); \cdots; up_{\ell_k}(n_k); [\![\mathbf{e}]\!]) = (up_{\ell_1}(n_1'); \cdots; up_{\ell_k}(n_k'); [\![\mathbf{c}]\!])$$

in the theory we have given in Table 4, minus the last two axioms. However, the full modal logic should come into its own when devising computationally adequate theories for languages with non-deterministic features, for example. Even for purely deterministic languages, evaluation modalities appear useful when we go beyond simple computational adequacy results and address the question of finding logical principles for reasoning about the behaviour of programs in all (observable) contexts. The rules of Evaluation Logic and the axioms in Table 4 are *more* than adequate for Proposition 4.6.2 (not all of them are used in its proof), but are not exhaustive for reasoning about observable equivalence (since the latter is not recursively axiomatizable). An interesting example of the need for the evaluation modalities can be found in [1, 2], where the necessity modality is used to express an induction principle for fixpoint computations.

References

[1] R. L. Crole and A. M. Pitts, *New Foundations for Fixpoint Computations*, Proc. 5th Annual Symposium on Logic in Computer Science, Philadelphia (IEEE Computer Society Press, Washington, 1990) 489–497.

[2] R. L. Crole and A. M. Pitts, *New Foundations for Fixpoint Computations: FIX-Hyperdoctrines and the FIX-Logic*, University of Cambridge Computer Laboratory Technical Report No. 204, August 1990.

[3] M. Dummett, *Elements of Intuitionism* (Oxford University Press, 1977).

[4] C. Gunter and D. S. Scott, *Semantic Domains*. Chapter in *Handbook of Theoretical Computer Science* (North-Holland, Amsterdam, 1990).

[5] G. Kahn, *Natural Semantics*. In K. Fuchi and M. Nivat (eds), *Programming of Future Generation Computers* (Elsevier Science Publishers B.V. (North-Holland), Amsterdam, 1988) 237–258.

[6] J. W. Klop, *Combinatory Reduction Systems*, Amsterdam Mathematical Center Tracts 129 (1980).

[7] D. Kozen and J. Tiuryn, *Logics of Programs*. Chapter in *Handbook of Theoretical Computer Science* (North-Holland, Amsterdam, 1990).

[8] J. Lambek and P. J. Scott, *Introduction to Higher Order Categorical Logic*, Cambridge Studies in Advanced Mathematics 7 (Cambridge University Press, 1986).

[9] F. W. Lawvere, *Equality in Hyperdoctrines and the Comprehension Schema as an Adjoint Functor*. In A. Heller (ed.), *Applications of Categorical Algebra* (Amer. Math. Soc., Providence RI, 1970) 1–14.

[10] R. Milner, M. Tofte and R. Harper, *The Definition of Standard ML* (The MIT Press, Cambridge Massachussetts, 1990).

[11] E. Moggi, *Computational lambda-calculus and monads*, Proc. 4th Annual Symposium on Logic in Computer Science, Asilomar CA (IEEE Computer Society Press, Washington, 1989) 14–23.

[12] E. Moggi, *Notions of Computations and Monads*, preprint, 1989.

[13] E. Moggi, Lecture notes on *An Abstract View of Programming Languages*, July 1989.

[14] P. D. Mosses, *Denotational Semantics*. Chapter in *Handbook of Theoretical Computer Science* (North-Holland, Amsterdam, 1990).

[15] B. Nordström, K. Petersson and J. M. Smith, *Programming in Martin-Löf's Type Theory, An Introduction* (Oxford University Press, 1990).

[16] G. D. Plotkin, *Call-by-Name, Call-by-Value and the λ-Calculus*, Theoretical Computer Science 1(1977) 125–159.

[17] G. D. Plotkin, *LCF considered as a programming language*, Theoretical Computer Science 5(1977) 223–255.

[18] G. D. Plotkin, *A Structural Approach to Operational Semantics*, Aarhus University Computer Science Department Report DAIMI FN-19, 1981.

[19] G. D. Plotkin, *Denotational semantics with partial functions*, unpublished lecture notes from CSLI Summer School, 1985.

[20] D. S. Scott, *A type-theoretic alternative to CUCH, ISWIM, OWHY*, unpublished manuscript, University of Oxford, 1969.

[21] R. A. G. Seely, *Hyperdoctrines, Natural Deduction and the Beck Condition*, Zeitschr. f. math. Logik und Grundlagen d. Math. 29 (1983) 505–542.

Conditional Control is not quite Categorical Control

J. Robin B. Cockett

School of Mathematics and Computing
Macquarie University
Australia N.S.W. 2109
rcockett@ mqccsuna.mqcc.mq.oz.au

Abstract

It is often the intent of an algebraic specification of a data structure to include an aspect of control. For example, a stack is either empty or non-empty and one expects to be able to perform different actions based on this test. The question of whether an algebraic specification correctly expresses the intended control is related to a categorical question concerning whether the equalizer completion of the theory is distributive.

A many-sorted algebraic theory $\mathbf{T}$ is distributive whenever its (product preserving) equalizer completion, or equivalently the dual of the category of finitely presented algebras, $\mathcal{E}(\mathbf{T}) = (\mathbf{Set}_f^{\mathbf{T}})^{\mathrm{op}}$ is a distributive category. This happens precisely when it has inhabited types and a weak form of "if...then...else" operator satisfying certain Horn clauses.

Of philosophical interest is the observation that if one drops the requirement that the types are inhabited the above correspondence fails. This means that the traditional method of adding control using conditional operators does not in general correspond to the categorical notion of control as given in distributive categories (or even locally predistributive categories).

1 Introduction

1.1 Background

In 1989 I was in Iowa city attending the AMAST conference and listened to a talk on "if...then...else" algebras. At the end of the talk I commented to the speaker that the models of these algebras formed distributive categories and that their properties could be best abstracted at this generality. Over the course of the next few days at the conference, I had several intense discussions concerning these issues with Bill Lawvere. We resolved that it was a fertile area to pursue. This, particularly, as we had to recognize that many of the equivalences which appeared so apparent to us in the heat of the conference were in reality still in the realm of mathematical folklore or worse unproven.

By a curious twist of fate, Steve Schanuel with Bill Lawvere, Bob Walters, and I had independently been pursuing results in the area of distributive categories. Each group had very different motivations and had used a different starting point. Bob Walters was also at the conference and, although at that time I did not know that this would happen, in December of 1989 I would go to Sydney to work with Ross Street and Bob Walters on distributive categories supported by the Sydney Category Theory Seminar.

Bob had made the important realization that distributive categories had an immediate application as a specification language. His favorite example is to contrast the classical specification of a stack with the distributive one. The latter simply states that $\langle \text{nil}, \text{push} \rangle : 1 + A \times \text{Stack}(A) \longrightarrow \text{Stack}(A)$ has inverse "pop" (we shall discuss this further below). Furthermore, he had recently embarked on a program of teaching distributive category theory to undergraduates at Sydney University under the guise of "Categories for Computer Science" [12]. The course was sufficiently popular that the Computer Science Department had been forced to take note of the increasing probability that their students might have this background. This article is heavily influenced by Bob's interest in promoting distributive specifications.

To my dismay Bob meant something slightly different from either Schanuel and Lawvere or myself by a distributive category. On my arrival in Sydney there was considerable consternation when I introduced the notion of a predistributive category as a possible starting point for the theory. Indeed, for a while it seemed that the different styles of definition would inhibit any real progress in the area. Fortunately, it has turned out [1] that all the notions are related closely by embedding theorems: so the results of the independent thrusts could begin to be consolidated. I think it is true to say that Schanuel and Lawvere have won on the naming front with Bob coming in a close second: the names I used have largely been expunged from the area!

There were many reasons behind Bill Lawvere's desire to pursue the subject. Undoubtably one was that he saw many interesting mathematical structures falling into the pattern of distributive categories. However, another was the niggling concern that although topos theory had given constructive mathematics a semantics, a topos was still very far from having its constructs computable. A simpler setting (even than a cartesian closed category) was needed to invest the issues of practical computability. Distributive categories looked like a promising avenue.

The present article follows in the spirit of the discussions I had with Bill at the

AMAST conference and provides some of the flesh to the "feeling" we then had that distributive categories and "if...then...else" algebras are related. Furthermore, coincidentally, it begins to bear out Bill's feeling that distributive categories play a central role in classical mathematics itself. Distributive theories seem to have been the focus of considerable classical attention.

1.2 Formalizing control

To illustrate the potential value of investigating distributive categories to computer science it is useful to trace the motivations of Bob Walters and in particular his realization that distributive specifications of data structures [11] could be useful. Before doing this, however, it is worth discussing why the coproduct in the form it arises in distributive categories has particular relevance to computer science.

1.2.1 Control, coproducts, and distribution

The purpose of a control statement in a program is to divide the program states into two (or more) disjoint sets from which the program proceeds in different ways. As the coproduct of two or more sets is their disjoint union, a control statement may be viewed as a map to a coproduct. That the control statements in programs can be modeled successfully by categorical coproducts has been known for some time. Given this realization it is not unreasonable to try and abstract those properties of the coproduct which make it suitable for expressing this control.

When a control statement divides the program states into two or more disjoint sets one certainly does not want to loose the results of calculations already completed as they may be of use down the branches of the program. Categorically this means that a strong coproduct, that is a coproduct over which the product distributes, is required in order that the results of the previous calculations can be made available down each control branch.

To illustrate this consider the following psuedo code:

```
write("What is the payment");
input(pay);
write("Is payee a national?");
input(national);
if (national = no) then tax = pay/2;
else tax = pay/3;
write("Tax withholding is");
write(tax);
end;
```

Notice that the value of `pay` is used down both branches of the conditional while the control decision is made on a completely different variable `national`. If we try to translate this into a series of (set) maps we obtain:

$$1 \xrightarrow{\text{(national,pay)}} (1+1) \times N \xrightarrow{\text{d}} 1 \times N + 1 \times N \xrightarrow{(b_0 \times \_/3; b_1 \times \_/2)} (1+1) \times N$$

where

$$d : (A+B) \times C \longrightarrow (A \times C) + (B \times C); \quad \begin{array}{l} (b_0(a), c) \mapsto b_0(a, c) \\ (b_1(b), c) \mapsto b_1(b, c) \end{array}$$

in which the disjoint union of two sets is represented as

$$A + B = \{b_0(a) | a \in A\} \cup \{b_1(b) | b \in B\}$$

and thus the map d is distributing the values of **pay** down each branch.

In fact the map d gives an isomorphism $(A + B) \times C \longrightarrow A \times C + B \times C$ which is the inverse to the natural map:

$$\langle b_0 \times i; b_1 \times i \rangle : A \times C + B \times C \longrightarrow (A + B) \times C; \quad \begin{array}{l} b_0(a,c) \quad \mapsto (b_0(a), c) \\ b_1(b,c) \quad \mapsto (b_1(b), c) \end{array}$$

The requirement that this last map is an isomorphism suffices to secure almost all the useful formal properties of the control of programs.

1.2.2   Sums

As the coproduct of two objects is often written $A + B$ it is often called the "sum." In this article we shall call a coproduct a **sum** only when the product distributes over it. Thus, a category has binary sums if it has coproducts such that

$$\langle b_0 \times i; b_1 \times i \rangle : A \times C + B \times C \longrightarrow (A + B) \times C$$

is an isomorphism. The inverse we shall denote

$$d : (A + B) \times C \longrightarrow A \times C + B \times C.$$

A cartesian category with sums is a **predistributive** category.

This is intended to be a suggestive use of names for indeed the coproduct can often be taken to be a structural form of addition which is a direct analogue of the quantitative form of addition (i.e. of "numbers"). Consider finite sets, there is an obvious number associated with each finite set, namely its cardinal, and the cardinal of the disjoint union of two sets is the sum of their cardinals. Thus, finite sets may be regarded as a structural version of the natural numbers. The requirement that products distribute over the coproduct in a distributive category is then a structural analogue of the distribution of multiplication over addition.

This analogy has been pushed much further in some fascinating work by Schanuel: he associates with an arbitrary distributive category a rig (ring without negatives), called the Burnside rig of the category. The rig represents the quantitative arithmetic of the structural setting. Some combinatoric problems can then be viewed as being concerned with the interplay of the structural setting (the distributive category) with the quantities in this Burnside rig.

1.3   Data structures

Every computer scientist knows what a stack is and yet if one looks in standard texts for the specification of a stack one often is surprised to find how unintuitive and complex the specification of this very basic data structure is. If one extrapolates this to providing a specification of a major software component one can quickly understand why the ability to specify might lag behind the ability to code. Bob Walters [11] observed that it was very simple to specify a stack if the constructs present in a distributive category are employed.

194

1.3.1 Algebraic specification

We start by considering the following algebraic specification given in Ehrig and Mahr
[5]:

```
Sorts:
    A,S
Operations:
    a1,...,an: 1 --> A,
    error: 1 --> A,
    empty: 1 --> S,
    pop: S --> S,
    top: S --> A,
    push: A * S --> S
Equations:
    pop(push(x,s)) = s,
    top(push(x,s)) = x,
    pop(empty) = empty,
    top(empty) = error
```

There are a number of obviously less than agreeable aspects to this specification.
It is not applicable to a general type A: not only must the elements be specified but
also a specified error element be present. This latter requirement makes it
rather a peculiar type – in fact a pointed type. One might reasonably continue by
complaining that stacks of the form

$$[a1, a2, error, a1, error, a3]$$

were surely not intended.

Having a specification of a stack in which the set A is general is of paramount
importance. Not only does it allow the reuse of the specification but it facilitates
the glueing of specifications.

1.3.2 Order-sorted algebraic specification

To obtain an algebraic specification of a stack on general type requires considerable
ingenuity and led to the development of order-sorted algebras which were subsequently used in OBJ3 [9]. To illustrate their effect consider the OBJ3 definition
of a stack given by Goguen [7]. Goguen states that "this seems about as simple a
program as one could desire."

```
STACK[X :: TRIV] is sorts Stack NeStack .
    subsorts A < NeStack < Stack .
    op empty : -> Stack .
    op push : A Stack -> NeStack .
    op top_ : NeStack -> A .
    op pop_ : NeStack -> Stack .
    var X : A .
    var S : Stack .
```

```
      eq top push(X,S) = X .
      eq pop push(X,S) = S .
endo
```

Notice that this description of a stack is now given for a general type A but at the cost of a Stack becoming a more complex type with a subtype NeStack.

Notice pop and top are only defined on the subsort NeStack. This means that when one pops a stack one must first know whether it is actually a NeStack: if it is not a typing error is reported. Therefore, one cannot guarantee that programs using stacks can be composed as the first program might pass a Stack when the next needs a NeStack. While all this can be detected by type checking, these subtleties may cause programmers (who believe that stacks are stacks) some frustration.

However, the situation from the point of view of specification is far worse. Notice that one cannot, using only the constructs of this description, exercise control according to whether the stack is empty or not. Of course OBJ3 does allow one to test the emptiness of a stack. However, a branch by testing whether the stack is empty presumes that a non-empty stack is a NeStack. The fact that this is so can be obtained only from the hidden assumption that the stack is implemented as an initial algebra. It is certainly not the case that a non-empty stack is a NeStack for non-initial algebras.

Thus, the fact that one obtains the correct intuitive notion of a stack from this OBJ3 description is almost a fortunate coincidence. It is not forced by the equations but rather by the special properties of the initial algebra. In fact, to provide a correct realization of a stack satisfying this definition the most important aspect is that it be an initial model. When the implementation does not automatically provide this, one may be faced with a non-trivial verification that it is in fact initial.

The Achilles heel of the initial algebra approach to the *specification* of data structures is that an initial algebra, while satisfying only equations provable from the axioms (called no confusion), satisfies many additional properties which are non-equational. Unfortunately, it is usually these properties which are fundamental to the use of the structure in programs.

To correct this defect one needs to introduce specifications which are satisfied by any implementation with satisfies its equations. In OBJ3 such things are called theories and they list the requirements, in the form of Horn clauses, that an implementation must satisfy. However, one cannot provide a purely algebraic specification of a stack on a general type without adding some form of control. In OBJ3 this is done by supplying a Boolean type which is (with the help of some built-in functions) the sum $1 + 1$.

Thus, to write an OBJ3 specification of a stack we need to add more equations to the above description which will involve the built-in functions for control. I leave it to the reader to ponder how this might be done such that a specification equivalent to the one described below is obtained.

1.3.3 Distributive specification

The specification of being a stack in a distributive category may be expressed as follows:

Sorts:

```
        A,stack(A)
Operations:
        empty: 1 --> stack(A),
        push: A * stack(A) --> stack(A),
        pop: stack(A) --> 1 + A * stack(A)
Equations:
        (empty ; push) . pop = i,
        pop . (empty ; push) = i
```

This is a short sweet specification: it says that a stack on A is any object with elements which are either empty or of the form push(A,X). The specification is done for general type A, does not introduce any extraneous types, and *all* its models are what we intuitively expect stacks to be! The cost, however, is that we have stepped outside equational logic. This I am arguing is a worthwhile investment.

The purpose of adding a Boolean type to OBJ3 was to obtain control. It is reasonable then, taking a categorical view, to ask whether this is equivalent to introducing sums into the semantics. If it were the argument for moving to distributive specifications is diminished. Significantly this is not the case.

It is rather obvious that having the sum $1 + 1$ has the effect of adding sums of the form $2^n \cdot A$. Mixed coproducts are not guaranteed: a counter-example is the theory of two sorts (besides $1 + 1$) and no maps. If we permit ourselves to consider Horn logic (which categorically is equivalent to adding formal equalizers while preserving products) this denial of equivalence still holds and the same theory serves as a counter-example. For the coproduct to be present in the Horn theory it already must be present as a formal equalizer.

The purpose of this article is to elucidate the relationship between the classical formulation of control, using conditional operators on a Boolean type together with purely algebraic notions, and the categorical formulation of control using the sum.

1.4 Specifications and models

Specifications using more powerful logics than equational logic have of course been investigated. There is a tendency to jump from equational logic straight to (first order) predicate logic as the next available alternative. However, in doing so one is passing over many intermediate logics whose more restricted natures have considerable value. Distributive logic, as such an intermediate logic, appears to have exactly the natural ingredients for program specification.

Distributive logic adds control to equational logic. The addition of control causes distributive specifications to cross an important conceptual boundary as distributive specifications will, in general, lack an initial model.

The great attraction of algebraic specification is that, despite giving a specification that has many models, there is always a unique distinguished model (to equivalence) namely the initial model. This means that by asking that models be initial one obtains a unique semantic denotation. This is, in turn, important as it is a necessary prerequisite for there to be a uniquely determined implementation.

The existence of initial models has been, quite rightly, a touch-stone for algebraic specification. However, the distinction between providing a construct in a programming language and a specification is important. Initiality (and finality) of programming constructs is vital: but this requirement does not carry through to the satisfaction of a specification.

1.4.1 Generic models

Despite there not being in general an initial model (in **Set**) for a distributive specification there is a **generic** model. This is a gadget satisfying the specification sitting inside a general distributive category. It has the property that given any model of the specification (in any distributive category) there is a unique distributive functor from the generic gadget which picks out that model. It is fairly obvious that the generic model sitting in its general distributive setting must be generated from the specification by allowing only those maps, types, and identifications which are derivable in distributive logic (see the formulation of Charles Wells [13]). Thus, what is true of the generic model must be true in all implementations.

The distributive algebraic theories discussed in the sequel are those distributive theories which may be described by an algebraic specification. It is the fact that they live in both worlds which makes them of special interest.

1.4.2 Sums, fixed points, and termination

It is a well-known fact, due to Bill Lawvere [10] and more recently emphasized by Huwig and Poigne [6], that a cartesian closed category with enough fixed points cannot have coproducts. It is a simple observation that this follows precisely because coproducts in a cartesian closed category are sums. This means that distributive specifications are only really applicable in situations in which types are not expected to have fixed points.

One reason for introducing fixed points into a semantics is to allow for the possibility of non-termination. Distributive specifications are, thus, particularly applicable to algorithms. Their use with processes should be more guarded.[1]

1.4.3 Distributive algebraic theories

A **distributive algebraic theory** is an algebraic theory, given by an algebraic specification, whose generic finitely complete model category is equivalent to the generic finitely complete model category of a distributive theory.

The reason for studying these theories should now be clear: if an algebraic specification is intended to express control then it should have an "equivalent" distributive presentation. If it does not then one might reasonably suspect that the specification does not faithfully convey the intended meaning. Furthermore, we may be able to tell, from general considerations, when it is undesirable to produce a purely algebraic specification!

---

[1]This does not actually mean that the description of processes using these specifications is impossible. It does means that one has to be careful that the processes involved have an external behavior: that is will always produce something (e.g. an infinite stream).

1.5   Technical introduction

1.5.1   Algebraic theories

A (many-sorted) algebraic theory **T** may be taken to be a small cartesian category, that is a category having finite products, whose types and maps are generated respectively by the primitive sorts and operations. If **T** is such a theory then a **T**-algebra in a cartesian category **X** is simply a cartesian functor with domain **T** and codomain **X**. The category of **T**-algebras in **X** has objects **T**-algebras and maps natural transformations. It is usual to take the category **X** to be the category of sets, **Set**: in this case the Yoneda embedding defines the finitely generated free algebras and finite colimits of these give the category of finitely presented algebras, $\mathbf{Set}_f^{\mathbf{T}}$.

The dual of the category of finitely presented algebras, $(\mathbf{Set}_f^{\mathbf{T}})^{\mathrm{op}}$, is equivalently the product preserving equalizer completion of **T** which we shall write as $\mathcal{E}(\mathbf{T})$. This category has the property that any cartesian functor from **T** to a finitely complete category **X** can be extended in an "up to unique natural equivalence" way to be a finite limit preserving functor from $\mathcal{E}(\mathbf{T})$ to **X**. It is also equivalent to the syntactic category for the Horn logic of **T**.

In the discussion of theories we must make some careful distinctions. A **presentation** of an algebraic theory is a particular collection of primitive sorts, operations, and equations used to describe the theory. Clearly a presentation of an algebraic theory is precisely the same as an **algebraic specification** of the theory. The **algebraic theory** itself is the small cartesian category which is generated from the algebraic specification: an **algebra** is simply a cartesian functor with domain the theory. Two algebraic specifications are **theory equivalent** if there is an equivalence of categories between their algebraic theories. This allows two very different specifications to have equivalent algebraic theories or, equivalently, an algebraic theory to have different presentations.

Two (presentations of) algebraic theories are **Horn equivalent** if they are equivalent as Horn theories. This is the requirement that the (product preserving) equalizer completions of their theories are equivalent. The equalizer completion is equivalent to the dual of the category of finitely presented algebras, thus we may also restate the condition by requiring that their categories of finitely presented algebras are equivalent. This condition has also been called **Morita equivalence** and has been studied in the context of modules of rings. If two algebraic presentations or specifications are theory equivalent they are certainly Horn or Morita equivalent but the converse is not true. A given theory (to Horn equivalence) can have many theory inequivalent presentations.

1.5.2   Distributive algebraic theories

An algebraic theory **T** is defined to be a **distributive algebraic theory** whenever its equalizer completion $\mathcal{E}(\mathbf{T})$ is a distributive category. These categories, at least in their cocompleted dual form, have been extensively studied by Yvres Diers in [4] as locally presentable categories. A **distributive category** is a finitely complete category with disjoint coproducts which are stable under pulling back. In particular this means that products distribute over coproducts, thus it is certainly predistributive.

An alternative rather elegant description, due to Schanuel and Lawvere, characterizes them as finitely complete categories with finite coproducts such that:

$$\mathbf{X}/(A + B) \simeq (\mathbf{X}/A) \times (\mathbf{X}/B) \quad \text{and} \quad \mathbf{X}/0 \simeq 1.$$

These conditions may be simplified [1] to requiring that $\mathbf{X}$ has finite limits and binary coproducts such that

$$\mathbf{X}/(1 + 1) \simeq \mathbf{X} \times \mathbf{X}.$$

The passage from predistributive to distributive is described in [1]. Excepting one technical difficulty which is overcome in this exposition with the assumption that all primitive types are inhabited, it is the case that one may fully and faithfully embed a predistributive category into a distributive category so as to preserve both products and binary coproducts.

1.5.3   Characterizing distributive algebraic theories

I shall show that an algebraic theory is distributive precisely when its primitive types are inhabited and the dual of its category of finitely presented algebras contains the sum $1 + 1$. This can be expressed equationally as the requirement that it has **preconditional operators** on all its inhabited primitive sorts. Preconditional operators satisfy certain simple Horn clause conditions.

The Horn clause conditions of preconditional operators can be eliminated when the idempotent completion $\mathcal{K}(\mathbf{T})$ already contains the sum $1+1$. When this happens we obtain **absolute conditional operators**. An obvious way in which this happens is if the type $1+1$ is directly represented as a primitive sort. In this case the absolute conditional operators become **conditional operators** and "if ... then ... else" or **conditional algebras** are obtained. These last directly implement the control on a Boolean type and give the classical formulation of control in programming languages.

It is worth emphasizing that it is not necessary to have a boolean type explicitly given in the presentation in order to simulate control purely algebraically. Absolute conditional algebras show how control can be based on a type which has a boolean type as a retract. A natural number object is an example of such a type.

There are many interesting examples of distributive algebraic theories: distributive lattices, Heyting algebras, Boolean algebras, various varieties of rings including commutative rings, and various varieties of rigs (semi-rings) are examples. Of classical computational interest are the conditional algebras.

When the types are not all inhabited the manner of constructing coproducts used here must be reconsidered. We show that having a conditional operator will not suffice to obtain even the predistributivity of the Horn theory (assuming that coproducts exist which itself can fail). This means there is a subtle difference between the control given by conditional operators and the categorical formulation of control and means, in general, that there are theorems provable in the categorical formulation which cannot be proven in the conditional formulation.

2   Distributive theories as categories

If every slice of a predistributive category is predistributive it is said to be **locally predistributive**. A locally predistributive category equivalently is a finitely complete predistributive category in which pulling back preserves coproducts. A locally predistributive category is **distributive** whenever the coproducts are disjoint. This is equivalently given by requiring that the category be **strict** in the sense that the category has all **preinitial objects** initial. A preinitial object is an object which has at most one map to any object. These properties and the categories involved are discussed in [1].

The main theorem of this section is a characterization of distributive theories in terms of the existence of conditional operators. The discussion starts by establishing a series of technical categorical results which are aimed at simplifying the task of this characterization.

The steps leading to this theorem are as follows: first we show that a predistributive category in which coreflexive equalization commutes with coproducts is locally predistributive (all slices are predistributive). It happens that in a predistributive category equalization commutes with coproducts if and only if coreflexive equalization is preserved by $A + \_$. The commuting condition explicitly is: if

$$E_i \xrightarrow{e_i} A_i \underset{g_i}{\overset{f_i}{\rightrightarrows}} B_i$$

for $i = 0, 1$ are equalizers then

$$E_0 + E_1 \xrightarrow{e_0 + e_1} A_0 + A_1 \underset{g_0 + g_1}{\overset{f_0 + f_1}{\rightrightarrows}} B_0 + B_1$$

is an equalizer. This allows the conclusion that a strict (all preinitials are initial) predistributive category with this commuting property is distributive.

In categories of algebras reflexive coequalization always commutes with products thus the required commuting condition described above always holds in the dual form. This means it is sufficient to check that the dual of the distributive law holds in the category of algebras to obtain the local predistributivity of the theory. To obtain full distributivity we must demand costrictness in the category of algebras. This is equivalent to the demand that the primitive types all be inhabited.

In the category of algebras the free algebras (obtained from the Yoneda embedding) are generators. Thus, it is natural to consider the (finite) regular cogeneration properties of distributive categories. In a category with regular cogenerators (in fact strong would suffice) a cocone is a colimit cocone if and only if it is for the cogenerators. This allows us to reformulate the existence of binary coproducts, over which the product distributes, in terms of the existence of conditional operators on the cogenerators. We may then establish the theorem which characterizes distributive theories.

2.1 Equalization in predistributive categories

The main result of this subsection is:

Theorem 2.1 *A predistributive category with coreflexive equalization is locally predistributive if and only if each coproduct functor $A + \_$ preserves coreflexive equalizers.*

A category has coreflexive equalization in case every parallel pair of arrows

$$A \underset{g}{\overset{f}{\rightrightarrows}} B$$

for which there is a common retract $q : B \longrightarrow A$ with $f.q = i_A = g.q$ has an equalizer.

The result shall be applied in the following form:

Corollary 2.2 *A predistributive category with equalization is distributive if and only if each coproduct functor $A + \_$ preserves coreflexive equalizers and the category is strict.*

The remainder of this section is dedicated to proving this result. A sketch of the proof is as follows:

That a locally predistributive category satisfies these properties is relatively easy as equalizers can be expressed as pullbacks over diagonal maps. When pulling back commutes with coproducts, equalization in general must commute with coproducts so certainly $A + \_$ must preserve equalization.

The difficulty is to establish the other direction. For this we need a number of preliminary observations. In any cartesian category the existence of coreflexive coequalization implies the existence of all equalization. This means that such a category is certainly finitely complete. Next we show that in a predistributive category $A + \_$ preserves coreflexive coequalization if and only if it preserves all equalization. This is then equivalent to demanding that $\_ + \_$ commutes with equalization. Finally, we observe that the pullback of a coproduct can be expressed as the coproduct of two equalizers allowing the equivalence of the theorem to be established.

We start the proof with the trivial observation that in predistributive categories, indeed cartesian categories, the existence of coreflexive equalizers implies the existence of all equalizers.

Lemma 2.3 *If a cartesian category has coreflexive equalizers it has all equalizers.*

Proof. Observe that

$$E \xrightarrow{\ e\ } A \underset{g}{\overset{f}{\rightrightarrows}} B$$

is an equalizer if and only if

$$E \xrightarrow{\ e\ } A \underset{\langle g,i \rangle}{\overset{\langle f,i \rangle}{\rightrightarrows}} B \times A$$

is an equalizer.

□

We now wish to show that if coreflexive equalization is preserved by $A + \_$ then $\_ + \_$ preserves equalization, in other words that coproducts commute with equalization. The following lemma is a well-known result concerning coreflexive equalization (see Peter Johnstone's book on topos theory [8] in which it is given in its dual form):

Lemma 2.4 *If all the horizontal and vertical equalizers are coreflexive and the diagram commutes in the obvious way, then the diagonal is an equalizer.*

$$
\begin{array}{ccccc}
B'_0 & \xrightarrow{\ e'\ } & B & \underset{g'}{\overset{f'}{\rightrightarrows}} & B' \\[4pt]
\scriptstyle a'_0 \,\|\, b'_0 \Big\uparrow\uparrow & & \scriptstyle a\,\|\,b \Big\uparrow\uparrow & & \scriptstyle a'\,\|\,b' \Big\uparrow\uparrow \\[4pt]
A'_0 & \xrightarrow{\ e\ } & A & \underset{g}{\overset{f}{\rightrightarrows}} & A' \\[4pt]
\scriptstyle h_0 \Big\uparrow & & \scriptstyle h \Big\uparrow & & \scriptstyle h' \Big\uparrow \\[4pt]
E & \xrightarrow{\ e_0\ } & A_0 & \underset{g_0}{\overset{f_0}{\rightrightarrows}} & \mathrm{b}_0
\end{array}
$$

Using this we can now observe that such an equalizer square is formed when performing componentwise coreflexive equalization over a coproduct:

$$
\begin{array}{ccccc}
A'+\mathrm{b}_0 & \xrightarrow{\ i+f_0\ } A'+B & \underset{i+f_2}{\overset{i+f_1}{\rightrightarrows}} A'+B' \\[6pt]
\scriptstyle a_1+i \,\|\, a_2+i \Big\uparrow\uparrow & \scriptstyle a_1+i \,\|\, a_2+i \Big\uparrow\uparrow & \scriptstyle a_1+i \,\|\, a_2+i \Big\uparrow\uparrow \\[6pt]
A+\mathrm{b}_0 & \xrightarrow{\ e\ } A+B & \underset{i+f_2}{\overset{i+f_1}{\rightrightarrows}} A+B' \\[6pt]
\scriptstyle a_0+i \Big\uparrow & \scriptstyle a_0+i \Big\uparrow & \scriptstyle a_0+i \Big\uparrow \\[6pt]
A_0+\mathrm{b}_0 & \xrightarrow{\ i+f_0\ } A_0+B & \underset{i+f_2}{\overset{i+f_1}{\rightrightarrows}} A_0+B'
\end{array}
$$

this allows us to form coreflexive equalizers component-wise.

Thus, in any category with coproducts the preservation of coreflexive equalizers by $A + \_$ is equivalent to the preservation of coreflexive equalizers by $\_ + \_$ In a predistributive category we now show that these preservations of coreflexive equalizers are equivalent to the preservations of arbitrary equalizers. Thus, the coreflexive assumption can be removed.

Lemma 2.5 *In a predistributive category* $\_ + \_ : \mathbf{X} \times \mathbf{X} \longrightarrow \mathbf{X}$ *preserves equalizers if and only if* $A + \_$ *preserves coreflexive equalizers.*

Proof. Obviously the former condition implies the latter. Thus the only difficulty is to establish the reverse implication.

Suppose, therefore, that $A + \_$ preserves coreflexive equalizers for every A. Let

$$
E_j \xrightarrow{\ e_j\ } F_j \underset{g_j}{\overset{f_j}{\rightrightarrows}} G_j
$$

be equalizers for $j = 0, 1$ then

$$
E_j \xrightarrow{\ e_j\ } F_j \underset{(g_j,i)}{\overset{(f_j,i)}{\rightrightarrows}} G_j \times F_j
$$

are coreflexive equalizers. This means that

$$E_0 + E_1 \xrightarrow{e_0+e_1} F_0 + F_1 \underset{\langle g_0,i\rangle+\langle g_1,i\rangle}{\overset{\langle f_0,i\rangle+\langle f_1,i\rangle}{\rightrightarrows}} G_0 \times F_0 + G_1 \times F_1$$

is an equalizer using the above lemma. Now if k equalizes $f_0 + f_1$ and $g_0 + g_1$ then k equalizes

$$F_0 + F_1 \underset{\langle g_0+g_1,i\rangle}{\overset{\langle f_0+f_1,i\rangle}{\rightrightarrows}} (G_0 + G_1) \times (F_0 + F_1).$$

However, we have the following identities:

$$\langle f_0 + f_1, i\rangle = \langle\langle f_0,i\rangle + \langle f_1,i\rangle\rangle.\langle\langle b_0 \times b_0\rangle; \langle b_1 \times b_1\rangle\rangle$$

$$\langle g_0 + g_1, i\rangle = \langle\langle g_0,i\rangle + \langle g_1,i\rangle\rangle.\langle\langle b_0 \times b_0\rangle; \langle b_1 \times b_1\rangle\rangle$$

where in any predistributive category $\langle\langle b_0 \times b_0\rangle; \langle b_1 \times b_1\rangle\rangle$ is an embedding into a coproduct and so monic. This means that the equalizer of $\langle f_0+f_1, i\rangle$ and $\langle g_0+g_1, i\rangle$ is the same as the equalizer of $\langle\langle f_0,i\rangle + \langle f_1,i\rangle\rangle$ and $\langle\langle g_0,i\rangle + \langle g_1,i\rangle\rangle$ but this is just the sum of the equalizers of f_j and g_j that is $E_0 + E_1$.

$\square$

By making the equalizer in one coordinate trivial we obtain:

Corollary 2.6 *In a predistributive category $A + \_$ preserves coreflexive equalizers for each A if and only if $A + \_$ preserves all equalizers for each A.*

We can now prove the proposition:

Proof(of 2.1). If X is locally predistributive it is certainly predistributive. Furthermore, equalizers commute with coproducts. This may be seen by expressing the equalizer as a pullback over the diagonal: as pulling back preserves coproducts the pullback is easily seen to be the coproduct of the equalizers in each component.

Conversely, we must show that if equalizers are preserved by coproducts that pulling back preserves coproducts. Consider:

$$\begin{array}{c} A_1 + A_2 \\ \downarrow {\scriptstyle \langle f_1; f_2\rangle} \\ C \xrightarrow{\ h\ } D \end{array}$$

then this pullback is given by the equalizer:

$$C \times A_1 + C \times A_2 \underset{\langle p_0.h; p_0.h\rangle}{\overset{\langle p_1.f_1; p_1.f_2\rangle}{\rightrightarrows}} D.$$

However, observe that

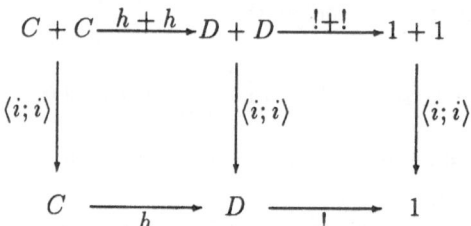

$$C + C \xrightarrow{h+h} D + D \xrightarrow{!+!} 1 + 1$$

is a pullback in each square as the right square and the outer square are certainly pullbacks (as $D + D \equiv D \times (1 + 1)$ and $C + C \equiv C \times (1 + 1)$). The above equalizer can be formed as the equalizer of the upper square in

$$C \times A_1 + C \times A_2 \xrightarrow{p_1 + p_1} A_1 + A_2$$

However, this is an equalizer of a coproduct which by assumption is the coproduct of the equalizers as desired. $\quad\square$

2.2 Reflexive coequalization in algebras

Let $\mathbf{T}$ be any many-sorted algebraic theory then the equalizer completion is equivalent to the opposite of the category of finitely presented algebras, $\mathcal{E}(\mathbf{T}) \simeq (\mathbf{Set}_f^{\mathbf{T}})^{op}$. An equalizer in this category is a coequalizer in the category of algebras. Thus, to ascertain how the equalizer behaves with respect to the coproduct in $\mathcal{E}(\mathbf{T})$ we may equivalently ask how coequalization behaves with respect to the product in the category of algebras.

Coequalization in any category of algebras is formed by constructing the congruence generated by the image of the equalizer in the product of the algebra with itself. The rules for this construction are as follows:

Let R be any relation on A an algebra then $R(S)$ is a relation on $A(S)$ for each sort S. We let E_R be the equivalence relation or **congruence** generated by R then $E_R(S)$ is the equivalence relation on the sort S.

Basis: $x \sim_R y \in R(S) \Rightarrow x \sim y \in E_R(S)$,

Reflexive: $x \sim x \in E_R(S)$,

205

Symmetric: $x \sim y \in E_R(S) \Rightarrow y \sim x \in E_R(S)$,

Transitive: $x \sim y \in E_R(S)$ and $y \sim z \in E_R(S) \Rightarrow x \sim z \in E_R(S)$,

Operational: $x_i \sim y_i \in E_R(S_i)$ for $i = 1, ..., n$ and $f : S_1 \times .. \times S_n \longrightarrow S_0$
$\Rightarrow f(x_1, ..., x_n) \sim f(y_1, ..y_n) \in E_R(S_0)$.

It is important to remember that in the category of algebras the relation R must itself be an algebra. If R is reflexive and $x \sim_R x'$ in some sort then certainly $f(x, y) \sim_R f(x', y)$ for any y. This means that for reflexive coequalization the operational requirement can be replaced by using the reflexivity and transitivity:

$$x_1 \sim y_1, ..., x_n \sim y_n$$

implies

$$\begin{aligned}
f(x_1, x_2, ..., x_n) &\sim f(y_1, x_2, ..., x_n), \\
f(y_1, x_2, ..., x_n) &\sim f(y_1, y_2, x_3, ..., x_n), \\
... &\sim ..., \\
f(y_1, ..., y_{n-1}, x_n) &\sim f(y_1, ..., y_n)
\end{aligned}$$

which by transitivity gives the operational rule.

This allows the rather surprising observation:

Lemma 2.7 *The congruence for a reflexive relation in a category of algebras is generated by symmetry and transitivity alone.*

Proof. For this we consider an arbitrary proof of $x \sim y$ and show that it can be replaced by one employing only a chain of generating relations and their opposites in the given type whose transitive composition is the desired relation $x \sim y$. This is true for proofs which state a generating relation, the opposite of a generating relation, or a reflexive pair (as the relation is reflexive). Next we show that it is true when adding any single step to the proof.

If the last step is symmetry then we may reverse the chain of the original proof to obtain a proof of the new pair in the desired form. For transitivity we may simply append the chains to obtain the new proof in the desired form. The only remaining difficulty is to show that an operational inference can replaced. However, using the technique described above we can certainly replace an operational inference on chains of length one by a proof of the desired form. However, given that we can translate an operational inference on chains of some given lengths we can always add one more step to any of these chains and add the basic step which modifies that coordinate of the function to obtain a new proof in the desired form. This means that an operational step can be replaced by a proof of the desired form.

□

When a congruence is being generated on a product from a product of two reflexive relations, the first of which is the diagonal, the transitive and reflexive rules will always preserve the diagonality of the first but close up the second into a congruence.

Proposition 2.8 *In any category of algebras reflexive coequalization commutes with the product functors* $\_ \times \_$.

Here we need to apply 2.4 in its dual form to obtain the bifunctorial version of preservation.

This implies that for any many-sorted algebraic theory $\mathbf{T}$, in $\mathcal{E}(\mathbf{T})$ the coproduct, in so far as it may exist, preserves coreflexive equalization. This allows the following simplification of what we must do to show that $\mathcal{E}(\mathbf{T})$ is locally predistributive.

Corollary 2.9 *An algebraic theory* $\mathbf{T}$ *has its equalizer completion* $\mathcal{E}(\mathbf{T})$ *a locally predistributive category if and only if* $\mathcal{E}(\mathbf{T})$ *has sums.*

In fact as every object is a reflexive coequalizer of objects in $\mathbf{T}$ it suffices to show that these objects have sums. Furthermore, we may use reflexive coeqalization again to show that it suffices to check that the objects of $\mathbf{T}$ distribute over these coproducts.

We are particularly interested in the case when the equalizer completion is distributive. In this case the initial object can have no non-trivial epimorphs. In the algebras this is the requirement that the final object has no non-trivial subobjects which happens precisely when every type is inhabited.

Corollary 2.10 *An algebraic theory* $\mathbf{T}$ *with inhabited types is a distributive theory if and only if* $\mathcal{E}(\mathbf{T})$ *has sums.*

As an arbitrary sort is a product of primitives it suffices to insist that the primitive sorts in $\mathbf{T}$ are inhabited.

If $\mathbf{T}$ is already predistributive we may conclude:

Corollary 2.11 *If* $\mathbf{T}$ *is predistributive then* $\mathcal{E}(\mathbf{T})$ *is locally predistributive.*

2.3 Regular inhabited cogeneration

If a category is of the form $\mathcal{E}(\mathbf{T})$ then the primitive sorts form a set of regular cogenerators. This may be more apparent when one takes the dual viewpoint: the finitely presented algebras are regularly generated by the finitely generated "free" algebras. This means that it is of some interest to investigate the properties of distributive (and locally predistributive) categories with a set of regular cogenerators.

Definition 2.12 *A cartesian category has a set of* **regular cogenerators** $\{A_i | i \in I\}$, *if each object* C *is the equalizer of a diagram*

$$ C \xrightarrow{\ c\ } \prod_{i=1}^{n} A_{j_i} \underset{h_1}{\overset{h_0}{\rightrightarrows}} \prod_{i=1}^{m} A_{k_i}. $$

Notice the restriction to finite products. The more usual notion of cogeneration does not have this restriction, however, as we are concerned, in the dual, with finitely presented algebras this is a natural restriction.

We shall say that a cocone is a **colimit cocone for an object** if for each cocone on the same base with apex that object there is a unique cocomparison map from the original cocone. A cocone is a colimit cocone for a set of objects if it is for each object in the set.

Lemma 2.13 *If* **X** *is cartesian with a set of regular cogenerators then* $\alpha : C \longrightarrow C_0$ *is a colimit cocone if and only if it is a colimit cocone for the regular cogenerators of* **X**.

Proof. The only difficulty lies in proving that being a colimit for the cogenerators implies that it is a colimit. Let $\beta : C \longrightarrow D$ be an arbitrary cocone on the diagram C then we have the equalizer:

$$D \xrightarrow{\ d\ } \prod A_i \overset{f}{\underset{g}{\rightrightarrows}} \prod A_j$$

and therefore the cones $\beta.d_i : C \longrightarrow A_i$ each of which has a unique cocomparison map by assumption. Thus, $\beta.d : C \longrightarrow \prod A_i$ has a unique cocomparison map as do $\beta.d.f$ and $\beta.d.g$. However, each map of the cone $\beta_D.d : C(D) \longrightarrow \prod A_i$ equalizes f and g and therefore factor uniquely through the equalizer of f and g. But this gives the unique cocomparison map to β.

$\square$

This means that in identifying coproducts it suffices to ensure that they are coproducts for the cogenerators. Indeed, if coproducts commute with equalization then it suffices to check that the cogenerators themselves have coproducts. We have already observed this phenomenon for $\mathcal{E}(\mathbf{T})$.

Proposition 2.14 *If* **X** *is cartesian has coreflexive equalizers which commute with coproducts (in so far as they might exist) and has an inhabited set of regular cogenerators* $\{A_i | i \in I\}$ *then* **X** *is distributive if and only if the sum* $1 + 1$ *exists.*

Proof. If **X** is distributive then certainly this is implied as the sum $1 + 1$ exists. For the converse we must show that there are distributive coproducts. We observe that if we can show that the products of cogenerators have coproducts over which the product distributes then all coreflexive equalizers of these object will have these properties. However, as they are regular cogenerators and coreflexive equalization preserves coproducts this means all the objects will have this property.

For a given product of the cogenerators we certainly have the existence of its coproduct with itself and the distributivity of this coproduct with respect to multiplication by a cogenerator. However, given two distinct products using the fact that each is inhabited we may view each as a coreflexive equalizer of their product. This means that the coproduct of two arbitrary products can be viewed as reflexively coequalized subobjects of the product of the two coproducts and $1 + 1$.

$\square$

It is amusing to observe that in this context the distributive law has become the associative law for the product in the sense that $(1 + 1) \times (A \times B)$ is $A \times B + A \times B$ while $((1 + 1) \times A) \times B$ is $(A + A) \times B$ and this distributivity provides the general distributivity.

An algebraic theory **T** is called a **conditional algebraic theory** whenever $\mathcal{E}(\mathbf{T})$ has the sum $1 + 1$. This provides the following characterization of distributive algebraic theories:

Corollary 2.15 *An algebraic theory is distributive if and only if its types are inhabited and it is a conditional algebraic theory.*

3   Conditional algebraic theories

We have discovered that a conditional algebraic theory in which all types are inhabited is a distributive theory. In this section we develop several axiomatizations
of conditional algebraic theories. We start with the assumption that the type $1+1$
is given in the presentation and show that this case is equivalent to the existence
of conditional operators. Next we assume that this type is not explicitly given and
show that there then must be preconditional operators. A class of examples of such
operators is given by the multiplicative algebras. Finally, we consider the case in
which the idempotent completion of $\mathbf{T}$ contains $1+1$ and show this is equivalent to
having a presentation of the theory having absolute conditional operators

3.1   Conditional operators

The sum $1+1$ has the following formulation using conditional operators in any
cartesian category:

Definition 3.1 *A* **conditional operator** *on A with base $(1+1, \top, \bot)$ is an operation $\mathrm{if}_A : (1+1) \times (A \times A) \longrightarrow A$ such that*

- $\langle \top, i \rangle.\mathrm{if}_A = p_0$ *and* $\langle \bot, i \rangle.\mathrm{if}_A = p_1$,

- *For any $g : (1+1) \times C \longrightarrow A$ the following identity holds*

$$g = \langle p_0, \langle \langle \top, p_1 \rangle.g, \langle \bot, p_1 \rangle.g \rangle \rangle.\mathrm{if}_A$$

Proposition 3.2 *A cartesian category has the sum $1+1$ if and only if there is an
object $1+1$ with elements*

$$\top, \bot : 1 \longrightarrow 1+1,$$

and a conditional operator with base $(1+1, \top, \bot)$ on every object.

Proof. The sum $1+1$ exist if and only if the base $(1+1, \top, \bot)$ has the property
that given any $f, g : X \longrightarrow Y$ there is a unique map

$$d(f,g) : (1+1) \times X \longrightarrow Y$$

with $\langle \top, i \rangle.d(f,g) = f$ and $\langle \bot, i \rangle.d(f,g) = g$. In particular this easily implies that
$d(p_0, p_1)$ is a conditional operator.

Conversely, given conditional operators we may formulate $d(f,g)$ as $i \times
\langle f, g \rangle$. The uniqueness of $\mathrm{d}(f,g)$ follows as, if $k(\top, y_1, ..., y_n) = f(y_1, ..., y_n)$ and
$k(\bot, y_1, ..., y_n) = g(y_1, ..., y_n)$ then

$$\begin{aligned}\mathrm{if}(x, f(y_1, ..., y_n), g(y_1, ..., y_n)) &= \mathrm{if}(x, k(\top, y_1, ..., y_n), k(\bot, y_1, ..., y_n)) \\ &= k(x, , y_1, ..., y_n).\end{aligned}$$

$\square$

Notice that once the choice of base $(1+1, \top, \bot)$ is made the conditional operators
are uniquely determined. It is also clear that if we are given a presentation of an
algebraic theory which includes the object $1+1$ that we need only assert the existence
of conditional operators on the primitive types to obtain such on all types.

In the subsection on absolute conditional operators we shall give an alternative
and more classical formulation for the conditional operator.

3.2 Preconditional operators

We have assumed that the object $1 + 1$ is in the presentation, however, this need not be the case. In general, what must happen is that $1 + 1$ occurs as an equalizer of the cogenerators which are given by the presentation.

To express a (finite) equalizer we must provided ourselves with the ability to write down a conjunction of equations. This puts us in the realm of Horn logic. To express a conditional operator without explicit access to $1+1$ results in the following definition:

Definition 3.3 *A* **preconditional operator** *on A with base $(\prod_{i=1}^n B_i, \top, \bot, H)$ is a map* $\mathrm{if}_A : \prod B_i \times (A \times A) \longrightarrow A$ *together with a set of preconditions:*

$$H(x_1, ..., x_n) \equiv h_1(x_1, ..., x_n) = h_1'(x_1, ..., x_n) \wedge ... \wedge h_n(x_1, ..., x_n) = h_n'(x_1, ..., x_n)$$

on $\prod B_i$ such that

- $\mathrm{if}(\top, x, y) = x$ *and* $\mathrm{if}(\bot, x, y) = y$,

- $\vdash H(\top)$ *and* $\vdash H(\bot)$,

- *For any map $g : \prod B_i \times \prod A_j \longrightarrow A$ we have :*

    $$H(x_1, ..., x_n) \vdash g(x_1, ..., x_n, y_1, ..., y_m)$$
    $$= \mathrm{if}_A(x_1, ..., x_n, g(\top_1, ..., \top_n, y_1, ..., y_m), g(\bot_1, ..., \bot_n, y_1, ..., y_m)).$$

It is now immediate from our previous results that:

Theorem 3.4   *An algebraic theory is a conditional algebraic theory if and only if it has preconditional operators on each type for a given base $(\prod_{i=1}^n B_i, \top, \bot, H)$.*

This can be specialized to obtain distributive algebraic theories as follows:

Corollary 3.5 $\mathcal{E}(\mathbf{T})$ *is distributive if and only if each primitive sort of $\mathbf{T}$ is inhabited and $\mathbf{T}$ has a preconditional operator on a given base $(\prod_{i=1}^n A_i, \top, \bot, H)$.*

As is demonstrated in the next subsection some important examples of distributive theories arise having just preconditional operators. An important observation is that if $\mathbf{T}$ is a conditional (or distributive) algebraic theory then any theory which is a quotient of $\mathbf{T}$ is also conditional (or distributive) as certainly the requirements above will still be satisfied. Thus, a strategy for finding examples of conditional (and distributive) theories is to find very general varieties which are conditional. This is the aim of the next subsections.

3.3 Multiplicative algebras

Many examples of distributive theories in mathematics occur as a subvariety or extension of a **multiplicative algebra**. This observation was made by Davey and Werner [3] and we introduce their results in order to exhibit some examples.

A **multiplicative algebra** is an algebraic theory $\mathcal{T}$ with, amongst others, constants $0, 1 : 1 \longrightarrow A$ binary operations $\cdot, + : A \times A \longrightarrow A$, where $\cdot$ will be referred to as the **multiplication** and $+$ the **addition**, and possibly other (non-constant) primitive operations $f_1, f_2, ...$ such that

[M.1] The multiplication is associative, commutative, and has unit 1 and zero 0,

[M.2] The addition has $0 + x = x = x + 0$,

[M.3] Multiplication distributes over all the other non-constant primitive operations, $+, f_1, f_2, ...$, that is

$$x \cdot f_i(y_1, ..., y_n) = f(x \cdot y_1, ..., x \cdot y_n).$$

Proposition 3.6 *Any multiplicative algebra is a distributive theory.*

Proof. Set $\top = \langle 1, 0 \rangle, \bot = \langle 0, 1 \rangle : 1 \longrightarrow A \times A$ then I claim that

$$\mathrm{if}(x_1, x_2, y_1, y_2) = x_1 \cdot y_1 + x_2 \cdot y_2,$$

with preconditions saying that x_1 and x_2 are orthogonal idempotents

$$H(x_1, x_2) \equiv x_1 \cdot x_1 = x_1 \wedge x_2 \cdot x_2 = x_2 \wedge x_1 \cdot x_2 = 0, x_1 + x_2 = 1,$$

is a conditional operator.

It is easy to check $\mathrm{if}(1, 0, y_1, y_2) = y_1$ and $\mathrm{if}(0, 1, y_1, y_2) = y_2$ thus it remains to check that each primitive operator commutes with the conditional. We have three cases to check: the constants, the multiplication, and the operations over which multiplication distributes.

Consider the multiplication on the assumption that $H(x_1, x_2)$:

$$
\begin{aligned}
&\mathrm{if}(x_1, x_2, y, z) \cdot \mathrm{if}(x_1, x_2, y', z') \\
&= (x_1 \cdot y + x_2 \cdot z) \cdot (x_1 \cdot y' + x_2 \cdot z') \\
&= (x_1 \cdot y \cdot x_1 \cdot y' + x_1 \cdot y \cdot x_2 \cdot z') + (x_2 \cdot z \cdot x_1 \cdot y' + x_2 \cdot z \cdot x_2 \cdot z') \\
&= (x_1 \cdot y \cdot y' + 0) + (0 + x_2 \cdot z \cdot z') \\
&= x_1 \cdot y \cdot y' + x_2 \cdot z \cdot z' \\
&= \mathrm{if}(x_1, x_2, y \cdot y', z \cdot z')
\end{aligned}
$$

For the operations over which the multiplication distributes we have:

$$
\begin{aligned}
&\mathrm{if}(x_1, x_2, f(y_1, .., y_n), f(z_1, ..., z_n)) \\
&= x_1 \cdot f(y_1, ..., y_n) + x_2 \cdot f(z_1, ..., z_n) \\
&= f(x_1 \cdot y_1, ..., x_1 \cdot y_n) + f(x_2 \cdot z_1, ..., x_2 \cdot z_n) \\
&= x_1 \cdot f(x_1 \cdot y_1 + x_2 \cdot z_1, ..., x_1 \cdot y_n + x_2 \cdot z_n) + \\
&\qquad x_2 \cdot f(x_1 \cdot y_1 + x_2 \cdot z_1, ..., x_1 \cdot y_n + x_2 \cdot z_n) \\
&= (x_1 + x_2) \cdot f(x_1 \cdot y_1 + x_2 \cdot z_1, ..., x_1 \cdot y_n + x_2 \cdot z_n) \\
&= f(x_1 \cdot y_1 + x_2 \cdot z_1, ..., x_1 \cdot y_n + x_2 \cdot z_n) \\
&= f(\mathrm{if}(x_1, x_2, y_1, z_1), ..., \mathrm{if}(x_1, x_2, y_n, z_n))
\end{aligned}
$$

The constants are included in this case, however, for them we have, letting k be a constant:

$$\mathrm{if}(x_1, x_2, k, k) = x_1 \cdot k + x_2 \cdot k = (x_1 + x_2) \cdot k = k$$

as desired.

The following are subvarieties of multiplicative algebras:

Distributive lattices: Conjunction is traditionally taken to be the multiplication and disjunction the sum. The top and bottom of the lattice are respectively the 1 and 0.

Commutative rings: This is immediately a multiplicative algebra. The traditional approach to discovering distributivity is to use the fact that the sum is given by the tensor product.

Rigs: These are sometimes called semi-rings. They differ from commutative rings in that their "addition" while being commutative and associative lacks negation. Thus, they have two commutative associative operations addition $x + y$ and multiplication $x \cdot y$ with units 0 and 1 respectively, multiplication distributes over addition, and 0 is the zero for multiplication.

The condition [**M.3**] is stronger than is actually required to obtain distributivity. Heyting algebras do not satisfy [**M.3**] as conjunction does not distribute inside implication, yet Andy Pitts pointed out to me that Heyting algebras are a distributive algebraic theory. The expected preconditional operator does have the same form and satisfies the conditions of the previous subsection.

3.4 Absolutely conditional algebras

An algebraic theory is **absolutely conditional** in case the idempotent completion $\mathcal{K}(\mathbf{T})$ has the sum $1 + 1$. The object $1 + 1$ must then be a retract of a product of cogenerators. This gives rise to algebraic theories with absolute conditional operators. This section provides a usable presentation of absolutely conditional theories and develops some of their more elementary properties.

Definition 3.7
   An **absolute conditional operator** *on* A *with base* $(\prod_{i=1}^{n} B_i, \top, \bot, e)$, *where* $e = \langle e_1, ..., e_n \rangle$ *is an idempotent endomorphism of* $\prod_{i=1}^{n} B_i$, *if there is a map* $\mathrm{if}_A : \prod_{i=1}^{n} B_i \times (A \times A) \longrightarrow A$ *such that:*

- $\mathrm{if}_A(\top, x, y) = x$ *and* $\mathrm{if}_A(\bot, x, y) = y$,

- *For any* $g : \prod_{i=1}^{n} B_i \times \prod_{j=1}^{m} A_j \longrightarrow A$ *we have*

$$g(e(x), y_1, ..., y_m) = \mathrm{if}_A(x, g(\top, y_1, ..., y_m), g(\bot, y_1, ..., y_m))$$

We use the shorthand $\mathrm{if}_A(e(x), y, z)$ instead of

$$\mathrm{if}_A(e_1(x_1, ..., x_n), ..., e_n(x_1, ..., x_n), y, z)$$

for obvious reasons. The following three equalities follow from the second condition immediately:

Lemma 3.8 *If an algebraic theory has absolute conditional operators on a given base for each type:*

(i) $\text{if}_A(e(x), y, z) = \text{if}_A(x, y, z)$,

(ii) $e(x) = \text{if}(x, \top, \perp)$,

(iii) $\text{if}(x, \top, \perp) = \text{if}(\text{if}(x, \top, \perp), \top, \perp)$

It is not hard to show that the following result holds:

Theorem 3.9 *An algebraic theory is absolutely conditional if and only if each primitive sort in* **T** *has a absolute conditional operator on a given base* $(\prod_{i=1}^{n} B_i, \top, \perp, e)$.

An **absolute** **conditional** **algebra** is a presentation of an algebraic theory having constants

$$\top, \perp : 1 \longrightarrow \prod_{i=1}^{n} B_i$$

and an operator (which we shall discover is an absolute conditional operator)

$$\text{if}_A : \prod_{i=1}^{n} B_i \times (A \times A) \longrightarrow A$$

for each primitive type A and other primitive operations $f_1, f_2, ..$ such that

[C.1] $\text{if}(\top, x, y) = x$,

[C.2] $\text{if}(\perp, x, y) = y$,

[C.3] $\text{if}(x, y, y) = y$,

[C.4] $\text{if}(x, \text{if}(x_1, x_2, x_3), \text{if}(y_1, y_2, y_3)) = \text{if}(\text{if}(x, x_1, y_1), \text{if}(x, x_2, y_2), \text{if}(x, x_3, y_3))$,

[C.5] Given any other primitive operation $g : \prod_{j=1}^{m} A_j \longrightarrow A_0$ the operator **commutes** with it in the following sense

$$\text{if}_{A_0}(x, g(x_1, ..., x_m), g(y_1, ..., y_m)) = g(\text{if}_{A_1}(x, x_1, y_1), ..., \text{if}_{A_m}(x, x_m, y_m)).$$

In particular, for a constant k this reduces to $\text{if}_{A_0}(x, k, k) = k$.

Notice that [C.4] simply says that the conditional operator commutes with itself: thus, [C.5] subsumes [C.4]. Notice also that the notation suggests that we are working in a conditional algebra with $n = 1$, however, I am abusing notation so that the equation used below:

$$\text{if}(x, y, z) = \text{if}(\text{if}(x, \top, \perp), y, z)$$

should really be written as

$$\text{if}(\text{if}(x_1, .., x_N, \top_1, \perp_1), ..., \text{if}(x_1, .., x_N, \top_N, \perp_N), y, z) = \text{if}(x_1, ..., x_N, y, z).$$

Our main objective is to prove:

Theorem 3.10 *An algebraic theory is absolutely conditional if and only if it has a presentation as an absolute conditional algebra.*

In order to approach this we begin by noting the following properties of the absolute conditional:

Lemma 3.11 *In any conditional algebra*

(i) *The condition is a choice:*

$$\text{if}(x,y,z) = \text{if}(\text{if}(x,\top,\bot),y,z),$$

(in particular this gives $\text{if}(x,\top,\bot) = \text{if}(\text{if}(x,\top,\bot),\top,\bot)$*),*

(ii) *The condition can be simplified:*

$$\text{if}(\text{if}(x_1,x_2,x_3),y,z) = \text{if}(x_1,\text{if}(x_2,y,z),\text{if}(x_3,y,z)),$$

(iii) *Negation:*

$$\text{if}(\text{if}(x,\bot,\top),y,z) = \text{if}(x,z,y),$$

(iv) *Conditional operators can be transposed:*

$$\text{if}(x,\text{if}(y,z_{11},z_{12}),\text{if}(y,z_{21},z_{22})) = \text{if}(y,\text{if}(x,z_{11},z_{21}),\text{if}(x,z_{12},z_{22})),$$

(v) *Repeated conditions can be eliminated:*

$$\text{if}(x,\text{if}(x,z_{11},z_{12}),\text{if}(x,z_{21},z_{22})) = \text{if}(x,z_{11},z_{22}),$$

(vi) *The conditional operation commutes with any (i.e. not necessarily primitive) operation* $g : A^m \longrightarrow A$*, that is:*

$$\text{if}(x,g(y_1,...,y_m),g(z_1,...,z_m)) = g(\text{if}(x,y_1,z_1),...,\text{if}(x,y_m,z_m)).$$

Proof.

(i)

$$
\begin{aligned}
\text{if}(\text{if}(x,\top,\bot),y,z) &= \text{if}(\text{if}(x,\top,\bot),\text{if}(x,y,y),\text{if}(x,z,z)) \\
&= \text{if}(x,\text{if}(\top,y,z),\text{if}(\bot,y,z)) \\
&= \text{if}(x,y,z).
\end{aligned}
$$

(ii)

$$
\begin{aligned}
\text{if}(\text{if}(x_1,x_2,x_3),y,z) &= \text{if}(\text{if}(x_1,x_2,x_3),\text{if}(x_1,y,y),\text{if}(x_1,z,z)) \\
&= \text{if}(x_1,\text{if}(x_2,y,z),\text{if}(x_3,y,z).
\end{aligned}
$$

(iii)

$$
\begin{aligned}
\text{if}(\text{if}(x,\bot,\top),y,z) &= \text{if}(x,\text{if}(\bot,y,z),\text{if}(\top,y,z)) \\
&= \text{if}(x,z,y).
\end{aligned}
$$

(iv)

$$\text{if}(x, \text{if}(y, z_{11}, z_{12}), \text{if}(y, z_{21}, z_{22})) = \text{if}(\text{if}(x, y, y), \text{if}(x, z_{11}, z_{21}), \text{if}(x, z_{12}, z_{22}))$$
$$= \text{if}(\text{if}(x, y, y), \text{if}(x, z_{11}, z_{21}), \text{if}(x, z_{12}, z_{22})).$$

(v)

$$\text{if}(x, \text{if}(x, z_{11}, z_{12}), \text{if}(x, z_{21}, z_{22})) = \text{if}(\text{if}(x, \top, \bot), \text{if}(x, z_{11}, z_{12}), \text{if}(x, z_{21}, z_{22}))$$
$$= \text{if}(x, \text{if}(\top, z_{11}, z_{12}), \text{if}(\bot, z_{21}, z_{22}))$$
$$= \text{if}(x, z_{11}, z_{22}).$$

(vi) **An easy structural induction.**

$\square$

The elimination of repetitions has another more useful form in which an arbitrary operation is interposed between the first occurrence and the later occurrence. This is called "deep repetition":

Corollary 3.12 *For any* $g : \prod_{j=1}^{m} A_j \longrightarrow A_0$ *we have*

$$\text{if}(x, g(y_1, ..., y_i, \text{if}(x, v, w), ..., y_n), z) = \text{if}(x, g(y_1, ..., y_i, x, ..., y_n), z)$$

Proof.

$$\text{if}(x, g(y_1, ..., y_i, \text{if}(x, v, w), ..., y_n), z)$$
$$= \text{if}(x, g(\text{if}(x, y_1, y_1), ..., \text{if}(x, y_i, y_i), \text{if}(x, v, w), ..., \text{if}(x, y_n, y_n)), z)$$
$$= \text{if}(x, \text{if}(x, g(y_1, ..., y_i, v, ..., y_n), g(y_1, ..., y_i, w, ..., y_n)), \text{if}(x, z, z))$$
$$= \text{if}(x, g(y_1, ..., y_i, v, ..., y_n), z)$$

$\square$

Using the fact that if commutes with every operation we obtain the last identity required of an absolute conditional operator:

Corollary 3.13 *For any* $g : \prod_{i=1}^{m} A_j \longrightarrow A_0$ *we have*

$$g(\text{if}(x, \top, \bot), y_1, ..., y_{n-1}) = \text{if}_{A_0}(x, g(\top, y_1, ..., y_{n-1}), g(\bot, y_1, ..., y_{n-1})).$$

Proof.

$$g(\text{if}(x, \top, \bot), y_1, ..., y_{n-1}) = g(\text{if}(x, \top, \bot), \text{if}(x, y_1, y_1), ..., \text{if}(x, y_{n-1}, y_{n-1}))$$
$$= \text{if}(x, g(\top, y_1, ..., y_{n-1}), g(\bot, y_1, ..., y_{n-1})).$$

$\square$

Corollary 3.14 *Any absolute conditional algebra is an absolute conditional algebraic theory.*

We have therefore established half the theorem:

Proof (of 3.10). We wish to show that an absolute conditional operator necessarily satisfies [C.1]–[C.5]. The first two axioms are immediate: for [C.3] observe that setting $g(x, y) = y$ we have

$$y = g(\text{if}(x, \top, \bot), y) = \text{if}(x, g(\top, y), g(\bot, y)) = \text{if}(x, y, y).$$

For [C.4] and [C.5] we set

$$g(x, x_1, ..., x_n, y_1, ..., y_n) := f(\text{if}(x, x_1, y_1), .., \text{if}(x, x_n, y_n))$$

that

$$g(\text{if}(x, \top, \bot), x_1, ..., y_n) = \text{if}(x, g(\top, x_1, ..., y_n), g(\bot, x_1, ..., y_n)$$

which when unwound gives:

$$
\begin{aligned}
&f(\text{if}(\text{if}(x, \top, \bot), x_1, y_1), .., \text{if}(\text{if}(x, \top, \bot), x_n, y_n)) \\
={}& \text{if}(\text{if}(x, \top, \bot), f(x_1, ..., x_n), f(y_1, ..., y_n)) \\
={}& \text{if}(x, f(x_1, ..., x_n), f(y_1, ..., y_n)).
\end{aligned}
$$

$\square$

A **conditional algebra** is an absolute conditional algebra with the added stipulation that the idempotent e is the identity. In this case $\prod_{i=1}^n B_i \equiv 1 + 1$ and we may express the conditions in the following well-known form:

[Cond.1] $\text{if}(\top, x, y) = x$,

[Cond.2] $\text{if}(\bot, x, y) = y$,

[Cond.3] $\text{if}(x, y, y) = y$,

[Cond.4] $\text{if}(x, \top, \bot) = x$

[Cond.5] Given any other primitive operation $g : \prod_{j=1}^m A_j \longrightarrow A_0$ the operator **commutes** with it in the following sense

$$\text{if}_{A_0}(x, g(x_1, ..., x_m), g(y_1, ..., y_m)) = g(\text{if}_{A_1}(x, x_1, y_1), ..., \text{if}_{A_m}(x, x_m, ..., y_m)).$$

4   Concluding remarks

The above discussion has still left open the question of whether the requirement that the primitive types be inhabited is absolutely necessary to obtain arbitrary sums. Certainly, if the requirement of habitation is dropped, $\mathcal{E}(\mathbf{T})$ cannot be guaranteed to be distributive as habitation is necessary to obtain strictness. However, this does not rule out the possibility that $\mathcal{E}(\mathbf{T})$ is locally predistributive. While the precise conditions for this to occur are still open we can make some relevant remarks:

(i) For a conditional algebraic theory coproducts may not exist in $\mathcal{E}(\mathbf{T})$.

This can be seen most easily by considering the effect on generation of emptying a type of an algebra by forming a product with another algebra in which that type is empty. The finite generation properties derived from that type are then lost. Thus, for example, if a type in a theory is uninhabited, has a free endomorphism (so that an element x finitely generates $\{f^n(x)|n = 0, 1, 2, ...\}$), and a map to an inhabited type then $\mathcal{E}(\mathbf{T})$ will not have coproducts.

(ii) Even if $\mathcal{E}(\mathbf{T})$ has coproducts they may not be sums.

To see this we may examine the lattice of preinitials of $\mathcal{E}(\mathbf{T})$. If $\mathcal{E}(\mathbf{T})$ has sums, it is not hard to see that this lattice is equivalent to the lattice obtained by flattening $\mathbf{T}$ itself [1]. As $\mathbf{T}$ is only cartesian, the lattice obtained by flattening is provided necessarily only with a meet structure. Of course, if there are only a finite number of elements of the lattice then it will also have joins. Notice, when 1 is indecomposable, the sum of two uninhabited types must be uninhabited. This means that the join of two preinitials associated with uninhabited types cannot be the top of the lattice as this would make it inhabited.

This immediately means that the theory generated by two disconnected uninhabited sorts with no operations (and the sum $1 + 1$) cannot have its equalizer completion predistributive as certainly 1 is indecomposable but in the lattice of preinitials the join of the two sorts is the top. Furthermore, as finitely generated algebras in this theory are finite, products of finitely presented algebras are certainly finitely presented so that coproducts exist in $\mathcal{E}(\mathbf{T})$. This means the distributive law itself breaks down!

In algebras the distributive law takes the dual form $A + (B \times C) \simeq (A + B) \times (A + C)$. Taking all the algebras to have $1 + 1$ interpreted as the two element set with the conditional operation interpreted in the only way possible, A to have the remaining sorts singletons, B to be an algebra with the first sort having more that two elements and the second sort empty, and C to be an algebra with the first sort empty and the second non-empty provides a counter-example to this form of distributivity. To see this note that the sum and product on the sorts with no operations are the underlying set sum and products whenever $1 + 1$ is interpreted as the two element set.

(iii) If $\mathbf{T}$ is predistributive then $\mathcal{E}(\mathbf{T})$ is locally predistributive.

This happens whether the types of $\mathbf{T}$ are inhabited or not. Thus, habitation is not necessary to obtain this weaker form of the result!

This means that adding conditional operators is not sufficient to guarantee the presence of coproducts let alone sums in the Horn logic. This is rather an important object lesson: it means that the common practice of adding conditional operators to obtain control in a purely equational way (or even Horn logic way) does not correspond to the natural categorical view of control. This is particularly relevant at the specification level when it is desirable to consider general and thus possibly uninhabited types.

References

[1] J.R.B. Cockett, *Introduction to distributive categories* Maquarie Computing Report 90-0052C (1990).

[2] S. Bloom and R. Tindell, *Varieties of if...then...else* SIAM Journal on Computing 12(4) (1983) 677-707.

[3] B.A. Davey and H. Werner, *Distributivity of coproducts over products.* Algebra Universalis, 12 (1981) 387-394.

[4] Y. Diers *Categories of boolean sheaves of simple algebras,* Lecture Notes in Mathematics **1187**, Springer-Verlag, Berlin, Heidelberg, New York(1985).

[5] H. Ehrig and B. Mahr *Fundamentals of algebraic specification I: equations and initial semantics.* Springer Verlag, Berlin (1985).

[6] H. Huwig and A. Poigne, *A note on the inconsistencies caused by fixed points in a cartesian closed category,* Theoretical Computer Science 73 (1989).

[7] J.A. Goguen "Higher-order functions considered unnecessary for higher-order programming." In *Research topics in functional programming* Ed. D.A. Turner, Addison-Wesley (1990).

[8] P.T. Johnstone *Topos Theory* Academic Press, London (1977).

[9] C. Kirchner, H. Kirchner and J. Meseguer "Operational Semantics of OBJ3." In *Proceedings of the 9th International Conference on Automata, Languages, and Programming.* Lecture Notes in Computer Science, vol. 241. Springer-Verlag, Berlin (1988).

[10] F.W. Lawvere *Diagonal arguments and cartesian closed categories,* Springer Lecture Notes in Mathematics 92, Springer-Verlag, Berlin (19) 134-145

[11] R.F.C. Walters *Datatypes in distributive categories,* Bull. Australian Mathematics Society 40 (1989) 79-82.

[12] R.F.C. Walters *Category Theory, Logic, and Computer Science,* course notes of lectures given at Sydney University 1988/1989.

[13] C. Wells *A generalization of the concept of a sketch,* Journal of theoretical Computer Science 70 (1990) 159-178.

Simple Type Theory in EVES

Mark Saaltink and Dan Craigen*

Odyssey Research Associates
265 Carling Avenue, Suite 506
Ottawa, Ontario K1S 2E1
CANADA

mark@ora.on.ca
dan@ora.on.ca

Abstract

This paper presents a brief description of a newly completed verification system called EVES. EVES is a formal system based on Zermelo-Fraenkel set theory with the Axiom of Choice. EVES supports the proof of mathematical properties, including proofs of program correctness. The development of EVES required the design of a new language, called Verdi, and of a heuristic theorem prover, called NEVER.

After introductory remarks on Verdi, NEVER and EVES, we present a combinatory version of Church's simple type theory in EVES as an illustration of the power and flexibility of the untyped set theory framework and of EVES.

*The development of EVES was sponsored by the Canadian Department of National Defence through DSS contract W2207-8-AF78/01SV.

1   Introduction

EVES is a new verification system that was delivered to the sponsoring agency, the Canadian Department of National Defence, in February 1990. Unlike many verification systems (e.g., HOL [9], EHDM [7], Veritas+ [11]) that have some form of higher-order logic as their mathematical framework, EVES is based on the Zermelo-Fraenkel axiomatization of set theory with the Axiom of Choice.

EVES is the successor system to the pedagogical verification system m-EVES [3, 5, 15]. The m-EVES effort was primarily meant to be a proof-of-concept exercise and was to set the foundation for EVES, which was to be developed more towards production-oriented concerns. For example, we omitted adding to the programming language component of m-EVES constructs that, while useful, were not absolutely necessary and added nothing to the research being pursued. In our view, m-EVES was a successful exercise; m-EVES has been distributed to over twenty sites in five countries, and has been applied to examples drawn from computer security, hardware verification, mathematics, and general computer science algorithms. Our experiences with m-EVES and those of other researchers have influenced our work on EVES. As with m-EVES, our primary goals were to insist on a sound mathematical foundation for EVES, to incorporate state-of-the-art automated deduction capabilities, and to develop a specification and implementation language that would satisfy many of the needs of our sponsors.

In this paper we will:

- discuss our choice of an untyped set theoretic framework rather than a type theory framework;

- discuss our use of a LISP-like syntax;

- present a brief overview of the newly designed language Verdi;

- contrast Verdi with m-Verdi;

- present a brief overview of other aspects of EVES; and

- demonstrate the expressibility of the untyped set theoretic framework through the presentation of a combinatory version of Church's Simple Type Theory.

Detailed descriptions of EVES and Verdi can be found in the Verdi reference manual [4].

2   Why Set Theory?

One of our main goals in designing Verdi was to improve expressibility (in comparison with m-Verdi) in both the specification and programming components of the language. From the specification perspective, we envisioned two options for achieving this goal: the use of a higher-order logic (specifically, type theory), or the use of axiomatic set theory.

Our initial feelings were to proceed with a type theory approach. However, further considerations—including the following—led to the choice of an untyped axiomatic set theory framework:

- Set theory has been widely used as a foundation for mathematics and is well understood. Many existing mathematics and computing science books use set theory to describe concepts; few use type theory.

- More is known about automated proofs within a first-order framework than in higher-order systems.

- While simple type theory is well-understood, in practice it is too restrictive. Many different ways of adding polymorphism have been tried (Cardelli claims that there are six independent design choices, and thus sixty-four different polymorphic type systems). The foundations and mathematical properties of these systems are not so well understood.

Consequently, we chose a ZFC axiomatization (i.e., a Zermelo-Fraenkel axiomatization with the Axiom of Choice) — and, hence, Verdi is based on a first-order logical framework.

From the programming perspective, the decisions for what to include in Verdi were much simpler. There were some obvious areas of improvement, in contrast with m-Verdi, which could be handled at (reasonably) low technical risk. These areas included **for**-loops, improved enumeration types, complete support of subvariables, mutually recursive executable procedures and a library facility.

Though certainly not as important an issue as our choice of a ZFC framework for Verdi, the choice of a LISP-like syntax for Verdi requires a few words. Effectively, we decided to proceed with an "abstract syntax" approach to Verdi. The abstract syntax is based on LISP with the intention that we can use some of the tools that have been designed for that language. The EVES R&D effort was not to include the development of a large collection of language specific tools.

Further, by defining an abstract syntax, we are opening the possibility for organizations that wish to enhance EVES to develop their own concrete syntax, to translate their concrete syntax into our abstract syntax (and the converse), and to use their proprietary tools. For example, an organization that has a bit mapped graphics screen might support a wide spectrum of mathematical notations. Moreover, the abstract syntax approach allows for greater commonality of notation between the mathematics document [18], reference manual [4], and the representation used within the verification system.

Interestingly, early experiences with Verdi have shown a marked preference for the Verdi notation when compared with that of m-Verdi. It is only fair, however, to add the caveat that the early experiences have been with individuals who are experts (or, at least, familiar) with LISP.

3 Verdi

Verdi is a formal notation that may be used to write programs that are to be verified formally using the EVES verification system. Consequently, Verdi consists of syntactic forms for expressing specifications (what effect a program is to have), implementations (how a program is to cause an effect), and proofs (justification that a program meets its specification).

An expression is a Verdi sentence that can be evaluated (using a structure and a state) to produce a value. The expressions are character literals, numerals, strings, identifiers (denoting variables), function applications, and quantifications. Some expressions are called *manifest expressions* and are mandatory in certain instances where expressions are syntactically required (i.e., case labels and array bounds). Manifest expressions can be evaluated at compile time. For each executable expression there is a related legality expression. If the legality expression evaluates to the truth value true then it is guaranteed that the corresponding executable expression can be evaluated without aborting. Legality is defined inductively on the syntactic structure of expressions.

Verdi declarations result in the modification of a theory by extending the vocabulary and adding further axioms. The proof obligations associated with each declaration mandate that each extension to a theory is a (semantic) conservative extension (see the formal description of Verdi [18]).

While Verdi is, in general, an untyped language, typing information is necessary for syntactic forms that are to be executed. A type name denotes a set of values. The Boolean, Integer and Character types belong to the initial theory. The Boolean type denotes the logical truth values. The Integer type denotes the set of mathematical integers. The Character type denotes the ASCII character set. Other types are introduced through an enumeration declaration (which denotes an isomorphic copy of the integers but where only those values denotable by the enumerands may be used in an executable context), an array declaration, or a record declaration. Type synonyms are also permitted. Verdi type sameness is a compromise between the extremes of name sameness and structural sameness since the structures of records and enumerations are not used in sameness checking.

Type specifiers may occur in the formal lists for functions and procedures. In addition to allowing the association of type expressions (effectively, either a type name or an array expression) with parameters, open-array associates are permitted. Hence, a form of type parameterization for procedures and typed functions is supported. For example, the formal list for a procedure that finds the minimum integer element of an array (indexed by integers) may look like:

```
((LVAR (a) (OPEN-ARRAY (INT) (INT))) (PVAR (x) (INT))).
```

The various function declarations introduce functions. Functions that are used in an executable context must have been introduced by a typed function declaration. Such a declaration associates type information with the parameters and the result of the function. The result of an executable function application is predictable only if the application is legal. By legal, it is meant that the parameters satisfy constraints (determined by a function pre-condition). Certain functions, defined as part of the initial theory, are called wide domain functions and are those functions that have more than one signature; these functions are similar to operators in classical programming languages. Non-executable functions may be defined recursively and, by using function recursion groups, through mutual recursion. ZF function declarations also introduce non-executable functions.

An axiom declaration restricts the possible structures for the names in a vocabulary. Additionally, heuristic information, used by NEVER, may be added. For example, through the axiom rule declaration an axiom will be treated as a conditional rewrite rule by NEVER.

A statement is a Verdi sentence that denotes one or more execution steps and determines, in part, the ordering of the execution steps. It is through the execution of statements (using a structure and a state) that the values associated with the observables and states are modified. The Verdi statements are **exit** (from a loop), **return** (from a procedure), **abort** (the program), **note** (a form of annotation), assignment, procedure call, **block**, conditional, **case**, **loop**, and two forms of **for**-loop.

A procedure declaration introduces a procedure and is always executable. Procedures may be defined recursively and, by using procedure recursion groups, through mutual recursion. Procedures may have open-array parameters.

A library is a repository for library objects. Library objects are collections of Verdi declarations and, through the use of the **load** command, may depend upon other library objects. The **load** command introduces the declarations of the associated library specification object (and any necessary subsidiary library specification objects) to a current theory. Library objects are one form of support for modularization and abstraction.

Verdi also supports the various system, prover, and library commands that are used to interact with EVES. Verdi is the interface language used with EVES. Most of these commands pertain to NEVER. So, for example, there are commands for performing induction, instantiating variables, simplifying formulae and applying conditional rewrite rules. Some of the commands are described in Appendix B.

Finally, the Verdi initial theory consists of function and axiom declarations that are common to all Verdi programs. Verdi supports fairly common functionality for manipulating Boolean, Integer and Character values. There are also functions that support the manipulation of elementary values (such as enumeration values). For sets, Verdi has functions supporting the following: adding an element to a set, creating a singleton set, membership, subset, union, intersection, difference, symmetric difference, powerset, cup (union of all elements in a set), makeset (of n elements), and nullset (denoting the empty set). There are numerous axioms pertaining to the above functions in the initial theory along with the Axiom of Regularity and the Axiom of Choice.

As mentioned above, a declaration extends a theory. As an example of such an extension, the type declaration

```
(TYPE ARRAY-ID (ARRAY (ENUM-ID.FIRST) (ENUM-ID.LAST) (INT)))
```

results in the following additions to a theory:

```
(RULE ARRAY-ID.TYPE-P () (= (TYPE-P (ARRAY-ID)) (TRUE)))
(RULE ARRAY-ID.DEFINITION ()
    (= (ARRAY-ID) (ARRAY (ENUM-ID.FIRST) (ENUM-ID.LAST) (INT))))
(TAG ARRAY-ID.VAL)
(FUNCTION-STUB ARRAY-ID.MAP (X))
(FRULE ARRAY-ID.TYPE-OF.MAP
        (X)
        ((TRIGGERS (ARRAY-ID.MAP X)))
        (IMPLIES (= (TYPE-OF X) (INT))
                (= (TYPE-OF (ARRAY-ID.MAP X))   ·
                    (ARRAY (ENUM-ID.FIRST) (ENUM-ID.LAST) (INT)))))
(FUNCTION ARRAY-ID.MAP.PRE (X) () (= (TYPE-OF X) (INT)))
(FUNCTION-STUB ARRAY-ID.PAD ())
```

```
(AXIOM ARRAY-ID.TYPE-OF.PAD () (= (TYPE-OF (ARRAY-ID.PAD)) (INT)))
(FUNCTION ARRAY-ID.PAD.PRE () () (TRUE))
(RULE ARRAY-ID.AREF.MAP
    (I E)
    (IMPLIES (IN I (RANGE (ENUM-ID.FIRST) (ENUM-ID.LAST)))
             (= (AREF (ARRAY-ID.MAP E) I) E)))
```

4 Verdi improvements over m-Verdi

To summarize the improvements and differences from m-Verdi, resulting in the Verdi design:

- The logical basis is untyped first-order logic, with Zermelo-Fraenkel set theory and the Axiom of Choice built-in. Hence, the specification component of the language is more expressive than the strongly typed, first-order predicate calculus basis of m-Verdi.

- Typing is not completely absent from Verdi, as executable constructs are still subject to type checks. The typing system is more flexible than m-Verdi's (a mix of name-sameness and structure-sameness) and includes a provision for open-array parameters.

- A library mechanism has been added. This addition goes much further than m-Verdi's package mechanism as it supports the separate development of library units.

- Procedures and non-executable functions can be recursive or mutually recursive.

- Domain errors during execution are handled. An implementation is allowed to abort during a calculation when a function is applied to arguments outside of its domain. Various Verdi proof obligations are generated to show that such mis-applications will not occur. This approach has allowed us to eliminate the separate executable, non-executable approach (e.g., plus and eplus) of functions found in m-Verdi.

- For-loops have been added and the definition of enumeration types adjusted to admit more reasonable proofs of procedures iterating over the full range of an enumeration type.

- Subvariables are fully supported. In m-Verdi, subvariables could be assigned, but not passed, to pvar parameters.

- The m-Verdi form of variable declarations has been removed.

- The loop proof rule has been strengthened, so that less information needs to appear explicitly in the invariant. Further, it is now possible to prove nested loops; this could not be done in m-Verdi.

It is important to note that, while we have substantially improved the expressibility of the language, we have maintained the sound mathematical basis [18]. As
those familiar with the m-Verdi mathematics [17] will observe, the mathematical
framework for Verdi is more complex (as a result of the additional capabilities) than
that for m-Verdi.

5   EVES

As reported above, the logical framework for EVES is quite different from m-EVES.
Perhaps the single most important distinction is the move away from a strongly
typed framework to one which is untyped. This distinction is also prevalent in
comparing NEVER with m-NEVER.

Once it was clear which logical framework was to be used for EVES, significant
research and development was focused on how one should proceed with automated
deduction within a typeless framework — especially since some of the most useful
capabilities of m-NEVER, the various decision procedures, are strongly dependent
on knowing the type of an expression.

Consequently, the typing framework, which was so integral to m-NEVER, was
removed. An analysis of approaches used by the Boyer-Moore prover, which is
also untyped, was undertaken and, based on that analysis, a type prescription
mechanism incorporated into NEVER. The basic idea was that NEVER (and Verdi)
would support type predicates and the type prescription mechanism could be used
to determine the type, if one exists, of an expression. The determination of typing
information for an expression allows for the application of the type specific decision
procedures.[1]

In addition to the major restructuring of the prover, a new initial theory needed
development and the prover needed to handle the changes to theories resulting
from the various Verdi declarations. The initial theory, besides consisting of the
vocabulary and axioms that are built into the language, has an extensive heuristic
component. Numerous experiments were performed to determine how the heuristics should be included. Many of the decisions resulted from earlier experiments
describing set theory within m-EVES (and using m-NEVER). (The initial theory
that was incorporated in EVES (Version 1.0) is described in the Verdi reference
manual [4].)

Various other modifications and experiments were conducted, including:

- The conversion of some small examples from m-EVES to EVES (including the
  flow modulator and arraymin examples (both described in the Verdi reference
  manual [4]) and sequence theory.

- The implementation of nested histories (needed for libraries).

- The implementation of a different way of handling Boolean equalities. Previously, the prover converted Boolean equalities into if forms, thereby causing
  numerous case splits. The new method for handling Boolean equalities, which
  uses the deductive database, does not cause case splits and is faster.

---

[1]Some parallel experiments involving the implementation of a Boyer-Moore mode on top of
the verification system [8] were performed. Feedback relating to performing proofs in a typeless
framework was obtained from these experiments.

- The implementation of short-circuiting of subgoals[2] and the caching of forward rules. For the system's handling of a quicksort specification, the running time of the system was improved by 50%.

- The modification of the `equality-substitute` command so that the substitutions used by NEVER are reported to the user.

In addition to the language and theorem prover work reported above, there were other modifications and improvements that differentiate EVES from m-EVES. These include the implementation of several features:

- A faster EVES parser and prettyprinter.

- A Zmacs interface to EVES (with improvements over that of m-EVES).

- A compression scheme to reduce the size of freeze files. The implementation of this compression technique increased the speed of the `freeze` and `thaw` commands.

- A library mechanism. However, it must be admitted that the implementation is not without fault. For example, by using different path names to identify the same file, it is possible to fool the verification system. Further study (especially into logical path names) of the library mechanism is necessary. Conventional use of the library mechanism is sound.

- A mechanism that catches keyboard interrupts and, hence, permits the interruption of proof commands that are taking too long.

6   Completed Examples

The EVES verification system is new and, consequently, the experience base is still limited. To date, the examples that EVES has been applied to are:

- Significant portions of an interpreter for the programming language PICO [12]. This is the largest example tried in either m-EVES or EVES and, to date, consists of 10,000 lines of Verdi. (Only the evaluator for PICO programs remains to be proven; type checking, data structures, abstract syntax, etc., have been specified, implemented, and proven correct.)

- A micro-flow modulator [4] and the arraymin example reported herein.

- The examples described briefly below in Section 8.

We have, obviously, had much more experience with the pedagogical m-EVES system. All of the examples that have been completed with m-EVES could be successfully proven using EVES. So, to give an indication of our experiences, a list of some of the examples completed by our research group follows:

---

[2]For example, if a conjunct in a subgoal is shown to be false, there is no need to prove the remaining conjuncts.

- a version of the Unix[3] TR program [13];

- a version of the Unix WC program [14];

- a simple real-time control system [19];

- a small flow modulator [2];

- a proof of the non-interference security property for the pedagogical low water mark system [5];

- an n-bit adder [15];

- various sorting programs;

- saddleback search; and

- axiomatic descriptions of theories of finite sets and finite sequences, along with model theoretic proofs of the consistency of these descriptions.

7   A Small Example

Prior to our presentation of Simple Type Theory in EVES, a small example of a Verdi program is presented. Through this example, we wish to present a flavour of Verdi and of performing proofs (in a typeless framework) in EVES. Appendix B describes briefly the commands used. Note the use of the open-array parameter in the **arraymin** procedure. The program finds the minimum element of an integer indexed array.

Prior to introducing concepts specific to the **arraymin** procedure, we need some general results pertaining to the concept of type and of open-arrays. The kinds of general results will, in due course, either be a part of the EVES initial theory or will be available in library units that will become part of each EVES release. As EVES is a new system, we are still investigating the approaches to present such results.

The first axiom states that if x, y are sets denoting types and x is a subset of y, then $x = y$. The proof of the axiom requires the use of two axioms that are part of the initial theory. The first axiom, **TYPE.NOT.EMPTY**, states that any set denoting a type is non-empty. The second axiom, **TYPE-OF.DEFINITION**, states that for two sets x, y say, if x is a member of y and y denotes a type, then the type of x is y.

```
(AXIOM type-p-subset (x y)
  (IMPLIES (AND (TYPE-P x)
                (TYPE-P y)
                (SUBSET x y))
           (= x y)))
(USE TYPE.NOT.EMPTY (X X))
(PRENEX)
(OPEN)
(USE TYPE-OF.DEFINITION (Y X) (X E))
(USE TYPE-OF.DEFINITION (Y Y) (X E))
```

---

[3]Unix is a trademark of AT&T Laboratories.

```
(INVOKE SUBSET)
(SIMPLIFY)
```

The next axiom is a property of open-arrays. The axiom states, under various type restrictions, that if x is an element of the set determined by a particular open-array then there exists an array corresponding to x. The subsequent rule states the same property in slightly different terms. Note that both these axioms are to be treated as conditional rewrite rules.

```
(RULE in-open-array-0 (x i t)
  (IMPLIES (AND (ELEM-TYPE-P i)
               (TYPE-P t))
          (= (IN x (OPEN-ARRAY i t))
             (SOME (lo hi)
                (AND (IN lo i)
                     (IN hi i)
                     (IN x (ARRAY lo hi t)))))))
(SPLIT (AND (ELEM-TYPE-P I)
            (TYPE-P T)
            (IN X (OPEN-ARRAY I T))))
(SIMPLIFY)
(REWRITE)
(INSTANTIATE (Y T))
(REWRITE)
(USE TYPE-P-SUBSET)
(INSTANTIATE (LO$0 LO) (HI$0 HI))
(SIMPLIFY)
(INSTANTIATE (X$0 Y$0) (Y T))
(SIMPLIFY)

(RULE in-open-array-1 (x i t)
  (IMPLIES (AND (ELEM-TYPE-P i)
               (TYPE-P t))
          (= (IN x (OPEN-ARRAY i t))
             (AND (IN (LOB x) i)
                  (IN (HIB x) i)
                  (IN x (ARRAY (LOB x) (HIB x) t))))))
(SPLIT (AND (ELEM-TYPE-P I)
            (TYPE-P T)
            (IN X (OPEN-ARRAY I T))))
(SIMPLIFY)
(REWRITE)
(PRENEX)
(REWRITE)
```

Having introduced the general properties about open-arrays, we now proceed with properties specific to finding the minimum element of an array. The concept of the smallest element in a range is then introduced (and is used in the post condition of the main procedure).

```
(FUNCTION is_smallest_in_range (x a lo hi) () ;no measure condition
  (AND (<= (LOB a) lo)
       (<= hi (HIB a))
       (SOME (y)
         (AND (IN y (INT))
              (<= lo y)
              (<= y hi)
              (= (AREF a y) x)))
       (ALL (y)
         (IMPLIES (AND (IN y (INT))
                       (<= lo y)
                       (<= y hi))
                  (<= x (AREF a y)))))))
```

The function min_in_range determines the smallest value in a range.

```
(FUNCTION min_in_range (a lo hi)
   ((MEASURE (- hi lo)))
  (IF (OR (NOT (IN lo (INT)))
          (NOT (IN hi (INT)))
          (NOT (<= hi (HIB a)))
          (<= hi lo))
      (AREF a lo)
      (IF (< (AREF a hi) (min_in_range a lo (- hi 1)))
          (AREF a hi)
          (min_in_range a lo (- hi 1)))))
(REDUCE)
```

The next two rules specify that the value determined by min_in_range for a specific array and range is, in fact, the smallest such value.

```
(RULE min_in_range_smallest_1 (a lo hi)
     (IMPLIES (AND (IN a (ARRAY (LOB a) (HIB a) (INT)))
                   (IN lo (INT))
                   (IN hi (INT))
                   (IN (HIB a) (INT))
                   (<= (LOB a) lo)
                   (<= lo hi)
                   (<= hi (HIB a)))
              (is_smallest_in_range (min_in_range a lo hi) a lo hi)))
(INDUCT)
(REDUCE)
(SPLIT (= HI Y$1))
(SIMPLIFY)
(INSTANTIATE (Y$0 Y$1))
(SIMPLIFY)

(RULE min_in_range_smallest_2 (a lo hi y)
     (IMPLIES (AND (IN a (ARRAY (LOB a) (HIB a) (INT)))
```

```
              (IN lo (INT))
              (IN hi (INT))
              (IN (HIB a) (INT))
              (<= (LOB a) lo)
              (<= lo hi)
              (<= hi (HIB a))
              (= y hi))
          (is_smallest_in_range (min_in_range a lo y) a lo hi)))
(EQUALITY-SUBSTITUTE y)
(REWRITE)
```

Finally, the main procedure **arraymin** is introduced. Note the use of the open-array parameter and the **for-loop**.

```
(PROCEDURE arraymin ((LVAR (a) (OPEN-ARRAY (INT) (INT)))
                     (PVAR (x) (INT)))
  ((PRE (< (LOB a) (HIB a)))                   ; a is non-empty
   (POST (is_smallest_in_range x a (LOB a) (HIB a))))
  (:= x (AREF a (LOB a)))
  (FOR-INCREASING y (RANGE (LOB a) (HIB a))
     ((INVARIANT (AND (<= (LOB a) y)
                      (<= y (+ 1 (HIB a)))
                      (= x (min_in_range a (LOB a) (- y 1)))))))
    (COND ((< (AREF a y) x) (:= x (AREF a y)))))))
(EQUALITY-SUBSTITUTE X-0)
(REWRITE)
(REDUCE)
```

8 Developing Set Theory in EVES

The EVES initial theory contains only the most basic rudiments of set theory: the usual ZFC axioms plus about twenty elementary lemmas. In addition, we have theories of Booleans, Characters, Integers, and the data structures used in Verdi programs. Using the library mechanism, we have begun to extend this primitive set theory to incorporate more of the commonly used elements of set theory.

To date, we have built up a library including the following units:

- **setrules**: Additional elementary properties of the basic functions on sets, such as the distributivity of union over intersection, and properties like $x \cup y \subseteq z \iff (x \subseteq z \land y \subseteq z)$.

- **cap**: The unary intersection function $\bigcap X = \{ y \mid \forall x \in X . y \in x \}$ (when X is nonempty).

- **nat**: Additional facts about the Natural numbers; for example, every nonempty set of Naturals has a least element.

- **pair**: Ordered pairs and the projection functions.

- **seq**: Finite sequences.

- **fn:** Functions and relations, domain and range, cross products, inverse relations, composition of relations and functions, image and preimage of a set through a relation, and function spaces.

In most cases we have followed the usual practice (see, for example, [10]) in our development. For example, pairs are implemented using the Wiener-Kuratowski representation $\langle x, y \rangle = \{\{x\}, \{x, y\}\}$, although this implementation is hidden by the library mechanism from users of pairs. Relations and functions are represented as graphs; thus $x R y \iff \langle x, y \rangle \in R$, and when f is a function, $(f(x) = y) \iff \langle x, y \rangle \in f$.

Our theory of ordered pairs has one unusual element. In addition to the pairing function and projections, we provide a `size` function, together with an axiom that the size of a pair exceeds the size of its constituents. This allows for induction over binary trees built by pairing. The existence of this `size` function, for the Wiener-Kuratowski representation of pairs, is a consequence of the Axiom of Regularity.

A sketch of the proof of the existence of the `size` function shows the kind of argument that we have succeeded in formalizing in EVES. Say x *has an n-path* for natural n, if either $n = 0$, or $n > 0$, x is a pair, and one of the constituents of x has an $(n - 1)$-path. Say x *has an infinite path* iff for all natural n, x has an n-path. Now if x has an infinite path, we can define a function $f(n)$ so that $f(0) = x$, and for all n, $f(n)$ is a pair with constituent $f(n + 1)$. Then define $g(n) = H(f(n))$, where $H(p)$ is the set of constituents of p: for all a, b, $H(\langle a, b \rangle) = \{a, b\}$. Then for all n, $f(n+1) \in g(n) \in f(n)$. (This is the only point in the proof where the specific representation of pairs is significant.) Then the set $X = \{f(0), g(0), f(1), g(1), \ldots\}$ is not regular. Thus, the assumption that x has an infinite path is contradictory. Let $P = \{n \mid x \text{ has no } n\text{-path}\}$. Then P is non-empty, and therefore it has a smallest element n_0. Define $\text{size}(x) = n_0$. Now it is easy to show that the size of a constituent of x is smaller than the size of x.

The transcription of this argument into EVES was fairly straightforward, except for the use of ellipses in the definition of X. In general, the informal expression $\{e_0, e_1, \ldots\}$ is expressed formally as $\bigcup\{e_n \mid n \in \text{Nat}\}$. Thus the formal definition of X is

$$X = \left(\bigcup\{f(n) \mid n \in \text{Nat}\}\right) \cup \left(\bigcup\{g(n) \mid n \in \text{Nat}\}\right).$$

The proof in EVES used two subordinate library units (one for naturals, giving the "least element" property used above, another with some extra lemmas about the arithmetic and comparison functions). We defined eight functions and proved fourteen lemmas, with a total of 113 user steps to complete the proof.

The theory of functions illustrates a weakness of EVES. In common practice, after defining functions and application, the mathematician can define the notational abbreviation

$$\lambda x \in S \, . \, e \equiv \{\langle x, e \rangle \mid x \in S\},$$

then go on to show that $\lambda x \in S \, . \, e$ is a function with domain S, and applying it to some $x \in S$ gives e. EVES lacks a capacity for syntactic extensions of this sort, and does not allow for this type of schematic proof. The best we can do is to provide a specific rote process for writing the appropriate set definition, lemmas, and proofs.

The EVES library is far from complete. We would like to see more of the commonly used elements of set theory represented in the library, including, for example, finiteness, the Real numbers, infinite sequences, and trees. Moreover, the existing library units could be further enriched.

9   Type Theory in EVES

As an experiment, we tried to represent Andrews' theory $\mathcal{Q}_0$ [1] in EVES. We knew, of course, that it is possible to represent higher-order objects in set-theory (at least when the domains of the functions considered are bounded, as they are in type theory or analysis). The point of the experiment was to discover how effective EVES would be in reasoning in the higher-order domain. In particular, we weren't too concerned about the purity of our representation of $\mathcal{Q}_0$ in EVES; we were more concerned with the effectiveness of proving.

Since we already had the theory of functionality available in the EVES library, much of the necessary development for this experiment was at hand.

One area of potential confusion in discussing this experiment (and in describing the theory of functionality) is in the two uses of the word "function". When it is necessary to be precise, we refer to the functions of the first-order language of EVES as "proper functions", and to the functions represented as sets as "internal functions". Thus, for example, union is a proper function, while a term f satisfying (function-p f) denotes an internal function.

9.1   Representing Types

Some of what is syntactic in $\mathcal{Q}_0$ is represented in the formulas in EVES. In particular, type information is represented explicitly. We defined terms for the types, (prop) and (ind) for Booleans (o) and individuals (ι), and the function type constructor fcn. If term t represents type α and term u represents type β, then the term (fcn t u) represents the type ($\beta\alpha$) of functions from α to β. We defined a function colon to express typing; thus the formula (colon x t) asserts that x has the type represented by t.

It is necessary to use special heuristics in EVES to manage the type information. In particular, the typing rule for applications

```
(implies (and (colon f (fcn t u))
              (colon x t))
         (colon (ap f x) u)))
```

is a poor rewriting rule because the variable t is not bound in the conclusion. (EVES is fairly weak in finding instantiations for such variables.) The solution is simple; use forward rules for colon. The above fact then is expressed as a forward rule triggering on the expression (ap f x). For each of the primitive constants, we express its typing as a forward rule. Since EVES uses innermost-first traversal ordering, when a well-typed application term is encountered, the types of the subterms have already been determined, its type is properly inferred using the forward rule for applications.

9.2 Representing Terms

Constant families are represented in a simple way. For example, for each type α there is a constant symbol $Q_{((o\alpha)\alpha)}$ of type $((o\alpha)\alpha)$. We defined a function Q of one argument, such that for all t we have

```
(colon (Q t) (fcn t (fcn t (prop)))).
```

Thus when t represents type α, (Q t) represents the constant $Q_{((o\alpha)\alpha)}$. This has the pleasant consequence that the (meta)theorems of $\mathcal{Q}_0$ that are expressed schematically with respect to type are simple theorems in EVES. For example, the schematic theorem $Q_{o\alpha\alpha}x_\alpha x_\alpha$ can be expressed in EVES as follows:

```
(axiom Q-reflexive (x t)
  (implies (colon x t)
           (= (ap (ap (Q t) x) x)
              (true)))))
```

The representation of applications is simple; the theory of functionality already provides the (proper) function apply. We shortened the name to ap for use here.

The representation of abstraction terms presented more of a problem. There is no simple way to define a variable-binding construct in EVES. This problem was "solved" by the crude trick of using combinatory abstraction to eliminate the bound variables [6, 20]. Thus, instead of the expression $\lambda x(f(gx)(hx))$, we write $S(Bfg)h$. The combinatory abstraction algorithm is not difficult to apply by hand, but the calculation of the appropriate type subscripts is tedious. We therefore wrote a small program to calculate these subscripts for us.

9.3 The Basic Axioms

Appendix A lists the axiomatization of $\mathcal{Q}_0$ in EVES. The axioms in EVES depart rather significantly from Andrews' axioms. Firstly, the axioms for λ-terms are replaced by the combinator reduction rules (such as $K_{\alpha\beta\alpha}\,x_\alpha\,y_\beta = x_\alpha$). Secondly, the axiom of Booleans ($g_{oo}\,T_o \wedge g_{oo}\,F_o \supset g_{oo}\,x_o$) was replaced by the simple expedient of using EVES Booleans as the values of type (prop). (This step is not logically necessary, but is heuristically essential. Other experiments with representing a "foreign" logic in EVES [8] showed the importance of using the EVES Booleans and numbers when possible; this allows the full power of the simplifier to be applied.)

The equality axioms and equality substitution rule were replaced by an axiom relating $Q_{o\alpha\alpha}$ with the EVES equality function. Again, this allows the EVES simplifier to apply equality reasoning during proofs. Also, this lets us state axioms about equality in $\mathcal{Q}_0$ in the form of EVES rewrite rules. Using the EVES equality function is essential for this.

The extensionality axiom can be represented in EVES, but only in an ineffective way. Combinatory abstraction applied to the axiom (written using Andrews' abbreviated notations)

$$(f_{\alpha\beta} = g_{\alpha\beta}) = \forall x_\beta(f_{\alpha\beta}\,x_\beta = g_{\alpha\beta}x_\beta)$$

results in

$$(f_{\alpha\beta} = g_{\alpha\beta}) = \Pi_{o(o\beta)}\left(S_{o\beta(\alpha\beta)(o\alpha\beta)}\left(B_{o\alpha\beta(\alpha\beta)(o\alpha\alpha)}\,Q_{o\alpha\alpha}\,f_{\alpha\beta}\right)g_{\alpha\beta}\right).$$

This illustrates a surprising difference between λ-calculus and combinatory logic. In the original version of the axiom, the functions f and g get applied to something; thus there is the possibility for the use of axioms about these applications. This is precisely what makes the extensionality axiom useful. In the combinatory version, f and g are not applied to new terms. Thus, we will not be able to use this axiom in the desired way. If, for example, we try to show the equality of the terms $S K a$ and $S K b$, the original rule lets us compare $S K a x$ and $S K b x$; the combinator rules then show both terms equal to x. In the combinatory version of the rule, we are invited to consider $\Pi (S (B Q (S K a)) (S K b))$. This does not bring us closer to a proof. (Since Π is defined as $Q (K T)$, we can use extensionality again, but we get nowhere.)

It is possible to provide enough axioms in combinatory logic so that the axiom of extensionality is unnecessary; Sanchis [16] lists such a set, and shows for any terms X and Y, if $X x = Y x$ is provable for some variable x not free in X or Y, then $X = Y$ is also provable. This approach was deemed not very useful for the current experiment; explicit use of extensionality seems to allow for more natural proofs.

If a strong axiom of choice is assumed, we can add a constant $\Gamma_{\alpha(o\alpha)}$ and an axiom

$$p_{o\alpha} (\Gamma_{\alpha(o\alpha)} \, p_{o\alpha}) \supset \Pi_{o(o\alpha)} \, p_{o\alpha}.$$

The idea is that $\Gamma_{\alpha(o\alpha)} \, p_{o\alpha}$ returns some value x for which $p x$ is false, if any such value exists; otherwise it returns some arbitrary value. This Γ-term acts as a kind of Skolem constant for the proposition p; the occurrence of p within it ensures that different quantified propositions are furnished with different constants.

This new axiom together with the combinatory version of the extensionality axiom and simple equality reasoning, gives

$$(f_{\alpha\beta} A = g_{\alpha\beta} A) \supset (f_{\alpha\beta} = g_{\alpha\beta}),$$

where

$$A = \Gamma_{\beta(o\beta)} \left(S_{o\beta(\alpha\beta)(o\alpha\beta)} \left(B_{o\alpha\beta(\alpha\beta)(o\alpha\alpha)} Q_{o\alpha\alpha} f_{\alpha\beta} \right) g_{\alpha\beta} \right),$$

and now proofs using extensionality are possible.

In the present experiment, we adopted neither of these two approaches, but rather expressed the extensionality axiom using quantification in EVES. This lets us make full use of the EVES mechanisms for handling quantification.

9.4   The Model

In the model, types are simply sets; (fcn t u) is the function space from t to u. The predicate (colon x t) is the membership test (in x t). Type (prop) is the set of Booleans and type (ind) the set of integers.

The basic combinators are defined by repeated λ-abstraction. As noted above, there is no direct way to define λ-terms in EVES, so for each λ-term defining a combinator, we defined a specific set, and proved the needed properties. Thus, for example, the typed K combinator, is defined by

$$K(a, b) = \lambda x \in a . \lambda y \in b . x.$$

In EVES, this is defined in two steps, one for each abstraction:

$$K1(x, b) = \{\langle y, x \rangle \mid y \in b\}$$
$$K(a, b) = \{\langle x, K1(x, b) \rangle \mid x \in a\}$$

Once the S and K combinators are defined, the others can be expressed in terms of them: $I_\alpha = S_{\alpha\alpha(\alpha\alpha\alpha)(\alpha(\alpha\alpha)\alpha)} K_{\alpha(\alpha\alpha)\alpha} K_{\alpha\alpha\alpha}$, and so on; the typing and reduction properties of these combinators can be proved directly from those of S and K.

The equality function $Q(t) = \lambda x \in t \,.\, \lambda y \in t \,.\, (x = y)$ is equally easy to define by abstraction:

$$Q1(x, t) = \{\langle y, (x = y) \rangle \mid y \in t\}$$
$$Q(t) = \{\langle x, Q1(x, t) \mid x \in t\}$$

The description operator $\iota_{\iota(o\iota)}$ is only a bit more difficult to define. We made use of the EVES facility for implicitly defined functions to define a proper function of an internal function $\mathbf{f}$, returning the unique element Integer x for which $(\mathbf{ap\ f\ x})$ is true, if such an element exists, otherwise returning 0. Then it was trivial to define an internal function corresponding to this.

9.5   Comments on the representation

The handling of type information has two drawbacks. Firstly, the prover must spend time establishing that terms are appropriately typed before applying rewriting rules (as most of these require type hypotheses). In a prover built for $\mathcal{Q}_0$, these hypotheses could be discharged during matching. Secondly, in order for the type of a term to be inferred, type hypotheses for all the free variables appearing in it must be available. Unfortunately, after some user steps in the course of a proof, the relative order of hypotheses is such that these variable type hypotheses appear after some terms using the variable. Then an additional user step is required to correct the order of hypotheses.

The axiomatization we used has some drawbacks and some advantages. One drawback is the absence of an induction principle for types. Andrews is able to prove a schematic theorem T_α by showing T_o, T_ι, and $T_{\alpha\beta}$ under the assumptions T_α and T_β.

Similarly, Andrews is able to define a family of constants by induction over types. In this manner he defines description operators $\iota_{\alpha(o\alpha)}$ for each type α, based on the primitive description operator for type ι. This development is impossible in the axiomatization here. In order to follow the advanced development of $\mathcal{Q}_0$ we would need to add the family of description functions to the basic axioms. This would force other changes to the axioms; given the description function we can write a closed expression of any type, namely $\iota_{\alpha(o\alpha)}(\lambda x_\alpha . T_o)$. Thus we can not allow nonempty types. The present axiomatization allows an arbitrary set to be used as a type; that would need to be changed.

On the plus side, since (in our model) types are arbitrary sets, we can easily add new primitive types, or even a subtype constructor.

9.6   Some Examples

With the primitive basis of $\mathcal{Q}_0$ paraphrased in EVES, we tried some elementary examples. Our first observation was the difficulty of writing (and reading) the necessary combinatory terms that represent λ-abstractions in the theorems and definitions of $\mathcal{Q}_0$. We wrote a very simple program to convert expressions written in Andrews' notation (without his abbreviations) to the corresponding EVES expressions. (Subsequent use of this program showed that it should really accept the abbreviations as well.)

A second observation was in the difficulty of following the development laid out in Andrews' book. Firstly, because of the way we expressed the axioms, much of the early development was unnecessary. Secondly, Andrews works mostly at the level of syntactic abbreviation and meta-theorem.

We defined the basic Boolean connectives as (internal) functions. For each connective, we proved its relation to the corresponding EVES function, e.g., for negation we proved the theorem

```
(implies (colon x (prop))
        (= (ap (Qnot) x)
           (not x)))
```

where `Qnot` is the $\mathcal{Q}_0$ negation function and `not` is EVES negation.

Negation is simple; Andrews defines it (as a notational abbreviation) as $\sim_{oo} = Q_{ooo}F_o$. It was simple to relate this to EVES negation.

Conjunction is rather more complicated. Andrews gives the definition

$$\wedge_{ooo} = \lambda x_o \,.\, \lambda y_o \,.\, (\lambda g_{ooo} \,.\, g_{ooo} \, T_o \, T_o) = (\lambda g_{ooo} \,.\, g_{ooo} \, x_o \, y_o).$$

We can use extensionality to show

$$\wedge_{ooo} \, x_o \, y_o = \forall g_{ooo} \, (g_{ooo} \, T_o \, T_o = g_{ooo} \, x_o \, y_o).$$

From this formula, it is obvious that $\wedge_{ooo}T_oT_o$ is true. We can show $\wedge_{ooo}x_oF_o$ false by instantiating g_{ooo} to the function $\lambda x_o \,.\, \lambda y_o \,.\, y_o$; the two applications of g result in T_o and F_o respectively. Similarly, we can show $\wedge_{ooo}F_oy_o$ false.

Figure 1 shows the definition of conjunction in EVES. The combinators and type information completely obscure the content of the definition; evidently, typed combinatory logic is unfit for human consumption. (The EVES formula was machine-generated.) Figure 2 shows that this above proof was simple in EVES. The first reduce command applied the definition of `Qand`, the combinator rules, and the extensionality rule, and split into cases. The case where both x and y are true was immediate. The two instantiations noted above were expressed using hand proof steps, then rewriting completed the proof.

With the rewriting rules relating the $\mathcal{Q}_0$ binary connectives with their EVES counterparts in place, rewriting reduces $\mathcal{Q}_0$ propositional logic to EVES propositional logic, where the built-in decision procedures apply.

We also tried some elementary set theory in type theory, using functions of type $(o\alpha)$ to represent sets of elements of type α. We defined the subset relation and the union operation, i.e.,

$$\cup_{(o\alpha)(o\alpha)(o\alpha)} = \lambda x_{o\alpha} \,.\, \lambda y_{o\alpha} \,.\, \lambda x_\alpha \,.\, \vee_{ooo} \, (x_{o\alpha} \, z_\alpha) \, (y_{o\alpha} \, z_\alpha).$$

We showed that every set is a subset of itself, that a set is a subset of its union with another set, and that union is idempotent. All of these proofs were completely automatic (using the reduce command).

```
(FUNCTION Qand () ()
    (ap (ap (B (prop)
                (fcn (prop) (fcn (fcn (prop) (fcn (prop) (prop))) (prop)))
                (fcn (prop) (prop)))
            (ap (B (prop)
                    (fcn (fcn (prop) (fcn (prop) (prop))) (prop))
                    (prop))
                (ap (Q (fcn (fcn (prop) (fcn (prop) (prop))) (prop)))
                    (ap (ap (C (fcn (prop) (fcn (prop) (prop)))
                                (prop)
                                (prop))
                        (ap (ap (C (fcn (prop) (fcn (prop) (prop)))
                                    (prop)
                                    (fcn (prop) (prop)))
                            (I (fcn (prop) (fcn (prop) (prop)))))
                        (TRUE)))
                    (TRUE)))))
        (ap (ap (B (prop)
                (fcn (fcn (prop) (fcn (prop) (prop)))
                    (fcn (prop) (prop)))
                (fcn (prop)
                    (fcn (fcn (prop) (fcn (prop) (prop))) (prop))))
            (C (fcn (prop) (fcn (prop) (prop))) (prop) (prop)))
        (ap (C (fcn (prop) (fcn (prop) (prop)))
                (prop)
                (fcn (prop) (prop)))
            (I (fcn (prop) (fcn (prop) (prop)))))))))
```

Figure 1: The definition of conjunction

```
(frule Qand-type ()
    ((triggers (Qand)))
  (colon (Qand) (fcn (prop) (fcn (prop) (prop)))))
(reduce)

(rule ap-Qand (x y)
  (implies (and (colon x (prop))
                (colon y (prop)))
          (= (ap (ap (Qand) x) y)
             (and x y))))
(reduce)
(instantiate (x$0 (ap (K (fcn (prop) (prop)) (prop)) (I (prop)))))
(instantiate (x$1 (K (prop) (prop))))
(rewrite)
```

Figure 2: The basic lemmas about conjunction

9.7 Conclusions of the Experiment

Both parts of the experiment were quite successful. We were able to define the model for Q_0 without too much agony, although there was a certain tedium in the repeated use of the five-step process for defining λ-abstractions. The proofs of propositions in Q_0 were also fairly simple, although the explicitly-typed combinator terms were very ugly. We never typed them in directly, using instead a small program to generate them from more reasonable notations.

While we only attempted some fairly easy theorems in propositional logic and elementary set theory, the simplicity of the proofs in EVES is encouraging. Most of the proofs were completely automatic, and any hand steps we used (such as those in the proof of rule `ap-Qand` above) seemed natural.

There is a reasonable possibility that EVES will provide "hooks" allowing input and output transformations to be specified. With such a facility, a usable "Q_0-mode" could be implemented with little trouble.

10 Acknowledgments

Verdi was designed by Mark Saaltink and Dan Craigen, with material assistance from Irwin Meisels. NEVER was implemented by Sentot Kromodimoeljo and Bill Pase. The EVES development was implemented primarily by Sentot Kromodimoeljo, Irwin Meisels, and Bill Pase.

References

[1] Peter B. Andrews. *An Introduction to Mathematical Logic and Type Theory: to Truth through Proof.* Academic Press, 1986.

[2] Dan Craigen. *A Description of m-Verdi.* IPSA Technical Report TR-87-5420-02, November, 1987.

[3] Dan Craigen, *et al.* m-EVES: A Tool for Verifying Software, in Proc. of *10th International Conference on Software Engineering*, April 1988, Singapore.

[4] Dan Craigen. *Reference Manual for the Language Verdi*, ORA Technical Report TR-90-5429-09, February 1990.

[5] Dan Craigen. *An Application of the m-EVES Verification System. 2nd Workshop on Software Testing, Verification and Analysis* (July 1988), Banff, Alberta.

[6] H. B. Curry and R. Feys. *Combinatory Logic*, Vol. 1. North Holland, 1958

[7] Friedrich von Henke, Natarajan Shankar, John Rushby. *Formal Semantics of EHDM.* Technical Report, Computer Science Laboratory, SRI International, January 1990.

[8] Jason Fischl. *A Boyer-Moore Mode in m-EVES.* EVES Project Technical Report TR-89-5429-07, Odyssey Research Associates, September 1989.

[9] Mike Gordon. HOL: A Proof Generating System for Higher-Order Logic. in *VLSI Specification, Verification and Synthesis*, G. Birtwistle and P.A. Subrahmanyan (eds), Kluwer 1987.

[10] Paul R. Halmos. *Naive Set Theory*. Van Nostrand, 1960.

[11] Keith Hanna. VERITAS+, A Specification Language based on Type Theory, in *Proc. of Workshop on Hardware Verification, Verification and Synthesis: Mathematical Aspects*, Cornell University, 1989, M. Leeser and G. Brown (eds), Lecture Notes in Computer Science, Vol. 408, Springer-Verlag.

[12] Sentot Kromodimoeljo and Bill Pase. *Using the EVES Library Facility: A PICO Interpreter*. ORA Technical Report TR-90-5444-02, February 1990.

[13] Irwin Meisels. *TR Program Example*. ORA Technical Report TR-89-5443-02, August 1989.

[14] Irwin Meisels. *WC Program Example*. ORA Technical Report TR-89-5443-03, October 1989.

[15] Bill Pase and Mark Saaltink. Formal Verification in m-EVES, in *Current Trends in Hardware Verification and Automated Theorem Proving*, G. Birtwistle and P.A. Subrahmanyam (eds), Springer-Verlag, 1989.

[16] Luis Elpidio Sanchis. Functionals Defined by Recursion, in *the Notre Dame Journal of Formal Logic* 8(3): 161–174, July 1967.

[17] Mark Saaltink. *The Mathematics of m-Verdi*. I.P. Sharp Technical Report FR-87-5420-03, November 1987.

[18] Mark Saaltink. *A Formal Description of Verdi*. ORA Technical Report TR-89-5429-10, October 1989.

[19] Mark Saaltink. *The Mechanical Verification of a Simple Control System*. ORA Technical Report TR-89-5443-04, December 1989.

[20] D. A. Turner. Another Algorithm for Bracket Abstraction, in *the Journal of Symbolic Logic* 44(2): 267–270, June 1979.

A The axioms of Q_0 in EVES

```
;;; The axioms of Q0              -*- Mode: Verdi -*-

;;; types

(function-stub ind ())
(function-stub prop ())
(function-stub fcn (x y))

(function-stub colon (x t))

(rule bool-in-prop (x)
  (= (colon x (prop))
     (in x (bool))))

;;; application

(function-stub ap (f x))

(frule ap-type (f x t u)
    ((triggers (ap f x)))
  (implies (and (colon f (fcn t u))
                (colon x t))
           (colon (ap f x) u)))

;;; combinators

(function-stub I (t))
(function-stub K (t u))
(function-stub S (t u v))
(function-stub B (t u v))
(function-stub C (t u v))

(frule I-type (t)
    ((triggers (I t)))
  (colon (I t) (fcn t t)))

(frule K-type (t u)
    ((triggers (K t u)))
  (colon (K t u) (fcn t (fcn u t))))

(frule S-type (t u v)
    ((triggers (s t u v)))
  (colon (S t u v) (fcn (fcn t (fcn u v)) (fcn (fcn t u) (fcn t v)))))

(frule B-type (t u v)
    ((triggers (B t u v)))
```

```
               (colon (B t u v) (fcn (fcn u v) (fcn (fcn t u) (fcn t v)))))

(frule C-type (t u v)
     ((triggers (C t u v)))
     (colon (C t u v) (fcn (fcn t (fcn u v)) (fcn u (fcn t v)))))

(rule ap-I (t x)
   (implies (colon x t)
            (= (ap (I t) x)
               x)))

(rule ap-K (t u x y)
   (implies (and (colon x t)
                 (colon y u))
            (= (ap (ap (K t u) x) y)
               x)))

(rule ap-S (t u v x y z)
   (implies (and (colon x (fcn t (fcn u v)))
                 (colon y (fcn t u))
                 (colon z t))
            (= (ap (ap (ap (S t u v) x) y) z)
               (ap (ap x z) (ap y z)))))

(rule ap-B (t u v f g x)
   (implies (and (colon f (fcn u v))
                 (colon g (fcn t u))
                 (colon x t))
            (= (ap (ap (ap (B t u v) f) g) x)
               (ap f (ap g x)))))

(rule ap-C (x y z t u v)
   (implies (and (colon x (fcn t (fcn u v)))
                 (colon y u)
                 (colon z t))
            (= (ap (ap (ap (C t u v) x) y) z)
               (ap (ap x z) y))))


;;; The primitives of Q0

(function-stub Q (t))

(frule Q-type (t)
     ((triggers (Q t)))
     (colon (Q t) (fcn t (fcn t (prop)))))

(function-stub IOTA ())
```

```
(frule IOTA-type ()
   ((triggers (IOTA)))
  (colon (IOTA) (fcn (fcn (ind) (prop)) (ind))))

;;; The axioms

(rule ap-Q (t x y)
  (implies (and (colon x t)
                (colon y t))
           (= (ap (ap (Q t) x) y)
              (= x y))))

(rule extensionality (t u f g)
  (implies (and (colon f (fcn t u))
                (colon g (fcn t u)))
           (= (= f g)
              (all (x) (implies (colon x t)
                                (= (ap f x) (ap g x)))))))

(axiom IOTA-Q (x)
  (implies (colon x (ind))
           (= (ap (IOTA)
                  (ap (Q (ind)) x))
              x)))
```

B Prover Commands

In this appendix we describe the commands used in the examples.

The descriptions are abridgements of the descriptions presented in the Verdi reference manual [4]. Primarily, we have removed mention of well-formedness requirements on each of the commands.

Equality Substitute Command

`equality_substitute_command: (EQUALITY-SUBSTITUTE [EXPRESSION])`

The `equality-substitute` command substitutes, for the expression, its equal in appropriate contexts of the current formula. The expression must appear as the left or right side of an equality within the current formula (otherwise the command has no effect). In the absence of the expression, a heuristic is used to substitute equalities automatically.

Induct Command

`induct_command: (INDUCT [expression])`

The `induct` command attempts to apply an induction scheme to the current formula. In the absence of the optional expression, an induction scheme is heuristically chosen based on calls to recursive functions occurring in the current formula. If the optional expression is present, then EVES attempts an induction using the expression.

The `induct` command will have no effect on the current proof if either the current formula or the optional expression contains a quantifier; if the free variables of the optional expression are not a subset of the free variables of the current formula; if the expression is not a recursive function application; or if the recursive function application has a quantified sub-expression.

Instantiate Command

`instantiation: (identifier expression)`
`instantiate_command: (INSTANTIATE {instantiation}+)`

The `instantiate` command performs the given instantiations on the current formula. To allow the instantiations to occur, the scopes of quantifiers in the formula may be modified. Logical equivalence is maintained by keeping the uninstantiated subexpressions as extra conjuncts or disjuncts.

Invoke Command

`invoke_command: (INVOKE expression)`

The `invoke` command replaces the application of a function, as specified by the expression, by its defining expression (instantiated by the actual parameters to the function application). The `invoke` command works for functions which have been disabled. In addition, the `invoke` command may be applied to an expression rather than to a function, in which case, it works like a selective invoke in that occurrences of the expression in the formula are replaced by the expanded version.

Open Command

`open_command: (OPEN)`

The **open** command removes leading universal quantifiers from the current formula and the quantified variables are consequently free variables.

Prenex Command

`prenex_command: (PRENEX)`

The **prenex** command converts the current formula into prenex form (as far as possible). If the result of this command is a completely prenexed formula with only universal quantifiers, then the **open** command may be used to make the formula quantifier-free.

Reduce Command

`reduce_command: (REDUCE)`

The **reduce** command applies the non-inductive heuristics of the prover to the current formula. This consists of simplification, rewriting, and invocation.

Rewrite Command

`rewrite_command: (REWRITE)`

The **rewrite** command rewrites and simplifies the current formula. Conditional rewrite rules may be applied, provided their condition can be proven using only simplification and rewriting. This command also applies any forward rules which are triggered and whose condition is provable.

Simplify Command

`simplify_command: (SIMPLIFY)`

The **simplify** command simplifies the current formula. This may perform the substitution of equalities as well as trying to instantiate variables in order to find a proof.

Split Command

```
split_command: (SPLIT expression)
```

The **split** command performs a case split on the current formula with the supplied expression. This results in a new formula of the form

```
(IF expression formula formula)
```

provided there are no references to the quantified variables of the formula within the predicate. If there are, the **split** command performs a case split on the largest subformula within the scope of the referenced quantified variables. In effect, a case split causes the current formula to be worked on under the two cases, the first with the expression explicitly assumed equal to true and the second with the predicate not equalling true.

The **split** command may also be used for placing a specific hypothesis before a subexpression. This proof step may be required because of the sensitivity of the prover towards the ordering of subexpressions within the formula being reduced.

Use Command

```
instantiation: (identifier expression)
use_command:   (USE identifier instantiation*)
```

The **use** command adds the axiom associated with the identifier to the current formula as an assumption. This results in a new formula of the form

```
(IMPLIES assumption formula)
```

where the assumption is the axiom instantiated with the instantiations.

Formal Synthesis

Michael P. Fourman[*]

M.Fourman@ed.ac.uk

&

Roberto A. Hexsel[†]

rh@lfcs.ed.ac.uk

Laboratory for the Foundations of Computer Science
Edinburgh University.

March 1991

Abstract

Most applications of formal proof to digital hardware have been aimed at proving the correctness of existing designs. Here, we address the application of formal methods to the *design* of digital systems. Our particular concern is to show how a formal approach can address the problems of system level design: complexity and abstraction. To relate the system-level behaviour to the behaviours of primitive components, we model and relate behaviours at different levels of abstraction.

We base our presentation on a small, but revealing, case-study; starting from a high-level specification, we design a digital stopclock. The stopclock is specified in terms of user-level time ticks, and is implemented in terms of a much faster system-level clock. A block diagram of the design is formalised at the abstract level. Abstractions are introduced to relate this to the low-level implementation. The 'glue' logic, necessary to connect components using different abstractions, is formally derived.

---

[*]This work was partially supported by SERC grant GRF35890
[†]Supported by a grant from CAPES, Ministry of Education, Brazil.

1 Introduction

The recent VLSI revolution is based on the MOS transistor, which may be modelled as a switch. Using this as a primitive, we build gates, registers, counters, state machines, controllers, microprocessors and systems. To understand the behaviour of a system as a function of the behaviours of its component parts, we need to model and relate behaviours at many levels. Models based on predicate logic and formal proof have been widely used to verify the correctness of digital circuits. A few examples are [Gordon85] [CGM86] [Gordon87] [BG90] [Cohn87] [Cohn89] [Hunt87]. In these works, the behaviour of a device is modelled by a predicate that expresses the constraints the device imposes on the signals on its external ports.

In this paper, we address the application of formal methods to the *design* of digital systems, continuing a programme started in [FPZ88], and developed in [FFFH90] [FM89] [Fourman90]. Our particular concern is to show how a formal approach may address the problems of system level design: complexity and abstraction. We base our presentation on a small, but revealing, case-study. Starting from a high-level specification, we design a digital stopclock. Consider the following informal specification:

> *Design a digital stopwatch with a three digit, seven-segment display (to read seconds, tenths of seconds, and tens of seconds), and two control buttons, 'reset' and 'start/stop'. When the reset button is pressed the display is cleared. The start/stop button is used to start and stop the clock.*
>
> *You are provided with a 1MHz system clock, and a 10Hz digital signal synchronised with the system clock. You may assume that the buttons also produce synchronised digital signals.*

We will:

- formalise the specification at the user level (10Hz clock);
- write abstraction functions to express the controls and display in terms of 1MHz signals;
- develop an implementation by refinement.

The interest of the exercise is to see that design can be started at a high level of abstraction. We then introduce the abstractions used to relate the high-level specification to a concrete implementation. These relate the two levels of time. The control signals are *asynchronous* with respect to the specification-level model of time, and the output must satisfy constraints imposed by other system components; in this case the output is the display, and the behaviour of the human eye requires a large 'hold time', if the display is to be perceived.

1.1 Modelling Behaviour

We begin with a review of established methods for the application of formal logic to the specification of digital behaviour, and then continue with our design.

To model the behaviour of combinational logic, we model an output signal as a boolean function of the signals on the inputs. Function composition models the connection of the output of one device to an input of another. Tools, based principally on Boolean algebra, allow us to implement a given function quickly, accurately and efficiently. A similar, functional model may be used at a higher level of abstraction, to reason about simple data-flow architectures. To model general patterns of connection, and the hiding of internal wires, we need more-sophisticated models of behaviour. For instance, we may not wish to distinguish inputs from outputs. The classic example is a MOS transistor, sometimes used as a bidirectional switch. Informally, we model its behaviour as a switch controlled by the signal on the gate. Although the gate can reasonably be regarded as an input, both source and drain can act as inputs or outputs. We cannot formalise this model as a function.

At higher levels of abstraction, we may want to allow the possibility that, for some inputs, the output is indeterminate. To represent a unit delay as a function, we have to say what logic value appears on the output at time 0. It is more realistic to say simply that all we know of the behaviour is that the value on the input at time t appears on the output at time $t+1$. This is not a functional relationship; the signal on the output is not determined by the signal on the input — it is however constrained by it.

We model behaviour by saying that a device only allows certain combinations of signals on its ports. This representation of the behaviour as a subset of the possible combinations of signals is analogous to the representation of the analogue behaviour of a power source by a curve showing what combinations of current and voltage it admits. The characteristics of a load are represented similarly, by another curve. To determine what happens if we connect the two, we intersect the two curves. This model works well — but it is only a model and should be applied with care; it will not tell us what happens when we connect a toy 12V DC motor directly to the mains voltage.

We model the interconnection of digital devices in the same way: the behaviour of a component is represented as a subset of the possible combinations of signals at its ports; when we compose components, their combined behaviour is given by intersecting their individual behaviours. Again, this is only a model, and it must be applied with care; it will not correctly predict the behaviour of a circuit that wantonly violates design rules.

Clearly, graphical or tabular methods do not provide a practical way of manipulating these subsets. However, formal logic provides a notation for describing and manipulating these models. Predicate Logic provides a formal language for expressing relationships between things, together with a mathematical model of deductive reasoning about these relationships. The behaviour of a device may be described by a formula in predicate logic; the behaviour of a complex module may be composed from the behaviours of its parts, using the logical operations, *conjunction*, $\land$, and *existential quantification*, $\exists$, to model connection and hiding of internal wires. We use notation borrowed from ML [MTH90] to specify types and functions, and leave it to the reader to translate this to her favourite formalisation of typed predicate calculus.

To analyse continuous change, it is usual to model time using real numbers. When modelling digital behaviour, we may only be interested in the discrete sequence of states of a system; or we may require more detailed models of time that allow us, for example, to talk about setup and hold times, or concurrent systems. In this paper, we take a simple view of time as a potentially infinite sequence of

248

clock ticks, modelled by the natural numbers — t ∈ nat represents the number of abstract *clock ticks* since an (implicit) global reset. The time-dependent sequence of values on a wire is represented as a function from times to values.

```
type time = N;
type 'a signal = time →'a
```

Representing behaviours by relating *signals* on the ports of a device makes the representation of state implicit.

This model of behaviour and composition is only valid under appropriate constraints on the circuits we consider, and on the the interpretation of our model. Design rules express some such constraints, others must be checked by lower-level analysis of details of timing and electrical behaviour. We use formal methods to reason about the functional behaviour of devices operating in environments that allow us to use a synchronous digital abstraction of behaviour. Other tools are needed to verify these environmental constraints.

1.2 Specification

Specifications are essential contractual and methodological tools. The primary use of a behavioural model is to *specify* the required behaviour. This specification is central to the work of an engineer; his basic task is to design a system that meets the specification. Because the specification provides the interface between customer and designer, it must be understood by both. Specifications have another, equally important, rôle. Specifications express abstraction; we may use a component without worrying about (or even knowing about) its inner workings, if we know that it satisfies its specification. This *behavioural abstraction* is crucial to the design of complex systems; it provides the basis for managing complexity using hierarchical decomposition. Specifications are also necessary for scientific project management; once the specification of a component has been fixed, its users and implementers can work in parallel. Well-specified components also form the basis for reusable libraries.

Product specification and design documentation are often confused. A *specification* specifies a behaviour which may be implemented in different ways. Any user relying on the specification should be able to substitute one implementation for another without affecting the correctness of the overall system. Design *documentation* describes an implementation, it is necessary for design debugging, maintenance and test-pattern generation, and documents features incidental to that particular implementation. Using design documentation as a basis for incorporating a component in a system is usually a mistake — if you rely on an incidental feature you have no freedom to improve your system design by later substituting a different implementation of the component specification, unless, by chance, it shares the 'feature'. Worse, the original part may become unavailable, being superseded by another that meets the specification but has different behaviour, and you may have to redesign your system.

1.3 Correctness and Abstraction

Current "silicon compilers" take as input a register-transfer level description of behaviour, in terms of concrete data representations. There is usually no machine-assistance for the refinement of a design to this, register-transfer, level. Without proper documentation of the abstractions used, design management is difficult. Moreover, bugs introduced during the refinement process can be subtle, and dangerous.

Specifications may express abstraction, by hiding implementation detail. Another type of abstraction is expressed by *abstraction functions.* The need for these arises as soon as our specifications are expressed at a level higher than the implementation. The specification stipulates a relation that must hold between abstract objects. In an implementation, these abstract objects will be represented by patterns of concrete data in space and time. We use *interface specifications* to express the *data abstraction* and *temporal abstraction* which relate the concrete signals of an implementation to the abstractions of the design specification. To express the abstractions that relate signals at differing levels of description we again use predicate logic.

In developing our case study, we will look in some detail at various examples of abstraction. Here, we make one simple, but subtle, point. A given concrete signal usually represents at most one abstract signal, so it is possible to think of abstraction as a function, from concrete to abstract signals. However, not all concrete signals will correspond to one of our *intended* abstract values. We have to take account of the fact that our abstract signals (sequences of abstract values, modelled as functions on time) may at some times take values outwith the datatype used in the abstract specification.

One solution would be to reason explicitly about partial functions and terms that may not denote; some patterns of concrete data may not correspond to *any* abstract value. Our current approach is slightly different; an implementation of a datatype from the specification is given by *embedding* the type of specification-level signals in the type of concrete signals — some patterns of concrete data may not correspond to any *proper* abstract value. While reasoning about the abstract level, we take account of the possibility of 'illegal' values. $\mathsf{E}\,\tau$ (read τ *exists*) expresses the assertion that τ denotes a value within the intended range — this assertion may be false. Quantifiers are (implicitly) restricted to this range, and we interpret equality to imply existence:

$$(\forall\, x \cdot \phi) \;\hat{=}\; \forall\, x \cdot \mathsf{E}\,x \Rightarrow \phi \qquad\qquad (\exists\, x \cdot \phi) \;\hat{=}\; \exists\, x \cdot \mathsf{E}\,x \wedge \phi$$

$$(\tau = \sigma) \;\hat{=}\; \mathsf{E}\,\tau \wedge \mathsf{E}\,\sigma \wedge \tau = \sigma;$$

We adopt the same convention for atomic relations; for example, if a datatype has an order then we assume this is extended vacuously to illegal values:

$$(\tau < \sigma) \;\hat{=}\; \mathsf{E}\,\tau \wedge \mathsf{E}\,\sigma \wedge \tau < \sigma;$$

2 Formally Specifying the Stopclock

We now formalise user-level specification. The user's view of the stopclock is that it changes state on each 1/10th sec. clock tick. We model user-level clock ticks as naturals, the display, the reset command and the start/stop command are modelled as signals `display`, `reset` and `stst` that depend on this implicit 10Hz clock.

```
type Utime = nat ; type 'a USignal = Utime →'a ;
```

reset and **stst** are boolean signals; for the **display**, the user sees (or hopes to see) a sequence of three-digit values:

```
datatype Digit = 0 | 1 | ... | 8 | 9 ;
type Display = {tens:Digit, secs:Digit, tenths:Digit} ;
display:  Display USignal ;
```

The specification relates **display**, **reset** and **stst**. For instance, we may specify that, at each clock tick, if the clock is running, unless the clock is reset the display is incremented; if the stopclock is not running, then the display is unchanged unless the clock is reset. To formalise the implicit state (is the clock running or not), we introduce an internal boolean signal, **run**. We specify how the next state and output depend on the present state and inputs, and how the stopclock looks when we switch it on:

```
val AbsS(reset, stst, display) =
    ∃ run:bool USignal.  ∀ τ:Utime.
        display(0) = {tens=0,secs=0,tenths=0}
        ∧ display(τ+1) = if (reset τ) then {tens=0,secs=0,tenths=0}
                                else if (run τ) then nextTime(display τ)
                                else (display τ)
        ∧ run(0) = lo
        ∧ run(τ+1) = if (reset τ) then lo
                            else if (stst τ) then not(run τ)
                            else (run τ)
        ∧ E(display τ) ;
```

nextTime is defined in the obvious way:

```
(* nextTime:  Display→Display *)
fun nextTime{tens,secs,tenths} =
    if (tenths < 9) then {tens,secs,tenths=nextDigit tenths}
    else if (secs < 9) then {tens,secs=nextDigit secs,tenths=0}
    else if (tens < 6) then {tens=nextDigit tens,secs=0,tenths=0}
    else {tens=0,secs=0,tenths=0} ;
```

Here, **nextDigit** is a partial function defined in the obvious way for n < 9, and Digits have the usual ordering. There is a dependency between the values of run, stst and display: stst τ influences run(τ+1) which in turn influences display(τ+2). Notice that the user-level specification is deterministic since it defines the behaviour of the stopclock for all combinations of the control signals.

3   Implementing the Stopclock

We are also given some implementation dependent information; the implementation will be in terms of 1MHz signals. The top-level specification, quite properly, ignores the 1MHz clock: the user of a stopwatch shouldn't have to be aware of its existence. To design an implementation, we will have to decide how to represent the user-level abstract signals concretely. For example, the high-level specification does not explain that the reset button may be pressed momentarily, asynchronously with respect to the 10Hz clock tick, nor that the output must remain well defined for long enough to allow the human eye, which forms part of the total system, to perceive the correct display. To refine the specification, we will formalise the relation of the abstract sequence of displayed values, to the the low-level sequence that can, potentially, change too quickly to be read. We also address the internal representation of reset and start/stop — relating the abstract signals of the specification to concrete signals on wires attached to the buttons.

Classifying Abstractions   There are infinitely many different abstraction functions we could use. However, many are common enough to be considered clichés, and Melham's work, [Melham88], shows that some systematic study is profitable. In general, we must explain how the high-level data of the specification is represented in terms of lower levels. It is useful, but often impossible, to factor this into separate timing and data abstractions. Melham presents four kinds of abstraction: *structural–, behavioural–, data–* and *temporal–*. These are all used in our development of the case study; we also have to introduce some *mixed* abstractions. We believe that these occur frequently in real designs.

3.1   Behavioural Abstraction

Suppose that $\mathtt{Spec}(a, b)$ is the *partial specification* of a device and $\mathtt{Imp}(a, b)$ is the design description. By partial specification we mean that $\mathtt{Spec}$ does not completely define the range of behaviour that the device can exhibit but only defines its behaviour in environments or states that are of particular interest. $\mathtt{Imp}$ is correct with respect to $\mathtt{Spec}$ if the following relation holds:

$$\forall\, a, b \cdot\ \mathtt{Imp}(a, b)\ \Rightarrow\ \mathtt{Spec}(a, b).$$

This asserts that whenever a and b satisfy $\mathtt{Imp}$ they will also satisfy $\mathtt{Spec}$.

A device with input *in* and output *out* is specified by a predicate $\mathtt{Dev}$, defined so that $\mathtt{Dev}(in, out)$ holds exactly when the combination of signals at *in* and *out* is one that is allowed to occur on the corresponding ports of the device. Modelling behaviours as relations on *signals*, that vary over time, makes the representation of state implicit. Thus, a **delay** with a propagation delay of δ time units between input and output can be defined as

$$\mathtt{Dev}(in, out)\ \triangleq\ \forall\, t \cdot\ out(t + \delta) = in\, t.$$

Note that we say nothing about the output at times $t < \delta$. The system clock is *implicit* in this description. We view t as time measured from some implicit system reset. A suitable formalisation of a delay with implicit reset might be

$$\mathtt{Dev}(in, out)\ \triangleq\ \forall\, t \cdot\ out(t + \delta) = in\, t \wedge \forall\, t < \delta \cdot\ out\, t = lo$$

3.1.1   Specifying the Components

The primitive components we use in the implementation are specified below, under the assumption of the existence of implicit clock and reset signals. The datatype **bool** consists of the set $\{\mathtt{hi}, \mathtt{lo}\}$ and the operations **and, or, xor, not, implies** on values of **bool**. $\mathcal{W}_4$ is a four-bit word.

```
NOT(x,z) = ∀t:time.  z t ≡ not(x t)
AND(x,y,z) = ∀t:time.  z t ≡ (x t) and (y t)
OR(x,y,z) = ∀t:time.  z t ≡ (x t) or (y t)
XOR(x,y,z) = ∀t:time.  z t ≡ (x t) xor (y t)
COMP(inp1,inp2,z) = ∀t:time.  z t = (inp1 t = inp2 t)
DELAY(x,z) = ∀t:time.  z(0) ≡ lo ∧ z(t+1) ≡ (x t)
LATCH(x,s,z) = ∀t:time.  z(0) ≡ lo ∧
                         z(t+1) ≡ if (s t) then (x t) else (z t)
```

A 4-bit incrementer/register has a hold/increment input inc:bool signal, a reset input clr:bool signal and a 4-bit register out:W_4 signal is specified below, where $\oplus_{16}$ is binary addition of four-bit words (corresponding to addition modulo 16 of the integers they represent).

```
INCR(inc,clr,out) =
    ∀t:time.  (not(clr t)
                  ⇒ out(t+1) = if inc t then (out t) ⊕16 1 else out t)
            ∧ (clr t ∧ not(inc t))  ⇒ (out t) = 0₄
```

We do not specify what happens when inc and clr are both hi.

3.2   Structural Abstraction

Structural abstraction is expressed by *hiding* internal signals in the design description (using $\exists$). Suppose an implementation $\texttt{Imp}(x, y, z)$ consists of the interconnection of two simpler devices $D_1(a, b)$ and $D_2(c, d)$ with port b of D_1 connected to port c of D_2. The behaviour of the resulting structure can be modelled by

$$\texttt{Imp}(x, y, z) \equiv D_1(x, y) \wedge D_2(y, z).$$

We might want to use Imp to implement a specification $\texttt{Spec}(x, z)$ that constrains just the values of the external ports x and z. To relate Imp and Spec, we must abstract the structural information, that Imp has an 'internal' wire y. The abstracted behaviour can be modelled by

$$\texttt{AbsImp}(x, z) \equiv \exists y.\texttt{Imp}(x, y, z))$$

that is, values x and z are allowed to occur on the external ports only when it is *possible* for internal signals to be generated such that $\texttt{Imp}(x, y, z)$ holds.

3.2.1   Specifying Submodules

The point of our case study is to show we may represent, formally, common design practice — which includes top-down and bottom-up design. Designing top-down, we devise parts of the design concurrently with the refinement of the abstraction mappings that relate specification and implementation. Designing bottom-up we compose primitives to build components that match parts of our problem, and infer the abstractions from the implementation.

We *could* combine the formal, high-level specification of the stopclock with the abstraction mappings for its inputs and outputs, to calculate a low-level specification. The low-level specification is derived by expanding all high-level signals in terms of their concrete representation, thus achieving *Spec(abs x)*. The disadvantage of designing in this way is that structure inherent in the specification may be lost. Instead of dealing with the whole design at the implementation level, we show, here, how it may be partitioned into smaller problems *before* the refinement step.

Top-down Design For the stopclock, our specification suggests a partitioning into two subcircuits: one for producing run from the reset and start/stop signals; and the other (`INC`) for storing and updating the counting of time. A block-level sketch of this 'high-level' design, corresponding to the partitioning implicit in the specification, can be made before further refinement – see Figure 1.

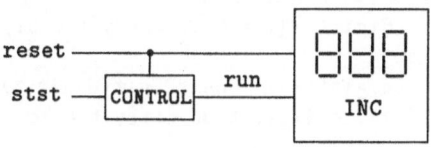

Figure 1: First partitioning.

Where,

```
INC(reset,run,display) =
    ∀τ:Utime.  display(0) = {tens=0,secs=0,tenths=0} ∧
               display(τ+1) = if (reset τ) then {tens=0,secs=0,tenths=0}
                              else if (run τ) then nextTime(display τ)
                              else (display τ) ;
```

and

```
CONTROL(reset,stst,run) =
    ∀τ:Utime.  run(0) = lo ∧
               run(τ+1) = if (reset τ) then lo
                          else if (stst τ) then not(run τ)
                          else (run τ) ;
```

Note that here we have only abstract, user-level, signals. Before introducing the lower level of time, we can further refine the implementation of `CONTROL`. We may replace the conditionals by equivalent boolean logic, and introduce a delay to store the state. This allows us to "design" `CONTROL` as follows – see Figure 2.

```
CONTROL(reset,stst,run) ≡ DELAY(nextRun,run) ∧
                          AND(resetBar,toggle,nextRun) ∧
                          XOR(stst,run,toggle) ∧
                          NOT(reset,resetBar)
```

We stress again that this 'implementation' is abstract. We will see soon how to refine it to a concrete level.

We can refine the design of `INC` similarly (Figure 3). Here

254

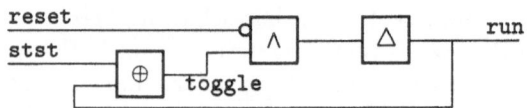

Figure 2: Implementing CONTROL.

```
NEXTₙ(reset,inc,carry,digit) =
    ∀t:time.  E digit t ⇒
        if reset t then carry t = 0 ∧ digit(t+1) = 0
        else if run t then
                if digit t = n then
                    (digit(t+1) = 0 ∧ carry t = hi)
                else
                    (digit(t+1) = nextDigit(digit t) ∧ carry t = lo)
        else digit(t+1) = digit t ∧ carry t = lo
```

Note that we require the carries to be generated with zero delay.

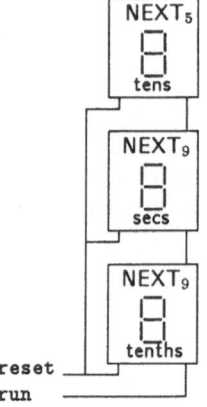

Figure 3: High-level view of the datapath.

3.3 Temporal Abstraction

Time is complex, partly because we have many different models of time, partly because the individual models may be complex, and, mostly, because we need to relate the different levels of timing abstraction, and the relation between different levels may be complex.

Temporal abstractions pervade digital design; an assembly code view of a microprocessor may abstract from the realities of prefetch, pipelining and microinstructions, and view each instruction as atomic. Each time-step at this level is implemented in terms of a variable number of microinstructions. Each microinstruction step may, in turn, be implemented in some number of system clock cycles. Finally, various submodules may be clocked at different multiples of the system clock frequency. Of course, we could continue further in the other direction and consider the compilation of a statement in a high-level language to a number of machine instructions, and so on. Timing abstractions, in addition to data abstractions, are needed to relate these levels.

The simplest temporal abstraction is *fixed sampling*; let f be a monotone increasing function, mapping each abstract time t to a concrete time $f\,t$. Sampling of a signal is given by function composition (Melham *op. cit.*) $Abs(x) \triangleq x \circ f$. For example, slow-down [Leiserson86] can be modelled by the abstraction function fn t => n * t, i.e. the abstract sequence of values consists of every n^{th} value of the concrete sequence. Often, the sampling function is not fixed; the mapping has complex dependencies on the overall behaviour of the device; in mapping behaviour at microinstruction level to instruction level in a microprocessor, the sampling function depends on the program executed.

3.3.1 Temporal Abstractions for the Stopclock

For our case study, the abstract, user-level ticks model rising edges of the 10Hz clock. We introduce some useful functions to formalise the relation between this and the model that considers the signals clocked at 1MHz:

rise x t is true if x changes from lo to hi at t

```
(* rise:  ('a→bool)→'a→bool *)
fun rise x 0     = x 0
|   rise x (t+1) = x(t+1) and not(x t) ;
```

This function can be "translated" into a circuit in a straightforward way – see Figure 4.

```
RISE(x,z) = ∃ y,yBar:bool signal.  ∀t:time.  DELAY(x,y) ∧
                                              NOT(y,yBar) ∧
                                              AND(x,yBar,z)
```

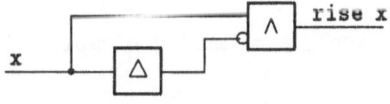

Figure 4: Implementing rise.

next p t returns the first time, t' ≥ t at which p t' holds

```
(* next:  ('a→bool)→'a→'a *)
fun next p t = if p t then t
                else next p (t+1) ;
```

nth s n returns the nth tick t' at which s t' holds:

```
(* nth:  ('a→bool)→'a→'a *)
fun nth s 0     = next s 0
|   nth s (τ+1) = next s ((nth s τ)+1) ;
```

Sometimes, we want to ignore the initial clock tick; n^+th s n returns the $(n+1)^{th}$ tick t' at which s t' holds:

```
(* n+th:   ('a→bool)→'a→'a *)
fun n+th s τ = nth s (τ+1)
```

The fundamental sampling functions we require, to relate abstract to concrete times, are defined in terms of the 10Hz clock signal, tick: smpl n returns the low-level instant t' at which the nth rise of the 10Hz clock occurs.

```
val smpl = nth(rise tick) ;
```

$smpl^+$ n returns the low-level instant t' at which the $(n+1)^{th}$ rise of the 10Hz clock occurs.

```
val smpl+ = n+th(rise tick) ;
```

3.3.2 Changing Levels of Abstraction

We now refine the CONTROL subcircuit to a physical level, where the signals vary with the 1MHz clock. This circuit will constrain the concrete signals, so that the abstract signals obtained by sampling them satisfy the constraints imposed by our earlier abstract decomposition. Because the connectives (conjunction and existential quantification) used to model composition of behaviours are monotone, this can be done component-wise, so we first consider how we might implement the abstract components:

Combinational Logic First note that, for a sampling abstraction, a concrete boolean logic gate implements the corresponding abstract logic gate. For example, recall the definition:

```
AND(x,y,z) = ∀t:time.  z t ≡ (x t) and (y t)
```

from this it follows that

```
AND(x,y,z) ⇒ AND(x o smpl, y o smpl, z o smpl)
```

Unit Delay To implement an abstract delay, we use a concrete latch. Recall the definitions:

```
DELAY(x,z) = ∀t:time.  z(0) ≡ lo ∧  z(t+1) ≡ (x t)
LATCH(x,s,z) = ∀t:time.  z(0) ≡ lo ∧
                         z(t+1) ≡ if (s t) then (x t) else (z t)
```

it is straightforward to show that

```
LATCH(x,s,z) ⇒ DELAY(x o (nth s),z o (nth s))
```

If we represent the user-level signals, `reset`, `stst` and `run`, by sampling concrete signals, `RESET`, `SS` and `RUN` on `rise tick`, we can use these implementations of the abstract components to obtain a low-level implementation of `CONTROL`.

This brings us to to a crucial point; the abstract reset and start/stop signals are not given by sampling the concrete signals from the buttons. We will require *glue logic*, to match the abstraction relation relating the the button and the abstract signal, to the abstraction we use to implement `CONTROL`. Since `run` is an internal signal, *we* can make sure we use the same abstraction at the interface to `INC` so that no *internal* glue is necessary.

For example, the abstract signal `reset` will be defined as an abstraction of the concrete signal `resetButton`. Unfortunately, because *outputs must depend causally on inputs*, we will see that it is not possible to implement glue logic for the reset signal such that

```
resetGlue(resetButton,RESET) ⊢ smpl s RESET = reset
```

We cannot produce the correct value at the beginning of the low level interval, as the value may depend on later inputs. We *will* be able to satisfy

```
resetGlue(resetButton,RESET) ⊢ smpl⁺ s RESET = reset
```

Since $smpl^+$ is again a sampling abstraction, this does not change our concrete implementation of the combinational logic, but we must take care to correctly implement the delay. The theorem we need is

```
LATCH(x,s,z) ∧ x(nth s 0) = 0 ⊢ DELAY(x o (n⁺th s), z o (n⁺th s))
```

Note that there is an extra hypothesis. This gives us the following low-level implementation of `CONTROL`.

```
NEXTRUN (nth s 0) = 0 ∧
reset = RESET o n⁺th s ∧ stst = SS o n⁺th s ∧ run = RUN o smpl⁺ ∧
RISE(tick,s) ∧
LATCH(NEXTRUN,s,RUN) ∧
AND(RESETBAR,TOGGLE,NEXTRUN) ∧
XOR(SS,RUN,TOGGLE) ∧
NOT(RESET,RESETBAR)
⊢ CONTROL(reset,stst,run)
```

Where the first line is a proof obligation that we must eventually discharge. This will be possible once we have implemented the glue logic for the buttons.

3.3.3 Timing Abstractions for the Buttons

It may be argued that the abstraction functions we are about to define should have been part of the initial specification. For our case study, this may well be true; however, in 'real life' not *all* abstractions will be specified before design begins. In any case, we believe that it is helpful to *structure* specifications by factoring them into high-level specifications and abstraction functions.

reset   The intention is that the reset button can be pressed asynchronously with respect to the user-level clock. Thus the abstract reset signal does not correspond to sampling the concrete signal produced by the button. The abstraction we use is

```
some s x τ = ∃t:time.  nth s τ ≤ t < nth s (τ+1) ∧ x t ≡ hi ;
```

We define the abstract signal `reset = some (rise tick) resetButton`, so

```
reset τ ≡ ∃t:time.  smpl τ ≤ t < smpl(τ+1) ∧ resetButton t = hi
```

Now we see why it is not possible to represent `reset` by sampling, on rising edges of the 10Hz clock, an internal signal generated by glue logic; we cannot produce the correct value at the beginning of the low level interval, as the value depends on later inputs. However, if we define

```
fun RESET 0    = false
|   RESET (t+1) = if s t then resetButton t else resetButton t or RESET t
```

then we *can* prove that

```
smpl+ s RESET = some s resetButton
```

We implement the recursive function directly to give our glue logic – see Figure 5.

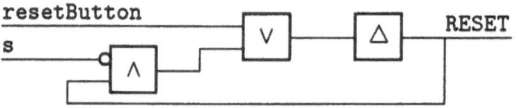

Figure 5: Glue logic for **reset**.

This gives us

```
resetGlue(resetButton,RESET) ⊢ n+th s RESET = some s resetButton
```

start-stop   The abstraction we use for start-stop determines what will happen if the user presses the start–stop button a number of times during a $1/10S$ interval. If this number is even, the stopclock should keep running normally; if the user presses the button an odd number of times within a $1/10S$ interval, then the state (running/stopped) should change. The abstraction we use is, where $\sharp t \cdot \phi$ is the *number* of times, t at which ϕ holds,

```
tgl s x τ = (♯t:time. nth s τ ≤ t < nth s (τ+1) ∧ x t = hi) mod 2 ;
```

We define the abstract signal `stst = tgl (rise tick) ststButton`. As we are counting the pressings modulo-2, a toggle behaviour is sufficient for keeping the count:

```
fun SS 0    = false
|   SS (t+1) = if s t then ststButton t else ststButton t xor SS t
```

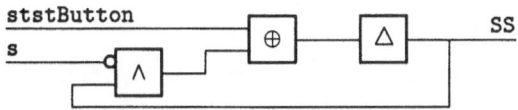

Figure 6: Glue logic for `stst` (start-stop).

This gives us

```
ststGlue(ststButton,SS) ⊢ n⁺th s SS = tgl s ststButton
```

Composing this glue logic with our low-level implementation of CONTROL, we can show

```
stst = tgl s ststButton ∧ reset = some s resetButton ∧
resetGlue(resetButton,RESET)) ∧ ststGlue(ststButton,SS) ∧
RISE(tick,s) ∧
LATCH(NEXTRUN,s,RUN) ∧
AND(RESETBAR,TOGGLE,NEXTRUN) ∧
XOR(SS,RUN,TOGGLE) ∧
NOT(RESET,RESETBAR) ∧
⊢ CONTROL(reset,stst,run) ∧
   reset = RESET o smpl⁺ ∧ stst = SS o smpl⁺ ∧ run = RUN o smpl⁺
```

3.3.4 Timing Abstraction for the Display

When the clock is running, the value shown by the display "should change from one valid value to the next at each clock tick". We *could* define

```
all smpl x τ = d ≡ (∀ t:time.  smpl τ ≤ t < smpl(τ+1)  ⇒  x t = d);
```

and use the abstraction `display = all smpl DISPLAY`. However, this would not leave us much time to update the display and our 'datapath' would be expensive to implement. If we take advantage of the behaviour of the human eye, we can use several system-level clock cycles to change from one valid display to the next, without the eye perceiving intermediate invalid values. However, *most of the time*, the display must be correct. This idea can be captured by an abstraction function relating the high-level behaviour of the display to the interval of low-level time in which the picture displayed is a consistent value except for a few low-level ticks at the start of each $1/10S$ cycle.

```
except kₐ smpl x τ = d ≡ (∀ t:time.smpl(τ+kₐ) ≤ t < smpl(τ+1)  ⇒  x t = d)
```

The parameter, k_d, formalises the 'few' in the English reading. The choice of the constant k_d has to be delayed until we have a better idea of how the implementation will behave; its value will depend on the delays associated to the incrementing of the display. But we could, right now, impose a constraint on the implementation that $k_d < 1000$, say, and be sure that the resulting flicker in the display would be imperceptible to the user.

3.4   Data Abstraction

Specifications may use abstract datatypes, such as `Digit`; implementations, in current technology, use binary bits. Data abstractions relate the abstract data and its concrete representation. A simple, and common form of data abstraction is to view the data appearing in parallel on a bus as representing an abstract data object.

Seven-segment Display   Our first example relates a seven-bit word to a single digit.

```
(* ssToDig:  W₇ →Digit *)
fun ssToDig w = case w of (hi,hi,hi,hi,hi,hi,lo) => 0
                        | ... |
                          (hi,hi,hi,hi,lo,hi,hi) => 9 ;
```

A seven-segment display implements this abstraction function

```
SSD(i,display) =
   ∀t:time.  E ssToDig(i₀ t, ..., i₆ t)
              ⇒ display t = ssToDig(i₀ t, ..., i₆ t)
```

This theorem states that *if the input is in the appropriate range*, then the value displayed corresponds to the number represented by inp.

Decoder   Our incrementer, INC, uses a different representation of the digits

```
(* w4ToDig:  word₄ → Digit *)
fun w4ToDig w = case w of (lo,lo,lo,lo) => 0
                        | ... |
                          (hi,lo,lo,hi) => 9 ;
```

The salient observation being that, with this abstraction,

```
w4ToDig word < 9  ⇒ nextDigit(w4ToDig word) = w4ToDig (incr word)
```

The decoder is just glue logic to relate the two data abstractions

```
DECODER(inp,out)
⊢ ∀t:time.  E w4ToDig(inp t)  ⇒ ssToDig (out t) = w4ToDig(inp t)
```

Joining these two circuits, we obtain

```
BINDISP(inp,display) = ∃v:W₇ signal.  DECODER(inp,v) ∧ SSD(v,display)
```

which satisfies the theorem:

```
BINDISP(inp,display) =
        ∀t:time.  E w4ToDig(i₀ t, ..., i₄ t)
                   ⇒ display t = w4ToDig(i₀ t, ..., i₄ t)
```

At the abstract level, we have just joined two bits of wire to produce a wire.

3.5 Datapath

In this section, we implement INC.

Bottom-up Design We use INCR and COMP to implement $NEXT_n$. We define
$NEXT_n IMP$ as follows,

```
NEXT_n IMP(reset,inc,carry,word) = ∃z:bool signal.
                                    OR(reset,carry,z) ∧
                                    COMP(word,incr(Rep n),carry) ∧
                                    INCR(inc,z,word)
```

then

```
NEXT_n IMP(reset,inc,carry word)
⊢ ∀t:time.  E(digit t) ⇒
   if reset t then carry(t+1) = 0 ∧ word(t+1) = 0
   else if run t then if word t = n then word(t+1) = 0 ∧ carry(t+1) = hi
                      else word(t+1) = incr(word t) ∧ carry(t+1) = lo
   else word (t+1) = word t ∧ carry (t+1) = lo
```

Here, Rep is the inverse of w4ToDig. If we use the right abstractions, $NEXT_n IMP$
implements $NEXT_n$. For the output, we want to combine the temporal abstraction
except k_d smpl with the data abstraction given by w4ToDig. For the control inputs
and carry output we must beware! Our concrete component generates the carry
after a unit delay. If we use a fixed sampling abstraction for the carry signals we
fall foul of the delay in generating the carries. However, if we use different sampling
abstractions for each carry signal then we can consistently maintain the abstract
view; that the carries are generated with zero delay. We define

$$\text{fun } \Delta^{-d} \ x \ t = x \ (t + d) \qquad \text{for } d \geq 0$$

The theorem has some constraints:

```
∀t:time.  RESET t = hi ⇒ ∃τ.  smpl τ = t ∧
∀t:time.  INC t = hi ⇒ ∃τ.  smpl τ = t ∧
NEXT_n IMP(RESET,INC,CARRY,WORD) ∧
digit = w4ToDig ∘ (except k_d smpl WORD) ∧
reset = RESET ∘ smpl⁺ ∧
inc = (Δ⁻ᵈ INC) ∘ smpl⁺ ∧
carry = (Δ⁻⁽ᵈ⁺¹⁾ CARRY) ∘ smpl⁺
⊢ NEXT_n(reset,inc,carry,digit)
```

The first two lines represent a requirement that, if the abstraction is to hold, RESET
and INC must only be hi at 10Hz clock ticks.

INC Finally, INC is implemented with three instances of NEXT_nIMP, three display-decoder pairs and some glue logic. INC takes as input the low-level versions of the reset signal RESET, the run/stopped signal RUN, the user-level clock tick and produces three "digits" as output Dt, Ds and Dss:

```
TEN,SIX:word₄
INC(RESET,RUN,tick,{tens,secs,tenths}) =
    ∃ clr,inc,ct,cs,css:bool signal, xt,xs,xss:𝒲₄ signal.  ∀t:time.
            AND(RESET,s,clr) ∧
            AND(RUN,s,inc) ∧
            NEXT₉IMP(clr,inc,xt,ct) ∧
            NEXT₉IMP(clr,ct,xs,cs) ∧
            NEXT₅IMP(clr,cs,xss,css) ∧
            BINDISP(xt,tenths) ∧
            BINDISP(xs,secs) ∧
            BINDISP(xss,tens)
```

The datapath contains three subcircuits, one for each digit, each consisting of a 4-bit register/incrementer, a decoder for translating from a representation of numbers by 4-bit words into one in terms of 7-bit patterns and a 7-segment display for output. The AND gates are there so we can discharge the side-conditions, on INC and RESET, introduced in the previous section. We can now observe that k_d can have the value 4 – which is well within the constraint we set ourselves earlier.

4   Putting It All Together

The sub-circuits comprising the stopclock will be timed by the 1MHz clock and yet behave as if synchronised by the 10Hz signal. This means, for instance, that the inputs to INC are 1MHz–level signals that change at the 10Hz ticks.

Notice that we are comparing the count for tenths and seconds to 10 (and the one for tens of seconds to 6, instead of 9 and 5, respectively. We are allowed to do so without violating our abstraction functions because, in the worst case ($59.9 \rightarrow 00.0$), the propagation of the carry-out signals ct,cs,css would take three 1MHz clock ticks. Suppose the count is 59.9. When the 10Hz signal occurs, the display changes to 59.0 and so remains until the next 1MHz tick; and then changes to 50.0 and then to 00.0. We assume that both the decoder and the displays can stabilise in less than $1\mu S$. Thus, the value displayed may not be consistent by, at most $4\mu S$ in $1/10S$.

The two and-gates are there to ensure that the controls to the datapath are only sampled on ticks of the clock. If this were omitted from the run input, it would quickly be apparent; if it were omitted from the reset input, it might not be a serious defect for our present application, but it would be a bug. This bug would only appear if the user noticed that sometimes, on reset, the last value of the display was not maintained for long enough for him to read it. A similar bug in a safety-critical system, where the last value of the 'display' was used by another program for real-time safe shutdown, could be fatal. The appearance of this bug would depend on the timing of the shutdown reset signal, and it might well evade quite thorough simulation.

5 Caveat and Conclusions

The development sketched in this paper has *not* been mechanically verified; there are certainly bugs to be found, and details to be refined. Nevertheless, we believe it has some value. In any case, such a paper-and-pencil exercise is a prerequisite for a more rigorous machine-assisted synthesis.

Acknowledgements We have to acknowledge conflicting pressures — from Stuart Anderson who has penetratingly criticised several versions of this paper, suggesting major improvements in organisation, presentation and substance (which we have tried to implement), and from Graham Birtwistle who has persisted in asking for camera-ready copy long after others would have given up in despair. We thank them both for their patience and help.

References

[AHLr90]   Abstract Hardware Limited, *LAMBDA Reference Manuals Ver. 3.1*, 1990.

[AHLu90]   Abstract Hardware Limited, *LAMBDA User Guides Ver. 3.1*, 1990.

[BG90]   G. Birtwistle, B. Graham, *Verifying SECD in HOL*, in "Formal Methods for VLSI Design", J. Staunstrup (ed.), North-Holland, 1990.

[BH90]   B. C. Brock, W. A. Hunt Jr, *A Formal Introduction to a Simple HDL*, in "Formal Methods for VLSI Design", J. Staunstrup (ed.), North-Holland, 1990.

[CGM86]   A. Camilleri, M. Gordon, T. Melham, *Hardware Verification Using High-Order Logic*, Univ. of Cambridge Computing Laboratory Tech. Rep. no.91, Sept. 1986.

[Cohn87]   A. Cohn, *A Proof of Correctness of the Viper Microprocessor: The First Level*, Univ. of Cambridge Computing Laboratory Tech. Rep. no.104, 1987.

[Cohn89]   A. Cohn, *Correctness Properties of the Viper Block Model: The Second Level*, in "Current Trends in Hardware Verification and Automated Theorem Proving", G. Birtwistle and G. A. Subrahmanyam (eds.), Springer-Verlag 1989.

[FFFH90]   S. Finn, M. P. Fourman, M. Francis, R. Harris, *Formal System Design – Interactive Synthesis Based on Computer Assisted Formal Reasoning*, in "Formal VLSI Specification and Synthesis", L. J. M. Claesen (ed.), Elsevier Science Publishers, 1990.

[FM89]   M. P. Fourman, E. Mayger, *Formally Based System Design – Interactive Hardware Scheduling*, in "Proc. of International Conference on VLSI", G. Musgrave and U. Lauther (eds.), Munich, 1989.

[Fourman77] M. P. Fourman, *The Logic of Topoi*, in "Handbook of Mathematical Logic", Barwise (ed.), North-Holland, 1977.

[Fourman86] M. P. Fourman, *Verification Using Higher-order Specifications*, in Proc. of the Silicon Design Conference, Wembley, 1986.

[Fourman90]   M. P. Fourman, *Formal System Design*, in "Formal Methods for VLSI Design", J. Staunstrup (ed.), North-Holland, 1990.

[FPZ88]   M. P. Fourman, W. J. Palmer, R. M. Zimmer, *Proof and Synthesis*, in Proceedings ICCD'88, Rye Brook, NY, 1988.

[Gordon85]   M. Gordon, *Why Higher-Order Logic is a Good Formalism for Specifying and Verifying Hardware*, Univ. of Cambridge Computing Laboratory Tech. Report no.77, Sept. 1985

[Gordon87]   M. Gordon, *A Proof Generating System for Higher-Order Logic*, Univ. of Cambridge Computing Laboratory Tech. Report no.103, Jan. 1987.

[Herbert88]   J. Herbert, *Temporal Abstraction of Digital Designs*, Univ. of Cambridge Computing Laboratory Tech. Report no.122, Feb. 1988.

[Hunt87]   W. A. Hunt, *The Mechanical Verification of a Microprocessor Design*, in "From HDL Descriptions to Guaranteed Correct Circuit Designs", D. Borrione (ed.), North-Holland 1987.

[Leiserson86]   C. E. Leiserson, J. B. Saxe, *Retiming Synchronous Circuitry*, DEC SRC Report no.13, 1986.

[Melham88]   T. Melham, *Abstraction Mechanisms for Hardware Verification*, in "VLSI Specification, Verification and Synthesis", Proc. of the Workshop on Hardware Verification, Calgary, G. M. Birtwistle and P. A. Subrahmanyam (eds.), Kluwer Academic Press, 1988.

[Mendler90]   M. Mendler, *Constrained Proofs: A Logic for Dealing with Behavioural Constraints in Formal Hardware Verification*, in "Designing Correct Circuits", G. Jones and M. Sheeran (eds.), Oxford, Sept. 1990.

[MTH90]   R. Milner, M. Tofte, R. Harper, *The Definition of ML*, MIT Press, 1990.

[Weise89]   D. Weise, *Constraints, Abstraction and Verification*, in "MSI Workshop on Hardware Specification, Verification and Synthesis: Mathematical Aspects", M. Leeser and G. Brown (eds.), Springer Verlag, 1989.

Proving (facts about) Ruby

Lars Rossen*

Technical University of Denmark
2800 Lyngby, Denmark

laro@id.dth.dk

Abstract

We describe a system for formal synthesis of digital circuits. This system
is based on the Ruby language and its implementation in a theorem
prover. We investigate what form a formal proof should have to ensure
correctness of circuits, and we devise a framework for doing these proofs.

*This work was supported by the Danish Research Academy and the Danish Technical Research
Council

1 Introduction

The Ruby language [12, 11] is a general relational specification language. The intended way of using the language is to derive a circuit description from a specification through a series of *calculations*. Each calculation step corresponds to a small refinement of the description. Successful examples of its use include the derivation of a variety of small scale DSP circuits [4]. It also seems possible to use it for real VLSI circuits as described in [5].

However all this work has been done as a paper exercise, and the primary reason for the work has been to show that the Ruby language was suitable for such specification and calculation. The logical next step is to construct a computer aided framework for doing these Ruby calculations.

Our first step towards a formal framework for Ruby designs was to implement the Ruby algebra in theorem prover. The theorem prover we chose was Isabelle [9, 8, 7], and we present the algebraic definition that was implemented in this prover. This work was originally described in [10].

Unfortunately a theorem prover usually does the opposite of helping a designer. The theorem prover might ensure that the design is correct in some sense, but the complication involved in theorem proving often drowns the creativity of the designer. This makes it infeasible to prove correctness of the calculation on the fly.

To overcome this problem we first describe what theorem we want to prove to ensure correctness of our circuit, and then we describe how to prove this. This leads to the concept of introducing *constraints* during the calculation of a circuit. To illustrate this we give an example of how a designer would construct such a correctness proof during the synthesis of a simple circuit. Finally we investigate how to construct a framework to aid the designer in this synthesis and we justify that it is both formal and easy for the designer to use.

Before we start the algebraic definition of Ruby, we give a short introduction to the notation used in this paper.

1.1 Notation

We will be using the notation commonly used in standard mathematical texts. $\exists, \forall, \in, \wedge, \vee$ etc. have their usual meanings. A typed expressions will be written as $F \colon \alpha$ denoting that F has type α. For integers, natural numbers and booleans we use the type symbols $\mathbf{Z}, \mathbf{N}$ and $\mathbf{B}$.

Usually we will write relations as infix for example. $a\,R\,b$ denotes a is related to b through the relation R. When defining relations in the Isabelle theorem prover we will use lambda abstractions, meaning that a relation between objects of type α and β (an $\alpha \sim \beta$ relation) can be defined as a function (predicate) of type

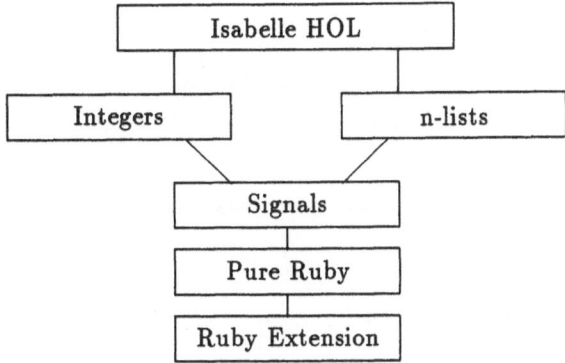

Figure 1: Ruby/Isabelle theory hierarchy

$\alpha \rightarrow \beta \rightarrow \mathbf{B}$. This means that relations can be defined through lambda abstractions. For example the identity relation can be defined as $\lambda\, a\, b \cdot\, a = b$. We allow a limited kind of pattern matching in the lambda definitions; we often define relations over pairs of data so the following are equivalent definitions:

$$\lambda ab \cdot (a = (a_1, a_2)) \wedge (b = (b_1, b_2)) \wedge P[a_1, a_2, b_1, b_2]$$
$$\lambda(a_1, a_2)(b_1, b_2) \cdot\ P[a_1, a_2, b_1, b_2]$$

The notation of proofs is inspired by [2].

2 Axiomatisation of Ruby

The implementation of a Ruby algebra in the Isabelle system is done by implementing a hierarchy of theories. This hierarchy is defined on top of the Isabelle Higher Order Logic (HOL). We have chosen the HOL object logic because Ruby has a natural definition in HOL. The Hierarchy we implement can be seen in figure 1.

The first two theory extensions (the theories of integers and n-lists) are not specific to Ruby but are needed as a basis for implementing the next theory.

The integer theory is a standard theory for operations on objects of type integer. Later we shall use integers to model time. The other theory is a theory of lists with fixed length. The type will be denoted by $\mathrm{list}_n(\alpha)$. The Isabelle system allows us to parameterise a type definition with a term (here n). The usual operations on lists are defined, and they are parameterised with a length indicator as well.

The following condition holds for an object of type $\mathrm{list}_n(\alpha)$:

$$L : \mathrm{list}_n(\alpha) \iff L : \mathrm{list}(\alpha) \wedge \mathrm{Length}(L) = n$$

nil and $\mathsf{cons}_n(,)$ are the two list constructs with some additional length constraints:

$$\vdash \quad \mathsf{nil}\colon \mathsf{list}_0(\alpha)$$
$$a\colon \alpha,\ b\colon \mathsf{list}_n(\alpha) \quad \vdash \quad \mathsf{cons}_n(a,b)\colon \mathsf{list}_{n+1}(\alpha)$$

We define the head and tail operation on lists and a notational abbreviation for lists:

Head:	$\mathsf{hd}_n(\mathsf{cons}_n(a_h, a_t)) \;=\; a_h$
Tail:	$\mathsf{tl}_n(\mathsf{cons}_n(a_h, a_t)) \;=\; a_t$
Lists:	$\{a_0, \cdots, a_n\}_{n+1} \;=\; \mathsf{cons}_n(a_0, \cdots \mathsf{cons}_0(a_n, \mathsf{nil}))$

After implementing a theory of integers and lists we are ready to define a theory of signals. A signal is a function from time, modeled as integers, to some data values. The type of signals is therefore

$$\mathsf{sig}(\alpha) \;=\; \mathbf{Z} \to \alpha$$

When dealing with Ruby expressions we are interested in reasoning about the structure of the data in the signal. In particular we want to reason about pairs and lists:

$$
\begin{aligned}
datatype \;=\;\; &primitive\ datatype \\
\mid\;\; &(datatype \times datatype) \\
\mid\;\; &\mathsf{list}_n(datatype)
\end{aligned}
$$

To be able to reason about the structure of a signal without actually applying the time to a signal, we define a set of higher order functions that operate on signals in the same way as we would operate on the underlying data.

First some signal type abbreviations:

$$
\begin{aligned}
\mathsf{sig}(datatype) \;&=\; \mathbf{Z} \to datatype \\
\mathsf{List}_n(datatype) \;&=\; \mathsf{sig}(\mathsf{list}_n(datatype))
\end{aligned}
$$

As we often want to construct signal lists from more simple signals we introduce Signal list operations that correspond to the operations on the underlying data.

Nil:	$\mathsf{Nil} = \lambda t\colon \mathbf{Z} \cdot \mathsf{nil}$
Cons:	$\mathsf{Cons}_n(a, b) = \lambda t\colon \mathbf{Z} \cdot \mathsf{cons}_n(a(t), b(t))$
Head:	$\mathsf{Hd}_n(\mathsf{Cons}_n(a_h, a_t)) \;=\; a_h$
Tail:	$\mathsf{Tl}_n(\mathsf{Cons}_n(a_h, a_t)) \;=\; a_t$

The following abbreviations are used as well:

Signal concatenation: $a:_n b = \mathsf{Cons}_n(a,b)$
Empty signal lists: $\langle\rangle = \mathsf{Nil}$
Signal–lists: $\langle a_n, \cdots, a_0 \rangle_{n+1} = a_n:_n \cdots a_0:_0 \langle\rangle$

2.1 Pure Ruby

Our next step towards an algebra for Ruby is to get a handle on what constitutes a Ruby–relation. The idea is that Ruby relation constitutes a subset of the general signal relations ($\mathsf{sig}(\alpha) \sim \mathsf{sig}(\beta)$). The way to make a precise statement of what constitutes a Ruby relation is to define a primitive set of Ruby relation and then define any extension to the Ruby language in terms of this primitive core language.

We have chosen 4 primitives as our core language and we call this language for Pure Ruby. The 4 constructs are:

$$
\begin{aligned}
ruby = \; & \mathsf{spread}(r) \\
| \; & \mathcal{D} \\
| \; & ruby;ruby \\
| \; & [ruby, ruby]
\end{aligned}
$$

$\mathsf{spread}(r)$ is used to construct combinational circuits, $\mathcal{D}$ defines a delay element, and the last two Ruby forms defines serial composition and parallel composition. We have found that a large selection of primitives and combining forms from [12, 11] can be defined through these 4 primitives. However there are forms that can not be defined this way, examples are pair and slow. We have deliberately chosen not to include these forms in Pure Ruby as they do not conform to to some nice algebraic properties. It is still possible to use them in our proof system as can be seen in [10].

The exact denotation of the 4 constructs are captured in the following 4 axioms:

Axiom

Spread: $\quad a\!:\mathsf{sig}(\alpha) \; \mathsf{spread}(f\!:\alpha \sim \beta) \, b\!:\mathsf{sig}(\beta) \stackrel{\triangle}{=} \forall t \cdot a(t) f\, b(t)$

Delay: $\quad a\!:\mathsf{sig}(\alpha) \; \mathcal{D} \, b\!:\mathsf{sig}(\alpha) \qquad\qquad \stackrel{\triangle}{=} \forall t \cdot a(t-1) = b(t)$

Ser.: $\quad a\!:\mathsf{sig}(\alpha) \; F;G \, b\!:\mathsf{sig}(\beta) \qquad\quad \stackrel{\triangle}{=} \exists c\!:\mathsf{sig}(\gamma) \cdot a F c \,\wedge\, c\, G\, b$

Par: $\quad a\!:\mathsf{sig}((\alpha_1 \times \alpha_2))[F,G]\, b\!:\mathsf{sig}((\beta_1 \times \beta_2)) \stackrel{\triangle}{=} \mathsf{Fst}(a)\, F\, \mathsf{Fst}(b) \,\wedge\, \mathsf{Snd}(a)\, G\, \mathsf{Snd}(b)$

We can only construct a subset of all possible (signal–)relations if we only use Pure Ruby when forming expressions (see figure 2). We want to be able to formally describe when we constructing expressions inside this Ruby–domain. We therefore

270

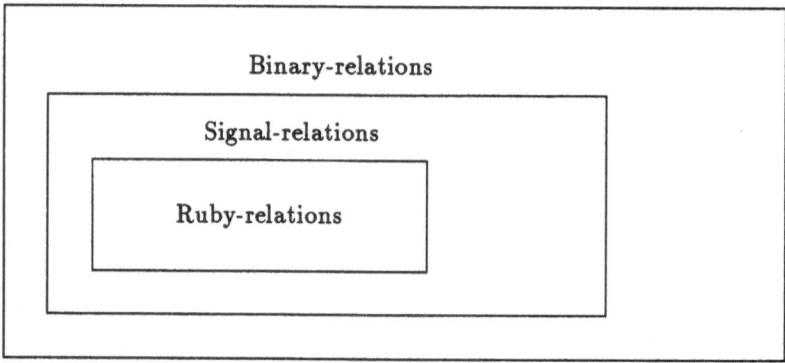

Figure 2: An illustration of how the ruby relations are a subset of the signal relations and signal relation are a subset of binary relations

introduce a Pure Ruby type: $\alpha \overset{Pure}{\sim} \beta$. A simple law is that all object of this type also are signal relations:

$$R: \alpha \overset{Pure}{\sim} \beta \ \Rightarrow \ R: \mathsf{sig}(\alpha) \sim \mathsf{sig}(\beta)$$

A more constructive definition of this type is given through the following 4 domaine axioms:

Axiom

Spread-type	$f: \alpha \sim \beta$		$\vdash\ \mathbf{spread}(f): \alpha \overset{Pure}{\sim} \beta$
Delay-type			$\vdash\ \mathcal{D}: \alpha \overset{Pure}{\sim} \alpha$
Composition-type	$F: \alpha \overset{Pure}{\sim} \beta,\ G: \beta \overset{Pure}{\sim} \gamma$		$\vdash\ F;G: \alpha \overset{Pure}{\sim} \gamma$
Par-type	$F: \alpha_1 \overset{Pure}{\sim} \beta_1,\ G: \alpha_2 \overset{Pure}{\sim} \beta_2$	$\vdash$	$[F,G]: (\alpha_1 \times \alpha_2) \overset{Pure}{\sim} (\beta_1 \times \beta_2)$

With these 4 axioms we can identify Pure Ruby relations but if we want to prove general things about Ruby relations then we need a Ruby induction and recursion theorem.

Ruby Induction

$$\forall f: \alpha \sim \beta \cdot \mathrm{P}(\mathbf{spread}(f)) \ \wedge$$
$$\mathrm{P}(\mathcal{D}) \ \wedge$$
$$\forall F: \alpha \overset{Pure}{\sim} \beta \ G: \beta \overset{Pure}{\sim} \gamma \cdot \mathrm{P}(F) \wedge \mathrm{P}(G) \ \Rightarrow \ \mathrm{P}(F;G) \ \wedge$$
$$\forall F: \alpha_1 \overset{Pure}{\sim} \beta_1 \ G: \alpha_2 \overset{Pure}{\sim} \beta_2 \cdot \mathrm{P}(F) \wedge \mathrm{P}(G) \ \Rightarrow \ \mathrm{P}([F,G])$$

$$\overline{\forall R: \alpha \overset{Pure}{\sim} \beta \cdot \mathrm{P}(R)}$$

Recursive functions are defined through the Ruby_Prim_Rec constant. Its denotation is captured in the following theorem.

Ruby Recursion

$\forall\,SD\,CP\cdot$ **Let** $fun\;=\;$ Ruby_Prim_Rec $S\,D\,C\,P$ **in**
$$\forall f\cdot\;fun\;\text{spread}(f)\;=\;S\,f\;\wedge$$
$$fun\;\mathcal{D}\;=\;D\;\wedge$$
$$\forall F\;G\cdot\;fun\,(F;G)\;=\;C(fun\,F)(fun\,G)\,F\,G\;\wedge$$
$$\forall F\;G\cdot\;fun\,([F,G])\;=\;P(fun\,F)(fun\,G)\,F\,G$$

If we want a function $\mathcal{F}$ to be defined recursively on Ruby relations, we make the following definition:

$$\mathcal{F}\;\overset{\triangle}{=}\;\text{Ruby\_Prim\_Rec}\,S\,D\,C\,P$$

Where S, D, C, P are functions that defines what the $\mathcal{F}$ evaluates to in the four Ruby cases. By instantiating the **Ruby Recursion** theorem we can derive a useful theorem about $\mathcal{F}$:

$$\forall f\cdot\;\mathcal{F}\;\text{spread}(f)\;=\;S\,f\;\wedge$$
$$\mathcal{F}\,\mathcal{D}\;=\;D\;\wedge$$
$$\forall G\;H\cdot\;\mathcal{F}(G;H)\;=\;C(\mathcal{F}\,G)(\mathcal{F}\,H)\,G\,H\;\wedge$$
$$\forall G\;H\cdot\;\mathcal{F}([G,H])\;=\;P(\mathcal{F}\,G)(\mathcal{F}\,H)\,G\,H$$

2.2 Ruby–extension

The next step in the process of making a Ruby system is to define the rest of the standard Ruby combining forms. First we illustrate how to define relational inverse in terms of the above four forms.

The normal definition is:

Theorem: Inverse $a\;F^{-1}\,b\;=\;b\,F\,a$

If we use that definition we could not use the Ruby type axioms on expressions involving inverse without extending Pure Ruby with that form. Instead we define inverse through Pure Ruby. First we define three spreads; $\mathcal{R}$, $\mathcal{L}$ and ID:

Definitions.

$\mathcal{L}$-def. $\mathcal{L}\overset{\triangle}{=}\;\text{spread}(\lambda ab\cdot\;\exists c\cdot b=(a,(c,c)))$

$\mathcal{R}$-def. $\mathcal{R}\overset{\triangle}{=}\;\text{spread}(\lambda ab\cdot\;\exists c\cdot a=(c,(c,b)))$

ID-def. $\text{ID}\overset{\triangle}{=}\;\text{spread}(\lambda ab\cdot\;a=b)$

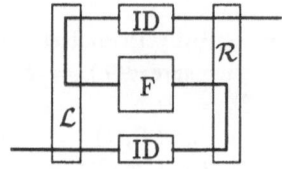

Figure 3: Inverse definition

If we look at figure 3 it seems reasonable to define Inverse as:

Definition: Inverse $F^{-1} \stackrel{\triangle}{=} \mathcal{L};[\mathsf{ID},[F,\mathsf{ID}]];\mathcal{R}$

To complete this definition one has to prove that the normal meaning of inverse is true from the definition. Furthermore it is convenient to prove a theorem stating that the inverse of a Pure Ruby relation is also a Pure Ruby relation. We have done this in the Isabelle theorem prover.

It is not the aim of this article to explain how to define the full Ruby language as an extension. Instead we list the definition of the relations and combining forms we will use in the rest of this article.

Conjugate is an abbreviation we often use, it is left associative:

$$R \setminus S \stackrel{\triangle}{=} S^{-1};R;S$$

Wiring primitives play an important role in designing circuits, and here are the definition of the ones we will use later:

$$\mathsf{Dub}: \alpha \stackrel{Pure}{\sim} (\alpha \times \alpha) \stackrel{\triangle}{=} \mathsf{spread}(\lambda a(b_1, b_2) \cdot\ a = b_1 = b_2)$$

$$\pi_1: (\alpha \times \beta) \stackrel{Pure}{\sim} \alpha \stackrel{\triangle}{=} \mathsf{spread}(\lambda(a_1, a_2)b \cdot\ b = a_1)$$

$$\pi_2: (\beta \times \alpha) \stackrel{Pure}{\sim} \alpha \stackrel{\triangle}{=} \mathsf{spread}(\lambda(a_1, a_2)b \cdot\ b = a_2)$$

$$\mathsf{apl}_n: (\alpha \times \mathsf{list}_n(\alpha)) \stackrel{Pure}{\sim} \mathsf{list}_{n+1}(\alpha) \stackrel{\triangle}{=} \mathsf{spread}(\lambda(a_h, a_t)b \cdot\ b = \{a_h\}_1 \mathsf{app}_{1,n} a_t)$$

$$\mathsf{apr}_n: (\mathsf{list}_n(\alpha) \times \alpha) \stackrel{Pure}{\sim} \mathsf{list}_{n+1}(\alpha) \stackrel{\triangle}{=} \mathsf{spread}(\lambda(a_m, a_l)b \cdot\ b = a_m \mathsf{app}_{n,1} \{a_l\}_1)$$

$$\mathsf{reorg}: ((\alpha \times \beta) \times \gamma) \stackrel{Pure}{\sim} (\alpha \times (\beta \times \gamma)) \stackrel{\triangle}{=} \mathsf{spread}(\lambda((a_1, a_2), a_3)(b_1, (b_2, b_3)) \cdot$$
$$a_1 = b_1 \wedge a_2 = b_2 \wedge a_3 = b_3)$$

$$\mathsf{Cross}: (\alpha \times \beta) \stackrel{Pure}{\sim} (\beta \times \alpha) \stackrel{\triangle}{=} \mathsf{spread}(\lambda(a_1, a_2)(b_1, b_2) \cdot$$
$$a_1 = b_2 \wedge a_2 = b_1)$$

$$\mathsf{NIL}: \mathsf{list}_0(\alpha) \stackrel{Pure}{\sim} \mathsf{list}_0(\alpha) \stackrel{\triangle}{=} \mathsf{spread}(\lambda ab \cdot\ (a = b = \mathsf{nil}))$$

The primitive Cross is often referred to as Swap as it swaps the component of a pair. If we chose to interpret Cross as a four sided primitive, where the left and top wire is represented in the domaine pair, and the bottom and right wire is represented in the range pair, then our **Cross** primitive is a real not connected wire cross.

fst and **snd** are abbreviations we often use. They put a Ruby relation in parallel with the identity.

$$\text{fst } F \ \stackrel{\triangle}{=} \ [F, \text{ID}]$$
$$\text{snd } F \ \stackrel{\triangle}{=} \ [\text{ID}, F]$$

Zip is another wiring primitive that converts a pair of lists into a list of pairs. It is defined recursively on the length of the lists:

$$\text{zip}_n \ : \ (\text{list}_n(\alpha) \times \text{list}_n(\beta)) \stackrel{Pure}{\sim} \text{list}_n((\alpha \times \beta))$$
$$\text{zip}_0 \ \stackrel{\triangle}{=} \ \text{Dub}^{-1}; \text{NIL}$$
$$\text{zip}_{n+1} \ \stackrel{\triangle}{=} \ [\text{apl}_n^{-1}, \text{apl}_n^{-1}]; (\text{Cross} \setminus \text{fst}(\text{reorg}^{-1}) \setminus \text{reorg}); \text{snd}(\text{zip}_n); \text{apl}_n$$

Loop connects the second signal of the domain and the range of the argument. It exists both in a two and a four sided version:

$$\text{loop}_2 H \ \stackrel{\triangle}{=} \ [H, ID] \setminus \mathcal{L}^{-1}$$
$$\text{loop}_4 H \ \stackrel{\triangle}{=} \ \text{loop}_2(\text{Cross}; (\text{Cross}; H) \setminus \text{reorg}^{-1})$$

Map is a generic combining form that expands according to the length of the signal it relates. We shall therefore define it in terms of number recursion:

$$\text{map}_0(F) \ \stackrel{\triangle}{=} \ \text{NIL}$$
$$\text{map}_{n+1}(F) \ \stackrel{\triangle}{=} \ [\text{map}_n(F), F] \setminus \text{apl}_n$$

Beside and **Below** are used to wire together two 4 sided circuits:

$$P \leftrightarrow Q \ \stackrel{\triangle}{=} \ \text{reorg}^{-1}; [P, \text{ID}]; \text{reorg}; [\text{ID}, Q]; \text{reorg}^{-1}$$
$$P \updownarrow Q \ \stackrel{\triangle}{=} \ (P^{-1} \leftrightarrow Q^{-1})^{-1}$$

Glue–left, –right, –over and **–under** $(\rightarrow \leftarrow \downarrow \uparrow)$ are notational abbreviations useful when connecting a two sided circuit to the side of a four sided circuit:

$$F \rightarrow H \ \stackrel{\triangle}{=} \ \text{fst } F; H$$
$$F \downarrow H \ \stackrel{\triangle}{=} \ \text{snd } F; H$$
$$H \leftarrow F \ \stackrel{\triangle}{=} \ H; \text{snd } F$$
$$H \uparrow F \ \stackrel{\triangle}{=} \ H; \text{fst } F$$

Glueleft ($\rightarrow$) and glueover ($\downarrow$) are right associative, glueright ($\leftarrow$) and glueunder ($\uparrow$) are left associative. Note that the symbol for glueleft ($\rightarrow$) are the same as

274

the symbol for function space in type theory, but the symbol will only be used in contexts where this conflict are easy to resolve.

Col is defined recursively like **map**, but it is a bit more complicated.

$$\text{col}_0(F) \triangleq [\text{NIL}, \text{ID}]; \text{Cross}$$
$$\text{col}_{n+1}(F) \triangleq \text{apr}_n^{-1} \to (\text{col}_n(F) \updownarrow F) \leftarrow \text{apr}_n$$

Bit values play an important role when designing circuits. Here we have chosen to model bit values as the numbers 0 and 1 representing the low and high value of a wire. These two values will be the only values we allow a wire to have.

We define a number of identity relations related to the domain of bit values. $\mathcal{B}$ is the identity on bit values, and it is defined through a relation that converts boolean values into bit values. ID_n is the identity on naturals, restricted to the range $[0, 2^n - 1]$. We define ID_n through the abstraction function Bits_n that converts a natural number to a list of bit values. **Bits** are defined as a column of cells that convert single bits:

$$\mathcal{B}: bool \overset{Pure}{\sim} \mathbf{N} \triangleq \textbf{spread}(\lambda in\ out \cdot (\neg in \land (out = 0)) \lor (in \land (out = 1)))$$
$$\mathbf{B}: \mathbf{N} \overset{Pure}{\sim} \mathbf{N} \triangleq \mathcal{B}^{-1}; \mathcal{B}$$
$$\text{bit}: \mathbf{N} \overset{Pure}{\sim} (\mathbf{N} \times \mathbf{N}) \triangleq \textbf{spread}(\lambda out(in, bit) \cdot out = 2in + bit)$$
$$\text{Bits}_n: \mathbf{N} \overset{Pure}{\sim} \text{list}_n(\mathbf{N}) \triangleq \text{col}_n(\pi_2; \text{bit} \leftarrow \mathbf{B}) \setminus \pi_2^{-1}$$
$$\text{ID}_n: \mathbf{N} \overset{Pure}{\sim} \mathbf{N} \triangleq \text{Bits}_n; \text{Bits}_n^{-1}$$

This definition of abstractions function is done ad hoc, it could be done in a more systematic way [3].

3   Rewriting rules

The proof system as described above is ideal for proving the rules that are traditionally used for Ruby calculation, and the process of proving such rules is described in [10]. Here we will list some of the rules that we are going to use in our next example. It is important to note that all the rules can be proven formally in the Isabelle theorem prover.

The rules we will be using can be put into different categories. In the following we will present 3 groups of rules:

- Often the same circuit layout can be described in different ways. The equivalence between these descriptions can be expressed in a series of laws:

$$[F, G]; [H, I] = [F; H, G; I]$$
$$\text{fst}(F; G) = \text{fst}(F); \text{fst}(G)$$
$$\text{snd}(F; G) = \text{snd}(F); \text{snd}(G)$$
$$\text{fst}(F); \text{snd}(G) = \text{snd}(G); \text{fst}(F)$$

- Other laws capture the idea that we can rearrange the components of a circuit without changing the circuit behaviour. It is easy to be convinced about the correctness of these rules by drawing the left and right side of the rule and then compare:

$$\text{loop}_4(\text{zip}_n \to \text{col}_n F) = \text{col}_n(\text{loop}_4 F)$$
$$\text{loop}_4(F \downarrow G) = F \downarrow \text{loop}_4(G)$$
$$\text{loop}_4(G \uparrow F) = \text{loop}_4(G) \uparrow F$$
$$\text{col}_n(\text{Cross}) \updownarrow \text{col}_n(F) = \text{zip}_n \to \text{col}_n(\text{Cross} \updownarrow F) \leftarrow \text{zip}_n^{-1}$$

- Certain changes to a circuit do not change its input/output behaviour. For example we can retime a Ruby circuit [11]:

$$F : \alpha \overset{Pure}{\sim} \beta \;\Rightarrow\; (F = F \setminus \mathcal{D})$$

4 Constraint based Calculation

The implementation of Ruby in a formal theorem prover makes it possible to formally prove the rules of the Ruby language. However we have not shown what kind of proof we want to develop when designing circuits.

The way the Ruby language is intended to be used is to have a specification written in Ruby and then apply a series of *calculations* to this specification until it is transformed into something that can be implemented.

$$spec \leadsto step1 \leadsto \cdots \leadsto impl$$

Usually most of these calculations are rewrites with equivalences. If we only use rewriting the arrows in the above diagram can be substituted with equals. This means that through calculating we have produced a circuit that is equivalent to the specification.

$$spec = step1 = \cdots = impl$$

Unfortunately this is not always possible. Often the specification is too general, and then through the calculating process one wishes to *constrain* the specification. A traditional way of handling this in hardware verification is to prove that the implementation satisfies the specification:

$$implementation \subseteq specification$$

What we say with this theorem is that anything the circuit accepts as a correct set of inputs and outputs is correct according to the specification. In other words; this theorem prevents us from constructing a circuit that computes incorrect results. It does not however prevent us from producing a circuit that are to restricted. In other words we do not now how much we have constrained the specification. Another problem is that the above theorem is difficult to produce through a stepwise calculation of the implementation from the specification.

A way to circumvent the problems is to modify the specification during the calculation of the implementation. We will allow modifications to the specification that reflect the constraints we want to introduced during the synthesis of the implementation. In this way the result of our calculations should be a theorem stating that our implementation is equal to a constrained specification.

The two questions that arise are what kind of constraint introducing calculation we allow and how to formally control this process ? Usually the constraint introducing calculations we are interested in are the introduction of restrictions on the domaine or range of the specification. This correspond to the following rules:

$$\frac{S \ = \ I}{C_d;S \ = \ C_d;I} \qquad\qquad \frac{S \ = \ I}{S;C_r \ = \ I;C_r}$$

The formal approach to calculating with constraint introduction will then be to conduct a standard forward proof using the above two rules and the following rules as well:

$$\frac{}{S \ = \ S} \qquad\qquad \frac{A = B \qquad S \ = \ I[A]}{S \ = \ I[B]}$$

The calculation process now looks like:

$$
\begin{aligned}
spec &= spec \\
spec' &= step1' \\
\cdot & \quad \cdot \\
\cdot & \quad \cdot \\
\cdot & \quad \cdot \\
spec''' &= impl
\end{aligned}
$$

We start out with a trivial theorem stating that the specification is equivalent to itself. Then during a series of calculations we transform the right hand side of the equation. Occasionally it is necessary to make a calculation that changes the left hand side as well. Let us illustrate it with an example.

5   Calculation example

In this section we will describe the process of calculating a "toy" circuit. The circuit is to take a stream of numbers and produce a output stream that represents the sum of the numbers. Furthermore it accepts a reset signal that initiates the start of a new sum. The circuit may also produce an overflow signal. The circuit could be a subcomponent of a DSP chip.

We start our calculation by writing down the specification in an algebraic notation:

$$
\begin{aligned}
[in, ins]\mathrm{SUM}_{spec}[ov, out] \triangleq \forall t \cdot (ins(t) = \text{``\textbf{add}''} \land \\
\neg ov(t) \Rightarrow out(t) = out(t-1) + in(t)) \\
\lor (ins(t) = \text{``\textbf{pass}''} \land out(t) = in(t))
\end{aligned}
$$

This description hopefully corresponds to our idea of what the circuit should do. Unfortunately it is not a Ruby description. We will however let this specification be the starting point for our calculations. So we set up our initial equation that is trivially true:

$$
\mathrm{SUM}_{spec} = \mathrm{SUM}_{spec} \tag{1}
$$

Our first calculation should translate this specification into Ruby form. An easy way of getting the specification into Ruby form is to combine a delay element and an arithmetic unit responding to the *pass* and *add* instructions in a loop. This gives us the following Ruby description of the circuit.

$$
\mathrm{SUM}_{ruby} \triangleq \mathsf{loop}_4(\mathsf{snd}(\mathcal{D}) \to \mathsf{ALU}_a \leftarrow \mathsf{Dub}^{-1})
$$
Where
$$
\begin{aligned}
\mathsf{ALU}_a \triangleq \mathsf{spread}(\lambda\,((in, d), ins)(ov, out) \cdot (ins = \text{``\textbf{add}''} \land \\
\neg ov \Rightarrow out = in + d) \lor \\
(ins = \text{``\textbf{pass}''} \land out = in))
\end{aligned}
$$

If we can prove that this Ruby specification is equivalent to our original specification ($\mathrm{SUM}_{spec} = \mathrm{SUM}_{ruby}$) we should be allowed to make a substitution on the right side of our equation:

$$
\mathrm{SUM}_{spec} = \mathsf{loop}_4(\mathsf{snd}(\mathcal{D}) \to \mathsf{ALU}_a \leftarrow \mathsf{Dub}^{-1}) \tag{2}
$$

This is not a simple calculation and we shall return to this problem in the next section.

Next we construct the inside of the ALU box. When looking at the abstract (spread) definition we see a case statement controlled by *ins* and an addition statement, so it must be reasonable to construct a concrete ALU_k through plumbing together a multiplexor and an adder:

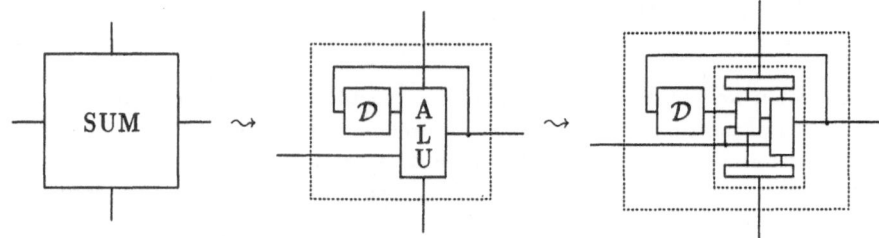

Figure 4: Calculating the SUM circuit

$$\mathsf{ALU}_k \triangleq \mathsf{Decode} \downarrow (\mathsf{fst}(\mathsf{Dub});\mathsf{reorg}) \to ((\mathsf{Cross} \updownarrow \mathsf{ADD}_a) \leftrightarrow \mathsf{Mux}) \uparrow \pi_1;\mathcal{B}^{-1}$$

Where

$$\mathsf{ADD}_a \triangleq \mathsf{spread}(\lambda\,((a,b),cin)(ov,s) \cdot \neg ov \Rightarrow s = a + b + cin)$$

$$\mathsf{Decode} \triangleq \mathsf{spread}(\lambda\,in\,(dum,out) \cdot (dum = 0) \wedge((ins = \text{``pass''} \wedge out = 0) \vee$$
$$(ins = \text{``add''} \wedge out = 1))$$

$$\mathsf{Mux} \triangleq \mathsf{spread}(\lambda((a,b),contr)(contr,out) \cdot (contr \wedge out = a) \vee$$
$$(\neg contr \wedge out = b))$$

With these definitions it should be possible to prove that $\mathsf{ALU}_a = \mathsf{ALU}_k$, and we can substitute ALU_k for ALU_a:

$$\mathsf{SUM}_{spec} = \mathsf{loop}_4(\mathsf{snd}(\mathcal{D}) \to \mathsf{Decode} \downarrow (\mathsf{fst}(\mathsf{Dub});\mathsf{reorg}) \to \qquad (3)$$
$$((\mathsf{Cross} \updownarrow \mathsf{ADD}_a) \leftrightarrow \mathsf{Mux}) \uparrow \pi_1;\mathcal{B}^{-1} \leftarrow \mathsf{Dub}^{-1})$$

The two calculations we have done so far are illustrated in figure 4.

Our circuit description is still a long way from anything that can be implemented. Most notable is the fact that the description still operates on general numbers, and not on a limited domain that can be represented by list of bits. The next calculation will therefore be to restrict the domain of numbers operated on by the circuit. We do this by applying a identity relation on a restricted range of numbers to both the original specification and the circuit description:

$$\mathsf{ID}_n \to \mathsf{SUM}_{spec} \leftarrow \mathsf{ID}_n = (\mathsf{Bits}_n;\mathsf{Bits}_n^{-1}) \to \qquad (4)$$
$$\mathsf{loop}_4(\mathsf{snd}(\mathcal{D}) \to \mathsf{Decode} \downarrow ((\mathsf{fst}(\mathsf{Dub});\mathsf{reorg}) \to$$
$$((\mathsf{Cross} \updownarrow \mathsf{ADD}_a) \leftrightarrow \mathsf{Mux}) \uparrow \pi_1;\mathcal{B}^{-1}) \leftarrow \mathsf{Dub}^{-1})$$
$$\leftarrow (\mathsf{Bits}_n;\mathsf{Bits}_n^{-1})$$

We have used the fact that $\mathsf{ID}_n = \mathsf{Bits}_n;\mathsf{Bits}_n^{-1}$ and now we can use some of the rearranging rewrite rules to move the Bits_n around the circuits description. That way it is possible to get some of the Bits_n into the adder multiplexor, and the cross over. We can also use the rules to move the Decode part of the circuit description outside the loop_4 body. We have done so in the next step, but it should be considered a series of transformations:

$$
\begin{aligned}
\mathsf{ID}_n \to \mathsf{SUM}_{spec} \leftarrow \mathsf{ID}_n \;=\; &\mathsf{Bits}_n \to \mathsf{Decode} \downarrow \qquad\qquad\qquad\qquad\qquad (5)\\
&\mathsf{loop}_4(\mathsf{snd}(\mathcal{D}) \to ((\mathsf{fst}(\mathsf{Dub});\mathsf{reorg}) \to \\
&\qquad (((\mathsf{Bits}_n^{-1} \to \mathsf{Cross} \leftarrow \mathsf{Bits}_n)\\
&\qquad\quad \updownarrow([\mathsf{Bits}_n^{-1}, \mathsf{Bits}_n^{-1}] \to \mathsf{ADD}_a \leftarrow \mathsf{Bits}_n))\\
&\qquad \leftrightarrow([\mathsf{Bits}_n^{-1}, \mathsf{Bits}_n^{-1}] \to \mathsf{Mux} \leftarrow \mathsf{Bits}_n))\\
&\qquad \uparrow \pi_1) \leftarrow \mathsf{Dub}^{-1})\\
&\uparrow \mathcal{B}^{-1} \leftarrow \mathsf{Bits}_n^{-1}
\end{aligned}
$$

We see that the adder, cross and multiplexor are now surrounded with Bits_n, this means that the can transform them into something that works directly on bit vectors. The rules to use are

$$
\begin{aligned}
\mathsf{fst}([\mathsf{Bits}_n^{-1}, \mathsf{Bits}_n^{-1}]);\mathsf{ADD}_a; \mathsf{snd}(\mathsf{Bits}_n) &= \mathsf{zip}_n; \mathsf{col}_n\, \mathsf{FA}\\
\mathsf{fst}([\mathsf{Bits}_n^{-1}, \mathsf{Bits}_n^{-1}]);\mathsf{Mux}; \mathsf{snd}(\mathsf{Bits}_n) &= \mathsf{zip}_n; \mathsf{col}_n(\mathsf{Mux}; \mathsf{snd}(\mathcal{B}))\\
\mathsf{fst}(\mathsf{Bits}_n^{-1});\mathsf{Cross}; \mathsf{snd}(\mathsf{Bits}_n) &= \mathsf{col}_n(\mathsf{Cross}; \mathsf{snd}(\mathcal{B}))
\end{aligned}
$$

Where

$$
\mathsf{FA} \;\triangleq\; \mathsf{spread}(\lambda((a,b),c_{in})(c_{out},s) \cdot s + 2c_{out} = a + b + c_{in})
$$

Let us do these transformations:

$$
\begin{aligned}
\mathsf{ID}_n \to \mathsf{SUM}_{spec} \leftarrow \mathsf{ID}_n \;=\; &\mathsf{Bits}_n \to \mathsf{Decode} \downarrow \qquad\qquad\qquad\qquad\qquad (6)
\end{aligned}
$$

$$
\boxed{
\begin{aligned}
&\mathsf{loop}_4(\mathsf{snd}(\mathcal{D}) \to ((\mathsf{fst}(\mathsf{Dub});\mathsf{reorg}) \to \\
&((\mathsf{col}_n(\mathsf{Cross} \leftarrow \mathcal{B}) \updownarrow (\mathsf{zip}_n \to \mathsf{col}_n(\mathsf{FA})))\\
&\leftrightarrow(\mathsf{zip}_n \to \mathsf{col}_n(\mathsf{Mux} \leftarrow \mathcal{B}))) \uparrow \pi_1) \leftarrow \mathsf{Dub}^{-1})
\end{aligned}
}
$$

$$
\uparrow \mathcal{B}^{-1} \leftarrow \mathsf{Bits}_n^{-1}
$$

A portion of the above equation has been framed: This corresponds to the parts that can be implemented directly in hardware (assuming a cell library with Full adders and bit multiplexors). The left hand side of the equation tells us that we have calculated the original SUM circuit with a restriction of the number domain to $[0, 2^n - 1]$. The portion of the right side that is not framed tells us how to interpret the signals in and out of the actual circuit.

The designer might stop here, but there is still room for improvement. The implementation as it stands is messy; it contains two zip_n, and it has a global loop with n wires. By using another set of Ruby transformations it is possible to move the zip_n outward and the loop inward. Again it is a series of transformations but we present it as one step.

$$
\begin{aligned}
\mathsf{ID}_n \to \mathsf{SUM}_{spec} \leftarrow \mathsf{ID}_n \;=\; &\mathsf{Bits}_n \to \mathsf{Decode} \downarrow \qquad\qquad\qquad\qquad\qquad (7)
\end{aligned}
$$

$$
\boxed{
\begin{aligned}
&\mathsf{col}_n(\mathsf{loop}_4(\mathsf{snd}(\mathcal{D}) \to ((\mathsf{fst}(\mathsf{Dub});\mathsf{reorg}) \to \\
&(\mathsf{Cross} \updownarrow \mathsf{FA}) \leftrightarrow \mathsf{Mux}) \uparrow \pi_1 \leftarrow \mathsf{Dub}^{-1}))
\end{aligned}
}
$$

$$
\uparrow \mathcal{B}^{-1} \leftarrow \mathsf{Bits}_n^{-1}
$$

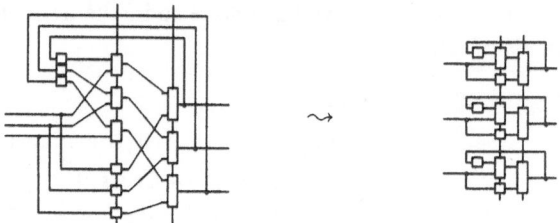

Figure 5: Layout optimising

This transformation can be seen in figure 5

Now let us step up a level and see what kind of calculation/transformation system we have described.

6   The Ruby Framework

With our small example we have illustrated how to synthesise a circuit from a specification. This was done through a series of calculation steps introducing constraints when necessary. Let us investigate what kind of operations we have used during our calculation:

1. Stating the formal definition of components.

2. Stating the existence of some theorems. These are either theorems that are proven or theorems that are believed to be true.

3. Setting up the initial specification equation to work on.

4. Manipulating the specification with the stated theorems. The manipulations should either be constraint introduction or equivalence rewriting.

We claim that it is the second operation that makes it feasible for a designer to use formal methods when synthesising a circuit. The second operation lets us state theorems *without proof*, theorems we need to proceed in our synthesis process.

Before explaining why we introduce a informal operation into our formal system we will investigate how a formally verified circuit is normally developed.

Formally verified circuits come in two flavors. Circuit that are verified after design, and circuits that are synthesised through the use of correctness preserving transformations. In the first method the circuit is synthesised with usual ad hoc methods, and the complete circuit is then proven correct with respect to a specification. The second method gives correctness by construction.

Ideally we would prefer to make a framework that supported the second method. We could do so by not allowing the designer to use unproven theorems. Unfortunately our experiments with Ruby has shown us the we use a large number of theorems during the synthesis process. It is unreasonable to expect a library to contain them all. This is especially true if the designer is to introduce new circuit components. For instance in the example our first transformation used a theorem stating the equivalence between a Ruby and a non Ruby description; it would be unreasonable to rely on the existence of such theorems. Nevertheless the theorem is intuitively correct and it should be easy to prove.

The logical solution would be to continue to enforce the use of proven theorems, but to allow the designer to prove theorems during the synthesis process. This should work in theory, but experiments with the Isabelle theorem prover have shown us that this is not feasible in practice. This stems from the fact that the process of formally proving theorem are a tedious process. Furthermore the process is very different from the synthesis process.

For the above reasons we still want to include the informal operation of using unproven theorems in the synthesis process. Fortunately we can still use the method to produce formally verified circuits. The steps necessary are:

- The specification phase: The intended behaviour of the circuit is captured in a formal description.

- The creative phase: The designer calculates the circuit using the four operations described earlier. This involves bringing the description into a Ruby form, and through a series of refinement steps to produce a Ruby description that can be implemented directly. During this step a number of theorems will be stated.

- The proof phase: The designer or a "proof hacker" formally proves the stated theorems in a theorem prover.

- The verification phase: The now proven theorems are combined with the calculation steps to produce a complete proof of the correctness of the developed circuit. This phase could be done fully automatically.

It is important to note that this method for developing formally verified circuits is not equivalent to the post–hoc verification method. The actual synthesis of the circuit (the creative phase) is done in a formal framework, through a series of transformations. Each transformation produces a small theorem to be proven. These theorems are much easier to prove than the huge proof obligations that arise in post–hoc verification methods.

The method has other advantages. By splitting the design up into a creative phase and a proof phase, we get the freedom to change the method used for doing proof without changing the synthesis procedure. This way we can use more than one theorem prover to prove our design. For example we might use tautology checkers;

they are usually fully automatic, but work only for a limited domain of theorems. By having a framework as a front end we can have an interface both to the powerful proof assistant Isabelle and to the more simple but automatic theorem provers. Furthermore when more advanced theorem provers are developed they can easily be introduced.

As an example of the flexibility of the method take the final step in our example section. This step was to do layout optimising of the circuit. We could imagine three ways to manage this step. The designer could break it down into small steps corresponding to pre–proven theorems. The designer could take it in a few (or one) steps and hope that a "proof hacker" could prove the steps in Isabelle. Finally the designer might rely on an automatic theorem prover that is designed to manage layout proofs. A theory for those kinds of proof is under development [6] and it is reasonable to expect other automatic theorem provers to appear.

7 Conclusion

We have devised a method for conducting a formal proof of correctness of a circuit with respect to a specification. We used Ruby as the formal language as we believe the easy graphical interpretation of Ruby descriptions makes the language easy to use for a hardware designer. We described what we consider a correctness proof in Ruby through a constraint–introducing calculation scheme. We implemented an algebra for Ruby in the Isabelle theorem prover, but our work with theorem provers convinced us that we needed a front end between the formal theorem prover and the designer.

As we investigated the operations this front end should have, we invented a method for doing formal proofs. This method corresponds more directly to the way a designer wants to work without sacrificing the formal aspect of circuit development.

In Lyngby we are currently developing the proposed formal framework; part of it is described in [1]. We also intend to implement other modules to aid the designer. These include a program for automatic drawing of the Ruby expression, and flow analysis programs.

We are also investigating how to interface this framework to a traditional design system, linking a library of pre–proven theorems to a cell library that can be used as the primitive cells in a implementable Ruby description.

8 Acknowledgements

Many thanks to Robin Sharp for helpful discussions about the form of the Ruby framework. Part of the paper was completed during my visit to Glasgow University funded by the Danish Research Academy; I am grateful for the help I received at Glasgow. I wish to thank Satnam Singh and Mary Sheeran for proof reading an early draft of this paper and giving constructive comments.

References

[1] Bent Warming Hansen and Jesper Jørgensen. Graphical and relational algebra for the synthesis of vlsi. Master's thesis, Technical University of Denmark, August 1989.

[2] Cliff B. Jones. *Systematic Software Development Using VDM*. Prentice/Hall International, 1986.

[3] G. Jones and M. Sheeran. Relations and refinement in circuit design. In Morgan, editor, *Proc. BCS FACS Workshop on Refinement*. Springer Workshop in Computing, 1990.

[4] Geraint Jones and Mary Sheeran. Circuit design in ruby. In J. Staunstrup, editor, *Formal Methods for VLSI Design*. Elsevier, 1990.

[5] David Murphy. Arithmetic on the a110. Technical report, Dept. of Computer Science, Glasgow University, 1990.

[6] David Murphy. Type refinment in ruby. In G. Hutton et al., editor, *Procedings of the 1990 Glasgow Functional Programing Workshop*. To appear in Springer Verlag Workshops in Computing series, 1990.

[7] Lawrence C. Paulson. Natural deduction as higher-order resulution. *The Journal of Logic Programming*, 3, 1986.

[8] Lawrence C. Paulson. The foundation of a generic theorem prover. *Journal of Automated Reasoning*, 5, 1989.

[9] Lawrence C. Paulson and Tobias Nipkow. *Isabelle Tutorial and User's Manual*, 1990.

[10] Lars Rossen. Ruby algebra. In G. Jones and M. Sheeran, editors, *Workshop on Designing Correct Circuits*. To appear in Springer Verlag, 1990.

[11] Mary Sheeran. Retiming and slowdown in ruby. In G. Milner, editor, *The Fusion of Hardware Design and Verification*. North Holland, 1986.

[12] Mary Sheeran. Describing and reasoning about circuits using relations. In *Proceedings, 1986 Leeds workshop on theoretical aspects of VLSI design*. Cambridge University Press, 1990.

Author Index